The SAGE Dictionary of Leisure Studies

The SAGE Dictionary of Leisure Studies

The SAGE Dictionary of Leisure Studies

Tony Blackshaw and Garry Crawford

Los Angeles | London | New Delhi
Singapore | Washington DC

First published 2009

SAGE Publications Ltd
1 Oliver's Yard
55 City Road
London EC1Y 1SP

SAGE Publications Inc.
2455 Teller Road
Thousand Oaks, California 91320

SAGE Publications India Pvt Ltd
B 1/I 1 Mohan Cooperative Industrial Area
Mathura Road, New Delhi 110 044

SAGE Publications Asia-Pacific Pte Ltd
33 Pekin Street #02-01
Far East Square
Singapore 048763

Library of Congress Control Number: 2008936954

British Library Cataloguing in Publication data

A catalogue record for this book is available
from the British Library

ISBN 978-1-4129-1995-1
ISBN 978-1-4129-1996-8 (pbk)

Typeset by C&M Digitals (P) Ltd, Chennai, India
Printed in India at Replika Press Pvt Ltd
Printed on paper from sustainable resources

Contents

Acknowledgements

Garry: For Victoria

We would like to express our sincere thanks to everybody at Sage for their support, encouragement and help with this project. We should also like to thank the two anonymous reviewers for their insightful and helpful comments on the first draft of the manuscript.

Introduction

During the last thirty years leisure studies has established itself as an area of academic study to be reckoned with, which as well as having an insatiable appetite for developing and applying ideas, concepts and theories ready-made from other academic disciplines, provides a forum for some exciting innovation and grounding of its own. Although the subject field is well served by introductory textbooks, which in general do an excellent job in acting as reference guides to this scholarship (see, for example, Rojek, 1985; Haywood and Kew, 1989; Haywood et al., 1995; Roberts, 1999; Harris, 2005; Rojek, 2005), there has hitherto been no dedicated dictionary for students and scholars working in this field. *The SAGE Dictionary of Leisure Studies* has been produced in order to fill this void.

In compiling this dictionary, we have had to be mindful that, despite its relative youthfulness, leisure studies is like any other subject field, in the sense that it is, to use John Updike's apposite analogy, always like an old world collapsing and a new world arising, and that we scholars have better eyes for the collapse than the rise, since the old world is the one that we know. With this in mind, one of our main objectives was to try to break this pattern of thinking and to reflexively question the meaning of *contemporary* leisure – what it means to scholars, students, managers, practitioners and ordinary men and women today. Practically, this meant that we were in the position of having to deal with a whole family of concepts from leisure studies which increasingly feel like the ghosts of those who haven't quite died – what the sociologist Ulrich Beck calls death-in-life zombie categories – lingering around a discursive formation that today only gives them a fitful and uncertain sense of still belonging to the world. There is often a tendency among leisure scholars to overlook the fact that some concepts, especially those developed under the aegis of 1970s and 1980s leisure studies, have been transformed by more recent societal changes and technological advances, in the process becoming grey areas of knowledge that have lost their former explanatory power. With this observation in mind we realized that, paradoxically, we were in the same position as anyone updating a previously published dictionary for a second edition. That is, we had to face up to the challenge that, if leisure studies needed a dictionary, it needed one for altered times.

The SAGE Dictionary of Leisure Studies is meant to be much more than a compendium of information about leisure studies: it is also inevitably an attempt to define the current identity of the discursive formation. The reader will see that it is written with the assumption that the contemporary world is one of constant 'disembedding' and 're-embedding' – as the sociologist Anthony Giddens would say – where men and women, freed from the shackles of the imagined 'social contract' that accompanied the virtues and the habitats of a modern society based on industrial production (which cast them 'ready-made' through their rank in the social class and gender hierarchies), have become the agents of their own destinies. Indeed, during the decades from the 1970s onwards men and women were increasingly becoming newly dislocated (or at least semi-assimilated) in the world and as a result the normative institutions associated with modern societies were transformed. Let us consider the influence of paid work on our leisure, for example. There is no doubting the fact that it still has a considerable bearing on our leisure opportunities and choices, but over the last twenty years particularly there has been a clear shift in what work means to us as individuals. Today it is the pursuit of pleasure – much more than work – that shapes our sense of ourselves.

This dictionary is also written with the conviction that leisure studies can no longer simply think of individuals as members of a category such as a social class, a 'race' or a gender (if this was ever the case). It is cultural variety rather than social uniformity that defines the *Zeitgeist*. This point of view is not entirely new in leisure studies of course. The leisure studies scholar Ken Roberts has always made a compelling case for a pluralist theory of leisure which recognizes that power and status are shared among a multiplicity of social groups and organizations in any nation state. The way in which our approach differs is that not only does it understand that men and women today are individuals first with all the rest after but also that their status is primarily as consumers to be seduced, rather than subjects of a state or citizens to be won over – that period when the boundaries of the nation state seemed to set the natural order of things has been outmoded by accelerated globalization.

If this is tantamount to saying consumerism is now the central business of life and that the nation state and its accompanying categories of subjectivity (e.g., social class, 'race' and gender) do not have the same resonance in people's lives as they once did, it does not correspond that we thought they should have no place in this dictionary. We simply decided that the amount of attention given to them had to be moderated so that we could deal with other more pressing issues of concern, particularly where current leisure students would expect entries. So, as well as giving due attention to individualization and consumerism, we also offer entries on a range of more freshly minted concepts which reveal the link between individual life-worlds and the larger sociality – celebrity, cool, digital gaming, event management, extreme leisure, governmentality, liquid modernity, performativity, queer theory, risk management, to name but a few – which have a growing currency in leisure studies today.

A dictionary is, of course, for the most part a practical resource, but in an interdisciplinary field like leisure studies its usability when subjected to a variety of scholarly demands is the real test of its worth. Accordingly this dictionary caters for the needs of those interested in sociological, philosophical and psychological understandings of leisure, as well as those whose specialized frame of reference is leisure management and economics and finance. In relation to the more general needs of students, it also deals with the full range of research methods and related concepts used by leisure studies researchers, dealing with the identification, explanation and application of both quantitative and qualitative approaches.

In writing this dictionary, we have also been particularly concerned to help students to both think through and make use of the key concepts, ideas, theories and methods by applying them to and locating them in leisure studies research. In this way the entries collectively form an interconnected study, encapsulating in detail both the interdisciplinary complexity of contemporary leisure studies with its ceaselessly shifting and expanding focus, while also charting current empirical developments in the field.

There will be readers who will no doubt disapprove of some of the material that has gone into the dictionary, while others will identify omissions which in their view should have been included. To draw the old world/new world analogy once again, it should be noted that all dictionaries are a product of their time. What this suggests is that dictionary writers, in focusing their attention on putting together their own state-of-the-discipline creations, are burdened not just with the baggage of historical consciousness but also with trying to capture the consciousness of the present-time in their particular field of study.

What this has meant in practice of course is that, in being confronted with the challenging task of forming our own accurate state-of-the-discipline representation of leisure studies, we had to decide what was going to be included and what was not. The reader's freely given, uncertain resolve could not be ours; and we, in so far as we had to make the decision about which key concepts and key thinkers to include, will have accurately represented leisure studies for some, while destroying an ideal for others. All we can say is that we can neither transcend time nor anticipate in advance any of these concerns, but we would simply reiterate that it is with leisure studies knowledge and issues of today that *The SAGE Dictionary of Leisure Studies* is primarily concerned. If some concepts traditionally associated with the subject field are not included it is because we thought that they no longer chime with the current needs of students on leisure studies courses.

Key thinker exclusions are less complicated to explain. These have been kept to a minimum simply on the basis of the limits imposed by the word count. Having said that, we have made sure that maximum attention is paid to the ideas of key thinkers in leisure studies when they do arise in the concept entries. With regard to the inclusion of key thinkers not usually associated with leisure studies (for example, Jean Baudrillard, Pierre Bourdieu, Zygmunt Bauman and Michel Foucault), it should be noted that we understand that it is a subject field of immensely wide range and, unlike many other subject fields, not only is it truly multidisciplinary but it is also not bound up with a long history of ideas upon which it has exercised a powerful influence. As we have said already, most of its knowledge and ideas have been borrowed from other disciplines and this trend is set to continue. With regard to the thinkers identified above, the enormity of the influence of their thinking on leisure studies at the current time simply demands their inclusion.

On a more practical note, the reader will see that we have individually written the majority of the entries, but that there are also a number of entries from other contributors. We would like to thank Rob Wilson and Mark Piekarz for writing the leisure management, economics and finance entries. We would also like to thank Gaynor Bagnall, Jeremy Coulton, Alex Dennis and Greg Smith from the Department of English, Sociology, Politics and Contemporary History at the Unversity of Salford for writing their individual entries on their own areas of expertise. As the reader would expect in a dictionary the entries are arranged in alphabetical order. Some of the entries are compact and efficient overviews, while most of them are more encyclopaedic in scope and are effectively more like mini-essays. Each entry is also cross-referenced to other *associated concepts* included in the dictionary in order to supplement critical assessment, facilitate broader in-depth study and hopefully excite further interest in leisure studies.

Tony Blackshaw

Associated Concepts Class; Consumer Society; Discursive Formations; Giddens; Globalization; Individualization; Pleasure; Work-Leisure; Zombie Categories.

A

A AND B ANALYSIS

This is a heuristic mode of investigation concerned with individuals' freedom to make leisure choices and the different ways in which they compete to achieve certain leisure ends. To this extent it is concerned with the characteristics of power relations in leisure. The central tenets of A and B analysis are implied in many studies of leisure relations, especially those which focus their attention on individual choices and tastes. At the most basic level, A and B analysts would be concerned with, for example, why A might choose to go to the pub against the wishes of B, who wants to stay in and watch a DVD, and how this might cause conflict in their relationship. More complicated applications also explore the multifaceted nature of relationships and the possibility of resolution and cooperation between individuals and social groups.

However, like game theory, A and B analysis is an unsatisfactory perspective on power relations because it fails to account for the structural inequalities and cleavages linked to political attitudes and cultural identification. These observations notwithstanding, Rojek offers a revised understanding for leisure studies which suggests that, by being more alert to the processes that accompany social stratification and how these are embedded and embodied in social interaction, we can develop clearer insights into the workings of leisure relations in terms of 'the *motivation* of actors, the *location* of trajectories of behaviour and the *context* of action' (2005: 25).

Tony Blackshaw

Associated Concepts   Game Theory; Leisure Bodies; Power; Rojek, Chris.

ABNORMAL LEISURE

The idea of abnormal leisure might be understood as the designation for all that is strange and deviant, unbridled and tempestuous and which in many cases is likely to be an infraction of the criminal law. It also constitutes the outlandish leisure pursuits that we are illicitly attracted to, but also fear and dare not try to fathom, yet we are often nonetheless fascinated enough to try these out. To this extent, abnormal leisure is the example *par excellence* of the unresolved, disturbing forms of our desires and fantasies, which are explored to good effect by Ken Kalfus in his post-9/11 novel *A Disorder Peculiar to the Country*. This not so simple story of adultery demonstrates how the psychology of domestic attrition stands for the paroxysm – the whole dying world of US security – as New Yorkers indulge in 'terror sex' in order to gain social advantage, and where the highest thrill is to bed somebody who survived the twin towers or served emergency duty in their aftermath.

Contextualizing his core argument around the concepts of liminality, edgework and surplus energy, Rojek (2000) outlines three key types of abnormal leisure: invasive, mephitic and wild leisure. *Invasive leisure* focuses on abnormal behaviour associated with self-loathing and self-pity and the ways in which disaffected individuals experience anomie and personal alienation from the rest of society through drink, drug or solvent abuse in order that they can 'turn their back on reality'. *Mephitic leisure* encompasses a wide range of pursuits and activities, from mundane encounters with prostitutes to the buzz of murdering through serial killing. To this extent mephitic leisure experiences involve the individual's self-absorbed desire for gratification at the expense of others. The reason why Rojek calls these leisure activities and pursuits mephitic is that they are generally understood to be 'noxious', 'nasty', 'foul' and 'morally abhorrent' by most 'normal' people, because they cause major offence to the moral order of things.

Rojek's third category is *wild leisure*, which involves limit-experiences through edgework and as such this tends to be opportunistic in character. But very much like mephitic leisure it involves the individual's self-absorbed desire for instant gratification. The experience of 'limit' is the name of the game with wild leisure, which includes deviant crowd behaviour such as rioting, looting and violence, particularly at sports events. Rojek also suggests that new technology presents individuals intent on pursuing wild leisure with ever more opportunities for instant gratification, typically in the form of video clips of anything from violence in sport to genocide, which supplies individuals with the vicarious 'delight of being deviant' (Katz, 1988).

There is an 'ethical' divide about the relative merits of the concept of abnormal leisure in leisure studies. Criticizing Rojek's work, Cara Aitchison has argued that 'violence, abuse and violations of human rights may well play a part in exploitative leisure relations but these acts themselves are not acts of leisure – they are acts of violence and should be named and researched as such' (quoted in Rojek, 2000: 167).

However, Rojek barks at the notion that we should ignore these kinds of leisure activities. In his view abnormal leisure may belong to the forbidden and the deadly, but it should not escape the notice of scholars of leisure that it *is* leisure all the same. Hannah Arendt coined the expression 'banality of evil' in order to bring to our attention the shocking ordinariness of such activities. In the light of Arendt's perceptive observation we can conclude that Rojek is merely tearing off leisure studies' veil of respectability to reveal what lurks in the hearts and minds of a good many men and women, which enables him to say something important about the infinite playfulness of the human mind. The mirror image this holds up to the rest of humankind may not be an ideal picture – it can frequently be dreadful and upsetting and often even morally repugnant – but, as Rojek makes clear, it is leisure all the same.

Tony Blackshaw

Associated Concepts Addictions; Desire; Deviance; Edgework; Football Hooliganism; Liminality; Rojek.

ACCULTURATION

This term emerged from cultural anthropology and has two principal and connected meanings. At its most basic level the concept of acculturation refers to the ways in which different cultures interact. The second, more sophisticated meaning, focuses on the process whereby different cultural (and we might say leisure) groups act together to create new cultural patterns, which may, or may not, create tensions or struggles between the old and new.

In recent years postcolonial critics, who are concerned with the effects of colonization and imperialism on the least powerful cultures and societies, and especially those in the poorest parts of the world, have suggested that, as with many other concepts from cultural anthropology, acculturation is limited by its quietism about the contested and uneven nature of cultural exchange, which often means the incorporation of minority cultures into the dominant hegemony of the Western cultural system. For that reason Bhabha (1994) replaces the concept with the idea of hybridity, which, as well as acknowledging the shifting expressions associated with ostensibly fixed cultural traditions, refers to the synergies of new transcultural forms – artistic, ethnic, linguistic, literature, musical, political, and so on and so forth – that emerge within the contact zones between cultures. According to Bhabha it is the 'in-between' or third space of these synergies that ultimately carries both the weight and the meaning of culture.

Notwithstanding the obvious strengths of Bhabha's critique, with the accelerated pace of globalization and associated technological change, it is becoming increasingly difficult to identify the unequal processes of cultural exchange associated with processes of acculturation, which are not only rarely fixed to specific localities but are also often transitory. To return once again to the topic of postcolonialism, take, for example, the traditional Punjabi musical and dance form of Bhangra, which many young Asian musicians in Britain have fused with a vast range of other musical forms (often hybrids themselves), such as disco, techno, house, raga, jungle and hip hop, to create new sounds and dance forms that are now being re-exported back to Asia.

Tony Blackshaw

Associated Concepts Edgework; Flow; Globalization; Hegemony; Liminality; Power; Racism and Leisure; Structure of Feeling.

ACTION ANALYSIS

This is a term used to understand and account for the nature of purposive or intentional activities in leisure. Action theorists are centrally concerned with concepts like freedom, choice, respect and responsibility. However, despite its focus on voluntarism and individual agency, action analysis is not as 'irredeemably individualistic' as some of its critics imagine. By and large its practitioners pay due attention to the structuration of social relations (e.g., Giddens, 1984). Accordingly, Rojek (2005: 49) uses the term 'to refer to grounded research that is committed to working with actors to understand leisure trajectories by exploring the interplay between location and context, and formulating leisure policies designed to achieve distributive justice, empowerment and social inclusion'.

Tony Blackshaw

Associated Concepts Action Research; Giddens; Individualization; Rojek, Chris Symbolic Interactionism.

ACTION RESEARCH

According to its adherents action research is not simply another methodology in the narrow and broad meaning of 'research methods', but is better understood as an *orientation* to inquiry, which 'has different purposes, is based in different relationships, and has different ways of conceiving knowledge and its relation to practice' (Reason, 2003: 106). If action research has one specific goal, it is to bring about social change. This observation notwithstanding, it might be said that the emphasis of action research is not merely social change (e.g. increased participation in leisure activities that lead to better health and well-being) but it is also on articulating the world through new ways rather than being caught in the entrenched vocabularies of either social science or politics. Reason suggests that to this end action research 'is an approach to human inquiry concerned with developing practical knowing through participatory, democratic processes in the pursuit of worthwhile human purposes, drawing on many ways of knowing in an emergent, developmental fashion' (p. 108).

Action research is invariably locally based and it often has a community as well as organizational orientation. Either way one of its primary purposes is to produce practical knowledge that is useful to people in the everyday conduct of their own leisure lives. As has already been suggested, on a wider societal level, action research can also be seen as an approach to inquiry that seeks to bring about the increased social, psychological and economic well-being of individuals and communities.

Central to the idea of much action research is the idea of cogeneration and it is a mode of research which aims to build democratic, participative, pluralist communities of inquiry by 'conscientizing' individuals and community groups whose lives are circumscribed by social, cultural, economic and political inequalities (e.g., Freire, 1970). Herein action research points to a kind of praxis where theory and practice meet in a kind purposive action to interpret 'practice', to make sense of it and find as yet 'hidden' possibilities for change. In this way, action research also points to the *possible* in the sense that it signifies something that has not yet happened. The idea of *possibility* also signifies a refusal to be constrained within the limits of 'how things seem to be' (see Bauman, 1976), which means that action research is also suggestive of a socialist politics (rather than a Marxist politics) that seeks to alter the world in ways that cannot be achieved at the level of the individual. That said, practitioners are also alert to the tension that may exist between praxis and necessity, namely there is not going to be a revolution so we need to get on with changing *our* world for the better. In

this second sense action research has close affinities with pragmatism.

Tony Blackshaw

Associated Concepts Class; Community; Community Action; Community Leisure; Marxism.

ADDICTIONS

The term addiction is generally used to describe the compulsive behaviour of somebody who is burdened by their adherence to an activity or substance, normally a narcotic drug, which is regarded as individually or socially harmful. While psychological studies have predominately been concerned with pathological explanations for addictions, sociological studies have been more concerned with analysing them in so far as they are societal phenomena.

The symbolic interactionist perspective has proved to be perhaps the most important sociological influence on exploring the extent and consequences of addictive leisure. Rather than ascribing addictive behaviours to individual pathologies, symbolic interactionists have explored the social contexts in which individuals become addicted to certain leisure activities. The work of the American scholar Howard Becker (1953) best exemplifies this tradition. He explored the deviant 'career' associated with 'Becoming a Marihuana User', arguing that drug use is like any other leisure activity, a socially acquired taste developed as a response to social processes and social milieu.

The sociological work of Anthony Giddens utilizes more explicitly psychological explanations to suggest that, if the frenzy of addictions that marks the contemporary world does not differ from that which fell foul of twentieth-century sensibilities, addictions do seem to be more widespread. Reminiscent of

Rojek's work on abnormal leisure, Giddens outlines the specific characteristics of addictions, which could include anything from narcotic drug use to alcohol, from sex (his own topic) to high-risk leisure activities.

- The 'high': the ecstatic experience or the thrill of being taken out of themselves that individuals seek out when they are looking for a leisure experience that is set apart from the mundane characteristics of everyday life.
- The 'fix': when individuals are addicted to a specific leisure experience all efforts to achieve a 'high' soon become translated into the need for a 'fix'.
- The 'high' and the 'fix': both can be understood as kinds of 'time out' when individuals are transported to another world. The upshot of this is that individuals may come to regard their ordinary day-to-day activities with 'cynical amusement or even disdain' or just the reverse – they might even generate a form of disgust towards their addictive pattern of behaviour.
- 'Giving up': the addictive leisure activity can also be understood as a kind of 'giving up', leading to the temporary abandonment of the care of the self. However, some forms of 'high' – those associated with flow, for example – might be understood by individuals as enabling them to penetrate the mystery of the self.
- The sense of 'loss': which is experienced in the aftermath of being taken out of oneself is often succeeded by feelings of embarrassment, shame and remorse.
- 'Layering': for all the apparent singularity of the ecstatic experience involved in individual highs, addictive experiences tend to be 'layered' in the individual's psychological makeup and can lead to compulsive behaviour patterns.
- Ambivalence: the loss of the self and the kinds of self-disgust typical of addictions are not necessarily just about indulgence. The pathologies of self-discipline characteristic of addictions can swing in two directions. For example, bulimia (compulsive overeating) and anorexia (compulsive fasting) are two sides of the same coin: each can coexist in the addictive behaviours of the same individual.

Tony Blackshaw

Associated Concepts Abnormal Leisure; Deviance; Extreme Leisure; Flow; Giddens; 'Into', the; Liminality; Symbolic Interactionism.

ADORNO, THEODOR

(critical theory)

AESTHETICS

Derived from the Greek words *aisthētikos*, which means 'perceptible by the senses', and *aisthēsthai*, which means 'to perceive', aesthetics, as it is understood in Western philosophy, is concerned with beauty in the arts and nature. The science of aesthetics, on the other hand, understands beauty as something absolute, which has the power to overwhelm any effort to treat it relatively. This modern disciplinary understanding of aesthetics is concerned with the concrete and it promises to offer an understanding of the meaning of beauty through the reconciliation of the rational and the experiential (Eagleton, 1990). As such the science of aesthetics concerns itself with asking questions such as: 'What is art?' and 'Can art be a vehicle for truth?'

According to its critics, the major problem with the science of aesthetics is not only that it is misguided in thinking that beauty is something absolute, but also it preoccupies itself with the sensory perceptual reaction that objects of art can offer rather than give a critique of the ways in which the cultural capital generated through artistic knowledge serves to sustain existing social inequalities, particularly social class. It can also be criticized for marginalizing the relationship between aesthetics and the passions of a wider human activity relating to our personal ethics and the political meaning of a life lived as a work of art, or in other words, the qualities arising from the experience of the art of life itself, which stimulate knowledge and self-discovery in order to liberate both memory and the imagination.

The work of Michel Foucault is of particular relevance to understanding the significance of leisure to this idea of the art of living. What Foucault suggests is that, with the onset of postmodernity, when we (modern men and women) were at last freed from the shackles of the imagined 'social contract' that accompanied the legislating virtues and the habitats of a modern society based on industrial production – from the social solidarity and community formations associated with the working classes, to the self-interest and propriety of the middle classes, to the mimicking 'aristocratic' virtues of generosity and courage of the upper classes – which cast us 'ready-made' through our rank in the class hierarchy, we were, for the first time in our history, in a position to think of ourselves as individuals *de facto*, which also meant exceeding the possibilities of the experiences of leisure in a world built on industrial production with its rigid class differences.

Foucault argues that, from this moment, it was inevitable that we would no longer be convinced 'that between our ethics, our personal ethics, our everyday life, and the great political and social and economic structures, there were analytical relations, and that we couldn't arrange anything, for instance, in our sex life, in our family life, without ruining our economy, our democracy, and so on', and that there could only be one practical consequence: we would have to create ourselves as a work of art: 'couldn't everyone's life become a work of art? Why should the lamp or the house be an art object, but not our life?' (1984: 350b). In other words, according to Foucault, today we inhabit a world in which aesthetics supersedes everything else,

where men and women are their own art and the performativity of life itself, often informed by our leisure choices (our dress sense, the holidays we take, the music and the artists we like best, the way we tattoo ourselves, how and who we love, whatever) is the foremost ethical principle. However, Foucault's critics would argue that, if it can be said that postmodern men and women are their own art, it is a form of art made to the measure of a consumer society and to this extent the art of living is mostly ready-made or off-the-peg.

Tony Blackshaw

Associated Concepts Authenticity; Bourdieu; Class; Consumption; Habitus, Field and Capital; Foucault; Performativity; Postmodernism; Postmodernity.

AGEING AND LEISURE

We all know that ageing refers to the process of growing physically older, but it is more difficult to suggest a formal definition that will deal adequately with the questions relating to the economic issues, cultural values and social and psychological concerns associated with the ageing process and the consequences of these for people's engagement with, and enjoyment of, leisure.

An ageing society is generally seen as one which is experiencing a decline in the birth rate and a concomitant increase in the longevity of the population as a whole. The UK and USA are good examples of this trend. The Office of Population, Censuses, and Surveys in the UK projects that, by 2011, almost 10 million people will be aged 65 or over and that, by 2020, there will be 30,000 centenarians. However, these bare statistics do tend to hide some anomalies. For example, in the UK, it is the white population that is ageing and ethnic minority groups are predominantly young, while in the USA, the US Census Bureau estimates that a white man born in 1970 can expect to reach 68 years, while for a black man it is just over 60 years.

Studies have also shown that the growing proportion of older people in a population leads to some significant changes in household structure, in particular an increase in one-person households (especially women) and shifts in the geographical distribution of populations where, on the one hand, poorer or less mobile older people are left in inner cities and, on the other, more affluent and mobile older people move to retirement areas, such as the popular seaside towns.

There are some major disparities in leisure opportunities associated with age, which can be summarized as follows.

- Health: implications of the lack of mobility, sight, hearing for leisure and leisure provision; increased dependence as confidence and mobility deteriorate; isolation due to loss of spouse, usually the male.
- Image: notions of the 'old age pensioner' and negative stereotypes of the elderly.
- Economic: reduced income with retirement, especially for those from working-class social backgrounds. Many older people live on the borders of poverty and for them leisure is a problem of excess time and a deficiency of resources, resulting in an enforced dependency on home-life.
- Psychosocial and cultural restraints: the old are not respected; leisure/work demarcation disappears and social contacts are subsequently reduced; a fear of crime, both real and perceived; increased feelings of being psychologically useless; increasing dependence on organized leisure; the implications of living with 'structureless' time and being a burden to the rest of society.

There are two key theoretical interpretations of the relationship between ageing and leisure. The first of these is identified by Clarke and Critcher (1985: 154–155), who point out that disengagement theorists have highlighted the relationship between older people and the rest of society, particularly the idea that once people retire they tend to withdraw in preparation for death. Focusing on the 'roleless' role that old age confers, disengagement theorists suggest that retirement is experienced by a large number of older people as largely negative, mixing elements of status loss with nothing to do. Retirees are said to have no roles once they lose the status of work and are depicted as 'old' people sitting around in 'cheerless' places, such as supermarkets and shopping malls, watching the world pass them by. The crux of this argument is that, in a production-orientated society, retired older people simply lose their central focus of life. Social processes also increase their sense of isolation (e.g., children move away; partners die; family becomes scattered), resulting in what Clarke and Critcher (1985: 155) call 'privatization with a vengeance'.

Contrary to this largely negative theoretical assessment, which by and large constructs older people as passive recipients of the ageing process, activity theorists (e.g., Forster, 1997) see them as active, engaged citizens. In this view retirement might be a period of transition and readjustment for many individuals but, far from withdrawing from the rest of society, it presents them with an unprecedented opportunity to take on new roles: old age is a time of potential. This optimistic approach assumes retirees have the necessary skills, social bonds, self-definitions and, crucially, the quality of time that can ensure they make leisure central to their retirement.

Tony Blackshaw

Associated Concepts Authenticity; Class; Leisure and the Life Course; Racism and Leisure; Serious Leisure.

AGENCY

(structure and agency)

ALIENATION

Alienation can be defined as isolation or a disconnection resulting from powerlessness. Theories of alienation are most commonly associated with the work of Karl Marx, who had built upon the writings of Hegel and Feuerbach. Marx suggested that human beings are distinguished from animals by their *creative activity*, but capitalism strips people of this creativity and, as a consequence, individuals are alienated in four key ways. These are, first, *alienation from the process of working*, where capitalism denies workers a say in what they produce and how they produce it and work is tedious and repetitive. Second, *alienation from the products of work*, where the product of the work (the object produced for sale) belongs to the capitalists and not the workers. Third, *alienation from other workers*, in that, capitalism transforms work from a cooperative venture into a competitive one. Factory work provides little chance for human companionship so workers become alienated from their co-workers. Fourth, *alienation from themselves* (or *human potential*), in that capitalist production techniques do not allow workers to fulfil their full creative potential as their roles become prescribed and set.

These ideas have been applied by several, and in particular (though not solely) Marxist, writers to the study of leisure. One notable example is Jean-Marie Brohm's (1978) consideration of sport participation. Brohm argues that sport participation in capitalist societies ultimately leads to athletes becoming alienated from their own bodies. The body is experienced by the athlete as an object and instrument – a technical means to an end and a machine with the task of producing the maximum work and energy. The result of this is that the body ceases to be a source of pleasure and fulfilment in itself. Instead, pleasure and fulfilment depend on what is accomplished with the body, namely satisfaction in terms of competitive outcomes rather than the physical experience of involvement. In particular, Brohm (1978: 18) writes of 'the total, not to say totalitarian mobilization of the athletes to produce maximum performance. Every sport now involves a fantastic manipulation of human robots by doctors, psychologists, biochemists and trainers. The "manufacturing of champions" is no longer a craft but an industry, calling on specialized laboratories, research institutes, training camps and experimental sports centres'.

Garry Crawford

Associated Concepts Class; Commodity Fetishism; Hegemony; Leisure Bodies; Marxism; Power; Sport; Work-Leisure.

AMATEUR AND AMATEURISM

The term amateur is most commonly associated with engaging in an activity without formal payment and/or having received no formal training. Traditionally, this term was used as a badge of honour to mark out an individual who had 'natural' talent (without needing to train) and was willing to engage in an activity out of love for the pursuit rather than monetary gain. This traditional idea of 'amateurism' is therefore very class based, as can be seen in the Victorian (and beyond) 'gentleman' (usually middle-class amateurs) versus 'players' (usually working-class professionals) cricket matches which began in 1806. However, in more contemporary times, the idea of professionalism has come to be associated with expertise and, consequently the term amateur is now most frequently used to denote a lack of skill or competence.

For Stebbins (1992) 'amateurs' are different from 'hobbyists' as, unlike hobbyists, amateurs constitute one part of the 'professional–amateur–public' (PAP) system. That is to say, their status as 'amateurs' is defined by the existence of others who get paid to do the same or similar activities. The classic example would of course be sport, where there is often a divide (though this is not wholly clear) between professional and amateur athletes. In particular, the ethos of 'amateurism' has been strongly defended in many sports, such as rugby, where disagreement over payments to players led to the split of codes into 'league' and 'union' in England in 1895 (and it was one hundred years later in 1995 when rugby union eventually removed all restrictions on the payment of wages to players). However, rugby union (and many other so-called 'amateur' sports) for a considerable amount of time allowed the payment of (sometimes considerable and excessive) 'expenses', which led many critics to refer to this system as 'shamateurism' rather than true 'amateurism'.

Garry Crawford

Associated Concepts Serious Leisure; Class; Consumption; Fanzines; Hobbies.

ANIMAL RIGHTS

The Aristotelian idea that the possession of reason separates humankind from the animal kingdom and allows it sole entry to the realm of the moral community has been challenged by animal rights activists. They place their faith in the sanctity of all life and argue animals should receive the same moral privileges as human beings.

It is undoubtedly the case that historically animals have quite legally been subject to abuse and neglect while people have pursued their own pleasures in leisure. Making leisure activities which are cruel to animals illegal has a long history but, as the recent ban on hunting with dogs in the UK showed, legislation has often been class-biased. As figurational sociologists Atkinson and Young

(2005) demonstrate in their discussion of greyhound racing in North America, cruelty towards animals in leisure settings is hardly a thing of the past and we need to understand that abuse and neglect are often embedded and hidden in sporting configurations which perpetuate our tacit tolerance of wrongdoings perpetrated against animals.

Tony Blackshaw

Associated Concepts Blood Sports; Elias; Ethics; Figurationalism; Mimesis.

ANOMIE

The concept of 'anomie' was introduced into sociology by Emile Durkheim in his discussion of the division of labour within a capitalist society. In *The Division of Labour* (1933 [1893]) Durkheim developed a theory of the historical progression of society from a state of 'mechanical' to 'organic' solidarity. This evolution is bound up with the development of the division of labour (i.e., the occupational structures) and also the social relations of society, such as friendships and communities. Mechanical forms of solidarity are essentially pre-industrial, where social organization is generally undifferentiated. The basis of organic solidarity is the division of labour and social differentiation – which sees the labour process divided into parts, with each individual performing a specific and differentiated role. In an organic society what Durkheim referred to as a 'normal' division of labour would develop, where the skills and abilities of individuals are equally matched to their professions and laws and rules would be more cooperative and fairer.

However, Durkheim recognized that there also existed 'abnormal' forms of the division of labour, which he referred to as 'anomic', 'forced' and 'uncoordinated' divisions of labour. The latter two 'abnormal' forms are quite similar and relate (respectively) to where individuals are forced to perform jobs that are not suited to their particular skills and abilities and where there is a rapid development in the division of labour and people's roles become uncoordinated and ill defined. However it is the 'anomic' division of labour which has received most attention.

Anomie, for Durkheim, refers to a state of 'normlessness' where there is a lack (or ineffective) set of social norms. In particular, Durkheim suggested that anomie could occur in times of rapid social change or crisis (such as class conflict), where a breakdown in social consensus occurs. Durkheim argued that human beings needed to be controlled, to rein in their 'insatiable appetites', and for Durkheim anomie was associated with individual and selfish desires and an absence of norms to control these.

However, while the concept of anomie was introduced into sociology by Durkheim it was not widely used until its adoption by the sociologist Robert Merton (1938). In particular, Merton formulated a theory of deviant behaviour that suggested contemporary American society was providing a mismatch between promoting certain cultural goals (such as individual success) and supplying inadequate means for every person to meet these. Hence, certain individuals would resort to deviant and/or illegal means and there would be a breakdown of social norms and regulations (or an anomie) to achieve these ends.

The concept of anomie has often been applied to leisure, most commonly in our considerations of how certain leisure activities (such as sport) can combat anomie by providing social norms and values. For instance, Schwery and Eggenberger-Argote (2003: 49) argued that 'sport could offer a simple societal framework to solve conflicts without having to resort to violence' and that 'sport serves to foster identity and can counteract the problem of social disintegration'. However, others have pointed to how leisure itself can be anomic. In particular, Gunter and Gunter (1980) have identified both anomic and alienated forms of leisure,

where anomic leisure is characterized by a general lack of structure in which individuals experience an abundance of unoccupied time. Anomic leisure suggests a 'lack of structural constraints and obligations, coupled with feelings of dislike, antipathy, confusion and possibly a sense of powerlessness to combat such conditions' (1980: 369). Examples of anomic leisure would appear in periods of high unemployment and rapid social transformation, where individuals are unable to move from their societal position and are 'condemned to leisure'. Furthermore, Eric Dunning (1999: 128) has suggested that many modern sports (and especially professional association football in the UK) have become locked into a situation that Durkheim would have called 'classic anomie' – as a result of the vastly increased amounts of money involved in sport, its rapid change and 'the standards whereby greed was kept in check' having broken down.

Garry Crawford

Associated Concepts Abnormal Leisure; Alienation; Deviance; Functionalism; Marxism; Sport.

ANSOFF MATRIX

The Ansoff Matrix, developed by Igor Ansoff in 1957, relates to the products on offer by an organization and strategies for diversification (see Ansoff, 1957). It is a tool that marketers will use if they have an objective(s) for growth, primarily because the matrix offers strategic choices to achieve this. Consequently, it is a good method of stimulating organizational growth. There are four main categories for selection: market penetration; market development; product development; and diversification. The matrix is particularly relevant in the leisure industry where market volatility and short product lifecycles mean analysis needs to be undertaken in a dynamic context. That is to say, organizations in the leisure industry must constantly evaluate both their products and their markets.

- In the context of the Ansoff Matrix, market penetration is about the marketing of existing products to existing customers in an attempt to increase revenue. Generally, this will be done by promoting the product more intensively and repositioning the brand. The product, however, will by and large remain in its current form and no changes will be made.
- Market development concerns the development of an existing product range in a new market(s). Fundamentally, this will mean using the same product but marketing it to a different audience. Common ways of attempting to do this involve taking a product overseas or to new areas of the country.
- Product development is probably one of the most straightforward strategies, but is also often one of the most expensive. New products are developed and targeted at existing customers as they generally replace existing ones. It is sometimes relatively simple to do this by developing an existing model, but sometimes this will involve developing new products completely.
- Diversification occurs when completely new products are targeted at completely new customers. In the matrix there are two types of diversification: related and unrelated. Related diversification means that the organization remains in its current industry and offers different products. Unrelated diversification means entering unknown industries with new products.
- Place strategies refer to how an organization will distribute the product or service they are offering to the end user. The organization must distribute the product to the user at the right place at the right time. Efficient and effective distribution is important if the organization is to meet its overall marketing objectives. For example, if an organization underestimates demand and customers cannot purchase products, its profitability is likely to be affected.

In essence, place strategies are generally concerned with distribution strategies, of which there are two main channels. Indirect distribution, which involves distributing products by the use of an intermediary, and direct distribution, which involves distributing direct from a manufacturer to the consumer.

Depending on the type of product being distributed and the channel chosen by an organization, there are three main distribution strategies: intensive distribution, exclusive distribution and selective distribution. Intensive distribution is commonly used to distribute low-priced or impulse purchase products, for example, chocolates and soft drinks. Exclusive distribution involves limiting distribution to a single outlet. The product will therefore usually be highly priced and requires the intermediary to place a significant amount of detail at its point of sale. A good example of a product associated with this strategy could be luxury cars sold by exclusive dealers. Finally, selective distribution involves the process of selecting a small number of retail outlets to distribute a product. Selective distribution is common with products such as computers, televisions and household appliances, where consumers are willing to shop around and where manufacturers want a large geographical spread. It is worth pointing out here that, if a manufacturer decides to adopt an exclusive or selective strategy, they should select an intermediary who has experience of handling similar products, is credible and is known by the target audience.

Rob Wilson

Associated Concepts Boston Matrix; Leisure Marketing; Marketing Mix; Market Positioning and Market Segmentation.

ART

(aesthetics; community leisure; modernism; postmodernism)

ASCETICISM

A formative term within historical leisure studies, asceticism – from the old Greek term *askein* meaning 'to exercise' – is understood as one of the most important features of the development of modern leisure. Put simply, the term refers to a set of guidelines to living that incorporate self-denial and an abstention from worldly pleasures in order to enhance individual spirituality. In his classic studies of the *Protestant Ethic and the Spirit of Capitalism* (1930), Weber linked ascetism with the puritan values embodied in early Protestantism (including, Lutherism, Calvinism and rationalization) to demonstrate, albeit controversially, its key role in engaging people in disciplined and productive work as modern capitalism emerged from the preconceptual and presystematic *zuhanden* world that preceded it. Leisure scholars have extended the Weber thesis to explore the key values associated with asceticism, such as discipline, diligence, hard effort and the systematic use of time, and the ways these have historically been linked to the promotion of productive leisure and modern configurations of social control.

Tony Blackshaw

Associated Concepts Aesthetics; Cool; Play Ethic; Social Control; Surveillance; Work Ethic.

ASSETS, LIABILITIES AND CAPITAL

Assets, liabilities and capital are three terms that you will often come across when you examine a set of financial statements. Wilson and Joyce (2007) demonstrated how these can have a significant impact on the success or failure of organizations' operations, particularly as they are the central figures that are used to construct a balance sheet. Put simply, assets are items or resources that have a value to the business, are used by the business and as such are for the business. They can be classified as either fixed assets or current assets, the basic difference being that a fixed asset is something that the business intends to keep and use for some time, whereas a current asset is held for the business to convert into cash during trading. Some good examples in the leisure industries are business premises (e.g., a swimming pool) and motor vehicles (e.g., community transport buses), which are fixed assets, and stock and cash, which are current assets.

Liabilities are essentially the opposite of assets as they are amounts owed by the business to people other than the owner. Normally liabilities are classified as either payable within one year (current liabilities) e.g., bank overdrafts and supplier accounts, or payable after one year (non-current liabilities) e.g., longer-term bank loans.

Capital (sometimes called equity) is the owners' stake in the business. This term is also used to describe the excess of assets over liabilities.

Rob Wilson

Associated Concepts Capitalism; Double-Entry Bookkeeping; Financial and Management Accounting; Financial Health and Ratio Analysis; Financial Statements.

AUDIENCES

This term is most commonly used to refer to the 'recipients' of mass media texts (such as radio, television or literature) or live performances (such as plays, concerts or sporting events). Often viewed as the end point of a production–text–audience process, audiences have until relatively recently often been marginalized in media and leisure research due to a preference for analysis of the production process and texts. However, in recent years we have seen an increased focus on the social importance of audiences and their potentially active role within this process.

A useful summary and categorization of the key theories and debates on audiences is offered by Abercrombie and Longhurst (1998). In particular, they suggest that there are three major paradigms (or groups of theories) that can be identified (historically) in the literature on audiences.

The first paradigm they identify is the *behavioural paradigm*. This concept covers many of the psychological theories of audiences and some of sociology's early thinking in this area and it includes the work of Katz, Blumer and Gurevitch (1974). This is often referred to as the 'syringe' model, where the media are seen as a stimulus from which audiences passively absorb messages.

A recognition that audiences are not passive, but can actively 'decode' and engage with texts, led to the replacement of this debate with, what Abercrombie and Longhurst refer to as, the *incorporation/resistance paradigm*. In this model audiences are seen as more active in their consumption, where the messages conveyed by the mass media are reinterpreted or even rejected (resisted) by audience members. Put simply, they suggest that the focus of this paradigm is on 'whether audience members were incorporated into dominant ideology by their participation in media activity, or whether to the contrary, they are resistant to that incorporation' (ibid., page 15). This paradigm includes many sociological and cultural studies discussions about audiences, such as the work of Stuart Hall and his colleagues at the University of Birmingham.

However, Abercrombie and Longhurst (1998) have argued that there are a number of weaknesses with this paradigm. First, that the power an audience has to resist or reinterpret the messages the mass media convey to them is often overstated within this paradigm; second, that there exists little empirical evidence to support this paradigmal framework and, on the contrary, as audiences become more skilled in their use of media, their responses and actions are less likely to conform to this simple model.

Abercrombie and Longhurst have proposed that there is now a shift occurring towards a new paradigm and this they refer to as the *spectacle/performance paradigm*. Within an increasingly spectacular and performative (postmodern) society individuals become part of a 'diffused audience'. That is to say, we draw on the mass media as a resource and use this in our everyday social performances, rendering us (and others) both performers and audiences to others' performances in our everyday lives.

The incorporation/resistance paradigm therefore recognizes that audiences are not the passive product of a production/text process, while more contemporary debates (within a spectacle/performance paradigm) allow us to breakdown the boundaries between production/text/consumption and to see audiences as both the consumers and the producers of texts and performances.

Garry Crawford

Associated Concepts Birmingham School; Celebrity; Communication; Consumption; Fans; Fanzines; Football Hooliganism; Ideology; Mass Media; Pardigms; Performativity; Power; Subcultures.

AUTHENTICITY

In the work of the existentialist philosopher Martin Heidegger (1962), authenticity is understood as that mode of human being-in-the-world (*Dasein*) of interest to those who wish to explore the existential qualities and possibilities that are uniquely their own as individuals; who cannot ignore the fact that as individuals they are 'thrown' into the world at a certain point in time and space;

and who recognize that their existence has a certain distinctiveness that nonetheless transcends simple analysis, description or perception. Heidegger contrasts authenticity with inauthenticity, which is a mode of existence whereby men and women flee from their responsibility to themselves by reducing their lives to the average or the typical or to believing they can understand it through the sciences.

As Agnes Heller (1999) has argued, to be authentic is not only to reject the risk of alienation caused by inauthenticity but is also a way of remaining 'true to oneself' in order to achieve the single most sublime virtue of life. As Heller points out, authentic men and women manage to remain faithful to their choices – they are those kinds of individuals 'who are pulled and not pushed, who are personalities', which means they are capable of achieving the sort of life that is as close to perfection as a modern person can get. In this way Heller is, in common with other existential thinkers, speaking of the possibility of moving from a state of 'having' to a state of 'being', in which men and women are rekindled with their own genuine, transcendent mode of being-in-the-world that is only possible through the engagement of the self with a life that is mystical and blends effortlessly with the collective.

That authenticity is increasingly important to people's leisure lives is demonstrated to good effect in Blackshaw's (2003) book *Leisure Life*, which traces the perceived sense of authenticity that marks the characteristic features of being one of 'the lads'. As Blackshaw demonstrates, just as it might be said that is not enough for an authentic Muslim man simply to pray, eat, drink and sleep and dress like Mohamed because he feels he must live like the prophet, it might also be argued that, for a modern secular working-class man, it is not enough for him have a leisure interest, he has to engage with it to the extent that it becomes an essential part of his spiritual being and communal life. As Blackshaw

demonstrates in his discussion, the notion of authenticity is wrapped up with 'the lads'' shared leisure experiences: just as they found their collective identity on them, they also justify their extremities through them.

On the face of it, Blackshaw's work seems to confirm Heller's argument that, just as authenticity is a matter of living a certain way, it is also an ethical way of life which involves treating others as you would expect them to treat you. In other words, taking responsibility for the Other: caring for and respecting those close to you, but also strangers. However, contrary to Heller, Blackshaw's research, drawing on Ricoeur's terminology, suggests that the constancy and resoluteness that accompany the authenticity of 'the lads'' leisure lives are marked by their own epistemology of 'attestation' that works in two ways which are mutually dependent. First, the discourse of the leisure life-world operates as 'the lads'' very own truth about the world, which is defined through a 'self-certainty' that enables them to give assurances to one another that it is in their leisure that they really can be authentic. Second, it is through the selfsame certainty of this discourse that 'the lads' can certify that 'their' leisure life-world is 'free' from those others whom it excludes – what 'the lads' call the 'flids', 'spastics', 'slags' and 'fanny' living 'solid' modern lives, barred from the discourse that has created them – which enables them to construct and schematize a collective leisure experience that is constant and which allows them to maintain their sameness at the same time as excluding and controlling the Other.

What Blackshaw's research also suggests, following Baudrillard (2001), is that, in an individualized society such as ours, pursuing an authentic existence is a form of dream making that is pathetically absurd. For all the determination of 'the lads' to live their leisure lives authentically, their capacity to form authentic loving relationships, to feel secure as well as free, is unlikely. This is because the existential import of the idea of authenticity emerges at its most potent in their lives when it transpires that there is no such thing: existentially 'the lads' may think they are authentic, but this authenticity is fated to be no more than fleetingly signifi- cant in a liquid modern consumer society. In other words, 'the lads', in common with other individuals, set themselves a circle that they can never hope to square: the ambivalence of being authentic in a world in which authenticity is just another (leisure) lifestyle choice.

Tony Blackshaw

Associated Concepts Alienation; Bauman; Crafts and Craftsmanship; Consumption; Individualization; Leisure as a Value-Sphere; Leisure Life-Style; Leisure Life-World; Serious Leisure.

B

BAUDRILLARD, JEAN (1929–2007)

Acclaimed as a genius in some quarters, dismissed as a talentless purveyor of postmodernist rhetoric in others, Baudrillard's status as a key thinker remains a matter of heated debate – something of an accomplishment in itself. Baudrillard was born in Reims in France. He was the first of his family to go to university, where he studied German and subsequently became a teacher and translator. He began to establish himself as a sociologist in the 1960s. One of his earliest central concerns was how to develop Marxist theory through an examination of reproduction and culture as well as production and structure vis-à-vis the work of Guy Debord and the Situationalists on the Society of the Spectacle and the cultural Marxism of Henri Lefebvre. Baudrillard subsequently expanded Marx's theory of commodity fetishism to argue that, in a consumer society, a symbolic realm of 'sign values' will supplement 'exchange values'. However, he was later to become disillusioned with Marxism and it became one of his prime targets of derision because of its epistemologically and ontologically naïve attempts to understand a society that had become postmodern (not his preferred nomenclature) and had in the process inadvertently become a simulacrum of itself.

On the vacillations of postmodern life, Baudrillard was brilliant. He met the paroxysm of the contemporary world on its own terms: knocked its wig off, twisted its private parts and spat in its eye. In the contemporary world, Baudrillard argued, leisure had been reduced to the status of 'any consumption of unproductive time' (Baudrillard, 1981: 76). 'Real' leisure had been replaced by an implosion of simulations and the upshot was that television had taken over human lives; like life more generally, leisure has become hyperreal or 'more real than real', merely a simulacrum of the 'real thing' it duplicates.

Critics have argued that Baudrillard's expiring of the social and 'reality' from his schema weakened these ideas almost to the point of extinction. However, this is to miss the point of Baudrillard. With his work it is difficult to unravel fact from fiction, fanciful musings from real issues – the counterculture of the 1960s suited his mood and style. The reader needs to be aware that his work is art, not science. He was the master of calculated irresolution. He did not want to put his readers' minds at rest – he wanted his ideas to puzzle and disturb us – and it is this that prevented his ideas tipping over into nihilism. Contrary to what his critics say, Baudrillard was not saying that life (or leisure) is fake or bogus, just that the hyperreality of the world we inhabit today renders null and void the opposition between truth and falsity.

When Baudrillard turned his critical eye to the absurdities of postmodern society, there was nobody else who could match his razor-sharp observations, especially about consumption. Indeed, the real subject of his work was not leisure at all but the pervasive power of consumer society – the habituation of a life that has been reduced to life-style shopping and the reduction of humankind to the status of commodities and insipid manufactured sameness.

Tony Blackshaw

Associated Concepts Bauman; Consumption; 'Into', the; Consumer Society; Cool; Leisure Bodies; Modernity; Leisure Life-Style; Performativity; Postmodernism; Postmodernity.

BAUMAN, ZYGMUNT (1925–)

Bauman is not a leisure scholar. He is a gifted practitioner of the sociological imagination who reads the world with the eyes of a poet and the mind of the most ardent of critics, arraigning the diminution of the public voice, and doing so with all the social force of witness he has at his command. To this extent he must be understood as the sociologist-as-man-of-action, admonishing us about the contingencies and ambivalences of modernity and postmodernity (re-described in his more recent work as solid modernity and liquid modernity) and how these resonate with people's experiences of leisure, as well as many of the issues confronting leisure studies.

Born into a family of Jewish origin in Poznan, Poland, in 1925, Bauman could be a character in a twentieth-century novel by the great Argentine writer, Jorge Luis Borges, an epic charting the peak and decline of the 'solid' *conjoncture* stage of modernity. As Keith Tester (2004: 1) has pointed out, by the 'time he was twenty, Bauman had confronted anti-Semitism, Stalinism, Nazism and warfare'. Despite fighting for his country against the Nazis during the Second World War, 'Bauman was expelled from the army in 1953 during an anti-Semitic purge which was carried out in the name of the policy of the "de-Judaising of the army"' (ibid). In 1968 he was sacked from his Professorship at Warsaw University and expatriated from his country during another anti-Semitic purge. Shortly after, he was offered a chair at the University of Leeds, and remained Professor of Sociology there until his 'retirement' in 1990.

Though Bauman has not written anything directly about leisure, some of his key ideas – liquid modernity, individualization, palimpsest identities, cloakroom communities, neo-tribes, sociological hermeneutics and hermeneutical sociology – have been taken up by leisure theorists, notably Tony Blackshaw in his (2003) book *Leisure Life: Myth, Masculinity and Modernity*, in order to make knowable the leisure life-world of a group of working-class men he calls 'the lads'. Drawing on these key themes, Bauman's work allows Blackshaw to not only make sense of how 'the lads' live their leisure lives in liquid modernity but also how they feel that collective experience individually and together.

Now in his ninth decade, Bauman's ability to ignite the sociological imagination remains undiminished and, not only that, he continues to be somebody with a marvellously acute sense of how contemporary life is lived. Indeed, his is the only sociology written today that comes close to depicting in its pages what the complexity of postmodernity (or as he calls it, liquid modernity) looks *and* feels like. If the true measure of the best sociology is the impossibility of examining and understanding life and leisure as it is lived just then, at that moment, before its ready-made theories and jargons get in the way, but which nonetheless tries to make its subjects live again as well as excite interest in their lives, then Bauman's sociology succeeds better than most. When you read him, imagine ontological and methodological questions don't matter; just savour his reading of the contemporary world and what it tells you about leisure and leisure studies – you can trust him.

Tony Blackshaw

Associated Concepts Baudrillard; Community; Consumer Society; Consumption; Individualization; Leisure Life-World; Liquid Modernity; Postmodernism; Postmodernity.

BINARY OPPOSITIONS

Though the consideration of binary oppositions originates in Greek philosophy, and specifically the observations of Parmenides, the basis of more contemporary discussions can be found in the structuralist work of Ferdinand de Saussure and Noam Chomsky, which suggests that language involves two-part systems, where terms, words or concepts are defined by their counterpart and, more importantly, by what they are not. For instance, male is defined as opposite and in contrast to female, as is black to white, high to low, good to evil, and so on ...

Lévi-Strauss (1966) suggested that these codes of opposition operate at a level that is not conscious or directly observable, but at a level that is sometimes described as that of deep structure. The study of culture, according to structuralists, consists of an examination of cultural forms. These cultural forms are the result of the human mind being brought to bear on particular environments. Lévi-Strauss argued that the resultant cultural forms all exhibit the same pattern, that of binary oppositions. What is significant is not the different contents, but the identical patterning of cultural forms and, hence, their structure.

The unequal nature of binary oppositions is developed further by Jacques Derrida, who points our attention to how one side of each binary pair is always 'preferred' to the other (such as 'good' over 'evil' or 'masculine' rather than 'feminine'), which is the product of imbalances of power and knowledge. Derrida suggests that this privileging of one component of a couplet is always based upon 'presence' and 'absence' – such as in Freudian psychoanalysis, when the female is defined as an absence of masculinity (and more specifically the phallus), which is seen as the 'norm'. However, Derrida suggests that binary oppositions are fundamentally flawed and unreliable and seeks to deconstruct these, pointing to how these oppositions are far from set or natural. In particular, Derrida breaks down the boundaries between binary pairs and argues that, rather than being understood as opposites, it is important to understand how these will blur and collapse into each other.

Given the focus of Derrida's own deconstruction of philosophy is 'Plato's Pharmacy', the issue of drugs in sport is an appropriate example to illustrate how this concept can be applied in leisure studies. Following Derrida, we can understand drug use as the scapegoat of sport. It is frequently seen as an 'evil' found in sport that must be cast out to maintain its 'purity' and 'true' 'essence'. However, Derrida deconstructs this order and in the process undermines the logic that there is some 'true' 'essence' of sport. Drug use has been prevalent in sport since its inception (both as a performance enhancer and as a remedy for injuries) and as a scapegoat it must belong inside sport, yet it must also belong outside because it undermines the 'true' ethos of sport. Deconstruction suggests that our ethical decision making about drugs in sport is socially constructed and based upon a set of judgments that rely on the invocation of existing frameworks of power and knowledge about what is 'deviant' and what is 'normal' in sport.

Garry Crawford and Tony Blackshaw

Associated Concepts   Decentring Leisure; Deconstruction; Freud; Postmodernism; Semiotics.

BIRMINGHAM SCHOOL, THE

The Birmingham School is a name given to a group of scholars working at Birmingham University's Centre for Contemporary Cultural Studies, which was established in the 1960s under the auspices of Richard Hoggart who was its first director. This Centre continued to produce influential and important work until its closure in 2002. However, it was in the 1970s and early 1980s that it became most prominent under the directorship of Stuart Hall and it was during this period that it became synonymous with the development of 'cultural studies' as a subject.

The work of the Birmingham School was diverse, but the output of most of those who worked there can be categorized into three key (interlinked) areas of interest: textual studies of the mass media, 'ordinary' life and political ideologies (Smith, 2001). First, it is evident that much of the work of the Birmingham School academics was influenced by Antonio Gramsci and that their studies of the mass media also combined this with semiotic analysis. In particular, much of this effort focused on the role of the mass media in producing and maintaining hegemony. Stuart Hall and other authors at the Birmingham School argued that the mass media provided ideological messages that portrayed a false ideology and prevented critical thinking.

Second, the Birmingham School had a tradition of ethnographic research into patterns of ordinary life, in particular subcultures. However, how this differed from traditional ethnography was that the studies of the Birmingham School often interpreted and located everyday action and practices within a wider political framework. For instance, the edited collection by Hall and Jefferson (1976) *Resistance through Rituals* saw members of the Birmingham School consider various forms of youth subcultures, such as their activities, dress, codes, drug use and so on, as cultures of resistance grounded in class relations.

Third, this work then crossed over into more specific considerations of the political economy and, in particular, the Birmingham School was also concerned with understanding right-wing politics, such as Thatcherism. In *Policing the Crisis*, written by Hall and his colleagues in 1978, the Birmingham School authors employed the neo-Marxist work of Gramsci and also Stanley Cohen's (1972) ideas on moral panics. Here, Hall et al. suggested that, from the 1960s onwards, a breakdown of consensus had started in British society. British life was becoming much more characterized by strikes, protests and demonstrations, which were causing major disruptions to the capitalist system and the status quo in British society. However, a series of moral panics was created in the 1970s onwards, which helped reconstruct a sense of national identity and restore social cohesion.

Of particular significance to leisure studies is the work of two Birmingham School scholars, John Clarke and Chas Critcher, and their book *The Devil Makes Work* (1985), who applied a neo-Marxist consideration of the political economy to leisure. In this they suggest that the degree of freedom of choice individuals had in their leisure was often exaggerated and that this (particularly for the working classes) was both shaped and constrained by capitalism. In particular, they suggested that, while middle-class leisure pursuits are heavily promoted and subsidized, working-class leisure activities are often restricted and/or licensed by the state. This can clearly be seen throughout the eighteenth and nineteenth centuries in the way traditional working-class folk sports, which were often seen as little more than dangerous gatherings, were either banned or institutionalized and controlled by the state and middle classes. Significantly, they also suggested that in more contemporary times leisure has become progressively commercialized, with leisure increasingly based around a consumption which is fed and controlled by multinational capitalist corporations.

The 1970s and 1980s have been seen as the golden era of British cultural studies and the Birmingham School, but, from the early 1980s onwards, there began a (greater) fragmentation and diversification of ideas and subject matter within the School (Smith, 2001). In many ways this was a logical development, but it also marked the beginning of the end of the Birmingham School as a group of scholars who shared similar interests and perspectives. In particular, authors began to move away from solely focusing on class to considering other areas such as gender and ethnicity. In *Women Take Issue* Angela McRobbie and her colleagues (Women's Study Group, 1978) 'took issue' with the marginalization of women in the Birmingham School's study of working-class culture. Race and ethnicity were also areas that had received little consideration in the early work of the Birmingham School. Though *Policing the Crisis* had touched on issues of race, it was Paul Gilroy and his colleagues in *The Empire Strikes Back* (1982) and later *There Ain't no Black in the Union Jack* (1987) who provided the first detailed consideration of race to come out of Birmingham.

Garry Crawford

Associated Concepts Capitalism; Class; Consumer Society; Consumption; False Consciousness; Folk Devils and Moral Panics; Hegemony; Hoggart; Ideology; Marxism; Mass Media; Power; Racism and Leisure; Semiotics/Semiology; Structure and Agency; Subcultures.

BLOOD SPORTS

Blood sports is a generic term applied to any sporting activity that involves the suffering or killing of animals or people, such as bull fighting and fox hunting. In particular, hunting provides us with a useful illustration of the contextual nature of 'blood sports'. For instance, a simple distinction is often drawn between hunting for subsistence and hunting for pleasure; however, throughout history, hunting has been an activity that has often been associated with ceremony and activities that go beyond the gathering of food alone. It is also the case that the word 'sport' is a term that has historically been most commonly associated with hunting and this continues to be the case for many people. Even the term 'game' is one that is frequently applied to those animals that are hunted.

Beyond hunting, other forms of killing for pleasure, such as bull, dog and cock fighting and bear baiting, have had a similarly long history. These 'sports' have their origins in pre-modern societies and in some cases were frequently linked with combat training (such as using dogs and other animals in warfare) as well as entertainment. Probably the most prominent historical example of blood sport (certainly in terms of our contemporary interest in it) was the gladiatorial and animal fighting events of ancient Rome.

Again, the origins of these activities lie in both combat training and entertainment, but in ancient Rome these took on new social, political and cultural significance. Gladiatorial events were common throughout Roman history across much of their empire, and these only came to an end with the fall of the Roman Empire (in around the fifth or sixth century AD). These events were used to dispose of 'undesirables' (such as criminals) as well as for entertainment and involved a variety of forms of combat between humans, or humans and animals or between various (often exotic) animals.

Romans of all social backgrounds and classes attended the spectacles of the arena, but it is difficult to judge the social role that blood sports played in Roman culture. Some historians (such as Barton, 1994) have indicated that these were closely connected to religion, as the origins of many blood sports lay in religious sacrifices to Roman gods. Others (such as Hopkins, 1983) have suggested these events were more to do with militarism and imperialism – by way of celebrating and commemorating great victories and battles. Sansone (1988) has viewed these events more notably as forms of sport and entertainment, while Clavel-Lévéque (1984) has highlighted their use as a form of social control and as a 'show of power'. Their 'true' purpose however is likely to have been a combination of these reasons and also dependent on the context of each particular event.

Beyond the Roman Empire, animal fighting has continued to be a popular form of entertainment throughout history in many different cultures and indeed the world over. For instance, bear baiting was a very popular leisure pastime in England between the sixteenth and nineteenth centuries and still continues today in certain parts of the world. Likewise hunting for 'sport', such as grouse and deer hunting, is still legal and popular in many countries, and even today the laws to outlaw fox hunting in the UK have had little real impact on preventing this activity from continuing in many rural locations. In particular, what is often significant about the control and regulation of blood sports is the class dimension to these activities, which means that, while many working-class leisure activities such as cock fighting and badger baiting have been deemed 'cruel' and are therefore banned in many countries, middle-class and aristocratic sports, such as grouse hunting and (to some extent) even deer hunting, have been allowed to continue.

Though blood sports are often seen as 'barbaric', it is important that these are understood in their historical setting and in the context that *all* societies will choose to kill – such as in state executions or slaughtering animals to eat. In many ways our own contemporary society is just as (if not more) barbaric as that of ancient cultures such as the Roman Empire, as modern society has turned the slaughter of animals into an industrial-scale process of cultivation and production-line mass killing.

Garry Crawford

Associated Concepts Abnormal Leisure; Carnivalesque; Deviance; Mimesis; Violence.

BODY/BODIES

(leisure bodies)

BOHEMIANS

'Just as none of us is outside or beyond geography', said Edward Said (1993: 6), 'none of us is completely free from the struggle over geography'. This is a statement that is pertinent to the idea of the bohemian. The term derives from Bohemia, the kingdom of central Europe which, under Hapsburg rule between the early sixteenth century and the end of the Second World War, included the Czech Republic and Slovenia. The idea of bohemianism was first used in the nineteenth century to describe the unconventional lifestyles of *demi-mondaine* characters – artists, writers and musicians, as well as the hybrids, misfits and one-offs – who had created alternative or deviant artistic communities or countercultures, typically in the zones of transition formed in major European cities. 'Bohemia' came into existence, then, so that people ill at ease with the prevailing conditions of modernity could have somewhere to call home. In this sense it could be said that bohemianism is a sign of authenticity because bohemians are men and women who refuse to live a false life or, in the contemporary world, refuse to conform to the conventions of consumer society. However, as Wilson's prescient (2000) work suggests, bohemianism today has been so thoroughly commercialized that it has become just another leisure life-style choice for individuals seduced by the idea of living a life that is off-the-wall: 'glamorous and sexy, unconventional and edgy, yet chic and cool'.

Tony Blackshaw

Associated Concepts Abnormal Leisure; Authenticity; Community; Consumption; Cool; Deviance; Edgework; Flow; Leisure Life-Style; Liminality; Zones.

BOSTON MATRIX

The Boston Matrix, much like the Ansoff Matrix, is a well-known marketing tool. Its primary concern is in developing and effectively managing a product portfolio in order to help organizations develop and control their market share. The matrix involves placing an organization's products into four categories: star, cash cow, problem child and dog.

The idea behind the Boston Matrix is that each of these categories can be useful to an organization in the sense that products can move freely between them depending on the market situation and the marketing objectives of that organization.

- *Star products* are characterized by a high market share and therefore a high turnover. This signifies an excellent state of affairs for an organization as high market growth presents an opportunity to obtain an increased market share. However, products in this category are also under an increased threat from both current and potential competitors.
- *Cash cows* are the breadwinners for an organization in the short term. Although the market growth is low and the product is likely to be in the latter stages of its life-cycle, potential competitors will be unlikely to enter the same market. This presents the organization with opportunities to squeeze revenues during the final stages of a product's life.
- *Problem child* products are those that perform badly at present. However, when product assessments are made, their future potential is often considerable, as indicated by high market growth. These products are often referred to as question marks in the sense that their futures are frequently uncertain. Organizations are normally advised to invest heavily in such products or to get out of the market altogether.
- *Dogs* are characterized by a low market share that is likely to dent the corporate bottom line. Market growth is low, so the situation is unlikely to improve. Organizations are usually advised to discontinue such lines.

Rob Wilson

Associated Concepts Ansoff Matrix; Leisure Marketing; Marketing Mix; Market Positioning and Market Segmentation.

BOURDIEU, PIERRE (1930–2002)

Pierre Bourdieu was an extremely influential French sociologist who contributed significantly to our understanding of many aspects of social life, including social practices, consumption, culture, leisure and sport and social class. Born in rural southern France in 1930, Bourdieu went on to study philosophy at the *Ecole Normal Supérieure* in Paris under the tutelage of Louis Althusser. Upon graduation he became a *lycée* (French higher school/college) teacher at Moulins from 1955 to 1958, before undertaking his military service in Algeria and becoming a tutor there. While in Algeria, Bourdieu undertook extensive ethnographic work that would not only form his first book *Sociologie de L'Algerie* (published in English as *The Algerians* in 1962) but also the foundations of his theoretical approach to society and culture. In 1960, on his return to Paris, he followed an academic university career path, teaching at the University of Paris until 1964, where he took up a post at the *Ecoles des Hautes Etudes en Sciences Sociales*. In 1981 he was appointed to the chair of Sociology at the *Collège de France*.

Though Bourdieu's work was largely structuralist, as he was interested in how cultures and practices produce and reproduce social domination he also sought to bridge the traditional divide between structure and agency. Bourdieu suggested that it was necessary to not only understand objective social structures but also to grasp how these were interpreted and practised by social actors. A good example of this is his work on habitus, which suggests that, while 'culture' is something that shapes and directs our behaviour, it also operates not on, but through and within, individuals – habitus is therefore 'embodied'.

Bourdieu offered several key ideas and theories that have been employed in the study of society and culture and, in turn, have been taken on board by leisure scholars. For example, Bourdieu recognized the composite nature of social class and how this is shaped not only by economic capital (such as in a Marxist understanding) but also by other forms of capital, such as social capital and cultural capital. Bourdieu is also most commonly associated with his seminal work on distinction, which, by drawing on extensive research into social practices, sets out an understanding of how culture produces and reproduces social distinctions and hierarchies.

Bourdieu turned his attention to numerous social and cultural practices, including education, art, film and sport, and was also politically active, particularly in his later life. He was an academic who believed it was important that intellectuals contributed to political struggle and amongst numerous other causes he championed the rights of French immigrants and farmers and suggested that it was important to fight against the creeping forces of globalization. Bourdieu consistently pointed out that in a global world politics is continually moving further away from the locality of the city to the international level, from the immediate concrete reality of people's everyday lives to a distant abstraction which renders it invisible.

Garry Crawford

Associated Concepts Class; Consumption; Cultural Capital; Culture; Distinction; Habitus, Field and Capital; Marxism; Social Capital; Structure and Agency.

BRANDING, BRAND AWARENESS AND BRAND IMAGE

Kotler (1997) describes a brand as a name, term, symbol or design – or a combination of these – that is intended to identify the goods or services of one seller or group of sellers and the way it is used to differentiate these from those of competitors. A brand is not a product; it is the product's essence, its meaning and its direction, that which defines its identity in time and space. As such, branding helps an organization differentiate itself from its competitors. Consumers will often make a connection with a brand, form relationships with brands and trust brands and will often go back to a brand time and time again – this is called brand loyalty. Gilbert (1999) suggests that brands have to be clearly positioned so as to give distinct signals and demarcations from their rivals. This requires a clear distinction encompassing the need to provide a focus and personality for the brand. As Gilbert points out, the success of a brand is not based on the number of customers who purchase that brand just once; this is instead determined by the number of customers who repeat their purchase. It is important in a crowded market, such as leisure, the right branding creates an image that 'cuts through' (e.g., Nike, Adidas, Disney, Mecca Bingo).

Aaker (1991) suggests that consumers tend to buy familiar brands because they are comfortable with things familiar. This makes the assumption that the most familiar brands are probably reliable and, more than likely, of reasonable quality. A recognized brand will therefore be selected in preference to an unknown brand. The awareness factor is particularly important in contexts where a brand must first enter the evoked set – that is, when it is inevitable it will be evaluated within a set of other esteemed brands. An unknown brand usually has little chance of this.

A key component of brand awareness is brand image. This is what can often make or break a brand. A brand image for an organization is the sum of beliefs, ideas and impressions held by consumers about the company and its products (Stotlar, 2001). This is based on the rationale that by creating a positive brand image organizations will benefit from increased brand loyalty.

Rob Wilson

Associated Concepts Ansoff Matrix; Boston Matrix; Leisure Marketing; Market Positioning and Market Segmentation.

BUDGETING

It is vital that all businesses have a plan so that they can make effective decisions and exercise control over management operations. A budget is simply a plan expressed in financial terms. Budgets may often be prepared in summary format by illustrating income and expenditure streams on a monthly basis, although occasionally they can be much more detailed and will outline the expected income and expenditure from very specific items. Once budgets have been prepared, the financial information can be communicated to staff and targets can then be set.

For any plan to be achieved it must be monitored and control programmes need to be initiated. Budgets must be treated in the same way to prevent them from becoming unrealistic and poorly managed. The most common method of budgeting in the leisure industry is called zero-based budgeting.

Zero-based budgeting (ZBB) was developed to overcome some of the common criticisms of standard budgeting techniques, whereby managers simply dug out the budget from the previous year and increased everything by the rate of inflation. ZBB takes a much more strategic approach, with budgets rewritten each year. Budgets begin at zero and each item of income and expenditure is appraised so that the contribution of all the departments involved is maximized. This method of budgeting is traditionally used in leisure organizations due to the volatile nature of the industry. It also enables these budgets to be flexible so that organizations can respond to changes in the external environment (e.g., changing government priorities).

Rob Wilson

Associated Concepts   Assets, Liabilities and Capital; Cash Flow Forecast; Double-entry Bookkeeping; Financial and Management Accounting; Financial Health and Ratio Analysis; Financial Statements; Profitability, Liqudity, Growth and Breaking Even.

BUREAUCRACY

This term refers to a form of administration organized through complex rules, regulations and hierarchies, involving the division of specific categories of activity and roles. Though the bureaucratic form can be found over a long historical period, dating back to ancient Greece (if not before), the contemporary concept of bureaucracy is most commonly associated with rationalized ideas of organization that developed in Europe with the Enlightenment in the eighteenth century. Though the features of bureaucracy are discussed by several key social theorists, it is a term most commonly associated with Max Weber. Weber described the 'ideal type' (i.e., how something should work in principle) bureaucracy as an efficient and rational form of legal domination. However, 'real' bureaucracies (as Weber notes himself) were far less efficient and rational than the ideal type would suggest and, in particular, high levels of division of labour can lead to an individual disinterest in the overall well-being of the organization, overcomplexity, rigidity and the exponential growth of rules and regulations, amongst numerous other individual and organizational pathologies, which will question the overall efficiency of these types of organization. In particular, the flaws and limitations of bureaucratic structures are evident in the 'red tape' and rule-bound nature of many governmental bodies and organizations, including sporting and leisure organizations and governing bodies.

Garry Crawford

Associated Concepts   Capitalism; Leisure in the Community; Leisure Policy; Modernity; Work Ethic.

BUSINESS ENVIRONMENT

Scanning the business environment should be a key activity for all leisure organizations, because it is through this process that the threats and opportunities that may impact on their success can be identified and managed. The environmental scanning process involves identifying drivers of change in order to assess their impact. The challenge is to try and identify these drivers while they are still weak signals so that windows of opportunitiy can be seized or imminent threats can be anticipated and more easily controlled.

The term environment is not used here in an ecological sense, but in a more general contextual manner. There are various ways that the business environment can be delineated, with the most common being the internal business environment (the layer within an organization which it has most control over) and the external environment (the layer beyond its control, such as the global economy). It is also possible to make a distinction between the intermediary environment and the external environment, with the former referring immediate competitors and key markets which the organization can seek to take some control of. Some writers use the terms macro and micro to refer to the internal and external business environment; however, this can create confusion as these are more generally used to delineate different levels of economic study and analysis.

There are various ways that the scanning process can be approached. Two of the most common are SWOT and PEST analyses. These are acronyms which can provide a series of headings to help prompt and focus an evaluation of both the organization itself and the business environment in which it operates.

SWOT (Strengths, Weaknesses, Opportunities and Threats) comprises a two-part analysis: an internal analysis of the strengths and weaknesses of the organization and an analysis of the external business environment. This analysis of the external environment can be given further sophistication by the use of a PEST framework. PEST is the acronym for the Political, Economic, Social and Technological environment and is simply a framework by which the external environment can be approached in relation to identifying and assessing the risks to an organization.

As the business environment has become marked by more complexity and rapid change, more variables have been added to the basic PEST framework, such as separating the legal environment from the political and, more recently, by identifying the natural environment, or ecological factors, as a potential source of threats and opportunities – hence the emergence of PESTLE. There are other variations of PESTLE: for example, SPECTACLES analysis, which is an acronym for Social analysis, Political, Economic, Cultural, Technological, Aesthetic, Customers, Legal, and the Environments.

A key criticism of these models is not so much the weakness of the frameworks themselves, but the fact that, notwithstanding their ostensible sophistication, they belie the complexity of the environmental factors which need to be considered. That is, these frameworks have a superficial simplicity which makes them attractive and relatively easy to understand, but much more difficult to actually use in practice.

Mark Piekarz

Associated Concepts   Leisure Policy.

C

CAPITAL

(habitus, field and capital)

CAPITALISM

Capitalism is an economic system, based upon the private ownership of the means of production, operated within a free market for the generation of profit. However, capitalism is more than just a system of production, it is also an ideological perspective. The birth of capitalism is frequently associated with the Industrial Revolution or before this the Enlightenment and, though it is inextricably tied to both of these historical periods, it predates both. The foundations of capitalism in Europe can probably be traced back to antiquity and, in particular, the mercantile trade (or 'mercantilism') of ancient Roman society and, in medieval times, from the Middle East.

The ideals of capitalism were wholly compatible with those of the Enlightenment, of social progression through rational and calculated means, and therefore we can see the continued growth of capitalist enterprise and ideology throughout the eighteenth century leading right up until the Industrial Revolution. Capitalist ideology and economics provided an important precursor to the Industrial Revolution, but it is with industrialization that we see rapid changes in society and the widespread adoption of a capitalist system of society.

Capitalism was of great interest to several nineteenth-century sociologists and social historians, most notably Max Weber and Karl Marx. In particular, Weber was interested in the origins of capitalism and the Industrial Revolution, and argued that the Reformation had laid the foundations for modern Western capitalism by promoting a privatized work ethic that suited capitalism. Marx's analysis of capitalism, while also rooted in an historical analysis of its development and foundations, was more focused on the consequences of modern Western capitalism and, in particular, on offering a critique of this. Marx argued that modern capitalism had led to a growing social inequality, where the working classes (proletariat) were exploited by those who owned the means of production (bourgeoisie) in order to maximize profits. However, it is suggested by Marxists that within contemporary capitalism class-based exploitation not only takes place within the workplace but also within our leisure time. For instance, Clarke and Critcher (1985) point to how leisure choices are shaped and constrained by capitalism, and how leisure within capitalism is used both as a means of hegemonic schooling and as a source of capitalist profiteering.

Though the fundamental nature of private ownership and the generation of profit have changed little, it is evident that other aspects of capitalism have changed significantly. For instance, we can see that many contemporary capitalist economies (such as in Western Europe and North America) are primarily based upon consumption rather than production. This has led some to suggest that the form of capitalism we now live in should be described as 'advanced capitalism' or 'late capitalism' or as Lash and Urry (1987) define it 'disorganized capitalism', which refers to the ways in which the structuring of society, the economy and social relations (and we might say leisure) have become less organized, more fragmented and characterized by risk and uncertainty.

Garry Crawford

Associated Concepts Alienation; Consumer Society; Consumption; Hegemony; Ideology; Marxism; Modernity; Risk Society.

CARNIVALESQUE

Carnivalesque is a blanket term that refers to those traditional, historical and enduring forms of social ritual, such as festivals, fairs and feasts, that provide sites of 'ordered disorder' (Stallybrass and White, 1986), where social rules are broken and subverted and where one can explore one's 'otherness', secret desires and most intimate pleasures. This term is most commonly associated with the Russian literary theorist, critic and philosopher, Mikhail Mikhailovich Bakhtin. Bakhtin was particularly interested in the European medieval carnival, where he suggested there was an inversion of the normal social order, with the normal social hierarchies, conventional roles and identities being transgressed, and a revelling in the obscene, vulgar and grotesque. Though Bakhtin suggests that these types of 'anarchic' carnival died out in the Renaissance period, the carnivalesque spirit continued in literature and, in particular, Bakhtin's most famous work *Rabelais and His World* (originally published in 1968) is a consideration of the sixteenth-century satirical and extravagant writings of Rabelais.

Bakhtin (1984b) describes four categories of the carnivalesque. The first is free and familiar contact between people, where the differences and hierarchies between people collapse. Second, is where there is a new mode of interpersonal relationship between people, where the normal restraints and expectations are transgressed. Third, is what Bakhtin (1984b: 123) refers to as a 'carnivalistic mésalliance', where 'free and familiar' attitudes spread over everything, bringing together and unifying things which are normally separated, such as the sacred and the profane. Fourth, Bakhtin identifies a 'profanation' in a whole carnivalistic system of debasing and blaspheming what is normally held as sacred.

The ideas of the carnivalesque have been applied to many aspects of leisure and in particular to discussions of social transgression and resistance – both in a textual sense and in terms of social phenomenon. For instance, Annandale (2006) considers the digital game series *Grand Theft Auto* as a carnivalesque text, in its parody, satire and subversion of social conventions, while Giulianotti (1991) applies the concept to his consideration of the carnival-like behaviour of Scottish football fans.

Garry Crawford

Associated Concepts Flow; Intertextuality; Liminality; Power; Semiotics; Spectacle.

CASTELLS, MANUEL

(network society)

CASUAL LEISURE

(consumption; crafts and craftsmanship; serious leisure)

CATHARSIS AND CATHEXIS

These two concepts belong to a word family that has a number of applications. From the Greek term *kathairein*, at its most basic catharsis means to purify or to clean. However, it is the psychoanalytical understanding of the concept that has generally been used in leisure studies. On the one hand, catharsis is used to refer to the release of pent-up feelings and emotions in order to reduce tensions and anxieties (e.g., when individuals play competitive sport), echoing Plato's premise that a cathartic experience involves 'removing the bad, and leaving the good'. On the other hand, it used to signify a purgative or liberating leisure experience accomplished through performing challenging and often distressing activities (e.g., completing a marathon). From the Greek *katekhein*, meaning to hold fast, cathexis (also in the meaning of psychoanalysis) refers to ways in which individuals can channel their energies on single goals and is similarly used to explain how people achieve remarkable sporting achievements.

Tony Blackshaw

Associated Concepts Authenticity; Flow; Liminality.

CELEBRITY

Today we are all familiar with this term and most of us will know what a celebrity is, but it is difficult to produce a concise definition that will cope adequately with the many questions arising from this awareness. The derivation of the term is undoubtedly religious, from the solemnity of holy celebration, but its contemporary usage is secular. Celebrity, and its shorthand equivalent 'celeb', are used to describe a specific kind of cultural figure whose fame or notoriety precedes them and whose distinguishing cultural quality is that of being watched. Celebrities will usually have found their fame in the entertainment industry or in the most popular sports – premiership footballers, for example, have recently completed the transfer from sportsmen to celebrities. Yet the term is no longer held in reserve solely for those individuals who it would seem have a special talent and whose rostrum of fame is

decidedly small. It is just as likely to apply to those who have the ability to fulfil our collective fantasies about stardom or some form of deviant activity for which they have become famous and, crucially, who come across to us as classy, sassy or just desirable, which in 'real-life' terms makes them, for most of us, tantalizingly just out of reach.

In his discussion of the successive stages of the development of the means and relations of media transmission, Régis Debray (2007) argues that, if the figures of the saint and the hero were respectively the identifying myths of pre-modernity (Logosphere) and modernity (Graphosphere), in the contemporary postmodern age (Videosphere) it is the figure of the celebrity that is central. Bauman suggests that what this means is that celebrity has become the new focal point of power and privilege in our global popular culture. If the 'flawed consumers' (the poor) are the neglected underside of postmodernity, the silent emblem of poverty, social exclusion, obesity and human waste, celebrity represents its overside: inclusion, skinniness and consumptive waste. Celebrities exist to remind us that we could be all of these things if we were also fabulously successful. For Bauman, it is consumerism that creates huge unconscious needs that only celebrity can satisfy (or so it seems).

Celebrities are the 'real-life' incarnations of Baudrillard's cult of the 'into': men and women who are obsessed with their appearance and who have become 'dedicated to the utopia of preservation of a youth that is already lost'. As Debray points out, youth is the canonical generation of postmodernity, so we expect the celebrity faces on our television screens – which on the one hand peddle the wares of the consumer capitalism and on the other feel the need to confess to us their every depravity as well as their addictions – to be youthful and wrinkle-free. In this way, celebrities are perceived to be the miracle of our contemporary obsession with individual self-construction, not least because they are the 'stars' who give hope to ordinary people who constantly long to reinvent themselves on youthful celebrity lines. In this sense it is easy to see why the world today is also the age *par excellence* of makeovers and botox, because celebrities lead us to believe that lines on a face are unpleasant on the eye – as well as being a constant reminder of mortality – and it makes perfect sense to airbrush them out.

Yet, because of their own mortality, celebrities are destined to move between the competing claims of ordinariness and specialness; they are like statues, simultaneously mighty and incapable, untouchable and all too touchable. The key is to try to achieve just the right balance between the two, but to also avoid at all costs the invisibility that is anathema to any celebrity: to disappear from the public consciousness or achieve the kind of familiarity which means that the public do not see you any more.

As the audience for celebrity has grown so has public interest in the private lives of celebrities, and celebrities themselves have come to understand that one of the best ways of maintaining their magnesium flare fame is to shamelessly confess themselves, by revealing all to an eager audience. Yet for all their want of trying most celebrities are condemned to suffer the fate of Porter in Shakespeare's *Macbeth*, opening the gate with a great deal of bluff and bluster but doomed to vanish after a brief moment centre stage.

Tony Blackshaw

Associated Concepts Aesthetics; Audiences; Desire; Fantasy Leisure; Flow; Happiness; Hedonism; 'Into', the; Liminality; Mimesis; Pleasure; Surveillance.

CIVIL SOCIETY

This is an imprecise and often contradictory term which Adam Ferguson, a leading philosopher of the Scottish Enlightenment, described as the processes by which humankind developed out of its 'rude' condition into a state of civilization. Writing in 1767, Ferguson held that, in any civil society,

the individual, while free to regard his or her happiness as a legitimate pursuit, should be willing to relinquish it if it interfered with the common good. In its more general usage the term refers to that realm of sociability and public participation outside the structures of the state which incorporates informal leisure interests such as dining out and drinking and more formal leisure institutions such as voluntary associations.

From a more critical perspective, Marx and Engels (1965 [1845]) described civil society as the 'true source and theatre of all history' that exists in opposition to the state and the economy. The more sophisticated versions of Marxism move beyond this dialectical understanding of civil society to argue that the state is not only a system of government but also an 'ideological' and 'repressive' apparatus (e.g., Althusser, 1977) or an amalgam of complex structures where the battle for hegemony is played out (e.g., Gramsci, 1971). This politics of civil society is perhaps best summarized by Keane (1988: 14) who describes it as 'an aggregate of institutions whose members are engaged primarily in a complex of non-state activities – economic and cultural production, household life and voluntary associations – and who in this way preserve and transform their identity by exercising all sorts of pressures and controls upon State institutions'.

In his book *The Fall of Public Man* (1977) Richard Sennett argues that, in the late seventeenth and eighteenth centuries, coffee houses were the places where civil society flourished, but this has since steadily declined. In a similar vein, Putnam (2000) observes that we have witnessed a decline in social capital. He points out that the bowling leagues of his youth with their legions of teams are no longer a dominant form of leisure participation and that people now tend to 'bowl alone'. Obviously they don't actually bowl alone, but in small, closed groups such that the activity does not involve any interaction with new people. Critics have argued that, like any other pillar of civil society, leisure rests on a complex foundation that state action can either fortify or undermine. While not talking about leisure directly, in his latest book of essays Sennett (2005) argues that the state has a key legitimating role to play in civil society and, drawing on the ideas of social capital and the critical social value of status, he argues that it needs to move beyond its current merely enabling function in order to play a key role in prompting usefulness as a public good.

Tony Blackshaw

Associated Concepts Community; Elias; Hegemony; Serious Leisure; Social Capital; Social Network Analysis.

CIVILIZING PROCESS

(Elias, Norbert)

CLASS

Edgell (1993: 1) argues that the concept of 'class' was originally used to refer to the division of the Roman population on the basis of property and for military purposes and that this was a set and prescriptive system. Contemporary notions of class are specifically linked to the reorganization of society that occurred along with the Industrial Revolution. In particular, studying and defining the nature of social class was of particular interest to early sociologists, such as Karl Marx and Max Weber. Marx offers one of the most famous analyses of the concept. His discussion of class was part of a wider consideration of the history and nature of societies and how these were shaped by the means of production within each historical period. Marx argued that with the Industrial Revolution there emerged two key social classes, which were both defined by their relations to the means of production – the capitalists (or bourgeoisie) who owned the means of production and the workers (or proletariat) who worked for the capitalists for a wage. Though Marx recognized internal conflicts between these classes, he suggested that the key feature of capitalism was that the bourgeoisie sought to exploit the proletariat as much as possible in order to maximize production and profit, thereby causing an inevitable conflict between these two classes.

It is a common misconception that Marx only recognized the existence of two social classes. He also acknowledged the existence of other social strata, such as the petite-bourgeoisie, the intelligentsia and the lumpen-proletariat. However, he saw these as transitional classes, because as the power of the bourgeoisie increased there would be a 'proletarianization' of society as all non-bourgeoisie become wage labourers (or in Marx's terms 'wage slaves').

Max Weber is generally seen to have developed Marx's work, both in adapting Marx's consideration of class and in recognizing the existence and importance of other forms of stratification such as status and ethnicity. For Marx, social class was defined by the relations to the means of production; similarly for Weber, the key defining feature of class was market position or, more specifically, the ownership (or lack of ownership) of property. However, Weber recognized other (both positively and negatively) privileged classes, such as those with a higher or lower education or social status. This then creates a much more complex and multifaceted understanding of social stratification (i.e., social ordering) than that set out by Marx.

To a significant degree, there has been some convergence between the definitions of class offered by both neo-Marxist and neo-Weberian writers. In particular, several neo-Marxist writers (such as Wright, 1976) have recognized the complex nature of class relations and composition. Furthermore, definitions and conceptualizations of social class have been offered and developed by numerous other authors who have each contributed their own understanding of this, such as Pierre Bourdieu who recognized the importance of other forms of capital beyond the economic (such as social capital and cultural capital) in shaping social class position.

Inevitably an individual's class position does have a significant impact and influence on their leisure. At its simplest level, the increased income and better work conditions that come with a higher class status can lead to greater leisure choices and opportunities than are afforded to those lower down the social order. However, as indicated, class is much more complex than simple economics, and so too is its relationship to leisure.

Class-based 'cultures' and traditions will also help shape leisure choices: for example, in England there is still a predominantly working-class following of rugby league as opposed to the more middle-class supporter base for rugby union. Clarke and Critcher in their classic (1985) study of leisure also highlighted several key class-based dimensions of leisure, such as how leisure is also shaped by middle-class ideals and capitalist commercial interest and can be used as a form of social control of the working classes.

Furthermore, it has been suggested that not only is leisure class-based but it can also play an important role in maintaining class hierarchies. For instance, Theodor Adorno and his colleagues at the Frankfurt School argued that the 'culture industry' (e.g., those who produced popular music, cinema and sport) produced cultural (leisure) products on the basis of maximizing profit and that these helped pacify the working classes – such as providing them with entertainment to alleviate their sense of alienation. A similar argument is offered by Clarke and Critcher (1985) who suggested that leisure has often been used as a form of social control, such as how ideas of 'rational recreation' were used to instil 'values' (i.e., compliance) within the working classes. However, writers such as Dick Hebdige and others at the Birmingham School have pointed out that leisure can also be used as a form of class-based resistance, such as working-class youths forming rebellious subcultures which are based around and utilize leisure activities, such as music and fashion.

In turn, certain leisure activities can be used to define and establish a person's class position. For example, playing golf may see an individual deemed 'middle class' by some, while membership of an exclusive golf club may enhance a person's social standing, networks and opportunities. The degree to which social class determines our leisure is characterized by the structure and agency debate, which questions to what degree social structures (such as class) determine our lives

and culture or to what extent this is based upon individual choices (agency).

However, there is general agreement that the nature of social class within most advanced capitalist societies, such as the UK, has changed significantly within recent decades. In particular, it has been suggested that there are now greater opportunities for individuals to be 'socially mobile' and move up (or down) the class hierarchy, undermining the rigidity of this system. It has also been suggested by some that the traditional class system, based upon an individual's relation to the means of production, is breaking down, and is increasingly being replaced by one based on an individual's ability to consume.

Garry Crawford

Associated Concepts Alienation; Birmingham School; Bourdieu; Capitalism; Consumption; Critical Theory; Cultural Capital; Culture; Marxism; Power; Social Capital; Status; Structure and Agency.

CLASS CONSCIOUSNESS

(false consciousness)

COLLECTIVE CONSUMPTION

(three-sector provision of leisure)

COMMODITY FETISHISM

Commodity fetishism refers to the exaggerated value of, and desire for, commodities which occurs within complex capitalist societies. The term is derived from the work of Marx and, in particular, the opening chapter to his seminal work *Capital* (originally published in 1867). Marx distinguishes between the 'exchange' and 'use' value of commodities. The exchange value relates to the economic value a commodity can command on the market, while the use value refers to the practical usefulness of the commodity. For Marx, the exchange value will always dominate in a capitalist system, as the production, marketing and consumption of commodities will always exceed and take precedence over people's real needs. This is an important distinction in understanding Marx's use and meaning of 'commodity fetishism'.

At the time of Marx, the word 'fetish' was primarily used to refer to primitive religious objects that were said to possess supernatural powers. Marx uses this term in a paradoxical sense, to highlight that the value of objects is not the result of some natural process, but, rather, the result of capitalist social and economic relations. However, in a capitalist system the production of a commodity seems 'natural' and, hence, the real social processes behind it are hidden, such as the labour and exploitation involved in producing it.

Marx's ideas of commodity fetishism were developed further by Adorno and his fellow writers at the Frankfurt School. In particular, Adorno extends Marx's ideas of commodity fetishism and applies this to understanding the 'culture industry' and how cultural forms, such as popular music, help to secure and maintain the continuing economic, political and ideological domination of capitalism. Hence, what Marx wrote about the industrial production process is also true (in Adorno's view) of the production of cultural goods. That is to say, they 'are produced for the market and aimed at the market' (Adorno, 1991: 34), where their exchange value is what dominates.

Garry Crawford

Associated Concepts   Alienation; Capitalism; Class; Consumption; Critical Theory; Ideology; Marxism; Power.

COMMUNICATION

Communication is the process of making meaning. The concept is used to explain how one individual (or a word, object, sign, gesture or similar) conveys meaning to another – whether that meaning is intentional or not. For instance, at its simplest, an individual speaks a word, which is heard and interpreted by a second person and this conveys a meaning to the listener. Similarly, an individual may wear a T-shirt or a hat, which conveys meaning to an observer – whether the wearer is the supporter of a particular sport team or whether the meaning conveyed may be unintentional, such as someone may think that the person in the hat or T-shirt looks silly or unfashionable.

However, this was not the original use of the term communication. Gunther Kress (1988) in *Communication and Culture* suggests that this term first came into popular usage in the nineteenth century to refer to physical means of connection, such as railways and shipping. However, it was with the development of new technologies, such as the telegram and later the radio and telephone, that the term became more commonly used to refer to the delivery of information rather than physical objects.

The origins of the term (as a simple process of passing on an object) strongly influenced early considerations of the communications process. In particular, one of the earliest studies of telecommunications was conducted by Claude Elwood Shannon who worked for the Bell telephone corporation in America in the 1940s. Shannon developed a mathematical model of communication that was concerned with the most effective way of transmitting information, which attempted to eliminate any disruption of the original message. This disruption in the transfer of a message Shannon referred to as 'noise'. This model therefore presents a very straightforward and simplistic understanding of communication, which at its simplest involves a three-stage process of 'sender–message–receiver'. First, there is an individual (the sender) who composes a message (such as a letter or a spoken sentence or phrase) and this is then delivered to and received by another individual (the receiver).

What this model fails to recognize or consider is the social context of message creation, conveyance and reception. For instance, the process of communication does not simply involve a message which is clearly intended by the sender and likewise clearly understood in the same way by the receiver. The meaning of a message will be determined by many different social factors, such as the context of the message, the form it takes, the power relations between the 'sender' and 'receiver' and the process of interpretation and reinterpretation undertaken by the receiver. All of these (and more) are what help to create the meaning of a message and also form important constituent parts of the communication process and therefore cannot simply be dismissed as 'noise' that needs to be overcome. The term 'mass communication' is generally used in academic studies to refer to the mass media. In particular, the consideration of processes of communication and reception have come to the forefront of many discussions of the mass media in recent decades, such as Stuart Hall's (1980) work on the process of encoding and decoding or Ien Ang's work on the reception of *Dallas* by television audiences.

Garry Crawford

Associated Concepts Birmingham School; Consumer Society; Consumption; Cultural Intermediaries; Mass Media; Network Society; Semiotics.

COMMUNITY

Isaiah Berlin once said that some things change and some things don't and it is important that we distinguish which is which. There is no doubting the fact that the way in which community is understood in leisure studies has changed markedly in recent years. When the concept was initially theorized by leisure scholars it largely mirrored orthodox sociological thought, which meant defining it first of all by breaking it down into the sum of its parts – namely the ideas of geographical propinquity, communities of interest and forms of common affective union – and second by explaining that these constituent parts should only be understood with the proviso that community is also more than these. Yet in defining the concept in leisure studies these days it may not even be obvious what its constituent parts are any more. For example, the idea of 'communities of leisure' can be used to refer to anything from locals drinking together in their village pub to a group of disparate individuals sharing a particular leisure life-style but not necessarily knowing each other.

This last observation notwithstanding, community is undoubtedly one of the front-line feelings of our age. As Bauman (2001: 1) points out, the concept is associated with mostly positive connotations: it has a warm and friendly sort of air about it, like a balmy summer's day it 'feels good: whatever the word … may mean, it is good "to have a community", "to be in a community"'. It summarily signifies a special way of being together, which seems as if it already has a room in our *doxa* (the knowledge we think with but not about) and not only that it is also endowed with an atmosphere all of its own: it stands out among other concepts.

Yet as that most discerning chronicler of the twentieth-century 'age of extremes' Eric Hobsbawm succinctly put it: 'Never was the word "community" used more indiscriminately and emptily than in the decades when communities in the sociological sense became hard to find in real life' (1995: 428). Hobsbawm's crucial observation suggests that when we come to ponder community today there is not only likely to be a certain elusiveness to the idea but also more importantly it also suggests that we cannot hope to deal with the concept in the orthodox sociological sense.

Cognisant of the limitations of the orthodox sociological way of defining its key ideas, Cohen (1985), drawing on the genius of Ludwig

Wittgenstein, alerts leisure scholars to the efficacy of exploring the ways in which concepts are used in everyday life rather than simply relying on normative definitions. This is the starting point for his own re-theorization of community, drawn mainly from his empirical research on the island of Whalsey, the Shetland Isles and at the Notting Hill Carnival, which led him to conclude that boundary marking processes, such as customs, habits and ritual, are vital defining features of community membership because they not only gesture at a shared sense of reality but also shape that reality, even though they are on the face of it merely the imaginary social constructs of both insiders and outsiders. In this respect, Cohen's conception is essentially that of a cultural 'imaginary' of community previously encapsulated in what orthodox sociologists meant when they talked about common affective union (see Bell and Newby, 1971). In Cohen's hands, however, the cultural 'imaginary' is something that is also constructed symbolically and, although its 'sense of community' does not necessarily have any spatial significance, putative membership is subject to shared symbolization, shared meanings and affiliation.

From the shared exploits of holidaymakers to football supporters, from nightclubbers to internet users, leisure scholars have identified various communities by drawing on Cohen's model. According to Bauman, however, these are merely *peg communities* – usually nothing more than holiday friendships or the 90 minutes or so that constitute a cup final win, ecstasy-fuelled love-ups or 'virtual' communities – which if they beg a certain intimacy, are unlikely to be reciprocated for long because they are too self-contained. For Bauman, leisure communities are not really communities (except symbolically or perhaps unintentionally), but at the very most spectacles (Debord, 1995 [1967]): seemingly palpable, but nonetheless constructed of individuals, first and foremost, everyone one of them.

Undoubtedly, the other most influential contemporary use of the notion of community in leisure studies has been Benedict Anderson's (1991) idea of the 'imagined community'. Despite any semantic similarities with Cohen's idea that community is to all intents and purposes 'imaginary', Anderson is here engaged with the ideas of nation and nationhood; he is not really talking about community in the way it has been conventionally understood in sociology. As Anderson famously pointed out, the development of print media was the precondition of all modern 'imagined communities' which 'are to be distinguished not by their falseness/genuineness, but by the style in which they are imagined' (1991: 6).

In common with Cohen's, Anderson's concept has been subjected to oversimplified applications in leisure studies, but one of the most compelling uses is Anthony King's (2000) work on the sociology of football. King clearly recognizes that, in a society which is no longer institutionally enclosed within the framework of the nation state as it was conceived in early modernity, it was perhaps inevitable that leisure, and in this case football, would come to play such a pivotal role in allowing individuals to express their cultural identities through both local and national versions of collective expression.

These observations notwithstanding, few concepts in leisure studies derive such consternation as the idea of community does from its critics. There are two main reasons for this. First of all, discussions about community in leisure are often nostalgic. Indeed any discussion of the concept cannot help but be shadowed and cross-cut by the past where it resides, its status securely sponsored and its fame family-friendly. In this sense we can say that community lives off its past. Its narrative is a hymn to a gentler, more innocent way of life, to days when folk knew their neighbours and stopped on the street to talk to one another. As Blackshaw's theoretical (2008) analysis of football and its communities suggests, most football fans know the upbeat story of the golden age of community in the people's game, when working-class communities nestled happily in terraced streets as approximately local cultures of identity and belonging made from the same red brick and mortar as the cathedrals in which they worshipped their local clubs.

Blackshaw's critique alerts us to a second problem with community. In highlighting the 'darker side' of community in leisure, he points out that most football fans also have some knowledge of the downbeat version of community, which has no necessary affinity to the past tense. This is the story which, if it also conjures the undeniable 'solidity' of football's 'communities', built on mutual identification and reciprocity, recognizes that football fans have always sought to express their solidarity in opposition to a supposedly threatening Other; and have always united themselves by vilifying and constantly mocking that Other. In other words, football, in common with many other collective leisure interests, and especially those in sport, has always had its own established outlets for prejudice and excessive emotionalism which are located in vicious rivalries that define themselves largely as and by resistance to their bitterest of opponents, blossoming whenever 'we' beat 'them', achieving their sensual union through the depredations of their necessary others – a sense of community that is essentially based on and stands for mutual hatred.

Tony Blackshaw

Associated Concepts Community Leisure; Identity; Leisure in the Community; Leisure Life-World; Liminality; Neo-Tribes; Nostalgia.

COMMUNITY ACTION

This is a term used to describe the organization of localized direct collective action, which sets out to achieve change through organization, mobilization and negotiation, in ways that can be both unconventional and unconstitutional. Community action presumes an active view of the participative citizen and is a political process based on four kinds of power relations with extant institutions or other forms of authority: conflict, cooperation, confrontation and change.

These challenges to authority tend to emerge in situations when leisure participants turn into leisure activists because they feel that they can no longer go on with things as they are; the catalyst for action is usually exploitation or changes to the way in which people experience their leisure which are more acute than normal. The 1932 mass trespass of Kinder Scout in the Peak District of England is a good example of this kind of community action. The trespass, organized by communist activist Benny Rothman, was in response to the power of rich landowners who wanted to keep the countryside for their own exclusive leisure and the laws that denied ordinary people access to what had historically been public rights of way. Looking back, the impact of this action has been enormous and was the impetus for the Access to the Mountains Act in 1939 and the establishment of the National Parks in the 1960s in the UK. Another more recent example is the growing prominence of community action in football, one of the most well-known cases being the establishment of FC United of Manchester, which saw a group of Manchester United fans withdrawing their support as a result of the corporate takeover by Malcolm Glaser to set up their own community-based club.

Saunders (1979) has suggested that much community action tends to be reactive and limited by its localized nature, holding little hope for the 'future transition to a qualitative different mode of organization of society'. Saunders' view reflects the other more general limitation of community action, which is that it often begins with a commitment to radical change but tends to drift back into more conventional politics, confirming Herbert Marcuse's astute observation of the way in which hegemony is maintained through a process of 'resistance through incorporation'. Basically, one of the major reasons why the status quo is maintained (and capitalism flourishes) is that it readily incorporates from dissenting movements those aspects which dovetail with its *modus operandi*, while being continually successful in resisting the remainder.

Tony Blackshaw

Associated Concepts Community; Community Leisure; Discursive Formations; Hegemony.

COMMUNITY LEISURE

Although the 'community' appendage has found widespread currency in the leisure domain, with the term just as commonly used to describe leisure facilities (e.g., community leisure centres, community pools and so on) as it is used to describe particular ways of working with individuals and groups in local communities through leisure (e.g., community arts, community sport and the like), it does not permit precise definition.

It has been suggested by some that the term is merely 'a fashionable label with virtually no recognition that a particular set of practices and values is implied' (Haywood, 1994). In the strongest use of the term, however, community leisure is suggestive of an orientation to a particular model of public policy, whose underlying rationale is to use leisure to promote those types of collective association that put the accent on the promotion of community values such as solidarity, affiliation, coherence, participation and active citizenship. As such it makes sense to give community leisure a general definition in relative terms, namely as regards the relationship between the community practice model of public service delivery as it is developed through different kinds of leisure.

Community practice is a set of 'distinctive methods and practices concerned with promoting, fostering and implementing community policies' (Glen, 1993). This involves working from a community-based approach, where the users of services have some control over the resources required to provide those services (Donnison, 1989). This ideal type model incorporates the following: 'top-down' community services which involve providing leisure opportunities and activities to a user public; 'bottom-up' community development which encourages communities to define their own leisure needs and make provisions for those needs; community action; multi-agency coordination, which stresses co-participation between different providers and users of community services; and an action research approach which operates as a reflexive tool to enhance practice.

Bramham (1994) has identified how the community practice model has been developed through the arts, pointing out that community arts have a local focus, take popular local forms, have their basis in an artistic rationale which is extrinsic rather than intrinsic (art is a process rather than an end in itself) and involve communal participation which is integrated with everyday culture and takes place on the streets, in parks and community centres. The role of the professional artist in the context of community arts is that of an *animateur* rather than an expert, whose central role it is to encourage individuals and communities to become more aware of their own circumstances in a society torn by conflicting interests and in the process encourage them to develop their own creative potential, so that they can harness this for their own individual benefit and that of their local community. As Bramham points out, this cultural democratic approach to developing community leisure through the arts not only challenges the elitism that tends to pervade traditional engagement (suggesting in the process that there are no universal criteria of what constitutes proper art), it also opens the potential for neglected or hidden cultural and artistic forms while celebrating them in the process.

It is with these kinds of values in mind that Haywood (1994: 131) outlines a set of strategies for engaging hard to reach groups in community sport.

- The discouragement of leagues and tables and the encouragement of 'one-off' encounters.
- The selection of sports in which the rules emphasize cooperation and teamwork rather than individuality.
- A deliberate stress on participation at the expense of performance (e.g., modifying the rules in order to include as many people as possible).
- The use of sports with a low TV/media/professionalized profile.
- In sports with a high media profile, such as football, the positive encouragement of fair play and respect for opponents and an

emphasis on attacking play and taking risks rather than safe defensive methods, since the former highlights the essential process of playing or the latter overstates the importance of the end product.

- The result should be an encouragement of diversity within the methods/rules that are part of sports.

Notwithstanding this recognition of the key role that community leisure has to play in the health and well-being of society by providing personal fulfilment to individuals and improving the quality of life in local communities, critics have argued that community interventions are often piecemeal and localized, conservative and unrepresentative, and often have a limited impact on public policy (i.e., community leisure more often than not operates as another variation of market-managerialism and that as a result its stress on equality of access to leisure opportunities tends to support the status quo or hegemony). However, there is little doubt that, as an alternative approach to public leisure provision, community leisure has the *potential* to be radical, in the sense that communities formed around leisure interests can lead to the arrangement of alternative kinds of collective consciousness raising and/or forces for political change.

Tony Blackshaw

Associated Concepts Action Research; Community; Community Action; Hegemony; Leisure in the Community; Social Capital.

COMPARATIVE METHOD
(OR COMPARATIVE ANALYSIS)

Comparative method or analysis is the comparison of two groups or subjects, with the express intention of finding or observing similarities or differences between them. Classic examples of comparative methods would be the use of a control and experimental

groups within 'scientific' experimental research, where the results of the control groups (where variables are kept constant) are compared with those of the experimental group (where certain variables are manipulated). Another would be cross-national comparisons, a good example of which would be an assessment of hours worked in different countries, and its impact on leisure patterns.

One use and advantage of comparative research is that it allows 'good practice' to be observed and learnt from other cases, such as discovering what leisure policies and initiatives work in one country or setting and applying them to another. However, as with all social research, it is impossible to take account of or control for every single variables. Therfore, what works or has certain effects in one context, group, or place, may not have the same effect or impact in another.

Garry Crawford

Associated Concepts Methodology; Quantitative Research; Qualitative Research.

COMPULSORY HETEROSEXUALITY

Compulsory heterosexuality is a term popularized by Adrienne Rich in her essay *Compulsory Heterosexuality and Lesbian Existence* (1981). This refers to the societal assumption that men and women are born biologically predisposed to being heterosexual – an assumption which authors such as Rich seek to challenge. Rich suggests that heterosexuality is 'naturalized', while homosexuality is seen as a psychological or biological dysfunction. However, she argues that more than this, heterosexuality is also a violent and patriarchal social and political system, which allows men physical and emotional access to women. For Rich, heterosexuality is therefore something imposed, particularly on women, which validates men's social and sexual rights over women. A good example and application of the use of the concept of 'compulsory heterosexuality' within leisure studies is the work of Wright and Clarke (1991) on the media representation of female rugby players. In this Wright and Clarke demonstrate how choices in language and visual representations in the mass media work to engage in a process of normalization, whereby female rugby players are represented in terms of hegemonic versions of heterosexual femininity.

Garry Crawford

Associated Concepts Feminism; Masculinity and Masculinities; Pornography; Queer Theory; Surveillance; Women's Leisure.

CONSUMER BEHAVIOUR AND CONSUMER RELATIONSHIP MARKETING

The ideas behind customer relationship management are not new. Many key theorists such as Kotler (1997), Gilbert (1999) and Brassington and Pettitt (2000) have widely acknowledged that how you treat your customers goes a long way to determining your future profitability, and companies are making bigger and bigger investments to do just this. This trend is attributable to the fact that customers today are savvier about the service they should be getting and tend to vote with their wallets based on the consumer experience they receive. Just consider how you made a decision relating to leisure recently. Did you choose one cinema over another? Did you choose to rent a DVD rather than go to the cinema? Did you choose to go to a restaurant instead of visiting the cinema or renting a DVD?

To this extent consumer relationship marketing (CRM) is concerned with consumer behaviour. This term is widely used in the leisure industry to describe the type of behaviour that consumers exhibit in searching for, purchasing, using, evaluating and disposing of products, services and ideas they expect will satisfy their needs. Such characteristics are ultimately used in order to make consumer choices – for example, which gym to use, where to go for a swim, what shop to purchase sport equipment from, and so on. However, consumer behaviour is also an important aspect of marketing as it helps organizations develop their plans to maximize sales and subsequent profits.

CRM involves using methods and tactics to develop a long-term relationship with customers in order to retain their loyalty. Once achieved the associated benefits of brand awareness and brand loyalty can be recognized. An organization must exceed customer satisfaction in order to retain them and develop a healthy relationship with its customers. Traditional transactional marketing tended to involve organizations focusing all of their marketing efforts on attracting each customer for one-off sales. However, customers who are loyal end up spending more in the long term so it makes sense – keep them happy!

In order to achieve effective CRM an organization needs to put tactics into place to attract customers, ensure that they are attracted to the organization and in the process make certain they are retained. The most common tactics used in leisure industry include: loyalty cards; a good customer service section; using individual account managers if it is a large client; and product variety and quality.

Rob Wilson

Associated Concepts Ansoff Matrix; Boston Matrix; Branding, Brand Awareness and Brand Image; Consumer Society; Consumption; Leisure Marketing; Market Positioning and Market Segmentation.

CONSUMER CULTURE

(consumer society)

CONSUMER SOCIETY

A number of scholars have argued that consumption has become the central concern of leisure studies, and that we are entering a new epoch which is based upon the construction of self-identity and social distinction through consumer goods. In particular, the work of sociologists such as Lash and Urry (1987) and Zygmunt Bauman (1997, 1998) inform this work.

Lash and Urry (1987: 2) suggest that Marx and Engels set out a useful consideration of 'organized capitalism' in the 'Manifesto of the Communist Party' towards the end of the nineteenth century. However, they also suggest that contemporary society can now be understood more accurately as being characterized by what they refer to as 'disorganized capitalism' which in turn is characterized by certain key developments in the nature of capitalist societies. First, there has been a decline in primary industries (for example, extraction industries such as coal mining) and secondary industries (for example, manufacturing industries), and a move towards greater emphasis on the tertiary (service) sector. Linked to this, there has been a decline in the 'traditional' working classes and a rapid growth in a more affluent (white collar, service sector) working class.

However, Lash and Urry (1987) argue that the most significant change in disorganized capitalism is the rapid growth of the service class (and the decline of the traditional working class) in most capitalist Western societies from the 1960s onwards. Crucially, the service class is not a class of producers, but a class of consumers. In particular, Lash and Urry suggest that, due to the rise in importance and the social dominance of this consumer class within society, individual identities have become more fluid and are increasingly based upon 'life-style' choices.

These life-styles are purchased ready-made through the huge range of consumer products and mass media resources available to choose from. This idea of the increasing fluidity of contemporary identities is developed most notably by Bauman (1997, 1998) who suggests that 'ours is a consumer society' (1998: 22). He would argue that all societies are consumer societies, to a greater or lesser extent, but there is something 'profound and fundamental' about the nature of contemporary consumer society that makes it distinct from all other societies (1998: 24). Most significantly, Bauman argues that all prior societies have been primarily producer societies. In the past for an individual to fully participate in society they had to be a producer of goods, or at least part of the production process, and social ranking was based upon an individual's position within the production process. However, in 'our' (consumer) society, an individual 'needs to be a consumer first, before one can think of becoming anything in particular' (1998: 26). According to Bauman, it is consumerism that defines who we are, who we can be, and our social hierarchies.

There is considerable evidence to suggest that we do indeed live in a consumer society. For instance, the mass media and telecommunications have led to a reduction in global time and space, where we are now able to shop 24/7 via the internet, the telephone and even via our mobile (cell) phones and digital televisions. Furthermore, the possibility of the almost immediate dissemination of information via the mass media and telecommunications means that we live in a rapidly changing world, where fashions, social relations and even identities have become ever-changing, and consumerism constantly responds to and informs these rapid changes.

In this view consumption is also an inevitable part of our leisure – as our leisure activities are increasingly based around the purchase and consumption of goods and services and shopping becomes a major leisure pursuit in itself. Consequently, our cities and landscapes become shaped around consumption, with city centres focused almost exclusively around shopping and consumption, the growth of shopping malls and retail parks, and other leisure venues (such as sport stadiums) becoming redeveloped to include greater consumer opportunities, such as shops, cafés and restaurants.

However, there are also significant social consequences to the growing importance of consumption in society. In particular, Bauman (1997) argues that contemporary consumer society is characterized by uncertainty and uncontrollability, and that there has developed a 'new world disorder' that has no visible structure and logic. There has been a general trend to privatization or what can be referred to as 'universal deregulation', where state-owned public services such as housing and the railways have been sold off to private companies. This has turned the political economy over to the supply and demands of capitalism, where the focus is less on providing public services and more on profit making, and the traditional safety nets, such as the welfare state and extended family networks, are increasingly eroded. Bauman suggests that our consumer society is one which is based on individualism, and on individual consumption. For Bauman, even when consumption takes place in the presence of other consumers ultimately these are all gatherings of individual consumers. As a consequence our identities become more individual, but also 'liquid' and fluid, and are increasingly based and constructed via individual consumer choices.

Bauman (1997) states that, in this ('postmodern' or 'liquid') consumer society, freedom of choice is what influences everything – but some have more freedom of choice than others. He uses terms such as the 'tourist' and the 'vagabond' as metaphors to describe the extent to which people participate in this consumer society and have choices. Most people are like 'tourists'. For the 'tourist' consumer, life is about never staying in any one place for too long, it is always temporary, and they are on a never ending journey of consumption and endless reinvention. It is an endless journey, as consumer desires are never fulfilled. Consumer desires do not desire fulfilment and completion, but rather 'desire desires desire' (1998: 25). At the other end of this continuum is what Bauman calls the 'vagabond'. Vagabonds are the people excluded from consumer culture. Vagabonds also move from place to place but not because of desire, but because they are not

welcome anywhere. They are excluded – 'flawed consumers' – who cannot afford to participate in what is essentially the only game in town.

Garry Crawford

Associated Concepts Bauman; Capitalism; Class; Communication; Consumption; Fashion; Identity; Leisure; Marxism; Mass Media; Shopping.

CONSUMPTION

The word consume dates from the fourteenth century and was used to mean something that was 'used up' or 'destroyed', such as to be consumed by fire. Similarly, the term consumption comes into usage in the sixteenth century to refer to any disease that causes 'wasting away', such as TB (tuberculosis) (Williams, 1976). Hence, 'consumption' is most often viewed as an end point (and implicit to this, the idea of waste), and the direct opposite of 'production', which is seen as the (often more important) process of 'creation'.

However, Lury (1996: 1) suggests that consumption needs to be understood as part of a wider 'material culture'. 'Material culture' is the term given to the study of 'person–thing' relationships. That is to say, the study of material culture is the study of objects and how these are used. Lury (following Warde, 1990, 1992) suggests that consumption, rather than being the outcome (and antithesis) of production, needs to be understood as a constituent part of a continuing process and cycle of various forms of both production and consumption. Hence, Lury (1996) argues that consumer objects should be seen to have a social life of their own. That is to say, consumer goods will have changing and different meanings throughout their lifespan, depending on who is viewing or using them and in what context they are located. Consumer goods are therefore (to varying degrees) 'polysemic' – open to multiple readings and meanings. People will use consumer goods in different ways and they will have different meanings for different people.

This is in many respects a development of the Birmingham School argument, such as that of Hebdige (1979), which suggests that subcultures engage in a process of 'bricolage', whereby they draw on existing consumer goods, but redefine and combine these to develop a distinct style to mark themselves out from the general public and use this as a form of social subversion and resistance. However, authors such as Lury and Warde extend this idea to suggest that it is not just subcultures, but most (if not all) consumers who engage in this act of (re)defining the meaning of consumer goods, and it also reconceives this as an everyday (often mundane) act, rather than necessarily an act of social resistance.

It is evident that consumption now plays a massive role in our contemporary society to the point that it has been suggested that we now live in a consumer society where consumption has become the key defining characteristic of our society. In particular, leisure has increasingly become a consumer activity. One of the most popular leisure pastimes is 'shopping', by physically walking around shops or browsing consumer items within catalogues or more commonly these days via the internet. Also, most other popular leisure activities involve the purchase and use of consumer goods, such as watching television, going to the cinema or pub, attending a theme park and so on. Furthermore, each of these acts often has associated consumer goods and practices – for instance, Crawford (2004) suggests that following sport also frequently involves numerous other related acts of consumption, such as going to a bar or pub before or after the game, consuming food and drinks at the game, using your car or public transport to get to the game, buying in beers and food to watch the game at home with ... and so the list goes on.

A particularly useful text on consumption is the work of Steven Miles (1998)

Consumerism – As a Way of Life. In this book Miles provides an excellent introduction to the key theories on consumption, noting the important foundation to this subject area as set out by Karl Marx, Max Weber, Thorstein Veblen and Georg Simmel, and then moving on to consider how this area was developed by the likes of Pierre Bourdieu (and in particular via his work on distinction), and the important work of writers such as Michel de Certeau on the role of consumption in transgression and resistance. Miles also highlights key postmodern writers on consumption such as Jean Baudrillard, as well as including other cross-disciplinary considerations such as the social psychological analysis of Helga Dittmar (1992).

Garry Crawford

Associated Concepts Baudrillard; Bauman; Birmingham School; Bourdieu; Capitalism; Consumer Society; Distinction; Fashion; Identity; Leisure; Marxism; Mass Media; Shopping; Subcultures; Veblen.

CONTENT ANALYSIS

Content analysis refers to the observation-based analysis of cultural texts, such as films, photographs or advertisements. The starting point of any form of content analysis is to establish a 'framework of analysis' in order to determine what will be studied, and what the researcher should be looking for. For instance, the portrayal of female athletes in British tabloid newspaper pictures could present a typical framework of analysis. The next stage then is to 'code' the components (i.e., identify key signifiers in each text), and then consider their 'meaning'.

However, there are several different types and approaches to content analysis with the main distinction being between quantitative and qualitative approaches. The traditional techniques of quantitative content analysis were most notably developed by Berelson (1952). Quantitative analysis involves determining beforehand a framework of analysis (what you are going to analyse and what you are looking for within this) and then counting (and 'coding') each occurrence of this in the material under consideration (for instance, in this case counting and coding images of female athletes in the British tabloid press).

This form of analysis then allows for large quantities of media to be looked at quite quickly and easily and enables the researcher to determine the level of media coverage a particular item gets. However, it cannot tell us what the mass media say about these stories or images, or whether some people or groups are portrayed positively or negatively in the mass media. For this, we need to employ qualitative methods. There are several forms of qualitative content analysis, including *discourse analysis*, *frame analysis*, *narrative analysis*, and *textual analysis*. However, these approaches share many similarities and therefore those undertaking content analysis will often draw on combined or multiple forms of these approaches.

Put simply discourse analysis involves the analysis of a cultural text or language and has two primary concerns. First, it is interested in the use of language in social life, and second, it is interested in investigating the relationship between language and social power. Frame analysis looks at how people make sense of their world by using frames of reference. In relation to content analysis, therefore, this approach would be interested in how a text (such as a newspaper story) is 'framed'. In other words, it would be concerned with the context and/or background where the text is located. Narrative analysis is similar to the other forms of media analysis, but is more specifically concerned with the narratives *within* texts. Narratives can be understood as themes or stories which sometimes unfold and develop over time. Therefore, for example, narrative analysis would be concerned with the way the mass media tell stories, and how these are developed. Finally, textual analysis (such as semiotics) is interested not just in the text in isolation, but recognizes that meaning is derived from both the text and how it is read and understood by the reader.

Garry Crawford

Associated Concepts Discursive Formations; Methodology; Qualitative Research; Quantitative Research; Semiotics.

CONVERSATIONAL ANALYSIS

Conversational (or conversation) analysis is a key method for studying conversational rules, patterns, structures and processes, and it originates in the work of the ethnomethodologist Harvey Sacks (1935–1975) and his colleagues at the University of California in the 1960s. Conversational analysis focuses mainly on spoken, but also non-verbal, aspects of communication. In particular, conversational analysis is interested in the structures and conventions of social interactions, such as turn-taking; repair (such as countering problems encountered in understanding, hearing, and so on); the sequences or ordering of actions; context; and the other fine details of ordinary communication and interaction.

Methodologically, converstational analysis usually involves the (either audio or visual) recording of conversations and interactions, which allows for careful, detailed and repeated analysis. Transcription of conversations and interactions involves paying careful attention to the details and using notations to signify a variety of interactional occurrences and phenomena.

Garry Crawford

Associated Concepts Communication; Ethnomethodology; Semiotics; Symbolic Interactionism.

COOL

Most student readers of this dictionary will be so familiar with the idea of cool that they will probably think that it barely needs to be explained. After all it is difficult to imagine anything young people do today that is not robed in the idea. Yet for all its popularity, and any ostensible certainty about its origins, cool is at best an elusive disposition. If ice and fire are binary extremes, cool is a zombie category somewhere in between. It is a way-of-being world which is designedly and teasingly (supposed to be) transgressive, but which is performed in a way that seems to take things neither too seriously nor too lightly. Just as there is no certainty about where cool is going to be found, or how long it is going to reside there once we have found it, there is no such thing as a hierarchical notion of cool. It is an attitude governed by a more plural and pragmatic aesthetic: if something works, 'hey, it's cool'. As this suggests, the idea of cool has a renegade quality: not only is it in awe to the idea of non-compliance, it is also hard to pin down and governed by an ephemeral currency that is susceptible to sudden shifts in the wind.

As Pountain and Robins (2000) point out, a cool attitude appears to be the dominant mind-set of the contemporary period. If rigid puritan asceticism was the abiding ethic of a 'solid' modern society dominated by industrial labour, 'liquid' aestheticism is the indispensable centre of cool. As Bauman has pointed out, the process of change from 'solidity' to 'liquidity' began once the majority of people recognized that it was in their grasp to find a place 'in that under-defined and under-determined social space stretched between the well-marked top occupied by the aristocrats who had their position guaranteed by heredity, and so *did not need* to "achieve" or "prove" anything, and the bottom – where people who for the lack of resources *could not* try, even if they wished, to achieve a position different from the one in which they were born, were cast – apparently once and for all, no appeal allowed' (Bauman, in Rojek, 2004: 294). Yet because this social space was to remain 'under-defined and under-determined' people would be charged with the task of having to continually prove themselves, precisely because they could never do so once and for all. So it was perhaps inevitable that cool would become the new arbiter of the proof of one's ability to fit in, in the process guiding what had become by now thoroughly individual quests for a durable identity.

In the event, though, most people have difficulty keeping on the right side of the line dividing cool from naff. One of the key reasons for this is the sense of having a certain independence from rational evaluation that is a critical component of cool. To talk of something as being intrinsically cool which is measured by universal standards is to misunderstand its shape-shifting nature – being a cool dresser, a cool dancer, having a cool music collection, cool friends, and so on is difficult to place – because proper effortless cool has no rational foundations. Rational logic would also suggest that cool multiplied by cool should mean something cooler, but in practice, an odd kind of polarizing effect often takes place. Rather than amplifying each other, cool multiplied by cool often cancel each other out. There is also the paradox that it can also be cool to be uncool – for example, revealing to your 20-something mates that you have a penchant for 1970s 'Glam-Rock' bands.

One of the upshots of the uncertainty surrounding cool is that it makes our cognitive activities seem somewhat (and always) self-conscious. It's as if we can't enjoy our own corporeal existence without worrying about whether we look cool or not. This is because in a performative society self-respect must be expressed in a carefully balanced out – as neither too hot nor too cold – outward appearance and demeanour. We inhabit a world in which aesthetics rule supreme and where people imagine that they will discover their individual sense of existential empowerment by creating their own chilled-out sense of coolness.

The cult of cool, of cultivating a cool appearance, criss-crosses all aspects of contemporary leisure: rappers justify their lyrical extremities with it; some football fans found their identities on it; consumers always seem to be on the look out for guides to living that will tell them the coolest ways to live and how to pose and what the coolest music is to listen to and where to shop for the coolest clothes and what to eat and drink in the coolest restaurants and where to go for the coolest holidays. But what is the real value of the concept in a consumer world in which it is radical to be cool but not cool to be radical?

For other critics, such as Bauman, cool, for all its quotidian popularity, is a problematic attitude, not only because it is exclusionary, but because it also implies a sense of detachment and perhaps emptiness, signalling 'a flight from feeling', because 'I need more space for myself' or because I must take flight from 'the real messiness of intimacy'. In a world dominated by the aesthetic of cool, it appears as if we can't aspire to anything stable or permanent any more for fear of looking foolish or outmoded. Indeed, the cool attitude comes with 'I can only *just* be bothered to engage with what you are suggesting' – offhand, shrugging and impervious, suggesting nothing really matters. This raises some key questions. What is leisure when it is chosen on the grounds of the objective of aesthetics, not moral evaluation? When the most alluring thing in life is to look cool, what is the role of politics?

Tony Blackshaw

Associated Concepts Aesthetics; Authenticity; Bauman, Zygmunt; Dionysian Leisure; Individualization; Liquid Modernity; Performativity; Zombie Categories.

COST ACCOUNTING

Understanding the terminology for financial accounting facilitates the compilation of financial statements. However, financial and management accountants undertake their work in two quite separate worlds. Ultimately they work with different terminology. In financial accounting the income statement, profit or loss are determined by deducting expenses from revenue. Cost accounting classifies the same expenses (and income) in a different manner as it attempts to illustrate the part of the business in which the expenditure is incurred. This is in order that costs can be redistributed throughout a business so that management can see which departments are doing well and which need to improve. For a local authority leisure centre, for example, this could mean identifying the costs associated with offering a swimming facility, the costs for operating dry-side facilities (five-a-side, badminton, trampolining, and so on) and the costs associated with outdoor spaces. Once clarified the management team will be able to determine opening times, the cost of such activities and ultimately whether or not to provide certain activities. The main classifications for cost accountants will be direct costs, indirect costs, fixed costs, variable costs, semi-variable costs, stepped costs and total costs. The definitions for all of these concepts are outlined below.

Direct costs are the most common costs that an organization will come across in its day-to-day business. These are costs that can be easily identified with a product or service delivered. Indeed the Chartered Institute of Management Accountants (CIMA) declares a direct cost as a cost which can be traced in full to the product, service or department that is being costed (CIMA, 2003). It is also necessary to be aware that:

Direct Material Cost + Direct Labour Cost + Other Direct Expenses = PRIME COST

In marked contrast, indirect costs are costs that cannot be identified as direct costs (also known as overheads). An indirect cost is a cost that is incurred in the course of making a product, delivering a service or running a department, but which cannot be traced directly and in full to the product, service or department. Be aware that:

Indirect Materials + Indirect Labour + Indirect Expenses = OVERHEAD COST

Fixed costs are costs that are incurred for a particular period of time which within certain activity levels is unaffected by changes in the levels of activity (CIMA, 2003), for example, rent or straight-line depreciation. However, variable costs tend to vary in line with the level of activity, for example, labour and materials. Semi-variable costs are likely to contain both a fixed and variable element and stepped costs are those fixed costs that increase incrementally over time.

If all of the fixed and variable costs are added together then the total costs will be achieved.

Rob Wilson

Associated Concepts Double-Entry Bookkeeping; Financial and Management Accounting; Financial Health and Ratio Analysis; Financial Statements.

CRAFTS AND CRAFTSMANSHIP

The word crafts, derived from the old English, meaning skills, refers to a particular set of abilities that are driven by human curiosity, unhurriedness and dedication to a job well done. What this suggests is that craftsmanship is creative only because it is facilitated by a particular kind of leisureliness. As Richard Sennett has suggested, what is also craftsmanlike is 'the desire to do something for its own sake', which epitomizes the special human condition of being engaged. Sennett (2008) argues that three abilities are the basis of craftsmanship: the ability to localize, the ability to question, and the ability to open up. When these three elements are combined men and women are capable of producing artifacts which are not only of stunning quality, they also carry with them the key to their production. Craftsmanship also brings with it the capacity to endow the lives of men and women with meaning.

In his most recent work Sennett has been concerned with developing these kinds of ideas to explore the extent to which people lack the cultural anchor of a more coherent and secure work existence. In the concluding part of his book of lectures, *The Culture of the New Capitalism* (2005), he offers three critical values that might just fill this void: narrative, usefulness and craftsmanship. As Scruton (2008) points out, Sennett is here continuing the critique which emerged in the nineteenth century, when commentators such as John Ruskin and William Morris extolled the crafts located in people's surnames (Smith, Cartwright, Thatcher, Mason, and so on) while at the same time criticizing the industrial labour process which was replacing them.

As Sennett (2005) points out, *narratives* are an essential part of what it means to be human and are repeated and retold by men and women in different ways. Narrative identities, like the stories which underpin them, are always accompanied with their own turning points, pursuits, dreams and desires, but the time-frames associated with the 'new capitalism' deprive men and women of this type of narrative movement, particularly in the workplace. In developing a critique of this situation, Sennett argues that the state has a key legitimating role to play in civil society and drawing on the idea of social capital and the critical social value of status further argues that it needs to move beyond its current merely enabling function in order to play a key role in prompting *usefulness* as a public good. Finally, drawing on Maslow's Hierarchy of Needs model, Sennett recommends reasserting the idea of *craftsmanship* as a key aspect of achieving fulfilment in the workplace.

It might be argued that from the perspective of leisure studies Sennett's analysis overemphasizes the significance of work at the same time as underestimating the extent to which people today are already achieving narrative coherence, usefulness and craftsmanship in their lives through serious leisure, and that perhaps it does not make sense to treat work and leisure as binary opposites any longer. Notwithstanding these observations, what Sennett has to say has some real import for thinking about the implications of the ostensible demise of craftsmanship (read: serious leisure), and the concomitant rise of consumerism (read: casual leisure) and what this implies for the ability of individuals to embrace the autonomy and the opportunities that come with experiencing leisure that is craftsmanlike and slow burn rather than consumerist and all too fleeting.

Tony Blackshaw

Associated Concepts Authenticity; Consumption; Hobbies; Leisure as a Value-Sphere; McDonaldization; Serious Leisure; Work Ethic; Work-Leisure.

CRIME

(deviance)

CRITICAL THEORY

As a concept in the social sciences, critical theory was developed by scholars at the *Institut für Sozialforschung* in the 1930s (or 'the Frankfurt School' as it is more commonly known, which included scholars such as Theodor Adorno, Max Horkheimer and Herbert Marcuse). The general thrust of the Frankfurt School critique is an argument against the Enlightenment idea that science and rational progress would be freeing for humankind – and hence they also offer a critique of modernity. The Enlightenment, otherwise known as the age of modern reason, was an epochal event which also brought with it a rational commitment to robust individualism and the right to freedom from religion and the state.

The Frankfurt School, located as it was in Germany at the time of the rise of the Nazi party, as well as fascism in Italy and Spain and Stalinist communism in the Soviet Union, saw that the legacy of the Enlightenment had been both a rise in the centralization of power in many nations and a rise in totalitarian states. The argument of the Frankfurt School was complicated, however,

because it also offered a criticism of traditional Marxist theory, though it is evident that Adorno and his colleagues were themselves offering a variation on Marxism. Where they varied most notably from Marxism is in attempting to move away from an economic deterministic model, which sees the economy as *the* major factor shaping the nature of society.

In particular, they have developed a consideration and critique of contemporary cultures and the culture industry. Hence, in offering a consideration of popular cultures and the industries that produce these, the Frankfurt School is continuing Marx's interest in production, but is also considering an area of society largely ignored by Marx. However, in doing so, it has begun to move away from a traditional Marxist perspective. In particular, they have turned their attention most notably to a critique of 'the culture industry' (such as the film and music industries). For the Frankfurt School the culture industry reflects capitalist values, and reinforces this through commodity fetishism and the rise of monopoly capitalism. This shapes the tastes and preferences of the masses, thereby moulding their consciousness by generating false needs. It therefore excludes real needs and any radically opposing political viewpoints. This is clearly illustrated in Adorno's writing on sport, where he writes that 'sport itself is not play but ritual in which the subjected celebrate their subjection' (1996: 77), and that it is 'the colourless reflect of a hard and callous life' (1996: 78). For Adorno our 'free time is nothing other than a shadowy continuation of labour' (1996: 77; see also Inglis, 2004).

Critical theory has developed methodologically, most notably via a later contributor to the Frankfurt School, Jürgen Habermas. From 1956 Habermas studied under Max Horkheimer and Theodor Adorno at the Frankfurt Institute for Social Research, but later split from both, as he believed that the Frankfurt School had become paralysed by its political scepticism and disdain for modern culture. As with interpretivist methodology, Habermas argued that the natural and social sciences were fundamentally different, and hence was critical of a positivist tradition that tried to draw on scientific methods. Therefore, Habermas suggested that the researcher should not be seen as a 'disengaged observer', but rather as a 'reflective partner' – in that they form a relationship with the research subject (such as through interviews and social interaction).

Critical theory is also an emancipatory theory, which suggests that to know the social world researchers need to take account of the historical, social and political contexts which constrain human thought and human action. The purpose of its research and theory therefore is to give a voice to these excluded and marginalized groups, and to help explain generalized oppression in order to bring about social change.

Finally, it is also important to note that 'critical theory' is a term and concept used (but applied differently) in literary studies which refer to textual analysis and in particular the application of theory to the analysis and understanding of texts (such as, books, stories and poetry).

Garry Crawford

Associated Concepts Class; Commodity Fetishism; Consumption; False Consciousness; Ideology; Marxism; Mass Media; Methodology; Modernity; Qualitative Research; Sport.

CRUISING

Adapted from the customary usage of 'making trips by sea for pleasure' into slang employ, this term is usually used to connote either walking or driving around a locality on the lookout for quick and anonymous sex, or has a specific reference to car cruising, which also involves a number of other interconnected leisure activities and forms stylistic expression, but particularly involves the parading and racing of motor cars.

It is the findings that emerged from Blackshaw and Crabbe's (2004) research that are the most informative about this leisure activity. They contend that car cruising is a 'deviant' leisure activity as much without a history as it is one without a future. For Blackshaw and Crabbe car cruises are consumerist peg communities, whose inspiration tends to spring from the performativity of individual cruisers: they are both events for consumption and things to be consumed by. Car cruises are in this sense reminiscent of Michel Maffesoli's (1996) neo-tribes and Scott Lash's (2002: 27) 'post-traditional' *Gemeinschaften*, in that they are 'mobile and flexible groupings – sometimes enduring, often easily dissolvable – formed with an intensive affective bonding'. Their affiliation is not really one of friendship, or of a community proper, but one of symbiosis, and their only glue is their incumbents' *individually constituted*, though insatiable, appetites to connect with others. Consequently, Blackshaw and Crabbe assert that car cruising is unequivocally *not* about community in its orthodox meaning and its narrative structure is sustained by a reflexive individualization.

If cruises are not the 'real stuff' of communities, neither are they institutions, nor even organizations. They are what Lash has called disorganizations, those more 'trivial' forms of social interaction which constantly come into being and just as quickly break off, maintained 'until further notice'. As such, Blackshaw and Crabbe argue that the disorganization of car cruising is made to the measure of postmodern times: a momentary stopping place more for gestures than consequences, of uncomplicated surface lives manufactured only for the time being, paraded as a *performative community* aching to be credible.

Cruising is merely about performing modified cars, performing bodies. Yet despite its apparent simplicity as a leisure activity cruising is difficult to locate. First, in its disorganization the culture of cruising is dislocated to no place in particular; it is always on the move and the theatre for its performativity is always an improvised stage set. There are 'official' cruises and 'unofficial' cruises and the latter tend to be more raucous than the former. Be that as it may, Blackshaw and Crabbe argue that *all* cruises seem to be characterized by their predictability. They tend more or less to take on the same attributes from one cruise to another and what goes on at cruises tends to be governed by the same principles. Indeed, all cruising is about performing the right 'look', the right 'style', which is defined by the coded and ever-shifting parameters of 'kroozin' kool', the constant balancing act of being able to read and perform how cars, clothes, driving, walking and talking should be.

On the one hand cruising is about the mundane rituals of displaying and checking out each other's motor cars and bodies and on the other hand it is centred on street racing. However, both these activities are closely related in the sense that each is about performance and performativity: a hybrid world where the mundane quotidian of performativity – display, gossip and tittle-tattle – collides with the apocalyptic and spectacular performativity of burning and street racing. This contrast of significance and absurdity, of the spectacular and the mundane, is what, for its followers, makes the whole event worth pursuing.

Blackshaw and Crabbe's research also suggests that the majority of cruisers are young working-class men, players who play out their own kind of magic which they have found with cars and women. Cruising has its own vernacular which is misogynist. As well as being sexist and fraternal, cruising is also a hedonistic feeling of freedom and irresponsibility. Cruisers attend cruises in search of a familiar truth, nothing mysterious as such, just something which can be made tangible with something on four wheels. Indeed, as Blackshaw and Crabbe point out, the discursive field in which cruising constitutes itself allows for the deconstruction of taken-for-granted hegemonic norms. It is in this process that individual cruisers are able to perform not only an augmentation of their existential capacities for the affectual and the imaginative, but also they can experience an atmosphere of intensified engagement with other like-minded people. However, the majority of what happens does not take place within an 'inner-circle' because there does not appear to be an 'in-crowd'.

On the face of it, then, cruising has no apparent hierarchies, only aesthetics, everyone included, nothing excluded, not even the fumes from the engines and burning tyres, which pervade the cruise scene as surely as a security blanket – just the amazing reality of an ephemerally flowing, magical leisure world played out with a creative intervention. Yet, when you begin to look a little closer, Blackshaw and Crabbe argue, car cruising is a flat and featureless leisure activity with few distinguishing characteristics or points of difference, a harsh mechanical environment in which it is easy for men to be sexist and obtuse towards women. Cruising is an ephemeral, optative leisure life-style which is on the face of it determined by choice, but is to all intents and purposes dictated largely by gender, age and the ability to afford the right performance kit. It is also a mode of performance that swaggers with an uncomplicated capitalistic atmosphere: a cultural mix of heady marketeering combined with trappy commercialism and personal aspiration, mass similitude dressed up as individual preferences.

Blackshaw and Crabbe reached the conclusion that in its commodification cruising reveals the unrelenting nature of capitalism, its vitality and vigorousness, and the opportunities it presents for individuals to live out their most imaginative fantasies of consumptive 'deviance'. In so doing it brings to our attention the most cherished commodity available to young men (and some women): the palimpsest desire for personal transformation, but one whose sensibility is inescapably attuned to consumer capitalism. And the actions and behaviours of cruisers can provide intimations of what the consequences of a fully privatized existence might bear a resemblance to. The key difference however is that this version of 'pure' capitalism is much like the anarchy and chaos found at cruises: it is staged and ephemeral rather than absolute.

Tony Blackshaw

Associated Concepts Abnormal Leisure; Aesthetics; Capitalism; Community; Cool; Desire; Deviance; Liminality; Neo-tribes.

CULTURAL CAPITAL

This concept derives from the work of Bourdieu (1984) and importantly has led to increased attention being paid to the cultural significance of consumption. Cultural capital is the cultural knowledge and understanding that people accumulate through their upbringing (or socialization) and their educational experience. Children are socialized into the culture that corresponds to their social class and this set of cultural experiences, attitudes, values, and beliefs represents a form of cultural capital that equips people for their life in society. The term cultural capital is used because, like money (or economic capital), this form of cultural knowledge can be translated into resources such as wealth, power and status. Cultural capital is a resource that can be drawn upon in the pursuit of power, and is a means by which social groups seek distinction from each other. Importantly, cultural capital is not secondary to economic capital as each may be important in different contexts. For example, people working in certain jobs may earn high wages yet may not be able to appreciate or understand classical music or fine art, whereas there are some people who are high in cultural capital but comparatively low in economic capital (such as teachers). It can be inferred from Bourdieu's work that distinctions between a range of groups may be based on differences in capital.

In *Distinction* (1984) Bourdieu provided a complex and impressive sociological study of cultural consumption and the role of culture in contemporary society based on large surveys carried out in France in the 1960s. People were asked to specify their personal tastes in music, art, theatre, home decor, social pastimes, literature, and so on. They were also asked about their knowledge about these arts. Using these data Bourdieu was able to identify a link between cultural practices and social origins, and demonstrate that a person's cultural tastes and preferences would correspond to their education level and social class. These cultural preferences or 'tastes' are an acquired cultural skill, a cultural competence which is used to legitimate the differences between different social groups. Cultural consumption fulfils the 'social function of legitimating social differences' (Bourdieu, 1984: 7). Groups inhabit a particular cultural space. Class-based cultural advantages are passed on from parents to children and cultural capital acts as the linchpin of distinction as cultural hierarchies correspond to social ones. In other words, people learn how to consume culture and this education is differentiated by social class (Jenkins, 2002). Bourdieu also developed the concept of habitus to refer to the way in which different social groups classify and view the world.

Gaynor Bagnall

Associated Concepts Bourdieu; Class; Consumption; Culture; Distinction; Habitus, Field and Capital; Marxism; Social Capital; Structure and Agency.

CULTURAL INTERMEDIARIES

This is the term used by Bourdieu to describe those members of the new and unrooted middle classes – postmodernity's ultra-cool set – who engage in the promotion and transmission of popular culture in order to legitimate relatively new leisure fields such as life-style shopping, fashion, popular music and celebrity as 'valid fields of intellectual analysis' (Featherstone, 1991).

In this sense, Bourdieu, like Gramsci before him, recognizes the gradual shift in the *modus operandi* of intellectual work, which sees the passing of the intellectual torch from traditional, legislating intellectuals to the intellectuals of a third culture who will not only shape the *Zeitgeist* but also act as go-betweens. As Featherstone has forcefully argued, these cultural intermediaries have to some extent been effective in collapsing some of the most enduring distinctions and symbolic hierarchies between 'high' and 'low' cultures of taste and have also been very successful in opening 'information channels between formerly sealed off areas of culture'. Notwithstanding the political activist potential of the cultural intermediaries, Bourdieu suggests that because of their class position and commitment to capitalist values they are unlikely to have any value beyond this largely self-absorbed communicative role.

Contrary to Bourdieu, some leisure scholars have argued that there is a central interpretive role for cultural intermediaries in dealing with social exclusion and poverty issues in a world where respect is arguably *the* pivotal value (Blackshaw and Crabbe, 2004; Blackshaw and Long, 2005). In this more critical meaning it might be said that the key task facing cultural intermediaries is breathing life into the cross-fertilization of cultures which might have taken place had it not been for ignorance, intolerance or distrust. There is the recognition with this approach that we need to pay people the compliment of taking them seriously as individuals and as communities with moral intelligence. Leisure has a key role to play in this process, because it does have the potential to communicate across those cultural boundaries that divide different social and cultural groups in a way that is at the same time respectful of the differences that separate them.

Tony Blackshaw

Associated Concepts Bourdieu; Communication; Community Action; Community Leisure; Cool; Postmodernity; Social Network Analysis.

CULTURAL OMNIVORES

The idea of the cultural omnivore is located in an attempt to develop and update the work of Pierre Bourdieu on cultural capital and taste. The general premise of the literature concerned with this concept is that in contemporary society there occurs a diffusion of cultural tastes, with members of society's elite acquiring more interest in middle- and low-brow tastes, and to a lesser degree those further down the social spectrum developing tastes in high- and low-brow culture and middle- and high-brow culture respectively.

Peterson and Kern (1996) suggest that this move from snobbishness to omnivorousness is occurring due to five main societal shifts. First, they point towards structural changes within society such as a broadening of education, geographical and social mobility and the growth of the mass media, which have all reduced cultural distinctions. Second, Peterson and Kern discuss how value changes have led to the tolerance of other cultures, outside of what is traditionally seen as the dominant culture (such as the cultural practices and values of ethnic minority groups). Third, they identify changes within the art world, where market forces have opened up art to a wider market and broadened its scope. Fourth, they point to generational politics and the liberalization of culture since the late 1960s. Finally, they look towards status-group changes and suggest that increasingly dominant social groups have sought to gentrify aspects of popular culture and incorporate these into their own cultural domain. It is these changes, Peterson and Kern (1996) suggest, that have led to a blurring and breaking down of cultural distinctions and hierarchies and are now leading to an increase in cultural omnivorousness. For instance, one example of this would be how in recent years the traditional class profiles of many sport supporters have (to some degree) begun to change, as many traditionally middle-class sports such as rugby union and cricket have received more 'popular' support, while sports such as professional football have increasingly marketed themselves towards a more affluent audience.

Erickson (1996) argues that we can no longer talk of a universal culture and universal cultural hierarchy on which cultural capital is based. What is the most useful cultural resource, Erickson argues, is a wide variety of tastes (and 'omnivorousness'), which is closely linked to social network variety. For Erickson it is social networks which define an individual's cultural resources, and the level of social prestige that they can obtain from these.

However, Warde, Martens and Olsen (1999) have suggested that Bourdieu should not be forgotten altogether and that this literature also needs to recognize that an expertise in forms of high-brow culture can still operate as an important source of cultural and social capital. The cultural omnivore literature, while introducing more fluidity and variation into Bourdieu's original theorization, does not develop his theorization of power relations any further. This literature still places cultural consumption on a (though now more complex) predominantly linear hierarchy of taste – where cultural variety and 'authentic' (e.g., 'ethnic') cultures are now the pinnacle of taste. Significantly, the emphasis within this literature is still most firmly placed on a cultural distinction rather than inclusion. It is also not a theory (unlike the original work of Bourdieu) that has been widely embraced or adopted in leisure studies.

Garry Crawford

Associated Concepts Bourdieu; Class; Consumption; Cultural Capital; Mass Media; Power; Social Capital.

CULTURE

In his lexicon of the 'language of cultural transformation', *Keywords,* the Welsh cultural theorist Raymond Williams (1976: 76) remarks that 'culture is one of the two or three most complicated words in the English language'. Culture is one of those 'things' that is everywhere and everything, and therefore it is quite difficult to pin down exactly what it is (and is not). Generally the term culture can be said to have three key and common usages. First, it can be used to

describe intellectual or more commonly artistic endeavours, such as poetry, art, music, literature, dance, and so on. Distinctions are often made here between what can be seen as 'high' (i.e., and hence often seen as 'important') and 'low' (i.e., 'common' or 'pop' culture, and hence often perceived to have less social significance). In particular, the tastes of social elites (such as opera, ballet and high art) are often seen as culturally more important than those of the lower classes (such as football, television and pop music), and in particular, these cultural forms in themselves can be used as the basis of social hierarchies and distinctions. It is also this use of the term 'culture' that Theodor Adorno and his colleagues at the Frankfurt School use in their discussion of the 'culture industry'. However, for Adorno and his contemporaries, what defined cultural production (such as popular music and cinema) was the capitalist machinery, which was profit (rather than artistically) driven.

Linked to this first definition of 'culture' is the second common usage of this term, that of seeing culture as 'progress' or 'development'. This, Williams (1976) alerts us to, is more in keeping with the original meaning of the term 'culture', where it was traditionally used to refer to the cultivation and husbandry of animals and crops. Hence, societies or individuals who are described as 'cultured' are understood to be more 'developed', more 'civilized', and/or have more 'refined' tastes.

Third, Williams identifies the idea of culture as 'a way of life' (see Longhurst et al., 2008). This refers to the practices, values and traditions of a particular social group. In particular, Williams highlights how this form of culture is usually 'symbolic', in that it is based upon common and shared symbols such as a shared language and meanings. In this sense nations can be seen to have a 'culture' such as a 'British' culture. But within this there will also be other cultures, such as Scottish or Welsh cultures, or immigrant and/ or religious cultures, such as Pakistani or Jewish culture, or cultures based around activities, groups or locations, such as a business cultures or nightclub cultures, music cultures, age-specific cultures, and so on and so on – all of which will in turn cross-cut and intersect with other cultures.

This recognition of the presence and existence of different cultures within a wider culture/society informs the basis of subcultural theory. However, it has been suggested that in an increasingly 'postmodern' or 'liquid' world our identities and cultural groupings will become more fluid and less fixed. Consequently, one updated version of subcultural theory is that of neo-tribes, which recognizes the increasingly fluid and temporal nature of cultural groupings.

Garry Crawford

Associated Concepts Birmingham School; Cultural Capital; Cultural Omnivores; Critical Theory; Distinction; Elias; Everyday Life; Habitus, Field and Capital; Neo-Tribes; Structure of Feeling; Subcultures; Youth.

CYBERCULTURE

'Cyber' is a prefix used to signify a 'computerized' or 'virtual' environment or encounters. It is a term that was most notably popularized by the novelist William Gibson with his coining of the term 'cyberspace' in his 1982 novel *Burning Chrome* and later in his 1984 novel *Neuromancer*, to refer to a hallucinogenic-like virtual world made up of human and computer networks and intersections. The ideas of the 'cyber', 'cyberspace' and 'cyberculture' have become synonymous with the rise of the internet and the World Wide Web in the 1990s, which in turn has raised a number of questions about the possibility of living out alternative lives or participating in virtual (or 'cyber') cultures. In particular, there has been considerable discussion and debate about the possibility of online or 'virtual' relationships and communities, such as in online 'worlds' like *Second Life*.

For instance, Rheingold (1994) sees the internet as offering a renewed sense of community participation, activity and democracy, and in contrast to more technological deterministic accounts he emphasizes the importance of personal choice and voluntary participation in these communities (Flew, 2002).

This online sense of community may be about forming new affiliations or for some may represent a strengthening of 'older' social links. For instance, Mitra's (2000) consideration of (ethnically) Indian users of the internet suggests that for some people this can provide an important link between them and their ethnic community and identity. This is particularly apparent with geographically mobile individuals who may live outside of their home country and culture.

However, it is important to recognize that the internet is in itself a cultural text, which is not simply or passively consumed by its users but is actively created and recreated by a significant proportion of users. While many individuals may simply draw on the internet as a source of information, many others will actively contribute to its structure and content. For instance, many internet users will frequently construct their own websites, newsgroups, mailing lists or discussion sites, or will actively contribute to those that already exist. Hence, internet communities often involve *active* participation within this culture, and this is particularly the case with many fan online mailing lists and newsgroups which will usually contain a limited number of contributors and users, further increasing the sense of coherence and community for members. For example, Hills (2002: 180) suggests that internet fan communities (and in particular he discusses the contributors to *alt.tv.X-Files*) need to be viewed as a 'community of imagination'. As he argues: 'this is a community which, rather than merely imagining itself as coexistent in empty clocked time, constitutes itself precisely through a common affective engagement, and thereby through a common respect for a specific potential space' (Hills, 2002: 180).

However, it is important not to fall into the all too easy trap of trying to emphasize the positive aspects of the internet as a means of stimulating and enabling new egalitarian cybercultures, as it is evident that not all communities are 'good'. Just as the internet may give access to a sense of community and help reinforce cultural identities for the ethnically Indian (Mitra, 2000) or *X-Files* fans (Hills, 2002), it can also do the same for racists, misogynists, criminals and various other deviant and hate groups or individuals. The anonymity of the internet also allows for (sometimes) high levels of bullying and threats to be made against individuals and, in particular, Jessica Valenti (editor of Femminist.org) writing in The *Guardian* newspaper (2007: 16) highlights how

several editors and contributors to 'women-friendly' or 'feminist' websites (including herself) have received threats of rape, murder and violence against them, again via the internet. It is therefore important to recognise that, as well as bringing people together, the internet (and other new technologies) can also help to isolate them as victims as well.

Garry Crawford

Associated Concepts Communication; Community; Culture; Fans; Identity; Mass Media; Network Society; Virtual Leisure.

D

DEADWEIGHT EXPENDITURE

Economic impact attributable to a sport event relates solely to new money generated by external visitors. Only visitors who reside outside the host city, and whose primary motivation is to attend the event or who stay longer and spend more because of the event, should be included (Crompton, 1995, 2001; UK Sport, 2000). Any expenditure by those who reside in the host community does not represent the circulation of new money, simply a re-circulation of what was already there. This is based on the assumption that, for example, if local residents had not spent money at the event that money would have been used to purchase other items in the host locality. A number of publications by LIRC (1997–2003) refer to local residents as 'deadweight'. The inclusion of local residents offers substantially different economic impacts, although event organizers frequently ignore this concept in an attempt to advocate the use of public funds and to boost political reputations (Crompton, 1995; 2001).

Rob Wilson

Associated Concepts Economic Benefit of Hosting Major Sport Events; Economic Impact of Hosting Major Sport Events; Event Management.

DECENTRING LEISURE

Decentring leisure appears in the title of Chris Rojek's seminal (1995) book which emphasizes a radical shift in leisure studies in the light of postmodernism, poststructuralism and deconstructionalism. The idea of decentring leisure is ambivalent in the sense that it not only assumes that leisure studies is a discursive formation that exists independent of individual leisure scholars but also that it should go about its day-to-day business by undermining the significance of its own unifying centre (the topic of leisure). In this sense Rojek is suggesting that, while leisure studies cannot help but be perspectival, it must always strive to remain open to various other culturally determined ways of seeing of the world. In other words, the modernist object of leisure 'as a bounded category of practice and experience' (Rojek, 1995: 146) needs to be subsumed into the subject of culture. Contrary to what its critics suggest (e.g., Roberts, 1999), the idea of 'decentring' neither 'relativizes' leisure nor undermines the discursive formation known as leisure studies, but instead both celebrates and advances the study of leisure, which in Rojek's hands is always in flux.

Tony Blackshaw

Associated Concepts Deconstruction; Discursive Formations; Rojek; Postmodernism; Postmodernity.

DECONSTRUCTION

This term is derived from the work of the poststructuralist philosopher Jacques Derrida. There is significant overlap between deconstruction and the idea of decentring. At its most basic the term suggests that the discursive formations (or what Derrida prefers to call texts) with which we are most familiar contain hidden and unexpected meanings which often signify points of resistance. Put simply, where structuralists set themselves the task of constructing alternative systems of thought which they deem to be truer than existing ones (e.g., a Marxist interpretation of leisure can be seen as a critical response to Functionalist understanding), poststructuralists aim to dismantle structures or systems of thought – that is, take them apart, to not only demonstrate how they are necessarily contingent and ambivalent but also to reveal the gaps and absences they render unintelligible.

It might be said that the central aim of deconstruction is to show how such texts do not come up to scratch under their own terms of reference. A successful deconstruction not only changes a text, it also conceives new ways of seeing. For example, Rojek's (2005) book *Decentring Leisure* is a deconstruction of leisure studies in the sense that not only does it call for a critique of taken-for-granted assumptions about leisure but, it also prompts changes in our perceptions about the potential and the limits of leisure studies. To this extent, we can see that deconstruction designates a mode of critical inquiry that attributes the meaning conveyed by texts to those who read them. It also signifies a transformative way of reading which assumes that there really is no reality outside what we say about the world.

Tony Blackshaw

Associated Concepts Binary Oppositions; Decentring Leisure; Deviance; Discursive Formations; Governmentality; Social Control; Surveillance; Postmodernism.

DEEM, ROSEMARY

(women's leisure)

DEMAND

The theory of demand, in conjunction with that of supply, is in part intended to explain how the prices and the quantities bought and sold in markets will vary in response to changes in the economic environment. Consequently, demand theory begins with the behaviour of individual consumers. It then extends its analysis to the market on the assumption that the 'market' demand curve is simply the sum of individual demand curves.

Demand for sport and leisure includes consumer spending in different leisure markets, such as clothing, footwear, televised sport and sports participation, and so on. At the core of the theory of demand is the idea of the utility-maximizing, rational, income-constrained individual consumer. Several core assumptions are made about consumers so that economists can derive clear, testable predictions about individual economic behaviour and hence market demand:

- Consumers receive satisfaction, welfare or utility from consuming goods and services.
- Consumers have complete sets of preferences or tastes associated with the consumption of goods or services.
- Consumers have perfect information about products, their prices and the effects of their consumption on their personal welfare and utility.
- Consumers only consider their own welfare or utility.
- Consumer preferences are given.
- Consumers are limited by expenditure constraints which make it impossible to spend more than their current income, which is 'fixed' in the short term.
- Consumers are individuals so small in relation to the whole market that their individual decisions (whether to buy or not to buy) do not affect the prices of goods.

The starting point for analysing demand is an examination of the quantity of the product demanded, the price of the commodity and the income of consumers. However, it has to be recognized that, for some aspects of the 'leisure market', consumers also need 'time', which can often pose a bigger constraint than money. Neo-classical economic analysis assumes utility-maximizing consumers are faced with many choices over how to allocate their time. Work is treated as a disutility and so they are faced with an income/leisure, leisure/time trade-off.

Rob Wilson

Associated Concepts Demand for Health Model; Income–Leisure Time Trade-Off and Time Dating; Neo-classical analysis; Supply.

DEMAND FOR HEALTH MODEL

This model relates to the fact that a great many of those who participate in sport, especially those over the age of 30, use it to maintain or increase their health status. This makes sport (and leisure) not just a consumption good, yielding utility, but also an investment good, where people sacrifice their present satisfaction in order to reap future benefits. Basically the return is better health in the future and potentially a longer life.

The Health Production Function is dependent on several inputs, including exercise, diet, housing conditions, work conditions and health services. The amount of exercise demanded will be related to the rate of return on the perceived longer-term benefits from improved health. This is dependent on both wage rates and the number of healthy days generated by increased exercise.

This model is useful for three reasons. First, it also gives us an insight into why income is an important determinant of demand.

Second, it also allows some insight into which activities will be substitutes or complements for one another. Third, the model indicates that people will respond differently to changes in certain variables depending on whether their motivation for participation is consumption rather than investment.

Rob Wilson

Associated Concepts Consumer Society; Consumption; Demand; Work Ethic; Work-Leisure.

DESIRE

At its most basic level of understanding this term is used to refer to things or persons we long or wish for. However, in the academic literature, desire is understood as an eternal and recurring plane of consciousness that reflects the vitalism of human creativity and experience, described by the philosopher James Conant (cited in Williams, 1993) as the manifestation of 'our most profound confusions of soul', and by the film critic Peter Wollen (2007: 93) as something which is always competitive and in the final analysis 'implies the possibility of struggle and, inevitably, the risk of death, as occurs in wars'. To this extent leisure scholars must be capable of understanding desire, because in doing so we also may understand how human beings think, speak, dream, imagine, live and die in the world.

Since Plato, desire has been understood as something that is invariably in conflict with reason, which 'operates as a distinctive part of the soul'. According to Freudian analysts it is desire rather than reason that is the driving force behind human existence, even if it is not always acted upon. There is no doubt that people often live their lives sandwiched between named duty and unnamed desire – wishes that just must be made true. Yet if desire is always the possibility of wish fulfilment this is often less than certain and expressions of desire tend to be intermittent and short-lived. What this Freudian understanding suggests is that there is something about desire that is irreconcilable with satisfaction.

Deleuze and Guatarri (1983) argue that human beings are much more than individuals who desire and refocus the debate about the *ways* we desire and the extent to which this could be split from memory and feeling and whether we should continue to acquiesce to being plugged into infernal desiring machines. According to Deleuze and Guatarri, to desire is to work for an ideology and we are desiring machines because we are modern men and women who desire in modern ways: nationally, patriotically, homophobically, and so on – but especially capitalistically.

It is in recognition of these different ideological influences that the philosopher and cultural critic Slavoj Žižek (2006) argues that cinema is the ultimate distorted leisure activity, because it doesn't give cinemagoers what they desire – it tells them how to desire. This could be said to be the same in leisure activities such as sport. According to queer theorists, sport is a system of desire that tends to exclude or 'de-naturalize' desires which are not heterosexual. The only acceptable forms of desire in sport, and particularly competitive sport, tend to be domineering and protective desires (Pronger, 1999). In male sport it is anathema to welcome other men into your own space. In other words, sport as a system of desire has no willing bottoms. The upshot is that the biggest insult in sport is the desire for the penetration of the arsehole. Metaphorically this is evidenced in most team sports, where the team with the most desire produces the most invasive phallus (offensive strategy) and the tightest arsehole (defensive strategy).

Tony Blackshaw

Associated Concepts Freud; Happiness; Queer Theory; Pleasure; Sport; Surveillance.

DEVIANCE

Notwithstanding the term's relative obscurity in everyday language, deviance, or more appropriately social deviance, has long held a fascination for students of leisure – if not leisure scholars. It is a concept much broader in focus than either 'crime' or 'law-breaking' which was developed in US sociology to describe any social behaviours or practices that deviate from those regarded as 'normal' within a particular society or other socio-cultural milieu. To this extent social deviance signifies those kinds of leisure activities, interests and life-styles which are condemned by the 'value consensus' of any dominant culture as 'wrong', whilst implying that they also need to be socially controlled.

In the 1960s there emerged what at the time was a radically alternative way of interpreting social deviance. Edwin Lemert (1967) turned this essentially functionalist understanding on its head when he suggested that it is not deviance that precedes social control, but it is social control that invariably leads to deviance. Following Lemert's lead the 'problem' of social deviance now changed to asking questions about how and why any society deems it necessary to socially control the leisure behaviours of particular individuals and social groups more (and in different ways) than others. It is also in this sense that the problem of social deviance has been seen as very much a 'leisure problem' (Clarke and Critcher, 1985), particularly with regard to the activities of working-class youth, because these take place in 'the streets, clubs and holiday resorts ... the places where their leisure activity has been most resented'.

Until recently social deviance has not been theorized to any great degree in leisure studies. Rojek goes so far as to suggest that, 'it is no exaggeration to claim that, throughout its history, it has effectively ignored the subject of deviance' (1995: 83). However, Coakley (1998) has drawn on the concept in the sociology of sport to argue that it is generally understood either in absolutist terms – 'it's either right or wrong' – or in relativist terms – 'it all depends on who makes the rules' – approaches. Coakley represents the absolutist approach as functionalist, placing an emphasis on the identification of social deviance as a departure from a predetermined social norm. By contrast the relativist position is represented in an over-simplified and theoretically naïve fashion as emanating from conflict theorists *vis-à-vis* Lemert who, in Coakley's over-simplistic view, presents deviance as a 'label' relating to certain behaviours or people who are identified as 'bad' or undesirable on the basis of rules made by those people in positions of power.

For Coakley, who appears to consider sport as being independent of its wider social context, the main problems with these two broad brush conceptualizations is that on the one hand they ignore social deviance which involves an over-comformity to rules and norms and on the other do not account for the ways athletes use these norms to evaluate both themselves and others. As a response, Coakley offers an alternative schema which draws on what he calls a 'critical normal distribution approach' to distinguish between 'positive deviance' involving overconformity or an unquestioned acceptance of norms and 'negative deviance' involving underconformity or a rejection of norms. These represent two ends of a continuum which in their extreme manifestations can be seen to lead to fascism (excess 'positive' deviance) and anarchy (excess 'negative' deviance) on either side of the 'normal' accepted range of behaviour. While undoubtedly showing a more sophisticated appreciation of the varieties of deviance in sport than many other studies, Coakley's approach is theoretically weak and ultimately too abstract, offering an objectivist, top-down analysis which essentializes certain types of 'deviant' behaviour and their sources.

While the ability to theorize social deviance in the sociology of sport has always remained limited, in sociology more generally the willingness to continue theorizing reached its highpoint in the 1970s. However, with the growing influence of postmodernism and cultural relativism by the late 1970s the sociology of deviance had reached a point in its history when it needed another kind of theoretical understanding, which could only be successfully written through a quite different language. This was because, as Sumner (1994) points out, with the shift to a more plural, postmodern world it was becoming increasingly untenable to make the case for the sociology of deviance.

In *New Perspectives on Sport and 'Deviance': Consumption, Performativity and Social Control*, Blackshaw and Crabbe (2004) reconceived the study of social deviance as a beginning enterprise, which not only enables us to consider that what it means to hold values is always open to question but also suggests that answering ethical dilemmas surrounding what is understood as deviance is made possible only by embracing and dealing with the complexity of the world of that which chooses to describe it. It is with this in mind that they place inverted commas around the concept of social 'deviance', not only to remind their readers of its 'undecidability', its shape-shifting quality, but also to reflect the contested nature of its use value as it is contingently stressed in their writings.

According to Blackshaw and Crabbe, the world of leisure itself must also be understood as a wholeheartedly contingent *set* of worlds. Not *a* world somehow separate from the rest of society, but a series of postulated worlds in which taken-for-granted assumptions about *the* world we oversimply tend to understand as 'reality' – with its prevailing norms, values, beliefs, behaviours and actions – are often subverted, changed or distorted. Adopting Rorty's position, which holds that any culturally grounded conceptualization of that truth needs to prove 'itself to be good in the way of belief, *and good, too, for definite, assignable reasons*', they argue that valuing contingency does not mean accepting the postmodern position that 'anything goes'. On the contrary, it means that, without the obligation of having to make their work take on an essentialist position, leisure scholars can get on with the task of constructing their own narratives about the world, about 'deviance'.

In other words, questions of what is or is not 'deviance' must be dealt with in the untidy realm of human interaction rather than in the tidy transcendental realm of universal reason. It is precisely because leisure scholars have this knowledge that we are in a stronger position to recognize and make explicit the ideological and the subjective to their understandings of social 'deviance'. In this way, Blackshaw and Crabbe demand a neverending dialogue between those who promulgate the most seemingly irreconcilable interpretations of social 'deviance' as well as a constant questioning of themselves, their own tacitly accepted assumptions and the institutions that surround their ideas. As they assert, what is perhaps the most important conclusion to be drawn from this reinventing of the study of this contested idea as a beginning enterprise is to refuse the more comfortable role of bystander to take on the active responsibility of engaging in unearthing and understanding even the most fiercely contested understandings of what is or is not social 'deviance' in leisure.

Tony Blackshaw

Associated Concepts Abnormal Leisure; Football Hooliganism; Power; Queer Theory; Social Control; Surveillance.

DIGITAL GAMING

Confusingly, the terms 'video games' and 'computer games' are sometimes used interchangeably to refer to all forms of electronic gaming. However, these are also used more specifically to refer to different types of games – where 'video games' is used to refer to games played on game consoles or on arcade machines, and 'computer games' is used specifically to refer to games played on PC or Apple Macintosh systems (Poole, 2000). To help avoid such confusion the term digital

gaming appears to be preferred, growing in acceptance within the literature on gaming to refer to all forms of electronic gaming including games played on games consoles, computers, arcade machines, mobile (cell) phones and other gaming hardware.

Though the origins of digital gaming can be traced back to the 1950s, it was not until the late 1970s and 1980s that it began to develop as a common leisure activity. Today, digital games are a major global industry. Global sales exceed $21 billion, and are now comparable to cinema box office takings (ESA, 2006). Today more digital games are sold in the USA and UK than books (Bryce and Rutter, 2001).

Contrary to popular belief, digital game playing is not solely restricted to male adolescents. The Entertainment Software Association (ESA) suggests that 69 per cent of digital game players are over the age of 18. Though digital gaming is by no means a level playing field when it comes to gender, the ESA also suggests that 38 per cent of gamers are female, and Fromme's (2003) study of over 1,000 German schoolchildren suggests that almost a third of girls claimed to 'regularly' play digital games (and 55.7 per cent of boys).

It is evident that a considerable amount of discussion has focused on the recurrence of violent themes in many digital games and, in particular, the concern that this could lead to heightened aggression in (young) gamers (see Emes, 1997). However, a relationship between violent games and gamers (as with violence on television) is far from conclusive. In particular, such research has been heavily criticized for its often inconsistent methodologies and small and unrepresentative sample groups. It has also been criticized for overestimating the ability of games to influence the specific attitudes and behaviour of individuals and/or groups, and for seeing gamers as passive and vulnerable to representations of violence within games.

Beyond these studies of violence and 'media effects', it is possible to identify a divide between those theorists who have sought to understand digital games by drawing on and developing a Film/Media Studies approach (such as Murray, 1997) and those who have adopted a more psychologically influenced focus upon patterns of play (a perspective called 'ludology') (see Frasca, 2003).

Adopting a Media/Film Studies approach to digital games does not simply mean that digital games are viewed as 'interactive' films, but it does provide certain 'tools' to help gain a more in-depth understanding of digital games. For instance, some would argue that games could be understood as a 'text' just as any other media form, such as a book, television show or film. This 'text' can then be studied to look for meanings, both obvious and hidden, within these.

However, there are those who question whether digital games can be understood as a 'text' in the same way as 'older' media forms (such as television, radio and cinema) because unlike these digital games are not set and rigid and can vary depending on how the player interacts with them (Kerr et al., 2005). This is a similar argument to that offered by a 'ludology' approach, which suggests that, while traditional media (such as films) are 'representational' (i.e., they offer a simple representation of reality), digital games are based around 'simulation', creating a world that gamers can manipulate and interact with. However, the degree of flexibility within a game should not be overemphasized. In particular, the degree of 'interactivity' a gamer has with, or over, digital games has been questioned by numerous authors – as the user's level of control or interaction with the medium is still restricted not only by the limitations of technology but also by the aims of designers and manufacturers.

Garry Crawford

Associated Concepts Audiences; Content Analysis; Cyberculture; Mass Media; Play; Violence; Virtual Leisure; Women's Leisure.

DIONYSIAN LEISURE

The adjective Dionysian is derived from Greek mythology. The way it is used when applied to leisure is as a kind of ecstatic release – whether it is through alcohol, drugs, sex, sport or dancing – from the limits of our own selfhood, which is circumscribed by the conventions of modern living and respectability.

Among the Greeks, Dionysus was the son of the ruler of all gods, Zeus, and was recognized as the god of prophecy, vegetation and wine, ecstasy and mindless pleasures, and fertility. He is often contrasted with Apollo, who was recognized as one of the most important deities: the God of light and life, giving being to purity and healing. In modern thought, the two terms arise in Nietzsche's Greek drama *The Birth of Tragedy* (1872). Here Nietzsche suggests that Apollo represents modern order, rationality, intellectual harmony and self-discipline (deferred gratification), while in marked contrast Dionysus represents the spirit of release and the spur-of-the-moment (instant gratification). As Rojek (1995) demonstrates, this provides a useful juxtaposition with which to explain how modern leisure activities are often circumscribed by the requirements of 'respectability'. He also alerts us to the ways in which Dionysian leisure activities not seen as 'respectable' are all too often understood as deviant and the consequences this kind of labelling can have for individuals.

In understanding the Dionysian spirit of ecstatic release and what it can tell us about leisure, however, it is perhaps more useful to look at the distinction between Dionysus and another Greek god, Pentheus. This arises in Euripides' (485–406 BC) tale *The Bacchae*, which contrasts two different ways of experiencing life. Dionysus was the last god to arrive in the Greek pantheon. In *The Bacchae* he is a young god, angry that his mortal family, the royal house of Cadmus, has denied him a place of honour as a deity. This is because he was exiled in Persia, where he became a 'foreigner' who found wine, dance, theatre, music and same-sex relations. In Euripides' tale, Pentheus is Greek while Dionysus is foreign. Pentheus is wholly male; Dionysus is undecidedly male and female. Pentheus is rational; Dionysus is playful.

The most significant part of *The Bacchae*, from our perspective, concerns Pentheus' anxiety to understand the mystery of the Dionysian spirit of release. Pentheus watches women dancing on a mountain and feels himself wanting to gain access to the undecidability of Dionysian sexuality but without losing himself. Dionysus suggests that the best way for him to do this would be to dress as a female and perform with the rest of the women. However, Pentheus remarks that this is impossible as he is a man. In the event, his curiosity overwhelms him and he does indeed dress as a woman. He joins the dancers, arrayed like a princess, but is humiliated because he refuses to lose himself in the dance – he can't recognize the Dionysian spirit within him for fear of looking stupid. The message in Euripides' tale is clear: if you do not recognize the Dionysian spirit within yourself, then it will find its own release and destroy you in the process.

In commenting on the continuing relevance of the Dionysian spirit in contemporary societies, David Greig (2007), who has produced *The Bacchae* for modern theatre, argues that at the cusp of the 1990s 'there was something truly Dionysian abroad in Britain'. Discussing his own version of what was to become known as the 'Summer of Love' of rave culture that hit Britain in 1988, Greig argues this period saw the emergence of 'illegal dances held in the open air, in nature; strange new songs that encouraged the participants to lose themselves in each other; and a culture in which masculinity and femininity evaporated into something much more ambiguous, open and strange', until it 'quickly degenerated into a horrible consumer parody of itself'. What this suggests is that there is something transcendent, something revelatory, something spiritual, something beautiful, about ecstatic forms of leisure – something Dionysian, a moment when individuals can truly be themselves, before the rationalities of social control and the entrepreneurial instinct set in.

Tony Blackshaw

Associated Concepts Catharsis and Cathexis; Consumer Society; Consumption; Desire; Deviance; Flow; Folk Devils and Moral Panics; Happiness; Hedonism; Pleasure; Postmodernism; Rojek, Chris; Social Control; Structure of Feeling.

DISCOURSES

(discursive formations)

DISCURSIVE FORMATIONS

Discursive formations are relatively autonomous configurations of power-knowledge which have sedimented and acquired a dominant societal or field-specific role. They are usually overly simplistically depicted in the literature as 'authorless' textual discourses of language and practice which in their decentredness are understood differently from 'top-down' ideologies based on the more rigid Marxist base–superstructure model. However, this view ignores the extent to which discursive formations are constituted in social and cultural practices and institutions.

According to Foucault every discursive formation has its own 'order of things' which it uses to perpetuate its own ostensible truths, its own 'innate' superiority over other discourses. Each discursive formation also has an obligation to those truths – the tacit assumption of the power-knowledge of those particular truths over others – to express its own perspective that reflects the specific nature of its thought, as well as its capacity to examine its own resources, which reflects the struggle it has with its own decentred existence. It should be noted, however, that discursive formations do not refer to 'things' by way of ideological statements, but instead constitute their own objects and subjects, concepts and strategies, and generate their own knowledge about them. To this extent power relations are involved at every level in discursive formations, which can mean that not only do some of them have the authority to represent the world but also that the knowledge they generate can make them seem as if their discursive products *are* the world. For Foucault, the relationship between power and knowledge associated with this ability to designate truth should never be underestimated and this is the basis of all discursive formations.

For example, the discursive formation known as leisure studies includes a wide variety of perspectives (e.g., historical, sociological, feminist, and so on) and institutions (e.g., leisure departments in universities, historical archives, key associations, journals, conferences, and so on) within the category of 'leisure' that it uses to produce its own ideas, concepts and theories, and to then generate its own strategies for dealing with this knowledge (e.g., ways of carrying out research, putative epistemological and ontological truths about the nature of leisure, and so on).

Notwithstanding their authority, discursive formations always generate their own forms of resistance which 'are all the more real and effective because they are formed right at the point where relations of power are exercised; resistance to power does not have to come from elsewhere to be real, nor is it inexorably frustrated through being the compatriot of power' (Foucault, 1980: 142). To contest discursive formations, whose structures and strictures are, as Foucault had argued, always imbued with a microphysics of power-knowledge, is to critically assess them not by reference to either the flickering surfaces of truth used to nourish their empirical validity, nor on the basis of their putative deeper ideologies or hegemony, but in relation to what they are in themselves as authorities of delimitation and government. What this also suggests is that discursive formations also exist in their performativity, that they are not merely textual. They communicate in a way that both reflects language and transcends it at the same time.

This can be illustrated with another leisure example. One of the incontrovertible challenges facing sports fans today is the problem of how to maintain that abiding devotion that makes them fans, when the professional clubs they support all seem to be trying their hardest to turn them into consumers. As Brown, Crabbe and Mellor's (2008) research on the foundation of FC United of Manchester suggests there are major variations in fans' commitment to their clubs, but for those inclined towards heavy commitment there is one cultural identity that is important in their lives, and not only are they fully committed to it but they are also insistent on politicizing it, as in this particular case, by contesting corporate power at Manchester United by withdrawing their support and setting up a community-based club. Indeed, drawn together in their rejection of consumerism and in their readiness to reject the success-seeking that goes with supporting Manchester United, the breakaway fans of FC United of Manchester can be said to have generated their own form of resistance to the discursive formation of consumerism in football through a form of community action-based politics.

Tony Blackshaw

Associated Concepts Community Action; Community Leisure; Consumption; Decentring Leisure; Deconstruction; Foucault; Governmentality; Hegemony; Marxism; New Social Movements; Performativity; Social Control; Surveillance.

DISNEYIZATION

Disneyization has been defined as 'the process by which the principles of the Disney theme parks are coming to dominate more and more sectors of American society as well as the rest of the world' (Bryman, 1999: 26). In defining the concept in this way, Bryman simply repeats Ritzer's (1993) definition of McDonaldization, but replaces the word 'McDonaldization' with 'Disneyization'. Hence, Bryman is seeking to define Disneyization in direct relation to Ritzer's concept of McDonaldization.

However, unlike Ritzer, Bryman is not providing a critique or criticism of a process, but rather is seeking to understand its social importance. In particular, he rejects the term 'Disneyfication', which has been used by other authors as a critique of the spread of Disney and its influences (Aldridge, 2003). However, as with Ritzer, Bryman suggests that the ideologies applied at Disney theme parks can be seen to be spreading to other industries, and also (again like Ritzer) sums up the characteristics of this in four key points, which he refers to as: 'theming', 'dedifferentiation of consumption', 'merchandising', and 'emotional labour'.

'Theming' relates to how the artefacts, characters or narratives are imported into an activity in order to create an image. For instance, Disney film characters are incorporated into 'theme' parks, such as Disneyland. However, theming is also becoming common in many sectors, such as shopping malls, casinos and restaurants who utilize 'themes' to create a concept and experience for their customers. The 'dedifferentiation of consumption' involves the breaking down of boundaries between different forms of consumption and institutional boundaries. For example, Disney theme parks intertwine shops, restaurants, hotels, merchandise and rides. The object is to create a whole Disney 'experience' which blends different forms of consumption together, and allows companies to sell consumers lots of different products and services under one roof.

'Merchandising' is key to the Disneyization process, and involves offering customers the opportunity to purchase a wide range of merchandise bearing a copyrighted logo or design, relating to the overall theme being sold. Finally, Disneyization involves 'emotional labour', which requires the employees of a corporation to perform in certain ways as part of their job. In particular, this involves being schooled in how to behave, such as always being 'friendly' or 'jolly' to guests/customers.

Garry Crawford

Associated Concepts Bureaucracy; Consumer Society; Consumption; McDonaldization; Modernity; Theming.

DISTINCTION

In its use in the social sciences, distinction refers to social differences and categories determined on the basis of 'taste'. In particular, the origins of academic interest in social distinction can be traced to the work of Veblen and Simmel. Simmel suggested that social elites develop a consensus of what is 'fashionable' and 'desirable' and these items are displayed as both a marker of their class membership and a distinction from other (lower) social strata. As Simmel wrote 'fashion is … a product of class division and operates … the double function of holding a given circle together and at the same time closing it off from others' (1997 [1904]: 189). Copying the trends, fashions and tastes of a social elite by those lower down the social scale then results in a continuous momentum as social elite's tastes and fashions change and develop to stay (at least) one step ahead. Similarly, Veblen (1934 [1899]) used the term conspicuous consumption to describe the way the *nouveaux riche* (newly rich) in nineteenth-century American society used their consumption as a means of social distinction.

However, the concept was developed more precisely and in a particular direction by Pierre Bourdieu in his key (1984) work *Distinction: A Social Critique of the Judgment of Taste*. Here Bourdieu drew on detailed empirical research he conducted in France in the 1960s and located this within a discussion of differing (but interrelated) forms of capital – economic capital, social capital and (most importantly in terms of distinction) cultural capital. While economic capital allows individuals the ability to purchase luxury items, it is cultural capital (which refers to learnt cultural knowledge and skills) that enables social elites to distinguish between cultural items (such as fashion, art, literature, and so on). Their cultural knowledge then allows these social elites to make more subtle and informed cultural choices and to utilize these as markers of social distinction, as well as to suggest that their preferences are a mark of 'taste' rather than simply choice. Unlike Simmel who saw preferences and 'tastes' as resulting from a social consensus, Bourdieu saw these as having their basis in social relations and experiences. For instance, Bourdieu suggested that a working-class interest in sport is often quite instrumental, seeing the development of their body as a means to achieve sporting ends, while the middle classes often see exercise as an investment in and development of their bodies and hence an end in itself. Their interests in sport and exercise reflect social class relations.

Garry Crawford

Associated Concepts Bourdieu; Class; Consumption; Cultural Capital; Cultural Omnivores; Fashion; Habitus, Field and Capital; Leisure Bodies; Shopping; Social Capital; Status; Veblen.

DOMINANT IDEOLOGY

(ideology)

DOUBLE-ENTRY BOOKKEEPING

Leisure organizations need to record economic transactions in order that they can produce financial statements and to do this they require an accounting system. To compile an income statement (P&L) and balance sheet a series of procedures needs to be established so that organizations can record every transaction that occurs during business operations. For each commercial transaction there is a requirement that the amount, date and description are recorded thereby allowing those responsible for the organization to be aware of what has happened, when it happened and the financial consequences. This involves entering all these transactions either as a debit on one account or as a credit in another. This basic accounting system is commonly known as double-entry bookkeeping and while most organizations now use computer programs they will still derive their 'logic' from this basic system. The specific application and style of the accounting system will depend on the type and size of business. Most large organizations will have accountants on their staff, but small businesses and organizations will be more likely to hire 'external' accounting advice.

Rob Wilson

Associated Concepts Assets, Liabilities and Capital; Financial and Management Accounting; Financial Health and Ratio Analysis; Financial Statements.

DROMOLOGY AND SPEED

The word dromology was coined by Paul Virilio to denote the growing importance of speed in modern day societies and especially the impact new technologies have on mobility. The root of the term derives from the Latin word for race (*dromos*); hence it might be said that dromology is the sociology of speed or the study of how innovations in a speeded-up modern world are experienced socially, culturally, economically and politically. According to Virilio, the 'dromocratic revolution' began with the invention of the steam engine, was established with the piston-driven internal combustion engine, and accelerated with the development of nuclear fusion. He also uses the term to refer to any means of engineering speed and the way it has dramatically changed the pace of life in modern societies, as well as the psychological, social and environmental impact it has had on individuals, communities and the world.

As Rojek (1995: 157–60) points out, this acceleration of life has impacted on people's leisure in a number of ways. Not only does the speed of modern life tear us from the stable anchors that formed us, it is also fraught with ambivalence: speed might have provided us with new leisure opportunities (e.g., cheap jet travel, access to global leisure events via information technology, and so on) but it has also increasingly mechanized our leisure experiences and subjects us to opportunity loss. However, what emerges most powerfully from dromological analysis is that in a global world in which speed is assumed to be a key repository of our individual freedom there are many things about it that should make us feel uneasy, not least the way it is leading us ever faster towards environmental catastrope.

Tony Blackshaw

Associated Concepts Aesthetics; Leisure and the Environment; Postmodernism; Postmodernity; Rojek, Chris.

DRUGS

(addiction)

DUNNING, ERIC

(elias; football hooliganism; mimesis; Rojek Chris; sport)

E

ECONOMIC BENEFIT OF HOSTING MAJOR SPORT EVENTS

Until the 1980s the hosting of major sport events such as the Olympic Games was viewed as both a financial and administrative burden on the organizing city or country in question. This view can be illustrated with evidence emerging from the 1976 Summer Olympic Games staged in Montreal, where it was confirmed that the event made a loss of £692 million, and the Summer Olympics held in Munich (1972), which recorded a loss of £178 million (Gratton et al., 2000). Following such confirmed and escalating losses, it seemed that any city wishing to host a major sport event would have to shoulder the financial burdens associated with it.

However, the 1984 Summer Olympics in Los Angeles changed the economic climate in relation to major sport events, when the Games made a surplus of £215 million through various avenues of visitor expenditure, including accommodation, food and drink, travel and shopping. This resulted in a change of opinion for those bidding to stage such events, when it was found that broader economic benefits to a city or country could result from the staging of a major sport event. The net effect of this was that the competition to stage major sport events began to intensify (Gratton et al., 2000).

Subsequently, the study of major sport events became an important focus of research in the area of leisure, sport and tourism throughout the 1990s and the economic benefits of such events have been specified in much of the literature (see Crompton, 1995; Mules and Faulkner, 1996; and Gratton et al., 2000). However, it is necessary to point out where and how this literature began and, perhaps more importantly, why it is still significant.

One of the first major publications was a study of the impact of the 1985 Adelaide Grand Prix (Burns et al., 1986). This was followed by a detailed review of the Calgary Winter Olympics (see Ritchie, 1984; Ritchie and Aitken, 1985; Ritchie and Lyons, 1987, 1990; and Ritchie and Smith, 1991), which suggested that the economic impacts of major events could be significant and far-reaching. These studies backed up the findings from the 1984 Los Angeles Olympics and supported the idea that the staging of major sport events could generate a significant amount of economic activity.

As Mules and Faulkner (1996) point out, however, sport events can still result in substantial losses, even when the cities themselves ostensibly benefit from significant additional expenditure. This view is supported with information gathered at the 1994 Brisbane World Masters Games, where the local authority invested A$2.8 million to stage the event and the region benefited from an additional expenditure of A$50.6 million, but the initial investment was never repaid.

Rob Wilson

Associated Concepts Deadweight Expenditure; Economic Impact of Hosting Major

Sport Events; Event Management; Multiplier Analysis.

ECONOMIC IMPACT OF HOSTING
MAJOR SPORT EVENTS

According to Crompton (2001), sport events can be seen as investments for both the organizations that sponsor them and for the communities that subsidize them. The potential economic benefits of such investments can be far-reaching since organizations invest in sport events in the belief that visitors will be attracted to a locality, bringing with them additional expenditure which will inject new wealth into the local economy.

In this sense, the term economic impact could simply be defined as 'the net change in the local economy resulting from spending attributed to a sport event or facility' (Turco and Kelsey, 1992: 9). UK Sport (2000: 12) argue that this so-called 'net economic change' can be expressed as 'the total amount of additional expenditure in the local economy generated by visitors to the event from outside the local economy', with change here being the outcome of an activity involving the acquisition, operation, development and use of sport facilities and services. Consequently the event will generate visitor spending, public spending, employment opportunity and tax revenue. As Crompton points out, this process illustrates the conceptual thinking that underlines the rationale behind economic impact.

This model is now widely used when commissioning economic impact studies as it has the ability to demonstrate the economic returns that a locality can potentially obtain. Specifically the total economic impact is made up of three components: direct, indirect and induced impacts (Howard and Crompton, 1995; UK Sport, 2000). The direct impact incorporates the initial visitor spending within the local economy on locally produced goods and services, including expenditure on accommodation, food, drink, entertainment, travel, and so on; the indirect impact represents the recirculation of initial visitor expenditure to other businesses and industries within the local economy; and induced impact refers to the increases in employment and household income that result from the economic activity fuelled by the direct and indirect impacts.

Rob Wilson

Associated Concepts Deadweight Expenditure; Economic Benefit of Hosting Major Sport Events; Event Management; Multiplier Analysis.

EDGEWORK

This term, as an expression of the ways in which people use leisure activities to deal with the 'edge' (the boundaries between order and disorder, life and death, consciousness and unconsciousness, subject and object) in the pursuit of voluntary risk taking and adventure, owes a great deal to Victor Turner's work on liminality. As expounded by Stephen Lyng (1990, 2005), the general principle of edgework signals the idea of getting as near as possible to the 'edge' without going over it. A good example of this is 'eyeballing', a term used by skydivers to determine the point when their parachute should be opened before 'ground rush' begins.

Written as a response to the limitations of psychologically reductionist accounts of risk-taking behaviour which operate with the tacit assumption that feeling alive is only possible in the presence of death, Lyng offers a sociological understanding of edgework that takes into account the ways in which individuals engage in extreme sports but also 'deviant' leisure activities, such as gambling and risky sex, which typically involve observable threats to their physical or mental well-being or 'sense of ordered existence'.

Lyng (2005) argues that the paradox of edgework is that, for some individuals, it signals a way of freeing themselves from the social conditions that can stifle the human spirit through social regulation and control, while for others it valorizes the risk-taking skills and activities which are demanded by the institutional structures of the risk society – the paradox being that some people seem to be pushed towards edgework practices while others are pulled. Lyng argues that we should not see these two ways of thinking in this 'edge-work paradox' as mutually exclusive or incongruous, but as a theoretical amalgam which helps us to better understand the ways in which individuals deal with the ambivalent relationship between freedom and security in the pursuit of play, 'particularly those forms of play that involve both risk and skill', in the contemporary world.

To this extent Lyng argues that edge-work not only emphasizes an element of personal control in the pursuit of action, it is also a rational and restorative practice which if it enables individuals to respond to the sense of helplessness they face in the light of the risk society appears to them as an 'innate response arising from sources deep within the individual, untouched by socializing influences. Thus edgeworkers experience this action as belonging to a residual, spontaneous self – the "true self" as it were' (1990: 879). What this suggests is that edgeworking in leisure is wrapped up with the modern search for authenticity in a world that is for many people experienced as inauthentic.

The idea that edgework has the potential to lead individuals to encounter some sort of transcendence, wherein they penetrate the very meaning of life itself to experience an unfettered or authentic sense of self, is challenged by postmodernism, which suggests that not only are limit experiences transient and lacking depth – people think they are living on the edge, but in reality they are firmly middle of the road – but also any idea that the self can have a 'solid' ontological status is itself illusory. A more serious criticism (and one which avoids the pitfalls of postmodernism), however, is that Lyng's thesis, in reserving faith for the 'edge' or borders of everyday existence, simply fails to address what it is that is at life's centre.

Tony Blackshaw

Associated Concepts Abnormal Leisure; Authenticity; Extreme Sport; Flow; 'Into', the; Liminality; Mimesis; Risk Management; Risk Society.

ELASTICITY

Common sense tells us that if the quantity of a product demand is high and its supply is low then prices are likely to be high. We only need to look at the example of the price of an England Rugby International match ticket to see this (i.e., demand is always much higher than the 80,000 tickets available, therefore the price of a ticket is going to be high). In light of this observation economists have developed a methodology to measure the responsiveness of quantity demanded and quantity supplied to a change in any independent variable, such as the price, the consumer's income and the price of substitutes. The general term used when referring to this measure is elasticity. The most common function of the calculation is to measure price elasticity of demand and price elasticity of supply. A simple formula can be used to apply the methodology:

$$\frac{\text{Percentage change in quantity demanded (or supplied)}}{\text{Percentage change in variable (price)}}$$

Such calculations can be particularly useful to leisure organizations as they give important insights into the most appropriate way of pricing products and services. Other measures of elasticity include: income elasticity of demand/supply and the price of other goods (cross price elasticity of demand).

Rob Wilson

Associated Concepts Demand; Supply.

ELIAS, NOBERT (1897–1990)

Norbert Elias was born in Breslau (which was then part of the Germany Empire, but is now known as Wroclaw and to be found in modern Poland) into a middle-class Jewish family in 1897. He served in the German army during the First World War, but after being discharged went on to study at the University of Wroclaw. By 1930 Elias was working with Karl Mannheim at the University of Frankfurt, but, as was the case for other 'Frankfurt School' (and Jewish) scholars, he was forced to flee from Germany with the rise of the Nazi party, going first to Paris and then later Britain. After the war he had several teaching posts, finally obtaining a full-time position at the University of Leicester in 1954 where he worked until his retirement in 1962.

In *The Court Society* (published in English in 1983, but based upon work he formulated in the 1930s) Elias considered aristocratic society in France in the century and a half before the Revolution, and argued that an extremely complex system of etiquette built up around court life during the reign of Louis XIV. To explain how this system had developed, Elias argued that a more comprehensive understanding of societal and social development was needed than presently existed, and set out to provide this in *The Civilizing Process* (1939), which was to form the basis of his subsequent writings.

Elias argued that the 'civilization process' was a result of structural changes within societies; as societies and the state became more complex, patterns of acceptable and civilized behaviour also changed in a particular and discernible direction. Elias suggested that since the Middle Ages we have seen greater control of people's social conduct and etiquette surrounding their bodily functions, eating and sexual habits, and violence. Our experiences and performances of these have become more 'civilized', and this is mediated through our 'habitus', which Elias viewed as a 'second nature' that we share with those who form our social group. However, the civilization process is not uni-directional and from time to time there can occur 'decivilizing spurts' where individuals will demonstrate less civilized beliefs or actions.

In understanding the nature of society, Elias drew on the idea of social (con)figurations – a term he first used in the original German edition of *The Civilizing Process* (1939), but did not set out explicitly until the publication of *What is Sociology?* (1978a). This suggested that society consists of interdependent individuals whose lives evolve into figurations which are in constant flux. Figurations also extend over time, therefore the social needs to be understood in terms of 'process' – but also as a long-term, unplanned and unpredictable process, where yesterday's unintended actions become the basis of today's society. Elias argued that one of the major shortcomings of conventional sociology had been that it made artificial distinctions between the individual and society. He suggested that one needed to understand the countless figurations that existed, interlinking individuals' lives, and the fluctuating balances of power moving through these.

Elias' theorizations have found particular applicability in the work of many contemporary sport sociologists, most notably the 'Leicester School' and specifically Eric Dunning. It is evident that from as early as 1939 Elias himself began using sport as a metaphor and site to apply his consideration of group dynamics and figurations. Though it was not until 1970 in 'Dynamics of Sport Groups with Special Reference to Football' that Elias (along with Eric Dunning) explicitly tackled the issue of the study of sport. Here, Elias and Dunning were able to use the metaphor of a football match as a site of reference to illustrate figurations, by showing how an individual's actions are both fluid and variable but also work within certain restraints applied by the laws and interactions of the social system.

Football also proved an important metaphor for understanding the civilizing process. Elias believed that the transformation of football from a pre-modern, violent, mass-participation free-for-all, to a more regulated and relatively non-violent sport, reflected the concurrent civilization and development of European societies.

Elias' consideration of the development of sport to a less violent form, through a process of civilization, saw its application from the early 1970s onwards to the growing debate concerning football hooliganism. Elias and Dunning argued that sport and leisure in modern society provided an opportunity not only for relaxation but also met certain 'socially conditioned psychological needs' (1986: 142) – being one of the few places in a civilized society where individuals were able to let their emotions run (relatively) free.

Mennell (1989) identified several (and defends Elias against) key areas of critique of Elias' work. In particular, Elias' theory of the civilizing process has been accused of being both ethnocentric and racist, seeing all that is Western as 'civilized' and for the 'good'. Authors have also argued that high levels of civilization could be seen in many small-scale, isolated, non-European societies, and therefore the arguments that link civilization invariably to the development of the (Western) state are fundamentally flawed. Others have also argued that rather than becoming more civilized Western societies are actually becoming more permissive, less moral and even barbaric. Examples cited include the breaking down of sexual boundaries, the decline of marriage, increasing protest and rebellion, ever-rising crime rates, as well as the harrowing scale of contemporary genocide witnessed in Nazi Germany, Stalinist Russia, Yugoslavia, Uganda and Cambodia, to name but a few.

Garry Crawford

Associated Concepts Critical Theory; Deviance; Football Hooliganism; Habitus, Field and Capital; Mimesis; Sport; Sportization; Structure and Agency; Violence.

ENJOYMENT AND FUN

(dionysian leisure; fantasy leisure; hedonism; pleasure)

ENTHUSIASMS

(community leisure; crafts and craftsmanship; hobbies)

ENVIRONMENT

(leisure and the environment)

ETHICS

In general terms, ethics is concerned with how we ought to act in order to be moral; and to this extent it refers to the moral code of an individual, a cultural group or a society. The term is also used to refer to the agreed set of ethical standards by which a particular research community decides to regulate its activities (e.g., the British Sociological Association has its own code of ethics).

Conventional wisdom suggests that it is only by belonging to a research community in which ethics are standard that leisure studies can progress as a discipline at all. Notwithstanding the official standing of any professional code of ethics, there are some ongoing ethical questions in leisure studies about what and how researchers study. Indeed, signing researchers up to a code of practice does not guarantee that they are going to be ethical. Codes of ethics made for 'good' research practice may appear to succeed and endure, but as is the case for many other sets of rules and regulations signed up to in the contemporary world, 'the durability of the goods', as Bauman might say, 'is often less than fully guaranteed and respondents' rights are often less than fully honoured'.

This raises several questions. To what extent do ethical codes of practice rob the researchers of their rights and obligations to act in responsible ways in the field? Does being ethical in the field merely imply being obedient and rule-abiding? To what extent do formal codes of ethics hold researchers beyond the reach of the intimate moral impulse? To what extent do formal codes of ethics lead to a process of dehumanization in the research process? To what extent does adhering to a code of ethics render the moral self 'dissembled into traits' (Bauman, 1993) to which we cannot ascribe any moral quality?

For Bauman, postmodern ethics is about trying to marry 'my' consciousness with what I find around me. Consequently, he is sceptical of organizations that 'contract out' ethical decision making to would-be experts, because not only does it invite researchers to mere proceduralism but it can also lead to the soporification of the moral impulse which is at the heart of morality. Following Bauman, we must continue to ask: to what extent does proceduralism incapacitate the moral impulse to act in a responsible way in the research process? Should individual researchers who follow their own moral impulse be prepared to back out of the disciplinary obligations imposed on them by the research community if this means that they can act responsibly towards the other in the field? What this tells us is that being ethical in research is no easy task.

Tony Blackshaw

Associated Concepts Bauman; Deviance; Methodology; Postmodernism; Postmodernity.

ETHNOGRAPHY

Ethnography is an empirical and theoretical research approach which has its antecedents in anthropology. At its most basic level it can be understood as one culture studying another culture. It is that methodological approach through which the researcher participates in the everyday lives of people over some length of time, either openly as a professional researcher or covertly in some masquerading role, watching things that happen, listening to what is said, smelling, touching and tasting, taking note of things that are tacit, and in the light of these observations asking pertinent questions, while linking all of this with what he or she knows already and has imagined as a consequence.

This definition can be summarized to suggest that ethnographic research typically involves the researcher participating in people's lives to learn the meanings and knowledge of their culture in order to produce what Clifford Geertz (1973) famously called 'thick descriptions' of the diversity and complexity of cultural life. To this extent, ethnography involves a process of penetration which is simultaneously that of translation, because in the person of the researcher it brings together two cultural traditions in a communicative contact – and thus opens to each other their respective contents which otherwise would have remained opaque.

The critique of ethnography as 'realism' or as a kind of *correspondence theory of truth* has been overwhelming in recent years and few if any ethnographers today believe that what they practise in their work is an approach to qualitative research which has as its central aim the 'discovery' of an accurate representation of some objective reality, in order to produce a 'true' picture of the cultural world under question. Indeed, one of the major problems with ethnography as 'realism' was that it assumed it could simply *translate* 'foreigners'' alternative cognitive frames into its own language rather than trying to imagine what those cognitive frames might mean if they remained *untranslatable*.

In light of this critique ethnographers have become less ambitious in their endeavours and ethnography today stands for the belief that the already existing reality exists, and that it does so in the knowledge that our ability to know that reality is fated to remain incomplete, because every ethnography, no matter how assiduously researched, is bound to be irredeemably ignorant of some matters. Correspondingly, ethnographers today have replaced the quest for epistemological and ontological certainty and methodological rigour with culturally grounded conceptualizations of truth that prove themselves to be, as Rorty (1991) would say, 'good in the way of belief, *and good, too, for definite, assignable reasons'*, and which ultimately help us to see that everyday cultural life is much more complex than we once imagined. Not only that, as Barker (2004) has suggested ethnography today tends to have personal, poetical and political rather than metaphysical justifications, and as a result ethnographers have focused their attention more closely on developing innovative political ways of writing about culture in all its diversity.

Indeed, while most enlightened ethnographers have come to recognize that their research findings will always remain partial, they have also become more aware of the limitations of traditional ethnographic forms of writing, which suggest that the meticulous and gradual observation of social phenomena provides a grounding for theory *vis-à-vis* Glaser and Strauss (1968) – an approach which assumes that theory emerges from research 'data', which is typically illustrated with characteristic examples of 'data' from field notes, such as interview quotations. Instead they have increasingly looked to develop ethnographic writing techniques which attempt to replicate the world under scrutiny as accurately as possible. The best ethnography works its magic through the ability of its author(s) to convince us about the reality under scrutiny, rather than through any correspondence with that reality. Like all good novels, ethnography must be well written, but its real strength and power lie in a researcher's ethnographic imagination.

This suggests a shift in ethnographic writing which means that if ethnography is as compelled as it ever was in its ambition to capture everyday life it also now has an ambition to

create atmosphere, whether it is a single consciousness or the atmosphere of a shared consciousness – even consciousnesses which are contingent, shape-shifting rather than enduring. Blackshaw (2003) argues that it is only by such staging ethnographers can reach a more profound level of truth that cannot otherwise be found. What some commentators now call ethnographic fiction relishes the task of transporting its readers by telling them how people who share a particular fate think, speculate, desire, understand and live their lives, but in a way which makes every gesture, every attitude, every word spoken by its respondents, part of its imaginative and deliberate study. Blackshaw's *Leisure Life* (2003), which is a study of working-class men's leisure, is a good example of this kind of ethnography. By alternating perspectives, seeing events unfold through 'the lads'' eyes and then from the view of the sociologist, Blackshaw manages to do more than simply analyse this leisure lifeworld. He enables the reader to walk in the shoes of 'the lads' and 'lad-like' to experience their worldview. This is nothing less than reinventing the ethnographer's writing craft by making fact read like fiction, using charged and poetic language which takes its readers on a cultural ride in order to find truth – physically transporting them. In this way this alterative way of writing ethnography permits and requires greater descriptive detail than was previously the case.

However, Blackshaw and Crabbe (2004) stress that this approach should not be understood as in any way deceitful on the part of ethnographers, but more precisely as ethnography looking at itself in the mirror and recognizing that it can still do everything it used to be able to do *and* much more. The trick of ethnographic fiction is that it is able to tell the 'truth' about the social world while not being exactly deceitful but by embellishing that 'truth'. In this sense, rather than trying to make the reader believe in the 'facts' of the reality it deals with in its pages, ethnographic fiction simply conjures the 'real' instead. As Blackshaw and Crabbe demonstrate through their own work, this changed economy of narration typically leads ethnographers to write in self-consciously cinematic ways, which will tend to draw on rhetorical devices, such as metaphor, metonymy and synecdoche, which they use *not* to replace the real, but to clarify, reinforce and enhance it.

Tony Blackshaw

Associated Concepts Action Research; Everyday Life; Flâneurs, Flâneurie and Psychogeography; Leisure Life-World; Qualitative Research.

ETHNOMETHODOLOGY

Ethnomethodology is the term coined by Harold Garfinkel, which literally means 'people's methods', and it refers to the study of the tacit practices by which people construct their everyday lives, make sense of what others do and, in particular, what they say. Ethnomethodology suggests that there is no 'natural' order to the social world, but rather a taken-for-granted 'sense' of order arises from people actively making sense of social life. Social order is understood as an elaborate fiction created by people to help them understand the nature of their social world. To this extent ethnomethodology is concerned with the analysis of how members of society make sense of, and understand, the world in which they live. This suggests that mainstream sociology has often overlooked the competencies and activity of individuals in creating their social world, often seeing them as merely passive products of society or 'cultural dopes' (Garfinkel, 1967).

A key difference from symbolic interactionism is that, where symbolic interactionism sees actors as drawing on existing resources in structuring their interactions, ethnomethodology emphasizes the active role of the individual in creating these. A good example is Garfinkel's famous study of a male-to-female transsexual ('Agnes'). He suggests that for Agnes to 'pass' as a woman there is only limited scope for planning

strategies, as 'she' can never know in advance exactly what will be required for her to pass. Hence, Agnes' status as a 'woman' is something that she has to continuously work at to create and maintain. What this suggests is that at the heart of ethnomethodology is the study of written and spoken communication, and a key method employed by many ethnomethodologists is that of conversational analysis, a method devised largely by Garfinkel's colleague Harvey Sacks (1935–1975).

Garry Crawford

Associated Concepts Conversational Analysis; Everyday Life; Symbolic Interactionism; Postmodernism; Qualitative Research.

EVENT MANAGEMENT

Among the key areas of leisure management at the beginning of the twenty-first century, events stand out as one of the most important, perhaps the most important. An event, according to Getz (1997), is temporary, can be planned or not, has a fixed length and, most importantly, is unique, a one-off, a spectacle, a showcase. It goes without saying that events have the potential to play a crucial role in any comprehensive leisure programme, not least because of their compelling ability to capture the public imagination in showcasing leisure. Commonly, events are categorized in three ways: hallmark/mega events (e.g., Olympic Games); major events (e.g., FA Cup finals); and minor events (e.g., national swimming championships).

As well as having the ability to bring added glamour to any managed leisure programme, at the same time as generating an enormous amount of income, entertainment, novelty, adventure and fun, events have the capacity to bring communities together and most importantly for investors to put places and people on the global stage. What this suggests is that events of any magnitude will need some sort of management process.

Essentially event management is the design and management of the event. It requires close attention to detail, working to tight deadlines and very often fast decision making, as well as the ability to respond to a full range of stakeholders, from local authorities, governing bodies and large companies who invest heavily, to the diverse needs of a user public who have become much more sophisticated and demanding in their consumption of leisure spectacles. It is in these crucial ways that there is a specialized demand for leisure event managers who are capable of generating opportunities for, and leading, controlling, planning and executing, successful projects, the core principles of which can be applied to the successful management of local and international events, both large and small. It should also be noted that due to their unique nature all events will be different both in terms of their size and objectives and that the job description for an event manager will differ from event to event. However, all events have to be promoted and held in a professional environment, meeting the needs of a range of different stakeholders.

Tony Blackshaw and Rob Wilson

Associated Concepts Carnival; Economic Benefit of Hosting Major Sport Events; Economic Impact of Hosting Major Sport Events; Management Styles; Risk Management; Spectacle.

EVERYDAY LIFE

Everyday life is the largely taken-for-granted world that often remains overlooked and hidden, what Lefebvre (1991) calls the 'common ground' or 'connective tissues of all conceivable human thoughts and activities' (cited in Gardiner, 2000: 2). The study of the everyday inhabits a remarkable territory in sociology

and leisure studies which has not been mined in any extensive way. Its spirit is what Hegel called the 'prose of the world', implying that there is something about the world that is ordinary rather than supernatural, mysterious or profound. It is the mundane recurring themes of everyday life that everyday life theorists are concerned with, capturing the humdrum fragments of life which encapsulate the human condition. They recognize that life can be exciting and spectacular, but that it is mostly mundane, unexciting and often disappointing. Accordingly everyday life theorists have an eye for the small moments of humanity that defy orchestration, ideology and indoctrination.

You might say that everyday life studies are in a sense an inversion of orthodox sociology. Its adherents have a desire to understand the quotidian of the ordinary world simply 'as it is' and to describe it through the use of ordinary commonplace language, to endow that reality with the immense significance of its insignificance. The origins of sociology lie in a consideration of 'systems' and macro-processes, such as is found in the work of Auguste Comte, Emile Durkheim and Karl Marx. By the late nineteenth century a more micro-sociological approach was developed through the work of social thinkers such as Max Weber and George Herbert Mead, and from this, the interpretive turn of the post-war era saw the birth of a number of approaches including ethnomethodology, phenomenology and symbolic interactionism. Though these microsociologies provided an important foundation for the study of the everyday, these continue to adhere to 'the pretence of objectivity' and 'scholarly detachment' (Gardiner, 2000: 5) – viewing everyday life as relatively homogeneous and attempting to impose order and structures on often highly complex social patterns.

However, in the past couple of decades there has been an increased interest in and awareness of the everyday and patterns of mundane consumption (such as eating). In particular, Lefebvre was one of the first writers to argue that the everyday was important and should not be taken for granted. However, when published (in French) in the 1940s his work was largely ignored in English-speaking academia until quite recently. Lefebvre, applying a neo-Marxist ideology in *Critique of Everyday Life* (1991 [1947]), highlights everyday life as a site of repression and social control, recognizing that dominant power relations operate not just in formal social institutions such as in the workplace or educational system. Other authors have also highlighted the everyday as a site of social resistance. In particular, Mikhail Bakhtin (1984a [1968]) and Michel de Certeau (1984) have suggested that everyday practices are not fully engulfed by 'false consciousness', and nor can the panoptic gaze peer into every aspect of our lives, but rather that everyday life can provide the opportunity for liberation and resistance.

While de Certeau recognized social life as constraining and oppressive, where individuals are largely 'marginalized' and have little say or control over factors such as market forces, he also suggested that everyday life was extremely complex and multifaceted, allowing room for manoeuvre and individuality. Where grand narratives tend to strip away the mundane, seeking some hidden and deeper truth or meaning, for de Certeau this hides what is truly important – as it is only at the level of the everyday that we can understand how social relations are experienced and lived out.

In theorizing everyday practices, de Certeau employs the concepts of 'strategies' and 'tactics'. Strategies for de Certeau are similar to Pierre Bourdieu's understanding and consideration of practices and social patterns (or habitus) within sociocultural fields. Hence strategies are linked to places, and the appropriate manners and actions specific to that particular place. However, in contrast to Bourdieu, de Certeau sees no 'single logic' to the social practices within these places, as there will always be room for multiple actions and practices, even if these are often 'unsigned, unreadable and unsymbolized' (Gardiner, 2000: 170). These multiple actions de Certeau refers to as 'tactics', which involve the disguises, deceptions, bluffs,

stubbornness and personalization of experiences that take place within sociocultural fields. De Certeau is not suggesting that tactics exist in opposition to or outside of strategies, but rather are a constituent part of these. Examples of the application of de Certeau to the study of leisure and popular culture include the work of John Fiske (1989) and Henry Jenkins (1992). For Fiske popular culture offers individuals fertile ground for resistance and rebellion, such as youths hanging round and being disruptive in shopping malls, while Jenkins (1992) highlights how fans of cult television shows will 'poach' storylines and characters from these texts and use them to create their own (often subversive, like pornographic 'slash fiction') material, such as new stories, poetry or art.

However, while theorists of the everyday do not look for the extraordinary in the ordinariness of everyday life, it is perhaps inevitable that by making the ordinary their topic of interest it becomes extraordinary. This can lead to a tendency to over-romanticize ordinary lives, and this is a particularly relevant critique of those who have applied the work of de Certeau, such as Fiske and Jenkins. In particular, authors such as de Certeau, and those who have drawn on his work, have been accused of being celebratory of popular culture and small acts of resistance, often overlooking the oppression, control and violence that exist within the everyday. Also, by identifying patterns in the everyday (such as de Certeau does with his discussion of strategies and tactics) it is difficult to see how these theorists significantly differ from other already well-developed interpretivist perspectives, such as symbolic interactionism and ethnomethodology.

Garry Crawford and Tony Blackshaw

Associated Concepts Bourdieu; Carnivalesque; Culture; Consumption; Ethnography; Ethnomethodology; False Consciousness; Habitus, Field and Capital; Flâneurs, Flâneurie and Psychogeography;

Ideology; Marxism; Power; Symbolic Interactionism.

EXTREME LEISURE

The centrality and utter banality of this term in popular discourse generally apply to its scholarly usage. From the Latin extrēmus, the word extreme signifies something at its outermost limits. When used in conjunction with leisure it appears to have one of two meanings. The first is the idea that individuals experience certain leisure situations differently because these bring them to the limit of their resources as human beings. Examples of this kind of extreme leisure include: abnormal leisure (Rojek, 2000); barebacking or unprotected anal intercourse in episodic sexual encounters among same sex-attracted men (Ridge, 2004); dangerous leisure (Olivier, 2006); edgework (Lyng, 1990, 2005); extreme sport (Le Breton, 2000); life-style sport (Wheaton, 2004); risk recreation (Robinson, 1992); and risk sport (Breivik, 1999). What all of these examples share in common is the idea that extreme leisure may lead to an encounter with some kind of transcendence beyond the limit of ordinary life situations, suggesting that there is something about leisure in its extreme forms that is profoundly revelatory of the human condition. The second meaning emerges from Baudrillard's work on hyperreality, which links extreme leisure with the idea of the postmodern obsession with the 'more real than real', in other words, not the beckoning hand of some alternative reality, but merely the allure of the spectacle of the consumer society performing itself through anything from extreme sport to extreme cuisine to extreme pornography.

What is most often overlooked in discussions is the politics of extreme leisure. As Laviolette (2006) argues, extreme leisure presents an ideal means for developing creative forms of radical political subversion. Through his ethnographic research into 'surfing against sewage', Laviolette explores how a surf culture in Cornwall in the UK uses extreme subversion as part of its environmental campaigns to protect the ecological sustainability of coastal leisure pursuits. Other research shows that developments in extreme leisure are just as radical but far less benign. As Franck Michel (2006) demonstrates, for example, sex tourism is a form of extreme leisure whose body trade is rooted in prostitution, and not only that, it is also an extension of the service aspect of mass tourism that is in itself a modern version of colonial exploitation.

Like edgework, the idea of extreme leisure is open to two other major criticisms. First, innumerable numbers of people have engaged in extreme leisure activities without ever encountering an authentic self or changing their understanding of themselves in some way. Baudrillard (2001) goes so far as to suggest that all extreme forms of leisure are merely nostalgic artificial re-creations of the life and death situations which were once the human fate but have since been ameliorated with the modern civilizing process. Second, in reserving their interest for the 'limit', the 'edge' or the borders of everyday existence, analysts of extreme leisure simply fail to consider what it is that is at life's centre.

Tony Blackshaw

Associated Concepts Abnormal Leisure; Acculturation; Authenticity; Consumer Society; Consumption; Edgework; Elias; Leisure and the Environment; Leisure as a Value-Sphere; Flow; Liminality; 'Into', the; Mimesis; Nostalgia; Pornography; Postmodernism; Risk Society; Spectacle; Tourism.

F

FALSE CONSCIOUSNESS

Although 'false consciousness' is a Marxist term, it is not one that was ever used by Karl Marx (at least not in his published work), but is rather a term coined by his friend and collaborator Friedrich Engels. For Engels false consciousness describes a consciousness or understanding that workers have, which is contrary to their 'real' interests. False consciousness is therefore in direct opposition to 'class consciousness', which for workers is an awareness of their collective exploitation and struggle.

For Marxists false consciousness is not a natural occurrence, nor is it the creation of the workers themselves, but instead is something imposed upon them by a 'dominant ideology'. That is to say, the attitudes and values (ideology) of the ruling (dominant) classes and their justification for their elevated social position are imposed upon the working classes. For instance, Marxists would argue that the idea we live in a 'meritocracy', where people succeed or fail on the basis of their individual abilities and efforts, is a dominant ideological attitude promoted in capitalist societies, and falsely believed by many. These are values which can be seen in numerous leisure pursuits, and in particular sport, which promotes the (misconception) that all are equal on the sports field, and also promotes capitalist values, such as competition, obeying rules and a 'winner takes all' attitude (see, for instance, Gruneau, 1983 and Hargreaves, 1995).

The idea of false consciousness is taken up and developed further by several neo-Marxist writers, including most notably Antonio Gramsci. In particular, he suggested that false consciousness could be overcome by re-educating the workers with a competing ideology (namely Marxism), which would open their eyes to their exploitation and shared class interests. As this last example suggests, though the term is primarily used by Marxists to refer to class-based relations, others have drawn on it to refer to other forms of ideological control, such as the feminist writer Efrat Tseëlon (1995), who employs the term to describe women's love of fashion and clothing, which operates as a means of subjugation and social control.

Garry Crawford

Associated Concepts Class; Consumption; Critical Theory; Feminism; Fashion; Hegemony; Ideology; Marxism; Power; Social Control.

FANS

What is a 'fan'? Hills (2002: ix) writes that 'everyone knows what a "fan" is, of course'. A fan is generally viewed as an 'obsessed' individual – someone who has an intense interest in a certain team, celebrity, show, band or similar.

The term fan is also one that is most frequently associated only with forms of popular culture. To be a fan most commonly signifies an interest in popular music, sport, television, films or similar. However, beyond simplistic dictionary definitions (such as that found in the *OED*), defining what is meant by the term 'fan' in a way that can be operationalized and sets a subject area for study can prove problematic. As Hills (2002: xi) suggests 'fandom is not simply a "thing" that can be picked over analytically'; being a fan is not just a label or category, it is also tied into individual and group identities and social performances, which are rarely set or coherent. Hence, numerous authors have avoided providing a clear definition of what or who constitutes a fan. However, one way in which fans are often defined is in terms of their relationship to 'consumers' and 'audiences'.

There has been a tendency in much of the literature on fans to identify these individuals and groups as distinct and different from wider audiences and consumers. This is particularly notable in the work of both Fiske (1989) and Jenkins (1992) who, though both drawing on the work of de Certeau (1984) who makes no such distinctions, have suggested that fans are different from 'ordinary' audiences or consumers in that fans 'actively' engage with the texts they consume. A similar attitude is evident in many studies of sport fan culture, and in particular in considerations of football (soccer) fans in the UK. Numerous authors such as Rogan Taylor (1992), Ian Taylor (1995), King (1998) and Giulianotti (2002) have drawn clear distinctions around dichotomies or typologies between what they define as 'traditional' fans (often white, male and working class) and 'new' (middle-class, often 'family'-based) consumers.

However, both Williams (2000) and Crawford (2004) suggest that these categories are often based upon subjective and romanticized ideas of 'authenticity', which see the celebration of one form of fan culture and the rejection of all that is seen as 'new' or 'consumerist'. As Grossberg writes (1992: 52): 'While we may all agree that there is a difference between the fan and the consumer, we are unlikely to understand the difference if we simply celebrate the former category and dismiss the latter one'.

Sandvoss (2003) suggests that what identifies (though crucially does not separate out) a fan from other readers of a text is their regularity of reading. Though numerous others use particular activities (such as those who attend live sport events as opposed to (so-called) passive 'armchair' supporters) or knowledge as the mark of distinction between fans and non-fans, Sandvoss argues that even the most active of fans will spend a great deal of time not actively engaging with the object of their fan interest. Ultimately, what defines a fan, for Sandvoss, is their *regular* engagement; such as regularly attending sports games or regularly watching these on television. He also provides us with what numerous other authors have avoided – a definition of what he sees as 'fandom': 'the regular, emotionally involved consumption of a given popular narrative or text' (Sandvoss, 2005: 8).

Garry Crawford

Associated Concepts Audiences; Consumption; Fanzines; Identity; Mass Media; Performativity; Power; Subcultures.

FANTASY LEISURE

We all know what fantasy leisure is. It involves the pleasure and enjoyment we get from identifying with great sportsmen and women, swashbuckling characters from the silver screen, the fuck-you-cool of gangsta hip-hop culture, the romantic love affairs depicted in classic nineteenth-century novels and the like, and the ways in which the creativity of the human imagination allows us to attach our own subjective meanings to these imaginings in order to make our own lives extraordinary.

Freud assumed that we are ashamed of such fantasies and we have no idea that what we fantasize about may well be common practice among other people. He hypothesized about our sexual fantasies in particular, suggesting that these are evidence of our mental turmoil: it is only those of us who live unsatis-fying lives who need to fantasize. We are all familiar with the stories of loners travelling in foreign lands – who in their most extreme man-ifestations Rojek (1995) calls fantasy voyagers – who assume a pretend identity that is not their own. For the duration of a holiday they are ace pilots rather than aircraft cabin attendants, doc-tors rather than nurses, single rather than mar-ried, rich rather than poor.

As Harris (2005) points out, though, it isn't necessarily the case that such people have social or psychological problems. He argues that we can safely assume that fantasy and wish-fulfilment are directed and controlled by the same motives and interests that drive all other leisure activities – the pursuit of pleasure. Nevertheless this is a particular kind of pleasure which arises from treating the world out there as if it is at the same time separate and 'other', but also customary and clearly recognizable. Harris also suggests that it is through making this distinction we can make sure our fantasies combine the allure of the unexpected with just the right amount of challenge.

Tony Blackshaw

Associated Concepts Aesthetics; Celebrity; Desire; Fantasy Leisure; Flow; Freud; Hedonism; Liminality; Pleasure; Rojek, Chris.

FANZINES

Fanzines or 'zines are non-professionally pro-duced publications, most commonly focusing on one or more specific fan interest, such as popular music, science fiction, role-playing and/or sport.

The origins of the fanzine can probably be found in nineteenth-century publications fea-turing short stories and poetry and often pro-duced by students. However, the first fanzines, as we understand them today, appeared around the 1930s, with *The Comet* (often cited as the first ever science fiction fanzine) appearing in

May 1930 in the USA. However (particularly in the UK), it is in the 1970s with the rise of punk music, as well as the technological develop-ments which made printing cheaper, that there was a significant rise in the number of fanzines produced – with key fanzines includ-ing *Ripped & Torn* and *Sniffin' Glue*. As with punk music, fanzines offered an alternative to mainstream culture and publications, and were a significant part of this music scene for many of its fans and followers.

Soon after this fanzines begin to appear for particular sports and teams. In particular, the history and rise of football fanzines are consid-ered at length by Richard Haynes (1995) who echoes the ideas of Raymond Williams in seeing these as an 'emergent culture' which challenges mainstream press and journalism, in particular in the way that their low circulation numbers allowed them to maintain (sub)cultural cred-itability and capital. Steve Redhead (1997: 91) specifically suggests that by the late 1980s foot-ball fanzines had 'displaced purely popular music fanzines at the cutting edge of fandom'.

The rise of the internet, and along with it 'webzines' and blogs (web-logs), has seen a new forum for non-commercial fan-based publishing, but has not diminished the popu-larity of fanzines which continue to be an important part of many fan cultures.

Garry Crawford

Associated Concepts Audiences; Cultural Capital; Fans; Mass Media; Subcultures.

FASHION

This term has two primary (and associated) meanings. First, fashion can refer to things that are 'fashionable' or, in other words, current trends or things that are 'in vogue'. Second, the term can also be used to refer to the contemporary global industry of cre-ating and promoting beauty, clothing and accessories.

The history of clothing begins with prehistoric humans draping their bodies with animal fur, and anthropologists would suggest that even then these were worn for decoration as well as protection (Lehnert, 1999). Clothing has always been an important form of display and decoration, as well as a marker of social status; however, the specific meanings and importance of fashion have changed significantly over history. For example, in fifteenth-century Europe 'fashionable' clothing was only worn by members of the aristocracy in court society, with no one below this having any form of dress or clothing that could be described as 'fashion' (Kawamura, 2005). By the nineteenth century fashion was no longer the preserve of the very rich, but still primarily operated as an indicator of social status; however, by the twentieth century fashion had become more 'democratic' and a concern for most (if not all) members of contemporary Western cultures (Kawamura, 2005).

Today, fashion is a major global industry that it is impossible to avoid: as Lehnert (1999: 8) writes: 'we cannot separate fashion from our daily lives. Even people who think they refuse to obey fashion commit themselves to it through their refusal'. Until very recently the study of fashion as an important social component has been quite marginal, but this does not mean that it has not been of interest to writers for a very long time. The English writer Thomas Carlyle published *Sartor Resartus* (1831) on the philosophy of clothes. The French writer Honoré de Balzac (1799–1850) wrote on the importance and nuances of fashions, such as the ways a cravat could be worn and tied, while the French poet and critic Charles Baudelaire wrote on women's fashions and also the *flâneur* – a subject later taken up from Baudelaire by the cultural theorist Walter Benjamin (Kawamura, 2005). Fashion was also the subject of early sociological consideration. For instance, Herbert Spencer (1966 [1896]) was (from an academic perspective) interested in clothing and fashions, as were Georg Simmel (1997 [1904]) and Thorstein Veblen (1934 [1899]) who saw clothing as a mark of social status and distinction.

Indeed, Bourdieu's *oeuvre* is essentially a sociology of taste and by implication fashion.

He has also convincingly argued that consumption in 'late modern' societies is 'predisposed ... to fulfil a social function of legitimating social differences'. To this extent Bourdieu helped to better theorize the ways in which people exercise 'cultural competence' in consuming fashion and the ways in which structures of taste are used to maintain boundaries and reinforce the social 'distinctions'. Bourdieu also made the point that in the 'status-differentiated' and 'market-segmented' culture of the new work economy, tastes are reflected in individual life-styles as much as (or more than) gender or class. The key concepts here are of course Bourdieu's notions of habitus, capital (social, cultural and corporeal) and field.

In more contemporary times fashion has become the subject of significant academic and popular feminist critique. For instance, Naomi Wolf in *The Beauty Myth* (1991) suggested that the emphasis placed upon women looking beautiful acts as a form of social control and oppression. Similarly, Tseëlon (1995) argued that women's love of fashion operates as a form of false consciousness. However, other writers have highlighted the role fashion can play in constructing our identities and our sense of who we are, and Wilson (1994) has suggested that fashion can be playful and transgress gender boundaries.

Some, such as Barthes (1957), have suggested that clothing and the adornment of our bodies can be understood as a language which conveys certain messages. As McRobbie (1989: 6) writes: 'what we buy and consequently wear or display in some public fashion, in turn creates new images, new, sometimes unintended, constellations of meaning. In a sense we become media forms ourselves ... '. Like a language, clothing has a 'syntax', where certain items placed together will construct a meaning (Caletato, 2004). This can be clearly highlighted in Hebdige's (1979) use of the idea of bricolage, where a collection of seemingly incongruous items taken together will create a meaningful image – such as Mods' appropriation of smart suits, short hair, army surplus 'parka' jackets and Vespa and Lambretta scooters (Caletato, 2004). However, as Edwards (2000) highlights, the meaning and 'messages' conveyed by clothing and body adornment are often confusing and highly ambiguous, and it is important to recognize that the 'intended' meaning of items can frequently be 'misread'. For instance, Wills (2000: in the British football fanzine *When Saturday Comes*) suggests that though the wearing of designer 'leisure' wear by some football fans is meant to signify their status as 'lads' or 'casuals' it simply identifies them as a 'pretentious prat' (cited in Crawford, 2004: 124).

Garry Crawford

Associated Concepts Birmingham School; Bourdieu; Communication; Consumption; Distinction; False Consciousness; Feminism; Flâneur, Flâneuire and Psychogeography; Habitus, Field and Capital; Identity; Shopping; Subcultures; Veblen.

FEMINISM

Feminism is the social, academic and political assertion that women should be seen and treated as equal to men. As a political movement, feminism can be understood to have gone through several key periods or 'waves' of action. Significant starting points in 'first wave' feminism were the publication of Mary Wollstonecraft's *Vindication of the Rights of Women* in 1792 and the first Women's Rights Convention in New York in 1848. This wave is said to have continued until 1920 when women were awarded the right to vote in the USA. 'Second wave' feminism is represented by the period of activity during the 1960s, starting with US President J.F. Kennedy's Commission on the Status of Women and the publication of Betty Friedan's *The Feminine Mystique* in 1963. 'Third wave' feminism refers to the contemporary feminist ideas and actions by both men and women that seek the emancipation of and equal rights for women (Lengermann and Niebrugge, 2007).

In academic terms, feminist research has significantly contributed to what we know about women's history, their experiences, participation, representation, the body, and power structures. Feminist research has also produced specific questions about methodology, such as the significance of the researcher's gender and the validity of experience.

In theoretical terms, patriarchal power, dominance and control are often the starting points for explaining women's experiences. A literal definition of 'patriarchy' is the rule of a social unit (such as a family or tribe) by a man; however, since the early twentieth century, feminist writers have used the term to refer to a social system of masculine domination over women.

Liberal, Marxist, radical, psychoanalytic, socialist and postmodern feminist (to name but a few) approaches have attempted to explain, describe and pose explicit challenges to all women's oppression. This observation notwithstanding, many black feminists have argued that much of the literature on gender focuses on white women and that greater understanding of the intersection of race/ethnicity and gender is needed.

In particular, liberal feminists have argued that subordination is rooted in customary and legal constraints that reinforce gender and sex role socialization and stereotyping, which then block women's entrance and success in social domains, such as the (so-called) public worlds of sport and leisure. However, this approach has been criticized for ignoring the wider social, political and economic structures.

Marxist feminists relate gender inequalities to the capitalist economic system, which requires and benefits from women's unpaid domestic labour. Similarly, socialist feminists recognize two systems – capitalism and patriarchy – which combine to oppress women. However, both Marxist and socialist approaches can be criticized for their reliance on economic reductionism and, even when married with a concern with patriarchy, they often ignore the differences of experience relating to individual women's choices.

Radical feminists believe neither liberals nor Marxists go far enough, and therefore argue that the patriarchal system oppresses women and that it is not possible to reform such a system. Patriarchy is seen as a primary, fundamental, universal and trans-historical power system, implying that there are essential and unchanging differences between all women and all men across time and space. Accordingly it is these patriarchal structures and institutions which must be demolished. Female biology and sexuality are viewed as a key to liberation, as men have controlled women as childbearers and rearers. But if women have biological qualities that they control, then these qualities can be used to affirm, celebrate, transform and support women. However, radical feminists fail to consider factors other than gender, such as class, age, ethnicity and education, which can also influence women's life experiences.

Black feminists offer a tripartite agenda constructed around racism, sexism and imperialism to address the implicit ethnocentrism and racism of existing feminist approaches, which are often informed by white middle-class personal experience. However, this approach can result in an essentializing of the experience of black women which itself then reinforces racist notions of biological difference.

Though the above feminist perspectives are themselves not necessarily homogeneous, postmodernists regard one specific feminist standpoint as neither feasible nor desirable – not possible because experiences cut across class, racial and cultural lines, and not desirable because the search for one form of truth is both meaningless and arbitrary. To this extent postmodern feminists seek to avoid patriarchal dogma and will choose not to use fixed categories such as 'women' and instead will emphasize diversity and difference. However, there is some conflict between postmodern feminists and others given that the postmodernists are willing to see all versions of truth as equal.

It is primarily socialist and liberal feminist perspectives that have dominated the discussion of women's leisure, particularly in the 1970s and 1980s. Specifically, studies such as Dixey and Talbot's (1982) have focused upon how patriarchy limits women's leisure in certain locations and at certain times, while other studies such as that of Green et al. (1990) have looked at dual system oppression through both capitalism and patriarchy.

However, in recent years there has been a growing engagement by feminist writers on leisure with more poststructuralist debates, which recognize that power is not uni-directional and simply the possession of a few individuals or agencies, but rather that power is more complex and multifaceted, and that leisure can actually be seen both to limit and empower different women, in a variety of different ways, at different times, and in different settings.

However, all feminists seek to identify relationships of oppression and to find ways of knowing and living that will avoid the subordination of women. In terms of leisure research, all tend to agree on the inadequacy of simply looking at participation rates as an answer to gender inequality given the bureaucratic and hierarchical factors. As such it can be said that the following concerns are central to feminist research: the social, economic and political structures that exploit, devalue and oppress women; the strategies committed to changing the condition of women; the critical perspectives towards research and intellectual traditions and methods that have ignored or justified women's oppression; explaining women's involvement in, and alienation from, particular leisure contexts and practices; and highlighting the engendered nature of leisure organization and bureaucracy.

Garry Crawford

Associated Concepts Marxism; Power; Postmodernism; Postmodernity; Racism and Leisure; Structure and Agency; Women's Leisure.

FIGURATIONS/FIGURATIONALISM

(Elias, Norbert)

FINANCIAL AND MANAGEMENT
ACCOUNTING

Owen (1994) contends that in the modern business environment leisure managers have to contend with the reality (and ever-growing importance) of money transactions. This is due to the continual state of change in the leisure industries, such as technological transformations, the varying economic climate and increasing customer expectations, which makes it more important than ever to steer an organization successfully through such transitions. In other words, the modern graduate leisure manager needs a practical understanding of money and its effect on the leisure industry.

Quite often a student will come across the terms financial and management accounting and will question the double appendage. The fundamental difference is explained when you consider that accounting information can look both forwards (namely, to the future) and backwards (namely, to the past) and that there are people both inside and outside the business who will use such information. In a nutshell, financial accounting is concerned with the preparation of information for external use, and is mainly taken up with reporting on past events (e.g., the publication of voluntary organizations' financial statements). Management accounting, however, is concerned with providing information that is primarily focused on the needs of management and will therefore be additionally concerned with the future planning and control aspects of the business (e.g., establishing how much of the budget was spent on promotional material). It should be noted, however, that management accounting is not a statutory requirement but a business tool.

Rob Wilson

Associated Concepts Assets, Liabilities and Capital; Double-Entry Bookkeeping; Financial Statements.

FINANCIAL HEALTH AND RATIO ANALYSIS

Financial health is a generic term which is used to describe how well an organization is performing and 'where the organization is' or,

in other words, its position in relation to its business objectives. Consequently we can use it to determine the financial health of a leisure organization, be it a leisure centre, a voluntary organization or a community intervention project. Generally, the financial health of an organization can be established by using the income statement and balance sheet to examine its financial performance and financial position. The income statement can be used to work out how profitable an organization has been over a given accounting period, thereby highlighting its financial performance; the balance sheet summarizes what the business owns and owes. Together these indicate financial health.

This observation notwithstanding, there is also a need to be aware of the importance of cash. Cash is different from profit and a cash flow statement needs to be used in conjunction with the income statement and balance sheet to show further details about the organization and its performance.

While the balance sheet and income statement will outline the financial health of an organization, they will not highlight the areas of strong (or weak) performance effectively. In order to achieve a more detailed understanding of an organization's financial health, then, it is also pertinent to undertake ratio analysis based on that organization's financial statements. This provides more detailed information about the profitability, liquidity, growth, defensive position and return on the capital employed for an organization.

Ratios are a quick and relatively simple way of examining the financial health of an organization. A ratio will express the relationship of one figure that appears on a financial statement with another or with another of the organization's resources (e.g., the number of employees to sales). Once a ratio has been calculated it can then be compared with budgets, previous information, other businesses and industry benchmarks.

Rob Wilson

Associated Concepts Profitability, Liquidity, Growth and Breaking Even.

FINANCIAL STATEMENTS

Wilson and Joyce (2007) argue that the sport and leisure industry is no different from any other industry when it comes from adhering to the principles of finance and accounting. Organizations – ranging from huge multi-million pound operations such as Manchester United Football Club to small voluntary sports clubs – are required to produce financial statements at least once a year. The objective of such final accounts is to provide information to a range of users (and not just the owner or shareholders. The information contained in the accounts is concerned with the resources held by the business and how these are used. The accounts demonstrate three crucial things: the organization's position at the end of a financial period; an analysis of changes during that period; and a reference point for the future prospects of the business. This information is of great importance to anyone who has an interest in the business because it shows whether or not the organization is achieving its goals.

A set of financial statements is usually part of a wider set of documentation called an annual report. This report will include the financial statements, the directors' report, the auditors' report and other information published by an organization on an annual basis. However, it is often the case that financial statements will provide the most important information as they are the most complete set of accounts. This set will include the balance sheet (showing the organization's assets and liabilities), the income statement (the profit and loss account in a previous life) and the cash flow statement. Also included will be notes on the accounting policies used and information about other significant activities.

The three major statements included as part of the financial statements can be classified straightforwardly. First, a balance sheet, which is a list of all of the assets owned by a business and all of the liabilities owed by that business at a specific point in time. This is often referred to as a 'snapshot' of the financial position of the business at a specific moment in time (normally the end of the financial year). Second, the income statement, which shows the profits (or losses) recognized during a particular period. This is calculated by deducting the expenditure (including any charges for capital maintenance) from the income. Finally, the cash flow statement, which is simply a financial summary of all of the cash receipts and payments over an accounting period.

Rob Wilson

Associated Concepts   Assets, Liabilities and Capital; Double-Entry Bookkeeping; Financial and Management Accounting.

FLÂNEURS, FLÂNEURIE AND PSYCHOGEOGRAPHY

The *flâneur* is the nostalgic figure found in Walter Benjamin's unfinished *The Arcades Project*, who is both a man of the crowd and the detached observer of it. He is the quintessential man of leisure, the introspective stroller, spectator, watcher and imaginer of the urban landscape. He is a wanderer who does not exist; he merely becomes when the opportunity offers itself. To this extent he is the strolling opportunist, the rifler of the quotidian par excellence; the experiencing subject whose subjectivity *is* his world, *is* the whole world.

The concept of *flâneurie*, or as it has recently become known, pychogeography, refers to the practice of 'urban wandering, the imaginative re-working of the city, the other worldly sense of spirit of place, the unexpected insights and juxtapositions created by aimless drifting, the new ways of experiencing familiar surroundings' (Coverley, 2006: 31). Behind this is the idea that there is some sort of reality beyond the everyday, which is not so much what Freud would have called uncanny but something mysterious and profound. To this extent the stories that *flâneurs* elucidate in their musings intertwine to form worlds more real than anything you could touch, taste or see. What *flâneurs* create are worlds that exist in the imaginative spaces of the mind and the geographies of the soul, which make the world rather than trying to imitate it. In this sense *flâneurie* is that point where the imagination and urban environment intersect – just as the *flâneur* moves from place to place, so does his restless mind, reflecting on the ordering of the city, its history, and its quotidian present.

The idea of *flâneurie* raises a number of questions. Does the concept ignore or marginalize women's experiences of the city? In response to the lack of women *flâneurs* in the literature, some feminist commentators have proposed the *flâneuse* or the 'woman of the crowd'. This leads us on to another question: should we distinguish between the figure of the *flâneur* as outsider and insider? Walter Benjamin said that in observing the urban environment outsiders concentrate mostly on the exotic and picturesque, while insiders always see the place through layers of memory. Is the story of the *flâneur* merely a story about humankind's sense of loneliness or the idea that because each and every one of us is subject to the same anxious burden of our own individual loneliness we must in self-defence enchant our lives with our own critical faculties of the imagination? Has the craft of *flâneurie* been superseded by consumer culture? Benjamin anticipated that the *flâneur* would eventually be caught up in the market forces that would destroy him. Bauman (1994) takes this view one step further and suggests that *flâneurie* has today been privatized, to the extent that it is a freedom to stroll that not only reinforces and rejuvenates our dependence on the market but also depends on it for its exercise.

In a different light, Sinclair (1997: 75) argues that the ideas of strolling and aimless urban wandering associated with *flâneurie* have been superseded by the hypermodern activity of stalking: in other words, journeys of the mind and geographies of the soul made with intent – 'sharp-eyed and unsponsored'. Today it is the stalker who is our role model: 'purposed hiking, not dawdling nor browsing'

is the order of the day. In a speeded up, liquid modern world, we have no time for strolling the streets looking for new sensations. We stalk instead. As Sinclair points out, stalking is walking with a thesis – it is *flâneurie* with a mission to seek out its prey. The *flâneur* knows where s/he is headed, even if s/he still doesn't know why or how.

Tony Blackshaw

Associated Concepts Abnormal Leisure; Bohemians; Carnival; Dromology and Speed; Edgework; Ethnography; Extreme Leisure; Flow; Liminality; Mimesis; Zones.

FLOW

This term is generally used to refer to the theoretical model of the psychology of optimal experience as developed by Csikszentmihaly (1974; 1990; 1997). Flow is used by Csikszentmihalyi to explore leisure (and other experiences) characterized by the existential feeling of total involvement in activities which are freely chosen and self-rewarding and contain a level of uncertainty of outcome that allows for individual creativity. The idea is that leisure allows individuals to enter a world of flow or a stream of super-consciousness – a relationship with time, space and experience that is far removed from everyday experience. As well as being current, flow is also open to possibility, allowing creativity to move through individuals who are at one with both the process and the content of the leisure activity in question. To this extent, flow is related to other humanistic psychological motivational concepts, such as the need for self-actualization associated with the work of Abraham Maslow and Carl Rogers, which has been used to explore opportunities for human innovation and creativeness.

In developing these ideas, Csikszentmihalyi argues that the level of leisure activities should be matched to individual skill. Tennis is the sport he commonly uses to illustrate how certain leisure activities promote flow and to demonstrate how it is possible to measure the value of flow to individuals. A game of tennis, he argues, is only enjoyable when two players are evenly matched, which suggests that uncertainty is a precondition of optimal flow and that satisfaction occurs at that borderline between boredom and anxiety, when the challenges of the contest are precisely balanced with each player's individual ability to act.

According to Csikszentmihalyi flow activities have as their prime purpose the pursuit of pleasure and happiness. Consequently individuals undergoing deep flow will often find the leisure activity so totally engrossing that not only does a transmogrification of time occur but they can also lose their self-consciousness. This is described as the autotelic experience of deep flow wherein engagement in a particular leisure activity ostensibly leads to individual transcendence. Csikszentmihalyi is also keen to stress that such experiences do not always need to give immediate gratification, noting that the journey to optimal or deep flow does not always feel pleasurable at the time (as in the case of a physically and mentally challenging sport or adventure activity), but can be achieved later, through reflection.

While Csikszentmihalyi's understanding of flow is undoubtedly helpful in making sense of the restorative emotional effects of leisure, as well as the ways in which it has the capacity to reveal to individuals existential insights into the way that they live their lives, it is for some critics ultimately too psychologistic (Rojek, 2000). What Rojek perhaps overlooks is that, in common with liminal experiences, what is the most powerful dimension of any flow experience is its solitariness – the way it emphasizes, not so much a sense of coming together, but the individual's existential separateness from others. This observation notwithstanding, what Rojek adds to this psychological understanding of flow is a sociological dimension which takes account of the quickening and slowing down of flow through the concepts of fast and slow leisure. As Rojek demonstrates, these enable us to account for the ways in which 'flow alters the quantity and intensity of our relationships with others, and, through this, the [ways in which the] character of leisure is altered' (ibid.: 22).

Tony Blackshaw

Associated Concepts Authenticity; Catharis and Cathexis; Edgework; Extreme Leisure; Fantasy Leisure; Happiness; Leisure; Liminality; Pleasure; Rojek, Chris.

FOCUS GROUPS

Focus groups (or focus group interviews) are interviews conducted with a group of people, rather than individually, and which often involve intense discussion around a key issue or debate. Focus group interviews usually consist of a group of between 6 and 12 individuals who have been selected for interview – groups that are too big may become difficult to manage, and those that are too small tend to simply replicate more traditional interviews. As with traditional (one-to-one) interviews, focus group interviews can take on a more or less structured format, but generally tend to be less structured than most one-to-one interviews. Group interviews will also tend to work best when the conversations are allowed to flow and develop naturally, with guidance and direction from the interviewer – also sometimes know as a *facilitator* or *moderator* in focus group research.

The advantage of focus group interviews is that they are more efficient in terms of time and resources than one-to-one interviews, as you can interview more people over a short period. Focus group interviews can also allow discussion between interviewees (group members), which can often raise issues and points that the researcher may not have thought of, or which may not have come out in a one-to-one interview. In particular, focus groups are often a good initial or preliminary research tool, which can be used to alert researchers to the key areas/subjects that they may then want to follow up in further research (such as via more in-depth, one-to-one interviews). Jonathan Long (2007: 87) in his book *Researching, Leisure, Sport and Tourism*, also points out that focus groups are advantageous in interviewing groups of children, as they reduce both the power imbalance between interviewer and interviewees and any risk of being accused of 'wrongdoing'.

However, disadvantages with this method include the following: certain (more dominant) individuals can often lead (if not 'take over') discussions, to the exclusion of quieter members or to the extent that some group members' opinions and comments are swayed by those around them; focus group research can also prove extremely difficult to transcribe as well as to identify individuals afterwards from audio-tape recordings of the session, making analysis more difficult.

Garry Crawford

Associated Concepts Interviews; Methodology; Qualitative Research.

FOLK DEVILS AND MORAL PANICS

Stan Cohen's original work *Folk Devils and Moral Panics* (1972) was developed through his research on the emergence of the 'Mods and Rockers' phenomenon in the UK during the mid-to-late 1960s. Cohen's work was drawn from labelling theory, which derives from the symbolic interactionist perspective.

The 'folk devil' is a cultural archetype analogous to the 'outsider', the perpetual villain of the peace. To what extent particular social groups are considered to be 'folk devils' is partly down to whether or not they have violated some law or tacitly understood social norm and partly down to what social reaction this evokes. Drawing on a range of empirical findings Cohen demonstrated to convincing effect how in times of societal upheaval involving unprecedented social,

cultural and economic change the actions of the control culture (official agents of social control and moral entrepreneurs, such as the mass media) combine to amplify social deviance and in effect create 'moral panics'.

That young people have historically tended to take the brunt of adult society's anxieties about its own predicament was not lost on Cohen who also demonstrated the special significance of the media role in this process and thus started to draw attention also to their ideological role in actively constructing meanings rather than merely 'reflecting' some supposedly shared reality. The 'folk devils and moral panics' thesis has characteristically been applied to leisure subcultures in the following ways.

- A group or individual gets involved in some deviant activity or breaks the law.
- The media as reproducers of the control culture pick up on this and convert it into a newsworthy story. A 'problem group' is identified.
- The causes of deviance are also simplified for easy explanation. The media produce headlines, stories and photographs that are of interest to a range of interpreters. In an effort to maintain interest, the original deviance is amplified through exaggerated and distorted reporting (e.g., misleading headlines) prediction (the deviance will occur again) and symbolism (drama, the power of words through labels, atmosphere, and so on).
- The media generate a ready-made history for events associated with social deviance and also engage in predicting that these will be followed by similar events, with the likelihood of even worse consequences requiring an institutional response.
- This generates more deviance as people become sensitized to stereotypes and as a result of media interest individuals are attracted or repelled by folk devils.
- The 'deviant' group are now typecast as 'folk devils', a 'moral panic' occurs and a campaign is established to stamp out the perpetrators.

What Cohen's model suggests is that to understand social deviance we must consider all the social actors involved, rather than ambiguously concentrating on the actions of 'folk devils'. In other words, from Cohen's position social analysis must examine the social audience and its reaction to social deviance since labels are not automatically imposed on all rule breakers and some escape labelling altogether. As Cohen points out, in the way that they are situated as 'folk devils' some social groups (e.g., youth subcultures, football hooligans, and so on) are time and again constituted as 'visible reminders of what we should not be'. One of the chief effects of this process is to lock them into 'deviant' roles and project them along deviant courses or careers by closing off legitimate opportunities and forcing the individuals involved to resort to social groups which offer support but which will, in due course, maintain their deviant status. Thus society creates social deviance in the sense that the application of the folk devil label is likely to produce more deviance than it prevents. Stigmatizing by labelling, then, places 'folk devils' outside conventional circles and sparks off a sense of uncertainty about them.

Furedi (1994) argues that today moral panics are not confined to distinct targets such as the young or specific leisure subcultures but can instead cover a whole range of social groups, so essentially no 'deviant' group can feel completely safe from possible persecution as a result of a future moral panic. As Blackshaw and Crabbe (2004) demonstrated, during a two-week period in 2003, a conflation of unrelated events in professional football included: an alleged sexual assault; one player's abusive behaviour towards a young female student outside a nightclub; Manchester United and England centre-back Rio Ferdinand missing a compulsory random drugs test; England players discussing the possibility of a strike following Ferdinand's subsequent omission from the national squad for a crunch Euro 2004 qualifying match against Turkey; a young Liverpool player being shot in a bar in the city at 1:30 in the morning; and a group of premiership players being accused of raping or 'spit-roasting' a 17-year-old woman at the Grosvenor House Hotel on London's Park Lane. This led to a moral panic and media calls for tighter controls on professional players. As those authors point out, in this instance the category 'footballer' became synonymous with 'deviant' behaviour, manifest in the 'deviant' practice of 'spit-roasting' in particular, and thus the professional footballer emerged as a new 'folk devil'.

McRobbie (1994) also develops Cohen's view of the notion of a moral panic. She still sees the moral panic as a means to control socially, but suggests that today we inhabit a society which is inundated with moral panics, 'to the extent that the panics are no longer about social control but rather about the fear of being out of control'. For McRobbie, however, the idea of the moral panic has become such common currency that nobody actually stops to ask whether the media are deliberately trying to provoke a panic for favourable publicity or just trying to be ironic. Either way, as she points out, with the absence of a hegemonic control culture it is difficult for the media to forge a consensus on even the most basic of issues, which leads her to conclude that for all its ostensible efficacy as a model for explaining patterns of social control Cohen's thesis is now out of date.

Tony Blackshaw

Associated Concepts Abnormal Leisure; Deviance; Football Hooliganism; Social Control; Surveillance; Symbolic Interactionism.

FOOTBALL HOOLIGANISM

It is difficult to define what actually constitutes 'football hooliganism', particularly since it has become such a value-laden and politicized concept. Generally, however, it is taken to refer to 'football-related disorder', including not just physical violence but also aggressive and threatening behaviour, the throwing of missiles, and sometimes even offensive and threatening language is classed as 'hooliganism'.

Giulianotti (1999) suggests that the sociology of football since the 1960s has been most closely associated with (if not largely dominated by) the study of 'football hooliganism'. Clarke (1992) has also suggested that the study of football fans has focused almost *exclusively* on the study of hooliganism. Since the early 1990s the focus on sport fans has (to some degree) begun to veer away from this academic fixation (particularly in the UK) with football hooliganism. However, it remains an intense topic of debate and discussion, both in and outside academia.

The first academic consideration of football hooliganism came with the work of Ian Taylor (1969, 1971), who attempted to locate the occurrence of football hooliganism within wider economic and social changes within British society. He argued that where once the football club existed as a focus of local working-class identity, the hijacking of the sport by new commercial interests and a general 'bourgeoisification' of the game (characterized by rising players' wages, the involvement of big businesses in the running of football and an influx of new 'middle-class' supporters) had seen its traditional working-class (most often young male *lumpen* proletariat) followers increasingly isolated and alienated from what was once 'their' sport. Taylor therefore argued that football-related violence could be seen as working-class 'resistance' to this process of bourgeoisification and an attempt by these young working-class men to reassert *their* ownership of football.

Taylor's position on hooliganism notably changed in the 1980s and 1990s, when it became increasingly apparent that hooligan activities were not solely participated in by working-class 'roughs', and Taylor (1982, 1987, 1989) recognized the presence of some more affluent (middle-class) individuals within hooligan groups. It is at this point that Taylor abandoned his view of hooligans as 'resistance fighters' to take up the alternative stance of seeing them as a 'serious social menace' (Giulianotti, 1999: 41).

Another academic perspective offered on football hooliganism is that of Peter Marsh (1978) who adopted a social psychological approach and argued that 'aggro' was an expected and accepted part of football culture – as was the case in many other aspects of human society. Marsh suggested that hooligans existed within an organized culture, where individuals were socialized along a 'career' path into their hooligan role. These individuals would engage in (often highly) organized and ritualized 'aggressive' behaviour, such as chanting or threatening behaviour, but actual violence at football matches was a rare occurrence (the seriousness of which was often amplified by the police, mass media and relevant authorities).

Elsewhere, both Stuart Hall (1978) and Garry Whannel (1979) point to the role of the mass media in helping create and reproduce the idea of the football hooligan as a folk devil and the cause of moral panic (Cohen, 1972), and probably the most well-known theorization of football hooliganism was developed by a group of academics at Leicester University, which most notably included Eric Dunning, Patrick Murphy and John Williams (until his departure from this team in the early 1990s to follow his own independent scholarly interests). The approach of the Leicester School was to adopt a figurational viewpoint, which drew heavily on the work of Norbert Elias.

Of particular relevance to this discussion is Elias' (1978b) theorization of the civilizing process, in which he suggested that Western societies since the Middle Ages had been undergoing a process of 'civilization' which had seen changing social norms and regulations, particularly in relation to the increased privatization of the body (and bodily functions) and growing intolerance towards acts of violence. Following on from Elias, the Leicester scholars (led by Dunning) suggested that supporter behaviour at football had undergone a process of civilization. They argued that at the turn of the twentieth-century violence at football matches was 'relatively high' (Giulianotti, 1999: 45). However, over time football crowds have become generally more 'civilized' and 'respectful' in their behaviour, and hence football fans (as well as the general public) have become more sensitized to acts of violence and aggression. The occurrence of violence at contemporary football matches is then explained as a 'decivilizing spurt', or a throwback to a less civilized era, and is most frequently conducted by the lower working-classes who trail behind at the rear of this civilizing process – violence that is now less tolerated by most people, and hence, is more socially visible.

However, Armstrong (1998: 17) suggests that after 1993 the Leicester School's position has moved away from forcefully locating hooliganism within working-class culture, as they too (along with Taylor) began to recognize that so-called 'football hooligans' were not just made up of the working classes.

In spite of these (and numerous other) attempts to understand football hooliganism, Armstrong (1998: 21) concluded that 'football hooliganism cannot really be "explained". It can only be described and evaluated'. However, while Armstrong offers a more in-depth account of football-related violence than most through his ethnographic study of Sheffield United fans, he still falls into the trap of seeking to 'explain' this phenomenon, and continues the academic as well as public and mass media obsession with this one 'relatively infrequent' (Wann et al., 2001: 102) aspect of sport fan culture.

Garry Crawford

Associated Concepts Alienation; Class; Elias; Fans; Folk Devils and Moral Panics; Mass Media; Power; Sport; Violence.

FOUCAULT, MICHEL (1926–1984)

Michel Foucault was one of the leading lights of a French philosophical moment in the second half of the twentieth century, the significance of which, according to Alain

Badiou, compares with classical Greek philosophy between Parmenides and Aristotle and the highpoint of German Idealism from Kant to Hegel. Born in Poitiers in France, he studied philosophy at the *Ecole Normale Supérieure* before embarking on a career as a psychiatrist in a Parisian hospital. This work left an indelible mark on Foucault and formed the basis of his doctoral studies on madness which he completed at the University of Hamburg in 1961. The subsequent publication of his doctoral thesis as *Madness and Civilization: A History of Insanity in the Age of Reason* brought Foucault critical acclaim and earned him a professorship at the University of Clermont-Ferrand in 1964. In 1970 he was elected to the prestigious *Collège de France* where he asserted himself as an authority on the history of systems of thought. However, this self-categorization was not as straightforward as it seemed, because in so far as Foucault can be called a philosopher who deals with history his is a history of an extraordinary kind with its own truth, the sort of truth Aristotle had in mind when he said that poetry is truer than history – truer because of its power to condense and represent the complexity of the world in the typical.

As a result Foucault is often described as a poststructuralist or a postmodernist, but this is to oversimplify the work of a man who always resisted labels. There is not the space here to explore the complexities of Foucault's work in any detail, but the student of leisure needs to be aware that there have been at least three Michel Foucaults, each concerned with the historical investigation of power and its resistance: Mark I, a structuralist or 'archaeologist' who suggested that history takes the form of *epistemes* (something akin to Khunian paradigms) marked by radical ruptures; Mark II, the poststructuralist or 'genealogist' version, who suggested that the practices which mark discursive formations need be interpreted in terms of their 'exteriority', especially at those points of resistance where repression is at its most powerful; and, finally, the Mark III version, who offered an explicit critique of the conception of sovereign power proposed by Machiavelli, and in whose work the emergence of the self is suggestive of a self-critique of his own earlier understandings of discipline, power, knowledge and the potential for resistance.

It is the Mark III Foucault who wrote about the 'desiring subject', the 'care of the self' and the 'use of pleasure' as a form of self-governmentality through which the 'art of living' must be understood, not just as a possibility but as the right of all men and women, notwithstanding their persisting economic differences, which on the face of it make the most explicit linkages with the study of leisure. However, this aspect of Foucault has not yet been developed in any extensive way by leisure scholars. What is well documented in the literature, though, is Mark II Foucault's work on surveillance and its role in controlling and maintaining 'docile' minds and bodies in the modern 'disciplinary society' which he developed in the book *Discipline and Punish* (1977). In leisure studies, one of the earliest applications of the idea of surveillance was Hargreaves' (1986) consideration of the British physical education system as a disciplinary regime which acts as a means of social control through the schooling of bodies to reproduce specific class, gender and ethnic divisions. Similarly Pronger (2002) draws on Foucault's work to illustrate how scientific-medical knowledges of the body have contributed to the transformation of the human body into a machine in the service of contemporary consumer capitalism, whilst Rinehart (1998: 42) identified the swimming pool as a mechanism of surveillance which when 'divided into areas for lessons (or lanes for the swim practice), became the symbolic of "hundreds of tiny theatres of punishment".

Tony Blackshaw

Associated Concepts Abnormal Leisure; Deviance; Discursive Formations; Governmentality; Leisure Bodies; Paradigms; Pornography; Sex; Surveillance; Social Control.

FRANKFURT SCHOOL, THE

(critical theory)

FREE TIME

This notion is central to most definitions of leisure. However, to say that leisure is simply free time, (namely, an occasion, opportunity or period free from other obligations, when an individual is able to organize his or her own time in whatever ways he or she sees appropriate) tells us nothing about the content and quality of the leisure experienced. Such a definition also ignores the fact that time free to make deliberative choices about what to do with one's free time is always accompanied by the implication that the individual's ability to enjoy his or her free time has been, or is potentially, open to restraint or constraint. Such a definition, if it is useful for identifying in broad terms the quantity of time available for leisure and how time is distributed among different social and cultural groups, also ignores, or at least marginalizes, how that free time has been created. For example, has the individual in question lost his or her job? Is he or she simply filling in time? Has he or she been forcibly retired? And so on. It is for these reasons that the notion of free time for leisureliness, like Bertrand Russell's dictum that liberty is 'the absence of obstacles to the realization of desire', is unsatisfactory.

Tony Blackshaw

Associated Concepts Decentring Leisure; Leisure; Leisure Class; Leisure Life-Style; Leisure Life-World; Leisure Society; Serious Leisure; Virtual Leisure; Women's Leisure; Work-Leisure.

FREUD, SIGMUND (1836–1939)

Sigmund Freud was one of the most influential thinkers of the modern era. Born in Freiberg and educated in Vienna, Freud initially took up a medical career and worked as a neurologist. However, he became increasingly interested in psychology and 'talking cure' methods which came to be known as free association. As a result he is mostly known as the originator of psychoanalysis. Significant attention has been lavished on his work on sexuality which he saw as the key to understanding human subjectivity and culture, and particularly his ideas about the repression of childhood sexuality as the root cause of neuroses in adults (i.e., the Oedipus and Electra complexes). However, there is much more to Freud's work than is often acknowledged. Not only does it reflect the complexity of the relation between science and literature which began to appear in debates about the meaning of knowledge from the mid-nineteenth century but it is also full of tensions and insights not merely particular but universal.

In his famous essay 'Civilization and Its Discontents' (1930), for example, Freud takes Rome to be a useful metaphor for the processes of modern civilization. Like Rome, Freud suggests, modernity might be evolving towards a newer and better society but it cannot shake off its past entirely. The modern world carries with it, beneath its foundations, the ambivalence of its own historicity. As he put it, 'nothing which has once been formed can perish – that everything is somehow preserved and that in suitable circumstances (when, for instance, regression goes back far enough) it can once more be brought to light' (Freud, 1995 [1930]: 725). What Freud's analysis suggests is that if at one level there is with the emergence of modernity the *progressive* affirmation of beauty, cleanliness and order, at another level, it has 'buried in the soil of its city or beneath its modern buildings' the *regressive* means of power and social control for their implementation.

This dichotomy is at the heart of the relevance of Freud's work for understanding leisure. As Harvie Ferguson (1989) demonstrates in an essay which begins by linking Freudian ideas with Freud's own favourite leisure activity of travelling, in the prototypical bourgeois modern world of passionate individualism, pleasure was not only turned into a self-possession and wrapped up with a kind of quest for wish fulfilment that was irreconcilable with satisfaction but it was also all too often based on the systematic repression of fun.

Tony Blackshaw

Associated Concepts   Desire; Fantasy Leisure; Happiness; Pleasure; Pornography; Sex.

FULL-TIME EQUIVALENT JOBS

When a sport or leisure event takes place it is often undoubtedly the case that many employment opportunities are created. Thus the staging of an event has a positive effect on the locality in question. Crompton (2001) suggests that an employment multiplier can be used to measure the direct, indirect and induced effect of an extra unit of visitor expenditure on employment in a city hosting an event. This shows how many full-time equivalent job opportunities would be supported in the locality as a result of visitor spending. However, the employment multiplier makes the assumption that all current employees are fully occupied, so an increase in external visitor spending will require an increased level of employment in the locality.

The use of this type of multiplier can be misleading when considering a sport event or facility, as local businesses are likely to respond by utilizing their current resources to a greater degree due to the relatively short duration of the event. New employees may not be hired and existing ones may be redeployed or asked to work overtime; at best only short-term appointments will be made (Crompton, 1995, 2001). This theory has been supported by empirical evidence from research conducted by Arnold (1986), which demonstrated that at the 1992 Adelaide Grand Prix there were virtually no new permanent jobs created. This research also found that several companies had organized the increased workload in such a way that they did not even have to pay overtime.

Rob Wilson

Associated Concepts Deadweight Expenditure; Economic Benefit of Hosting Major Sport Events; Economic Impact of Hosting Major Sport Events; Invisible Exports; Multiplier Analysis.

FUNCTIONALISM

Functionalism is a sociological theoretical perspective which advocates the positive 'functions' performed by social structures (e.g., institutions, hierarchies, norms) in producing and reproducing social order and cohesion. To this extent functionalism can be understood as a form of positivism, which suggests that society can be understood and studied by utilizing the methods and philosophy of the natural sciences. For instance, key figures in the development of functionalism, such as Herbert Spencer and Emile Durkheim, emphasized the similarities between society and biological organisms. An example of this is Spencer's discussion of economics, in which he coined the phrase 'survival of the fittest' in comparing how certain businesses will survive competition and others will fail with Charles Darwin's evolutionary concept of 'natural selection'.

Two key contemporary functionalists are Robert K. Merton and Talcott Parsons, who at Columbia and Harvard universities (respectively) developed functionalist analysis and helped make this the most widely accepted social theory in post-war sociology (particularly in the USA), right up until the mid-1960s when its dominance was challenged by a resurgence in more critical perspectives such as Marxism and feminism. Elements of a functionalist argument can be found in many theories and discussions of leisure (such as in the work of Stanley Parker (1983) who discusses the functions leisure can have for society, such as social integration and rule learning). However, there are few writers on leisure who have clearly or consistently advocated a functionalist perspective – though of course there are some exceptions, such as the sociologist Gunther Lüschen (1967) who offered a more traditional functionalist consideration of the role of sport in pattern maintenance and social integration.

A functionalist attitude to sport and leisure (though it is rarely if ever acknowledged as this) is evident in many governmental and non-governmental organizations' attitudes towards the positive functions of sport and leisure for individuals and society more generally. A good example of this would be the Victorian idea of 'rational recreation', which suggested that sport and leisure could be used in such a way as to promote good social values and morality in participants (see Bailey, 1989). It is also evident that most social science (and within this leisure studies) approaches involve some degree of functionalism in their quest to understand the role and functions of various social practices and institutions. For instance Rojek (1984), in his discussion of Marx and leisure, frequently highlights the social 'functions' leisure is suggested to have in Marxist arguments.

Garry Crawford

Associated Concepts Feminism; Marxism; Sport; Work-Leisure.

G

GAMBLING

Gerda Reith (1999: 1), in her book *The Age of Chance*, defines gambling as 'a ritual which is strictly demarcated from the everyday world around it within which chance is deliberately courted'. Gambling has a very long history, and there is evidence that it has existed in nearly all cultures, in every period of time – as McMillen (1999: 6) writes: 'in this respect it can be said to be a universal phenomenon of human history'.

Generally, gambling can be viewed from two contrasting perspectives, either as a form of leisure and recreation or as a serious social problem. These two contrasting viewpoints can be seen in the attitudes towards gambling exemplified in the philosophies of Plato and Aristotle towards gaming and play – where Plato saw gaming as a form of play, and an intrinsic and even 'sacred' aspect of human culture, Aristotle saw game playing as involving 'sordid greed' and 'meanness' (Reith, 1999).

Reith suggests that the idea of gambling as a 'social problem' has a long history, which dates back to the Middle Ages, if not before, where it was often seen as an unproductive activity, and hence of less value than more combative pastimes. During the Reformation gambling was seen as morally objectionable, while the philosophies of the Enlightenment saw it as fundamentally irrational. However, in more contemporary times it is the Protestant ethics of the nineteenth century which see gambling deemed as an ungodly vice, a position reinforced further by the work of Sigmund Freud (1928) who introduces the idea of the gambler as a 'compulsive neurotic', and links gambling addiction to the 'primal addiction' of masturbation.

However, there are also several sociological considerations of the social significance of gambling as a form of play and leisure. For instance, Veblen (1934 [1899]) discussed gambling as one way by which the leisured classes displayed their superior wealth. Likewise, Goldthorpe et al. (1969) considered the dramatic increase in the opportunities for gambling for 'affluent workers' in post-war Britain. Erving Goffman in his essay 'Where the action is' (1967) also recognized the centrality and importance of play in social life, and suggested that the opportunities for risk are limited within contemporary society, leading many to deliberately seek out risk, such as through gambling. Furthermore, he suggested that gambling involves a 'maintenance of self' where these situations of heightened risk and pressure can be taken as a measure of character and courage.

In more contemporary times, Reith highlights the central role gambling now plays in our society. Tying her discussion into debates about the changing nature of society and culture, such as the rise of a risk society, she argues that gambling is seen today as a common and constituent part of our culture. It is no longer a distinct and discrete activity engaged in solely in casinos and betting shops, but instead invades our everyday lives through lotteries, scratch cards, raffles, bingo, arcades, television, newspaper and radio competitions, stock market and currency speculation, the internet, and many other sources. As Reith concludes: 'chance has become an irreducible aspect of daily life: risk, speculation, indeterminism and flux are our constant companions in social, economic and personal affairs: we have entered the Age of Chance'. This echoes Bauman's (2004: 52) observation that liquid modern men and women are destined to live life as a 'casino culture' that 'wants from you nothing but to stay in the game and have enough tokens left on the table to go on playing'. A life that is messy, uncertain, fragmented, and where everything seems to happen as if by chance.

Garry Crawford

Associated Concepts A and B Analysis; Bauman; Freud; Game Theory; Goffman; Modernity; Play; Risk Society; Veblen.

GAME THEORY

This is defined as a theory of the optimal decision-making behaviour of two or more 'players' in situations where strategies have to be chosen in ignorance of other players' choices, but with the knowledge of the costs and benefits of taking different options. In the event, players have to act to achieve the outcomes they would prefer given the actions of other players. As a theory of decision making and human interaction, game theory is analogous with what has been broadly described as the psychology of interpersonal behaviour, as well as the ways in which individuals respond to information about which they have no direct acquaintance. It has been applied to a number of different contexts and is of interest to practitioners in academic fields as diverse as business management, moral philosophy and evolutionary biology. Critics of game theory focus on its embracing capitalistic accumulation, managerialism and its assumptions about the selfish nature of humankind. All of this was critically brought to bear by Adam Curtis in his documentary series *The Trap*,

which focused especially on the work of game theorist John Nash, who designed one particular game, 'Fuck You Buddy', in which the only way to win was to betray one's playing partner.

Tony Blackshaw

Associated Concepts A and B Analysis; Capitalism; Gambling; Individualization; Play; Play Ethic.

GATEKEEPERS

The challenge of gaining access to different organizations and other social contexts governed by hierarchical structures and power relations in order to carry out their studies means that researchers often have to rely on gatekeepers. Gatekeepers are those who are placed in crucial positions who have the power (often far beyond that based on any formal foundations) to grant (or deny) access to particular information, groups or places. Most social research will inevitably encounter gatekeepers – people who will need to be negotiated with in order to successfully undertake research. For instance, in William Foote Whyte's (1993 [1943]) classic study of street corner gangs in Boston in 1930s' America, one of the gang members 'Doc' operated as an initial contact and gatekeeper for Whyte, introducing him, and allowing him access to the street corner gang culture he wished to study.

Researchers should never presume that gatekeepers will provide access, as people can often be suspicious of outsiders, and therefore it is important to have alternative strategies or methods if the intended research is blocked by certain individuals or organizations. One way of negotiating access is to offer gatekeepers something in return. However, Fielding (2001) warns about the danger of promising too much to gatekeepers as making too many promises or concessions may mean that they (and not the researcher) will start to dictate the direction and outcome of the research.

Garry Crawford

Associated Concepts   Ethnography; Methodology; Qualitative Research; Quantitative Research.

GENDER

(feminism; women's leisure)

GIDDENS, ANTHONY (1938–)

Lord Giddens of Southgate was until 2004 Director of the London School of Economics (LSE). While since the early 1990s he has published a good deal of work on the 'Third Way', which drew him into the inner circle of New Labour politics in the UK and led to his appointment at the LSE in 1997, he is best known for his work in social theory which he developed while working at Leicester and Cambridge Universities in the 1970s, 1980s and early 1990s, leading to his reputation as one of the most important figures in sociology in the second half of the twentieth century.

It is impossible to summarize the content of Giddens' writings here. However, what any reader needs to grasp is that it is in his ambition to break free from the sociological conventions which lie at the heart of Giddens' brilliance. His work has never been hamstrung by the need to heed either theory or method in their conventional sense. Instead, sociology has always been a place for experiment and innovation. This is reflected in his idea of the double hermeneutic, which stresses the importance of the interface between the measure of the social world as it is developed on the one hand by sociologists in order to 'understand and explain social action' and on the other as it is constituted by lay actors.

In the 1970s Giddens worked with the aim of overhauling classical social theory by offering sociology some *New Rules of Sociological Method* (1976). Drawing on eclectic sources, including the meta-sociologies of Marx, Durkheim and Weber and the micro-sociologies of Goffman and Garfinkel, as well as the work of various philosophers, psychologists and semioticians, and developments in structural linguistics, Giddens outlined his theory of the subject which criticized orthodox sociology for failing to recognize that social actors not only conceptualize their own conduct reflexively but also produce social structures. In this sense he argued that society is not structured but structuring and that 'social life ... is continually and contingently reproduced by knowledgeable human agents – that's what gives it fixity and that's what also produces change' (Giddens, 1998: 90).

This work paved the way for his subsequent theorization of power and state, which was concerned with the modern ways in which nation states are capable of exercising power through information storage, surveillance, policing and the modern unbinding of time and space, which involves 'the lifting out of social relations from local contexts of interaction'. This work was also the basis of his theory of structuration which was his attempt to overcome the dichotomy between structure and agency that has dogged sociology since its inception. According to Giddens, structure must be understood as structuration because it is both the medium and the outcome of social practices of knowledgeable actors (the double hermeneutic again) which operate to both facilitate and constrain action. Structure then refers to the rules and resources recursively implicated in the processes of social reproduction.

Bauman (1989b) has suggested that the problem with Giddens' *New Rules of Sociological Method* was that they remained part of the self-same crisis that sociology was attempting to break away from. Bauman's point was that what Giddens should have been giving his attention to was the problematic that if 'society' continues to exist in the worn-out concepts, theories and methodologies that still fill the heads of sociologists, its members – the ordinary men and women of that sociality – by and large will have no idea today that they belong to it. As Bauman succinctly put it, 'to claim the right to speak with authority, sociology would have to update its theory of society' (p.55).

Although Giddens does not refer to leisure directly in his published work, his observations on modernity, on love and intimacy, on politics and on the many other matters which occur boldly and frequently, his writings have a direct resonance for understanding leisure and raise some key questions for leisure scholars. For example, how can the concept of structuration be used to understand issues surrounding leisure bodies – that is, how do processes of bodily structuration work in leisure? In his critique of modernity, Giddens (1990) draws on his ideas about time and space to argue that re-embedding mechanisms necessitate the establishment of new social relations which are not necessarily traditional or locally bound. How might we use such ideas to explain newly emerging patterns of community involvement in leisure? How does the concept of globalization impact on leisure and sport? Does Giddens' concept of the double hermeneutic exaggerate the significance of sociology in the way people see the world? In relation to his theory of the state, what role does leisure play in processes of information storage, surveillance and the policing of modern societies?

Tony Blackshaw

Associated Concepts Addictions; Bauman, Zygmunt; Leisure Bodies; Modernity; Sex; Semiotics; Surveillance; Symbolic Interactionism; Third Way.

GLOBALIZATION

There exists a great deal of ambiguity and confusion surrounding a clear definition of globalization. Sabo (1993: 2) defines it as a 'growing interdependence among the world's societies' and Giddens (1990) as an intensification of social relations at the world level, while Robertson (1995) calls this 'the compression of the world and the intensification of consciousness of the world as a whole' (cited in Harvey et al., 1996: 259). Likewise, there is considerable disagreement over the origins of this process.

Mennell (1990: 359) suggests that globalization is a 'very long-term process' that has existed for as long as the human race, while Kern (1983) argues that it has occurred since the standardization of space and time that was negotiated through the technological advances at the turn of the twentieth century. Harvey et al. (1996: 260) point out that globalization has significantly intensified since the early 1980s with the increased power and scope of neoliberal forces, such as transnational corporations, international capital, neoliberal economists and new-right political movements. However, whatever definition we choose to accept, or however early we wish to place the origins of this process, there is little doubt that leisure today is an increasingly globalized phenomenon. Moreover, there is also little doubt that the processes of globalization have rapidly increased within the previous few decades, primarily due to the ease of international travel, advances in new technologies and the growing similarities and interdependencies of political and economic systems around the world.

In particular, many leisure industries, such as those dealing with music, film and digital gaming, are largely controlled by multinational global corporations and the standardized products, such as Hollywood films, that are distributed and consumed the world over. Therefore, for some, globalization can be seen as a one-way process of cultural domination or colonization. In the past few decades the most common form of cultural domination discussed within the globalization literature is that of 'Americanization'. For instance, Tunstall (1977: 57) argues that 'authentic, traditional and local culture in many parts of the world is being battered out of existence by the indiscriminate dumping of large quantities of slick commercial and media products, mainly from the United States'.

However, other theorists have suggested that globalization can be better understood as a form of negotiation or hegemony between two different cultures. A strong advocate of the cultural hegemony debate within the sociology of sport is Donnelly (1996: 243) who states 'rather than engaging in an overdetermined view of Americanization, a more subtle approach is to regard Americanization in terms of cultural hegemony'. In particular, hegemony as a theoretical tool helps explain how dominant ideology is either incorporated, modified or resisted by the local, and 'provides pertinent insight into the issues of dominance and subordination in modern capitalism' (Minseok and Sage, 1992: 373). Here, for instance, Crawford (2002) highlights that while ice hockey in the UK is heavily dominated by North American players, styles of play and presentation, many aspects of the game and its presentation have been adapted to fit into British (sporting) culture.

And yet, even this approach sees globalization as too much of a neat, linear and structural process. Other authors have attempted to apply a more post-structuralist and fluid theorization of globalization, and most notable here is the work of Appadurai (1989, 1990, 1993), in particular, by suggesting that globalization should be understood as a series of multidirectional and fluid 'flows', which he refers to as 'scapes'. These scapes include the global flow of people (ethnoscapes), the media (mediascapes), technology (technoscapes), finance (financescapes) and ideas (ideoscapes). However, all of these flows and scapes are invariably connected and increasingly indistinguishable.

Garry Crawford

Associated Concepts Consumer Society; Elias; Hegemony; Ideology; Mass Media; Network Society; Risk Society; Sport; Sportization; Power.

GOFFMAN, ERVING (1922–1982)

Through a series of brilliant writings, including *The Presentation of Self in Everyday Life* (1959),

Asylums (1961a) and *Stigma* (1963), Erving Goffman became one of the best-known sociologists of the mid-twentieth century. He was probably the most ingenious of the post-war cohort of Chicago graduate students who were linked to symbolic interactionism. Goffman's abiding focus was the sociological analysis of face-to-face interaction, a realm he termed 'the interaction order'. When we are in the presence of other persons, we are as uniquely positioned to observe their attitude, dispositions and intentions as they are of ours. We do this through the expressions we 'give' about ourselves (the information we tell others) and the expressions we 'give off' (through our tone, accent, posture, facial gestures, and so on). Deploying many well-chosen illustrations and perceptive observations, Goffman demonstrated that the rules governing such expressive conduct are comprehensively social in character: face-to-face interaction is an expressive order that is constantly consequential for the identities of the interactants and their relationship to one another.

In *The Presentation of Self*, Goffman's first book, these themes were developed through a dramaturgical metaphor. The details of ordinary conduct in face-to-face encounters are dissected as elements of a 'performance' staged for an 'audience' occupying a 'front region'. Meanwhile, in the 'back region' interactants prepare themselves for performances that they must usually accomplish in collaboration with other members of the team. The 'impression management' mobilized by such performances sometimes involves elements of 'idealization' and 'mystification'. These are thoroughly social competences acquired through socialization. Goffman insists that 'the very obligation and profitability of appearing always in a steady moral light, of being a socialized character, forces one to be the sort of person who is practised in the ways of the stage' (Goffman, 1959: 251).

Goffman's contribution to an understanding of leisure derives from his longstanding interest in games as a model of the key properties of social life. Games were of course the source of Goffman's notorious interest in the calculative and strategizing aspects of interaction. What is sometimes overlooked is that he also saw games as phenomenological models for encounters more generally. Games are 'world-building activities' (Goffman, 1961b: 27) that can create a realm of meanings experienced as real by participants. Serious activity also has this quality. Games (again like encounters) are organized by rules and not just created 'on the spot' by participants. Games are meant to be fun, just as encounters ideally should be experienced as smooth, unproblematic, even euphoric. But such states do not simply happen automatically. They are produced through the 'work' of the interactants. For there to be fun in games, and euphoria in interaction more generally, elements of chance and risk need to be included. For a game to be compelling or a party interesting, people need to be a little different from each other and something needs to be at stake.

Goffman developed the link between fun and risk in his 1967 essay, 'Where the action is', which drew upon his participant observation fieldwork as a gambler and dealer in the casinos of Reno and Las Vegas. Gambling is the prototype of 'action', that is, freely chosen conduct that has a problematic outcome and is consequential for a person's subsequent life. Action in this special sense affords opportunities for the display of 'character', the capability to handle oneself during fateful moments. Since 'serious action is a serious ride and rides of this kind are all but arranged out of everyday life' (Goffman, 1967: 261), opportunities for action and character displays are largely confined in modern societies to carefully regulated leisure settings.

Goffman's enduring fascination for games as occasions for the licensed expression of 'fun' and 'action' has impacted on leisure studies in numerous ways.

Goffman's essay on action rekindled sociological interest in gambling and helped to reorientate sociology towards the study of a range of risk-taking activities, such as skydiving (Hardie-Bick, forthcoming). It also contributed to the development of research on 'edgework' (Lyng, 1990), although Lyng is careful to distinguish his concept from Goffman's. Edgeworkers, according to Lyng, typically minimize the scope of fate and emphasize the element of personal control in their pursuit of action.

This centrality of the notion of involvement to Goffman's sociology of interaction points to a further significance in his ideas for leisure studies. The notion that an activity is what a person gives concerted attention to, (that is, is involved in) helps clarify some of the terminological disputes around what counts as leisure, often expressed as variants of the 'what is fun for the golfer is work for the caddy' dilemma.

Goffman was indeed a major intellectual figure in the second half of the twentieth century. Birrell and Donnelly (2004) describe the broad reach of Goffman's influence on the sociology of sport. In particular, they show how Goffman can be reclaimed for critical and feminist perspectives on sport. The implications of Goffman's work are still being unpacked (Smith, 2006) and its relevance as a productive and provocative resource for studies of leisure is far from fully exhausted.

Greg Smith

Associated Concepts Edgework; Flow; Identity; Participant Observation; Performativity; Play; Symbolic Interactionism.

GOVERNMENTALITY

This term does not permit a precise definition, but is perhaps best summarized by Mitchell Dean who defines it as 'a novel thought-space across the domains of ethics and politics, of what might be called "practices of the self" and "practices of government", that weaves them together without a reduction of one to the other' (Dean, 1994: 174). This basic concept of governmentality comes from the work of Michel Foucault who offered it as a 'guideline' for analysis which has generally been applied to the mechanisms of governance, power, liberalism and the state.

Liberalism emerged out of the Enlightenment and the massive social, political and economic changes that developed in Europe from the seventeenth century onwards. In common with all other political doctrines it operates with its own *doxa* (the knowledge it thinks with but not about) that makes some fundamental assumptions about human nature and human knowledge. Most important among these is the recognition of the existence of the individual and the claims to individual liberty, such as the right to private property. While liberalism is a contested political doctrine most versions demonstrate a suspicion towards the activities of the state, and Foucault argued that this could be seen as a critical response to excessive interventionist policies in the eighteenth century.

Foucault's basic premise was that the rationality underpinning the liberal doctrine (taking as its key starting point the existence of self-interested individuals) not only exposed the dilemmas of a nascent modern Western democracy but also ushered in a process of governmentalization which broke with the *raison d'être* of the state as a monolithic institution and effectively changed the way in which it operated. To put it briefly, liberalism took advantage of growing concerns about 'how' and 'how much' to govern in the face of the quandaries posed by the emergence of a multiplicity of 'population' issues, for example, concerns about *social* dependency (e.g., the fear of the 'Mob', of the propertyless), the *political* franchise (e.g., the 'tyranny of majority rule') and *economic* expediency (e.g., the increasing financial costs of public welfare). As a result it was able to influence the state's concerns, about a range of issues, but especially those tied to the economy and individual freedom. In the event these came to be seen as matters of public concern, which also meant they were effectively 'decentred' from the direct responsibility of the state.

As Rose (1990: 5) points out,

with the entry of the population into political thought, rule takes as its object such phenomena as the numbers of subjects, their ages, their longevity, their sicknesses and types of death, their habits and vices, their rates of reproduction ... [which in effect marked] the birth and history of the knowledges of subjectivity and intersubjectivity ... intrinsically bound up with programmes which, in order to govern subjects, have found that they need to know them.

As sociologists have pointed out, this process of classifying 'problem' populations appealed to modern standards of universal reason which with its passion for taxonomy was typically corrective and exacting, revising and adjusting individual subjects and social relationships alike to its normative 'scientist' values. As Bauman demonstrates, once forged in modern liberal states, classification's coin quickly became the common currency and all aspects of life have to get their required doses of its classifying zeal in order to guarantee their legitimacy (Blackshaw, 2005).

In his earlier studies Foucault (1977) had argued that this systematic ordering of everyday life was achieved through a 'carceral archipelago' or a capillary network of power-knowledge established and also made tacit through 'normalizing judgements' and 'self-evident' truths which were embedded in the 'panopticonisms' (schools, prisons, hospitals, and so on) of modern disciplinary society. However, with a new interest in the 'art of government' (Foucault, 1991), he then suggested that social problems characteristic of liberal democracies were being increasingly marked by the 'conduct of conduct', whereby various social actors sought to affect the action of themselves ('governing the self') and others ('governing others') politically.

Expert knowledge is central to governmentality. Specifically, Foucault came to be concerned with how this 'decentred' and 'contingent' form of government impacted on the day-to-day lives of individuals and their own 'practices of the self' *and* specific social groups, in particular the way in which it facilitated a govern 'mentality' through the creation of specialist knowledge in the form of experts (e.g., doctors, health professionals, librarians, talk show hosts) and institutions (e.g. hospitals, gyms, libraries, talk show programmes), whose authority leads them to control the function and responsibility of governmentality and in effect the regulation of human 'subjects' and social relationships.

Given Foucault's assertion that *contra* liberalism freedom and power are intractably mixed means that his ideas on governmentality have a particular resonance for leisure scholars. A good contemporary application of governmentality in leisure studies is Simone Fullagar's (2002) research which explores how freedom and power operate in relation to leisure and life-style choices in Australian health policy. Fullagar's basic thesis is that physical leisure activities (e.g., sport, aerobics, gym work) need to 'be understood as political in the sense that

they are neoliberal practices implicated in the everyday exercise of power over the self', and also analysed by leisure scholars to explore the ways whereby they are used to promote 'specific individual leisure practices via health policy discourses [as] a means through which neoliberal rule is exercised over population groups' (2002: 69–70).

Tony Blackshaw

Associated Concepts Deviance; Discursive Formations; Individualization; Foucault; Social Control; Surveillance.

H

HABITUS, FIELD AND CAPITAL

Bourdieu's social theory of distinction is an explicit attempt to understand the nature of social class and social class divisions in a complex world where production has largely given way to consumption. Essentially, he offers a treatise on taste. For Bourdieu (1984) social class, like 'race', ethnicity and gender, needs to be understood as much by its *perceived* existence as through its *material* existence in the classical Marxist sense. To make this synthesis he draws on a theoretical toolkit featuring the concepts of field, habitus and capital. Field theory has its roots in the work of Kurt Lewin, who used the idea to explore the extent to which an individual's activities and conduct are determined by the totality of their lived experiences. *Fields* for Pierre Bourdieu (1977) are the constituent parts of a society or 'social space' – and some of the examples he discussed include the contemporary fields of art, politics, sport and economics. Society, for Bourdieu, consisted of multiple interrelated fields, where social collectives (such as social classes) are understood as occupying various positions within these fields.

Fields reflect the various social, cultural, economic and political arenas of life, which form their own microcosms of power endowed with their own rules. Power struggles emerge in fields as a result of the belief of social actors that the capital(s) of the field are worth fighting for. Analogous to fluctuations in the stock market, the 'currency' or rate of exchange attached to particular capitals is vulnerable to change as this is continually contested.

For instance, social classes are understood in relation to their position within the political or economic fields. However, dominant positions within one field can carry a significant influence (and hence an increased position) within other fields – as capital in one field can be converted to capital in another. Each field will posses its own power relations, and within each there will be the dominant and the dominated, mechanisms of control and reproduction and struggles for power (Jenkins, 1992: 88). Power relations will also exist in-between fields, with some (such as the political field) holding a dominant power over lesser, weaker fields.

For Bourdieu, each field would have its own *habitus*. The term habitus was first introduced by the French sociologist (and nephew of Emile Durkheim) Marcel Mauss, and then developed further by Norbert Elias. However, it is a concept associated most closely with the work of Pierre Bourdieu. A habitus is similar to what other authors have described as the 'culture' of a particular group or society. However, key to Bourdieu's understanding of habitus is that this is embodied. Jenkins (1992: 74) writes that habitus is Latin to mean 'a habitual or typical condition, state or appearance, particularly of the body'. Bourdieu maintained much of this original meaning of the word, and a particular emphasis was placed upon the embodiment of habitus.

This, Jenkins (1992: 74) argues, is manifested in three ways. First, habitus only exists 'inside the heads of actors' – for instance, ways of behaving and modes of practice are learnt and internalized by social actors. Second, habitus only exists through the practice and actions of social actors – their ways of talking, moving, acting and behaviour. Third, the 'practical taxonomies' actors use to make sense of the world are all rooted in the body – such as male/female, hot/cold, up/down, which are all linked to our senses and physically located in relationship to our bodies.

This Bourdieu linked to the term *hexis*, which referred to individuals' deportment, their stance, grace and gestures. While habitus is located within the body it is not a form of innate human behaviour, but rather is a way of behaving and understanding the world that is taught to us through social interaction. Unlike theories of socialization, for Bourdieu habitus was achieved primarily through instruction rather than by experience. In this sense the habitus constitutes only an 'assumed world', captured as it is through the confines of the individual social actor's 'horizon of possibilities' (Lane, 2000: 194).

With respect to art, a 'sophisticated' observer will have been taught the mechanisms and language for decoding the symbolic meaning of an art form, through their social network, education and interaction with others. This, therefore, is crucial to our understanding of why certain social groups (such as social classes) possess the skills to 'understand' and interpret art (linked to their cultural capital), and others do not.

However, it is also important to recognize that the habitus is not a set inflexible culture, which remains static throughout people's lives. As Bourdieu and Wacquant (1992: 133) suggest, 'habitus is not the fate that some people read into it. Being the product of history, it is an open system of dispositions that is constantly subjected to experiences, and therefore constantly affected by them in a way that either reinforces or modifies its structure'.

The application of ideas of habitus, field and hexis to the study of leisure are numerous, and Bourdieu himself used these concepts to consider areas of leisure such as art and sport. However, beyond Bourdieu, other examples include Gary Robson's consideration of the habitus of Millwall FC football (soccer) supporters, or Winlow and Hall's (2006) book on the violent leisure lives of young people.

Garry Crawford and Tony Blackshaw

Associated Concepts Bourdieu; Class; Consumption; Cultural Capital; Culture; Distinction; Elias; Marxism; Power; Social Capital.

HAPPINESS

As the great adventurer, spy, librarian and philanderer, Casanova, is reported to have once said: 'If pleasure exists, and we can only enjoy it in life, then life is a happiness'. However, in its modern usage, the word more often tends to be used to refer to those activities by which individuals can express feelings of joy during occasions of pleasure. What this kind of understanding suggests is that happiness is something that can never be grasped intellectually but only experienced fleetingly: the ultimate happiness is temporary and intense. As Agnes Heller (1999) points out, though, this is a relatively recent understanding of happiness which emerged with the development of modern subjectivity. In modern societies the idea of happiness can no longer be understood as objective: we *feel* happy or unhappy. This echoes Wittgenstein's observation that the world of the happy person differs from the world of the unhappy person, because they each inhabit different worlds. Yet we should also recognize that if happiness is personality-dependent it is an entirely precarious business, and often dependent on our material circumstances, although most recent books written on the topic of happiness and material wealth have suggested the law of diminishing returns – that more material wealth actually means less happiness (see Layard, 2005).

It is clear that our leisure experiences also have an important relationship with happiness. We can see this at a most basic level in the way that the notion of happiness is used as a marketing tool in the leisure industry, for example, by pubs, bars and restaurants to designate particular periods of time – 'happy hours' – when they sell their merchandise at reduced prices. It is also apparent in the ways that theorists have tried to understand the relationship between leisure and happiness at a more discursive level. Terry Eagleton (2007) and Richard Sennett (2003) have both gone as far as to suggest that leisure activities (such as playing in a jazz band) can constitute the very meaning of life because they involve individuals coming together and engaging in a kind of collective endeavour in pursuit of happiness through the mutuality of love. What these thinkers tend to overlook, however, is that some kinds of happiness cannot be repeated or the exceptional feelings they provoke will diminish if repeated too often – but this is certainly not always the case.

Tony Blackshaw

Associated Concepts Aesthetics; Asceticism; Desire; Flow; Hedonism; Leisure Marketing; Pleasure.

HAWTHORNE EFFECT

(observations)

HEDONISM

From the Greek *hēdonē*, this term is generally used to describe an excessive indulgence in leisure pursuits, which by the words of the great novelist-cum-philosopher Milan Kundera are motivated by and confer 'an amoral tendency to a life of sensuality, if not of outright vice'. As Rojek points out, the ideas of narcissism and selfishness are closely related to this definition of hedonism, which in contemporary

leisure formations 'prioritizes the wants of the individual above the wants of the community and it associates commodity consumption with life-satisfaction' (1995: 114). There is, however, a second understanding, which by putting a moral value on leisure compulsions focuses its attention on the ethical dimensions of hedonistic behaviour to ask, on the one hand, what import can be defined from the pursuit of pleasure and, on the other, if pleasure is inherently good or at least involves the absence of suffering, does it mean that it should take precedence over pain (which is inherently bad)?

The latter of these ethical understandings takes pleasure to be a form of manumission which is not merely concerned with achieving direct bodily gratification but is also about the satisfaction of any kind of desire. But as all human beings know, pleasures often bring more unhappiness than happiness. What these more sophisticated understandings suggest is that hedonism is not something that can be simply written off as selfish, trivial or irresponsible, motivated *only* by leisure life-styles given to instant gratification, but when we take into account that it is an unavoidable feature of a world dominated by the work ethic, turbo capitalism and social control, and when all of this is examined empirically and carefully, such tacit assumptions might be called into question.

Tony Blackshaw

Associated Concepts Consumption; Desire; Dionysian Leisure; Happiness; 'Into', the; Pleasure; Postmodernism; Work Ethic.

HEGEMONIC MASCULINITY

(masculinity and masculinities)

HEGEMONY

Hegemony refers to the authority of one group over others, and as a concept is used to explain how this domination is maintained and legitimated. Crucially, hegemonic domination is a two-way process of struggle and negotiation and often involves contradictions, thus hegemonic control is never total nor complete. The most famous (and most commonly cited) source on hegemony is the Sardinian writer and political activist Antonio Gramsci. For Gramsci, the state rules through a process of coercion (e.g., force, or the threat of it) and hegemony. Here, hegemony is understood as sociopolitical power, which helps ensure 'spontaneous' or 'natural' consent. This is obtained through ideological control, where the dominant ideological ideas become promoted as 'commonsense', neutral and natural explanations. Hence the state rules through consent, but it is a false consent which has been engineered through promoting the values and ideology of the dominant group.

In contemporary society the mass media play a key role in maintaining hegemonic domination, by prompting dominant ideological values, resolving societal tensions, and constructing a sense of shared identity and common interest. One of the most famous applications of the work of Antonio Gramsci on hegemony has been the work of the Birmingham School of authors such as Stuart Hall. For instance, in 1978 Hall and his colleagues argued that a 'moral panic' was created in the British mass media of the 1970s, which saw 'black muggers' as a 'folk devil' (Cohen, 1972) and vilified in the British press. This folk devil not only unites people against a common enemy, but also allows the state to introduce new and tighter social controls which can then be applied to the whole population (and not just the perceived 'wrongdoers'). Similarly, Clarke and Critcher (1985) have argued how the political regulation of leisure allows popular activities (such as football) to be controlled and commercialized, by using these as vehicles to promote the dominant ideological values at the same time as a source of capitalist profit. Furthermore, Harris (1982) has discussed how football can be used to resolve national tensions (such as between North and South) and also to act as a means of uniting the nation (such as when watching international football).

However, hegemony still constitutes a zero-sum linear theorization of power, where this is largely understood as existing within the hands of certain individuals or organizations which are accepted, negotiated or resisted by weaker individuals or agencies. More contemporary theorizations of power, such as is found in the work of Michel Foucault on discursive formations, however, see power as much more fluid and multidirectional, and operating through knowledge rather than against people per se.

Garry Crawford

Associated Concepts Birmingham School; Discursive Formations; False Consciousness; Ideology; Marxism; Mass Media; Power; Social Control.

HERITAGE

Since the 1970s there has been a significant 'heritage boom' in Britain, resulting in a vast expansion of sites representing the past, including museums, open-air museums and heritage centres. This interest in heritage is also apparent on a more global scale. The United Nations Educational, Scientific and Cultural Organization (UNESCO) has a World Heritage mission to ensure the protection of natural and cultural heritage across the world. Alongside this there has been an expansion in academic and more journalistic writing on heritage (Hewison, 1987; McCrone et al., 1995; Urry, 2002; Wright, 1985, 1989).

Yet heritage is a difficult, slippery and value-laden term, the definition of which is contested. Dictionary definitions revolve around ideas of the past, inheritance, history, historic and natural sites, tradition and the idea of something being transmitted from the past. We can conceptualize these into tangible (physical assets) and intangible (culture, people, tradition) forms of heritage. We can think of heritage as located in the cultural arena with material forms, such as monuments, historical or architectural remains and artefacts on display in museums, or with immaterial forms, such as philosophy, traditions, the arts, the celebration of great events, historical personalities, distinctive ways of life, education, literature, folklore, and so on. We can also conceive of heritage in a natural context, for example in the guise of gardens, landscapes, national parks, wilderness, mountains, and rivers. However, even these have a cultural component (Nuryanti, 1996).

According to the Department of Culture, Media and Sport (DCMS), heritage can be defined as 'properties and artefacts of cultural importance handed down from the past'. Such a definition assumes that there is a 'national heritage' which needs conserving for present and future generations. Inherent within this 'official' definition are ideas of unity, conservatism and nationhood. This version of heritage is often equated with nostalgia. The invocation of nostalgia is seen as a key, even a defining, characteristic of many heritage sites, where a sanitized version of the past is presented giving a 'rosy-glow' to history. It could be suggested that heritage is shaped by social, cultural and economic forces, and that in a consumer society for example, heritage increasingly takes the form that is required for it to be consumed as a cultural product (McCrone et al., 1995; Urry, 2002). Indeed, commentators such as Hewison (1987) and Wright (1989) claim that heritage has become a commodity, one that has diminished our critical capacity for understanding the past: history has therefore been turned into heritage.

However, these accounts of heritage take little note of the bedrock of popular support it receives or the different forms of heritage offered to the public gaze, the different historical narratives that are now available for consumption. Consider for example the growth and rise in popularity of museums representing the heritage of football clubs. Heritage sites do vary in their style, content and ability to offer a less 'sanitized' version of the past. Hence, it is important to recognize the diversity and heterogeneity of heritage-based sites, and the contested nature of the term (Bagnall, 1996).

Gaynor Bagnall

Associated Concepts Aesthetics; Commodity Fetishism; Disneyization; Flâneurs, Flâneurie and Psychogeography; Leisure; McDonaldization; Non-Place; Nostalgia; Theming; Tourism.

HOBBIES

A hobby is a leisure activity that is engaged in most commonly for pleasure and relaxation, but as Stebbins (1992: 10) highlights, unlike the multitude of other leisure activities that individuals regularly engage in, a hobby is a 'serious ... and committed ... specialized pursuit beyond one's occupation' that is 'durable'. Hence, hobbyists are usually quite dedicated to their particular interest and this interest will commonally persist over (sometimes a considerable) period of time. However, Stebbins also suggests that hobbies are not part of a 'professional–amateur–public' (PAP) system. In other words, hobbies are defined by their distinction from other pastimes that have become substantially professionalized (such as football) as monetary interest will always be (at best) secondary for hobbyists.

In particular, Stebbins (1992) identifies four different types of hobbyists: 'collectors' (e.g., stamp or cigarette card collectors); 'activity participants' (e.g., fishing or dancing); 'makers' and 'tinkers' (e.g., model builders, or even tropical fish keepers); and 'players' (e.g., role-players, computer gamers or target shooters).

Though the typical image of a hobbyist is of a collector amassing a sizable collection of items that they will never part with, hobbies should not only be seen as a process of consumption but can also involve significant acts of production. For instance, many hobbies are primarily about production. This can take the form of model building for its own pleasure, but within some subcultures hobbyist production can become semi-professional, such as the example of producers of fanzines, clothing and music as highlighted in Hodkinson's (2002) discussion of the goth scene in the UK.

In particular, and contrary to Stebbins' insistence that monetary gain will always be of secondary importance for hobbyists, Gelber (1992) identifies three forms of collecting which are motivated, to varying degrees, by monetary gain. The first is a 'merchant' model, where collectors buy, trade and sell items out of a desire to increase/improve their own collection. Second, 'investors' will build up a collection over a long period of time as an investment, almost by way of a life insurance policy, which they will then seek to 'cash in' at some point. Third, 'speculators' gain no direct pleasure from building up a collection, but instead regularly buy and sell items purely to make a profit.

Bishop and Hogget's (1986) consideration of hobbies moved away from the individual towards an emphasis on the importance of group membership. In particular, they emphasized that for many hobbyists it is often the opportunity to make friends and meet people through their hobby that is of primary importance, and thus the activity itself may be secondary (Bishop and Hogget, 1986: 33). This image of hobbyists would tie into that highlighted in Maffesoli's 'neo-tribes', in which contemporary (and often temporary) groupings are joined primarily out of searching and desiring to belong.

Garry Crawford

Associated Concepts Amateur and Amateurism; Authenticity; Casual/Serious Leisure; Consumption; Crafts and Craftsmanship; Digital Gaming; Fanzines; Leisure as a Value-Sphere; Subcultures; Neo-Tribes.

HOGGART, RICHARD (1918–)

Hoggart was born into a working-class family in Leeds. On the death of his mother at 'seven or eight' years of age, he went to live with his 'grandma' in a small through terrace house in Newport Street in Hunslet. Hoggart received his formative education at Jack Lane Elementary School, where he failed the eleven plus examination because of the maths paper that 'floored' him. Hoggart's headteacher Mr Harrison had been counting on him to be the first boy from Jack Lane to gain a scholarship to Cockburn, the local grammar school, and he immediately went down to the offices of the City of Leeds Education Authority, Hoggart's essays in hand, and came back with a place for his young protégé. To paraphrase Hoggart, once he was at Cockburn and on 'the prescribed route', the successive steps, since he worked hard, seemed to follow one another with near inevitability. He left Cockburn for Leeds University and after graduating from there was employed in the Adult Education Department at Hull. After a spell at the University of Leicester he became Professor of Modern English Literature at Birmingham University, where he founded the Centre for Contemporary Cultural Studies.

Tracing Hoggart's biography in this way alerts us to one of his most enduring gifts, which is his recognition that we need to grasp the contingency that small things, like saying or not saying the right things, or making the right gesture or not making the right gesture, can send a life down a different path. It happens all the time: we rarely notice it, but we should. It is with such a heartfelt and empathetic attention to the minutiae of everyday life that Hoggart will most be remembered, especially his classic study *The Uses of Literacy* which recollects a vision of working-class community life in the forty years after the First World War. Today his work might read as somewhat out of date – ham teas, evenings out at the pub and the pictures, charabanc trips to the seaside – but his legacy is a formidable one. Indeed, as an examination of the quotidian, Hoggart's books offer a tantalizing territory for leisure studies which has not been mined for a number of years. Few current studies have the ambition or the confidence for reviving the illusions of revealing the real to which Hoggart once aspired. This is a shame because, as reading him reminds us, the heart of leisure studies should be the culture and everyday lives of men, women and children, not the grandeur of its conceptions, but the subtle and inventive ways in which people can realize their leisure lives.

Tony Blackshaw

Associated Concepts Birmingham School; Culture; Ethnography; Everyday Life; Nostalgia.

HOUSEHOLD PRODUCTION FUNCTION APPROACH, THE

Developed in the 1960s, Becker's approach uses a household production function, which demonstrates that any activity (Q) undertaken by households or individuals, involves inputs of market goods (M) and time (T). He terms these activities 'composite commodities'. Each composite commodity involves different inputs of M and T, so that when the prices of M and T alter, the effect of consumption of different activities is varied. In the long run, as real wages increase, the price of T rises relative to the price of M: T is a finite input to household production, whereas M can be continually expanded. A change in the relative prices of M + T cause consumption patterns to change.

Substitution and income effects operate to give a change in the optimum consumption pattern. As the relative prices of T and M change, household production and consumption also changes to a different package of time and goods-intensive commodities. Basically this means that as the prices of time and goods change, people will alter what they buy and how they use their time. If wage rates increase, the substitution effect dominates and so there is a fall in consumption of time-intensive commodities. As time becomes relatively scarcer and more expensive, household production and consumption of goods-intensive activities will increase.

For leisure we can see that this model suggests that the greater goods-intensity in activities is a rational household decision, because rising wage rates make time more expensive relative to goods. The time-intensity of particular leisure activities is often not reducible, (e.g., playing or watching football). Additionally, the evidence suggests that as incomes rise participation rises more than proportionately. Therefore, we can suggest that participation in leisure will continue to increase despite the rising relative scarcity and value of time.

This approach provides an alternative model of consumer demand for leisure. It includes not only the demand functions for activities but also generates a derived demand for facilities, travel and recreation goods. It is a hierarchical demand model, with the demand for the leisure activity playing the role of the parent demand function and the time input playing a crucial role in the analysis. This approach has been adapted further by Grossman (1972), whose demand for health model has direct implications for the demand for sport.

Rob Wilson

Associated Concepts Budgeting; Cost Accounting; Deadweight Expenditure; Multiplier Analysis; Profit and Utility Maximization; Public and Private Goods.

HUIZINGA, JOHAN (1872–1945)

(play)

HUMAN RESOURCE MANAGEMENT

While this is a relatively new phenomenon, the idea of human resource management (HRM) has caused debate among theorists since its first appearance in the early 1980s. Consequently it is a concept where it is difficult to find a common definition. As a starting point, however, Bratton and Gold (1994) make a useful contribution, suggesting that HRM is part of a management process that specializes in the management of people. They also make the key point that employees are the backbone of any organization, veritably a human resource that will help it achieve a competitive advantage, as well as help managers to meet efficiency and equity objectives.

With these observations in mind, HRM seeks to develop a strategic approach to the management of people. Previously people management systems had centred on the welfare of employees and support to management in terms of recruitment, administration, training and industrial relations. The new strategy of HRM proposed a resource-focused approach which placed the emphasis on the employers' demands rather than the needs of employees. Thus the subjectivity around operationalizing a definitive version of HRM

exists due to the debate as to whether HRM is in fact a new paradigm or, as Armstrong (2003) believes, part of the continuing process of personnel management.

In terms of the leisure industries, HRM has been recognized and implemented through a variety of measures and with different levels of success. Many organizations will often still focus on personnel management as opposed to a more rounded strategy. As a service-sector industry this is not surprising since the associated spin-offs from a contented workforce will more often than not help the organization meet its wider operational objectives.

Rob Wilson

Associated Concepts Quality Systems; Training and Development and Appraisals.

IDENTITY

This is one of the most debated and complex concepts within the social sciences. Generally, identity, or more appropriately the idea of social identity, can be seen to refer to our sense of 'self', or 'who we are'. Where our sense of identity comes from relates closely to debates about structure and agency, and to what degree 'who we are' is determined by social structures (e.g., class and gender) and personal choices (i.e., who we choose to be).

For structuralists our identity is primarily defined by social forces. A good illustration of this is the work of Birmingham School authors (such as Hebdige, 1979) on youth subcultures, who see these groups (and the shared identity of their members) as the product of class relations. Hence, from this perspective, social structures shape social groupings, which in turn shape leisure and cultural interests.

Theorists aligned with symbolic interactionism (such as Mead, Becker and Goffman) see identity as both the outcome and a resource for social interactions. For instance, Mead suggests that our ideas of 'self' are developed through the use of significant symbols (such as language). Mead also suggests that symbols provide the basis by which individuals interact and give meaning to their social world. In order for interaction to take place, each person must interpret and understand the meanings and intentions of others. This is accomplished by the existence of common symbols and 'role-taking'. Role-taking involves imagining oneself in the position of the person you are interacting with – that is, imagining his or her role and position – this Mead refers to as 'the generalized other'. By adopting the role of the generalized other, the individual imagines how others would expect him or her to behave and adapts behaviour to fit. In other words, we understand our social situation and role by placing ourselves in the position of 'the other', and Mead argues that through this process of role-taking individuals will develop a concept of 'self'. This, Mead suggests, can be understood by making a distinction between what he refers to as the 'me' and the 'I'. The 'me' is the individual in a specific social role, while the 'I' is a sense of self as a whole. Hence, the 'I' is our self concept, which is built from the reactions of others, providing a stability and structure to identity.

However, poststructuralist and postmodern writers tend to emphasize the increasing fluidity in identity formation and maintenance. For instance, authors such as Zygmunt Bauman have argued that within our consumer society identities have become less stable and fixed as traditional markers, such as regional identity, social class and family, have become less certain. Also, in a fast-changing and liquid world, fixed identities have become less useful and fluid. For many poststructuralist and postmodern writers identity has then become based upon consumer and leisure choices, where it can be bought 'off the shelf' ready-made and discarded and replaced just as easily.

However, it is important to note that not everyone agrees with Bauman's arguments. For instance, Warde (1994, 1996) points out that our identities are not necessarily constructed simply by what we buy. Many consumer goods can be selected with little impact on an individual's identity, and other factors such as nationality, ethnicity, occupation, family and friendships continue to play important roles in shaping our identities. For example, Blackshaw (2003) illustrates the complexity of identities forged through enduring friendship in leisure in his book *Leisure Life*. Drawing on Ricoeur's hermeneutical philosophy, Blackshaw explores the dialectic of self and 'other' that constitutes what he calls the leisure life-world of 'the lads'.

For Ricoeur (1988) the idea of 'narrative identity' suggests the idea of a self as 'storied', made up of stories told by the person about themselves and their lives, stories told by others about them and wider social and cultural narratives. Each individual therefore develops a life narrative and a sense of who they are (their identity) through narratives. This then recognizes the temporal nature of identity, for, as with a never-ending story, this is always being constructed and developed and, hence, is ever-changing. It also overcomes the dualism of fiction and history, recognizing that our own personal narrative identities are a construct of both of these. Likewise, narrative identity mediates both 'sameness' and 'selfhood', locating individuals within a wider community and cultural narrative, but identifying the individual's specific location and personal narrative within this.

Garry Crawford

Associated Concepts Bauman; Birmingham School; Class; Consumer Society; Consumption; Structure and Agency; Subcultures; Symbolic Interactionism.

IDEOLOGY

Ideology is a shared belief system, or a way of looking at and understanding things. The origins of the term 'ideology' can be traced back to Antoine Destutt de Tracy in eighteenth-century revolutionary France, who used this to describe a 'science of ideas' which, drawing on the political, economic and social sciences, would replace theology and provide a universal understanding of human behaviour. Though Tracy saw ideology as a neutral scientific tool, many have pointed to the political connotations of ideology. Probably the most famous of these is the work of Marx, who along with Engels offered a critique of ideology, most notably in *The German Ideology* (1965 [1845]). In particular Marx and Engels argued that 'the ruling ideas are the ideas of the ruling classes'.

This suggests that the dominant ideology within a society will be that of the ruling classes, which not only favours this elite but is also used to legitimate their dominant social position. These ideas on 'dominant ideology' have been developed by numerous neo-Marxist writers, such as Althusser (1969), Gramsci (1971) and Habermas (1976). The dominant ideology thesis, though often diverse and complex, is summarized by Abercrombie et al. (1980: 2) as the idea that the dominant class which controls the means of material production also controls the means of mental production and, through its control of ideological production, this dominant class is therefore able to supervise the construction of a set of coherent beliefs.

The Marxist (and neo-Marxist) critique of dominant ideology therefore highlights the role of ideology in social power relations. In particular, Gramsci (1971) locates his critique of dominant ideology within a consideration of hegemony. This is the domination of one social group over others, but crucially this is a legitimated and negotiated process and ideology plays a key role in this. Specifically, this version of the dominant ideology thesis found particular favour in the 1970s and 1980s with Birmingham School writers such as Stuart Hall and his colleagues, who considered the role the mass media played in maintaining the hegemonic domination of the ruling classes by conveying dominant ideological messages and creating 'folk devils'.

However, Mannheim (1936) highlighted that every social theory is potentially an 'ideology', as each offers their own set of social beliefs and a 'true' understanding of the world and human behaviour. Hence, a number of authors (e.g., Abercrombie et al., 1980) have pointed to the lack of relevance and importance of ideology within contemporary debates. In particular, poststructuralism and postmodernism have proclaimed the futility of trying to find one 'true' reality (and ideology) as Marxism does, as it is better to recognize that multiple belief systems will always exist, and it is therefore better to understand these as competing discourses or discursive formations.

Garry Crawford

Associated Concepts Discursive Formations; False Consciousness; Folk Devils and Moral Panics; Hegemony; Marxism; Power; Religion.

INCOME–LEISURE TIME TRADE-OFF AND TIME DATING

Any time spent playing or consuming leisure means losing potential earnings. In this respect, the opportunity cost or price of engaging in leisure is foregone earnings. The more someone works, the less leisure time they will have. However, there will eventually come a point when the additional income earned from an additional hour at work is not sufficient to compensate for the loss of another hour of leisure time. At some point an individual will reach a point of optimum trade-off. This is the moment where the subjective valuation of an hour of leisure time is equal to the hourly wage rate. Working longer hours would then mean that consumers were irrationally choosing to trade an hour of leisure time for an income that was less than their valuation of that hour of leisure time. This choice mechanism is used in economics to analyse individuals' decisions concerning whether or not to work; whether to work part- or full-time;

whether to work more hours in the form of overtime; and whether to take a second job (moonlighting).

One particular qualitative constraint on leisure choices is the fixed time of day, week and year that many activities are limited to. This is called time dating. Most leisure activities are undertaken by the majority of people at specific times (e.g., many sports have their own seasons). As a result, all or most leisure activities and sports will display a peak demand at certain times. For many outdoor leisure activities, time dating will lead to demand peaks in the evenings and weekends. If people have the opportunity to work at these times, they will often get paid overtime, and so they are willing to forego their leisure time.

Rob Wilson

Associated Concepts Schor.

INDIVIDUALIZATION

This term has come to categorize the two phases of life, experience and perception, reflected respectively in modernity (or solid modernity) and postmodernity (or liquid modernity). It is not clear whether Foucault ever read Elias, but it appears to have been Elias' (1991 [1939]) crucial observation that it is the interdependency between society shaping individuals and individuals forming their own society out of their life (including their work and leisure pursuits) that is the central feature of the modern 'society of individuals', which led him to suggest that individualization emerged once human beings began (to paraphrase Foucault) to exist within themselves, inside the shell of their heads, inside the armature of their limbs, and in the whole structure of their physiology – when they began to exist at the centre of their own labour, the principles of which now governed them and the products of which would now elude them (Foucault, 1986: 318). What Foucault is describing here is the emergence of the Enlightenment, otherwise known as the age of modern reason and justice, which brought with it a rational commitment to robust individualism and the right to freedom from religion and the state. In relation to understanding modern leisure, what this means is that even if a society attempts to regulate the kinds of leisure activities that can be pursued, it has little hope of precluding the discovery by individuals of those leisure activities which they individually think can best be explored.

What Foucault was also suggesting was that casting society's members as individuals is the trademark of modernity. As Bauman (2002) points out, though, this casting was not to be a once in a lifetime act and in a modern society the activity of individualization is something that has to be re-enacted on a daily basis. In Lash's (2002) view, the major difference between solid modern and liquid modern individualization is that the former is *reflective*, mirroring the underlying tensions between individual agency and the structural determinants of a modern society built on differences such as social class, gender, ethnicity and age. Leisure subcultures are examples of the way in which reflective individualization works, especially in relation to particular style groups, such as the Teddy boys, Mods and Skinheads, as they emerged respectively in the 1950s, 1960s and 1970s. With the emergence of postmodernity or liquid modernity, however, individualization has become *reflexive*. As Lash points out, reflexes are indeterminate and immediate and as a consequence of liquid modern change reflexive individuals are those individuals who have to cope with living in an uncertain, speeded-up world, which demands quick decision making. Neotribes, otherwise known as the 'little masses' of the uncertain and fragmenting consumer society, are good examples of this reflexive individualization in action.

Bauman argued that with the processes of change associated with liquid modernity, individualization ends up transforming human identity from a 'given' into a 'task'. While being

well aware of Adorno's crucial observation that 'the illusory importance and autonomy of private life conceals the fact that private life drags on only as an appendage of the social process', Bauman insists that those living in an individualizing, liquid modern world are always on the verge of being struck by lightning: you never know where or when it is going to strike, only that is has happened. What he also insists is that getting struck by lightning is more common than people are prepared to imagine. Consequently, what this suggests is that liquid modern identities, through which nearly everyone reveals themselves in the leisure forms that they choose, are liable to be protean and palimpsest, sometimes confused, sometimes desperate for attention, but always self-absorbed and total in their devotion to self-authorship. In the event, it makes sense to see liquid modern men and women as shape-shifters whose individualized identities do not lie within them, so much as in the current form they assume, at any particular moment, and in their ability to metamorphose, while defying any tacit expectations about differences with respect to social class, ethnicity or even gender.

Tony Blackshaw

Associated Concepts   Bauman; Dromology and Speed; Elias; Foucault; Identity; Liquid Modernity;   Modernity;   Neo-Tribes; Performativity; Postmodernity; Subcultures.

INTERTEXTUALITY

Intertextuality is often used (in a strict sense) to refer to the intersection and cross-referencing that exist between texts. Intertextuality is a component of many older media forms such as novels, television and radio, where the understanding or 'decoding' of any one text may often refer to, or even require, the understanding of another text or texts. For example, to fully understand and appreciate the *Scream* (1996, 1997, 2000) trilogy of films, it is important to have an understanding of other horror films (texts). Similarly, to understand the film parodies of this, *Scary Movie* and its sequels (2000, 2001, 2003, 2006) it is necessary to have at least a rudimentary knowledge of *Scream* as well as the multiple other movie narratives and themes they draw on. However, intertextuality is particularly apparent in new forms of media, (such as digital gaming) which frequently draw on the narrative of, or make reference to, other texts. For example, many digital games are based on film or television narratives, such as those taken from *The Simpsons*, *Star Wars* or *Star Trek*. However, significantly the 'texts' which most sport-related games draw on are 'real' rather than fictional sports and teams.

Yet beyond this more 'strict' use of the term intertextuality the concept has also been employed in a fundamental/wider sense. In particular, the ideas of Mikhail Bakhtin that any text contains 'multiple voices' within it have been developed by Julia Kristeva in relation to intertextuality. Here, Kristeva suggests that any text can be analysed in terms of the other texts that it has absorbed and transformed. This then relates to the ideas of Roland Barthes and others, who would assert the 'death of the author' as all texts are constructed from a 'mosaic of citations' (Kristeva, 1969), where each text quotes, borrows, echoes, alludes to, parodies and pastiches other texts.

Garry Crawford

Associated Concepts Carnivalesque; Communication; Deconstruction; Digital Gaming; Discursive Formations; Mass Media; Semiotics.

INTERVIEWS

An interview is a social interaction between people based around the process of asking and answering questions. Interviews are probably the most commonly used form of research method in the social sciences (including leisure studies). While observations can help uncover how groups or individuals behave and questionnaires can reveal demographic and basic attitudinal information, it is via interviewing that most social and leisure research is undertaken, as it is this that brings us closest to an understanding of people's meanings and their attitudes towards their own and others' social lives.

Most interviews are usually one-to-one, but can involve an interviewer speaking to more than one person, though beyond two or three interviewees this then is usually classed as a focus group interview. Interviews can also sometimes involve multiple interviewers (such as an interview panel in a job interview). However, interviews need not be in person and can take place via telephone or the internet, and these forms of 'mediated' interview have both their individual advantages and disadvantages. Most interviewing involves the gathering of qualitative data, but can take a number of forms, usually categorized as *structured*, *semi-structured* and *unstructured* interviews. Structured interviews (as the name suggests) consist of a more formally organized interview, where the researcher will ask each interviewee exactly the same questions, worded in the same way and in the same order each time. This is typically done as it helps to increase the reliability of the interview process. Semi-structured interviews introduce some flexibility into the interview process, where the interviewer may vary the wording or ordering of questions. Unstructured (or *non-standardized*) interviews involve an even less formal structure and usually consist of the interviewer having a list of topics or subjects that he or she can more freely discuss with the interviewee (rather than sticking to a rigid Q&A-style format).

However, when undertaking most research, interviews will tend to vary in style and structure, with most involving varying degrees of structure and fluidity within them. In particular, Bell (1993: 51) suggests that the major advantage of the interview is 'its adaptability' where a 'skilful interviewer can follow up ideas, probe responses and investigate motives and feelings, which a questionnaire can never do'. Interviews specifically allow the interviewer to prompt or probe interviewees, following up answers or specific lines of questioning and enquiry which would not be possible with questionnaires or observations.

In any research process it is important for the researcher to consider their influence upon the research, but this is particularly important in interviews, where they can have a very significant effect on what the interviewer says or does not say. Interviewers must be aware of not 'leading' interviewees into providing certain desired answers, either via leading or biased questions, or simply through approving or disapproving body language or tones of voice.

Garry Crawford

Associated Concepts Focus groups, Method-ology; Observation; Qualitative Research; Questionnaires; Sampling.

'INTO', THE

The concept of the 'into' does not permit precise definition. It was developed by Jean Baudrillard and is tied to his penetrating critique of the 'fatal strategies' of the consumer society in which being 'into' leisure or 'into' sport is not only a manifestation of a narcissistic self-love of the body and a dedication to the preservation of youth, but it is also something much more than that as well. Implicit (if not explicit) to Baudrillard's thesis of the 'into' is the idea that not only do most of us today feel an inner emptiness in our lives, and that as such we are often given to existential self-doubt, but that the body is a depiction of the dance we do with our own transience, and the accommodations we make with ourselves in order to just get through the day. In this sense, we believe that

being 'into' the body will operate almost to protect us against the predictable fatefulness of death. The upshot of this is that the way we have become phobically concerned with the body prefigures the way in which it will be made up in the 'funeral parlour on our death': 'where it will be given a smile that is really "into" death'.

The point is not to be, nor even to have, a fit body, but to be 'into' your own body, 'into' your sexuality, 'into' your desire. With the hedonism of the 'into, the body is a 'scenario'; the curious 'hygienist threnody' (lamentation for the dead) devoted to it runs through innumerable fitness centres and gyms, bearing witness to a mass individualist asexual obsession. As Baudrillard suggests, 'this is how it is with bodybuilding: you get into your body as you would into a suit of nerve and muscle. The body is not muscular, but muscled. It is the same with the brain and with social relations of exchanges: bodybuilding, brainstorming, word-processing' (quoted in Horrocks, 1999: 54). A similar scenario surrounds joggers and jogging: 'you can stop a horse that is bolting. You do not stop a jogger who is jogging. Foaming at the mouth, his mind riveted on the inner count down to the moment when he will achieve a higher plain of consciousness, he is not to be stopped ... Jogging is a form of self-torture ... Like dieting, bodybuilding and so many other sports, jogging is a new form of voluntary servitude (it is also a new form of adultery)' (Baudrillard, 1989: 37–8).

Consequently, our expenditure of energy is no longer related to work but to leisure, to 'gymtime', where the virtually disabled can work off 'stress' in bodybuilding, step classes or other novel exercise regimes. In the gym, as we work out, the video screens dominate. And everyone is aware of this. According to Baudrillard, no performance can be without its control screen: what he describes as the New International Hygienic Order wants to be seen and it is 'everywhere jogging or walking, phobically concerned with bodies, self-maximization and self-inflicted servitude ... There are no more heights – just dangerous sports' (Horrocks, 1999: 55–6).

Baudrillard is also concerned here with a contemporary obsession with risk which is symptomatic of the contemporary world. First, material risk is *individualized* as the responsibility of the nation state to its populace diminishes while at the same time the global network of capital and commodities continues to grow independent of international borders. Second, 'new' risks abound. The contemporary world is the age of global warming, terrorism, HIV and AIDS, CJD, BSE, SARS, to name but a few 'new' risks. These risks take on an added dimension when we take into account the central importance of body-cultivation discussed above, which means that now we not only pay more attention to the body but also to anything that it is consumed by or that comes into contact with it. What Bauman (1994: 154) calls the liquid modern 'horror of disease and toxic substances that [may vandalize the individual] by entering the body or touching the skin'.

These observations notwithstanding, Baudrillard takes Bauman's observation one step further, by suggesting that, by being predestined to exact both physical and symbolic violence on the self, the individual invents extreme *risks* rather than face destiny and in the process fritters him or herself away in an 'exhaustion of possibilities'.

Tony Blackshaw

Associated Concepts Baudrillard; Deviance; Edgework; Extreme Leisure; Hedonism; Individualization; Leisure Bodies; Nostalgia; Postmodernism; Risk Management; Risk Society; Social Control; Surveillance; Work Ethic

INVISIBLE EXPORTS

In addition to direct economic impacts there is also a case to be made for the relevance of invisible exports. The Leisure Industries Research Centre (now the Sport Industry Research Centre) at Sheffield Hallam University (1998) defines invisible exports as the additional expenditure attributable to foreign residents attending a sport event. The nature of this expenditure is such that a contribution is made to the host country's Gross Domestic Product (GDP), whereas domestic spending tends to divert expenditure from one area to another with the resultant effect being no change in GDP. As the LIRC's research demonstrates, the value of invisible exports was clearly in evidence at the 1998 European Short Course Swimming Championships, where 66 per cent of the total additional expenditure was in the form of invisible exports. Consequently, the LIRC suggested that the argument for prioritizing international events is well founded as they lead to an influx of visitors and clear economic benefits.

Rob Wilson

Associated Concepts Economic Benefit of Sport Events; Economic Impact of Sport Events; Event Management.

INVOLVEMENT AND DETACHMENT

In the context of carrying out social research from a figurational perspective, the relationship between these two terms refers to the process of interdependence between researchers and their respondents (see Rojek, 1986, for a fuller discussion). In relation to the research process more generally, it also refers to the frequently perceived need for some element of detachment. Obviously all social research involves some kind of involvement – or an attempt at involvement – with others. In this way just as complete detachment is inconceivable, so is any attempt to remain completely objective. Yet researchers will often feel that they need to detach themselves from the field in order to make their 'data' intelligible, and others may attempt to detach themselves simply to make the whole process manageable.

In their research with football ticket touts, Sugden and Tomlinson suggested a gonzo research approach, which enables the researcher to get 'close to the centre of the action without ever being totally incorporated within it ... to be part of the scene ... *at the same time* being semi-detached from that experience' (1999: 390). Supportive of Giddens, they seem to be suggesting that the fusion between the knower and the known in the research process is never complete and in every epistemological relation there is and should always be some element of detachment. This stance assumes the modern individual perceives that he or she is the centre of the social world and external subjects and objects are taken into the self to be constituted reflexively in terms of that individual's cognitive (and ethical) understanding. Indeed, for Giddens it is this existential contradiction that marks off individuals in modernity from their traditional counterparts: modern men and women reflexively understand themselves as being both part of and yet detached from the social world of others.

As Blackshaw and Crabbe (2004) suggest in their retheorization of 'deviance' in sport, the best that researchers can do in attempting to detach themselves practically is to try to contemplate the field of research from an *ironic* distance. After all, an *ironic* distance is the best researchers can achieve, because, as Foucault insists, in reality there is no magical 'buffer zone' between the knower and the known: just as we cannot isolate any part of the world from any other part, we cannot isolate ourselves from the world. However, in approaching the issue of involvement and detachment pragmatically to achieve an *ironic* distance between themselves and the field, social researchers can still open themselves up to the possibility of an awareness of some of the contingencies and ambivalences within the research process. As Blackshaw and Crabbe point out, this is a reflexive task which cannot and should never be avoided.

Tony Blackshaw

Associated Concepts Elias; Figurations/Figurationalism; Foucault; Giddens; Methodology; Postmodernism.

J, K, L

LEISURE

There are three distinct but not unrelated etymological sources of modern understandings of leisure. There is the more obvious old French term *leisir*, itself derived from the Latin root *licēre*. *Licēre* is especially interesting because in its duality it reveals that the idea of leisure abounds with ambivalence: on the one hand it relates to freedom but on the other it is also a term which, as its root suggests, signifies permission or license. There is also a sense of ambivalence reflected in the distinction between the two other etymological sources, both of which are less noticeably related to the modern word. The first of these is the term *ōtiōsus*, meaning 'leisured'. *Ōtiōsus* is a transfiguration of the older Latin term *ōtium* which until the eighteenth century simply meant leisure. From this historical juncture, however, *ōtium* and its derivatives become synonymous with leisure time which may or may not be used for self-improvement. This shift in meaning was no doubt a reflection of changing social and cultural attitudes towards free time and work in light of the Reformation in Western Christianity and the development of modern capitalism (see Work Ethic). The other is the Greek term *skholē*, which at its most basic level of understanding simply means to be free from obligation. Like *licēre*, however, *skholē* has a more complex meaning and was considered by the Greeks to be an ideal state guided by the appreciation of moderation. In this sense *skholē* was an elitist theorization that in its rebuke to the *ōtiose* life considered leisure to be a serious business – both a privileged and studious occupation – which was suggestive of a restrictive economy of pleasure. As this observation suggests, if seriousness was a vital aspect of *skholē* what it also contained was the tacit acknowledgment of an affiliation between leisure and work.

In modern social thought the significance of work for understanding leisure has loomed large. In his *Theory of the Leisure Class* (1934 [1899]), Thorstein Veblen established the notion of leisure as a means of conspicuous consumption for those who had no need to work and who used it as means of acquiring reputability and status. In their neo-Marxist account of leisure in industrializing Britain, Clarke and Critcher (1985) suggest that for the majority of working-class people at this time leisure did not exist in the modern sense and 'work and leisure intermingled'. The public house was the wellspring of most popular working-class pastimes which were often accompanied with overt violence and brutality as well as drink. But by the early to mid-1800s the kinds of leisure forms that popular culture had traditionally promoted were increasingly seen through the eyes of establishment figures as problematic, signifying a social class struggle over leisure. In explaining this change in outlook scholars have identified two major factors: on the one hand, the emergence of a civilizing trend (Elias, 1994) in relations between state formation and changes in individual conduct, including new forms of morality and controlled, ordered and self-improving leisure forms (Cunningham, 1980) and, on the other, the suppression of the threat posed by extant forms of popular culture to the emergence of clock-time paid work.

What could not have been anticipated at this time was what would (from the 1900s onwards) become a mass consumer market for leisure and with it the idea of leisure as cultural competition for *distinction* between different status groups across the social spectrum (Bourdieu, 1984). Writing from a neo-Marxist perspective, Herbert Marcuse described such practices as the requirement of capitalism 'to promote consumerism and the inculcation of false needs and wants, of ever new desires, so we will keep working for the money to *buy* more, rather than stop working in order that we may *do* more. The result, for Marcuse, is that work and leisure remain alienated because they are restricted, through consumer culture, to false necessity' (Slater, 1998: 400).

Notwithstanding these critical observations, as leisure studies came to be established as a serious area of academic study in the 1970s some theorists continued to understand the concept as a residual category of time left over from other obligations – no more or no less than a domesticated functionalist understanding of *skholē*. In continuing with the theme of work, Parker's (1983) functionalist analysis suggested that, although work takes up only a portion of people's lives, their leisure activities nonetheless tend to be conditioned by the various factors associated with the ways in which the work that they do is structured, to the extent that their leisure tends to be opposite, neutral to, or an extension of that work.

From the late 1970s feminist scholarship began to expose the tendency of 'malestream' leisure studies to overlook the ways in which the structural and everyday features of patriarchal capitalist societies combined to prevent women from having the same freedoms as men and how this results in the structuration of their opportunities for leisure being for the most part circumscribed by their gender. Feminist scholarship revealed both the contingency and the multi-levelled ways in which women's leisure is constrained, not only directly due to the narrow range of activity options open to them but also because of the temporal, spatial, economic, ideological, sociopsychological factors involved, as well as the influence in this process of the categories of social class, 'race' and ethnicity and familial and other prescribed gender roles (see, for example, Deem, 1986).

Also, in response to Parker, other scholars suggested that leisure activities are not necessarily prescribed by the demands of work, but instead are often less defined and are expected by individuals to reflect their own individual choices and tastes. For example, Csikszentmihalyi (1974) argued that the definitive illustration of leisure of this kind is that characterized by flow, or the existential experience of total involvement in leisure activities, freely chosen, which are self-rewarding and contain an uncertainty of outcome that allows for individual creativity.

Most leisure scholars have avoided this elitist and individualist understanding of leisure and have developed some innovative analyses to uncover the inequalities of class, gender, ethnicity, age and ability which tend to establish and limit opportunities for leisure. This has spawned a range of empirical studies, but some of the best theoretical work on leisure has come from Chris Rojek. His *Capitalism and Leisure Theory* (1985) helped to establish leisure studies as a serious area of academic study, while his *Decentring Leisure* (1995) provided a radical critique suggestive of a postmodern theory of leisure which recognizes that if human lives today are marked by their freedom from the hegemony of any one specific meaning it is concepts such as risk, contingency, fragmentation, speed, change and de-differentiation which can best reveal the complexity of leisure in those lives. This decentring of leisure is also related to another key aspect of Rojek's critique, which argues that if leisure cannot be separated from other aspects of people's lives then the study of leisure should better proceed as cultural studies.

Tony Blackshaw

Associated Concepts Bourdieu; Capitalism; Commodity Fetishism; Consumer Society; Consumption; Decentring Leisure; False Consciousness; Feminism; Flow; Leisure Class; Leisure Education; Leisure Life-style;

Leisure Life-World; Leisure Society; Marxism; Postmodernism; Postmodernity; Serious Leisure; Rojek, Chris; Veblen; Virtual Leisure; Women's Leisure; Work-Leisure.

LEISURE AND THE ENVIRONMENT

Using its ecologist meaning, the environment refers to the ecological backdrop in which plants, humans and other animals coexist and act. It is often used interchangeably with related terms such as ecosystem, ecology, the ecological system, eco-friendly and eco-topia to describe the actual and potential environmental patterns that emerge as a result of this inter-reliance. Concern about the exploitative effects of leisure on the environment has grown exponentially in recent years, not only particular worries about ground, water, air and noise pollution, but also those encompassing environmental degradation and resource depletion. The message that emerges most powerfully from the environmental movement, which is concerned for and acts on behalf of the environment, is that there are many things about our leisure exploits that should make us feel uneasy – flying pollutes the atmosphere, the intensification of tourism has had catastrophic consequences for local cultures, much of our leisure involves consuming which creates a great deal of waste, and so on – and if we were prepared to ask ourselves such questions, we would find out a good deal about the environmental consequences of our leisure choices that we did not know before or were not prepared to admit to ourselves. This would go some way to giving us the confidence to recognize that even if we have left our children a planet more environmentally damaged than when we inherited it, things could still be different.

Tony Blackshaw

Associated Concepts Abnormal Leisure; Animal Rights; Consumer Society; Consumption; Deviance; Extreme Leisure; Leisure Education; Shopping.

LEISURE AND THE LIFE COURSE

This term refers to the process of change relating to leisure interests and activities, from childhood through to old age, brought about as a result of the interface between biographical events and wider socio-historical processes. It was preceded in the literature by the idea of the leisure lifecycle, which refers to the processes of change and development that see most people experiencing three careers in their lifetime: work, family, and leisure (Rapoport and Rapoport, 1975). The Rapoports argued that the key lifecycle transitions in our lives can be associated with starting work, getting married and becoming a parent, and that these are the most important moments for leisure because with them our patterns of day-to-day living are likely to offer themselves to change and reconstruction.

To this end the Rapoports focused their analysis on the family, because in their view not only is it an important agency in how people learn social values and norms but also it is equally important with regard to what they do in terms of their leisure choices during their lives. The family lifecycle involves a number of key stages, such as getting married and starting a family, leaving school and going to work or being unemployed, starting university, starting school, and so on. According to the Rapoports, it is also important to note that the family lifecycle can dominate and cut through other social variables, such as social class and gender.

The Rapoports also suggested that each of us has certain psychobiological *pre-occupations*, (namely gender, ethnicity and culture, wealth and the income of the family) which we will adapt to and change as we mature. The link between these *pre-occupations* is achieved through the life-line which represents our passage from birth to death. The three major pre-occupations can impinge upon our lives and our progress at different times and with different intensities. The Rapoports also identified groupings of phases that have particular pre-occupations: young people aged 10 to 18 years; young adults aged 17–18 to 23–25 years; the establishment phase of 23–25 years to 55 years; and the later years of 55+.

Here they studied social groups relating to these categories to reflect the interest arising out of these pre-occupations in order to explore how issues relating to health, image, economic inequalities and cultural change become significant issues at different points in our lives. Their research suggested that the first phase often tended to involve tension between rebellious youth and the family and that this was also reflective of the second phase, which involves a search for freedom. The third phase involves increasing responsibilities and as a result leisure interests will often take a backstage in people's lives. The fourth stage tends to centre on issues regarding health and having sufficient economic stability.

As Haywood et al. (1995: 134–5) show, for all its strengths the Rapoports' thesis is limited for at least three reasons. First, it views age not so much as a social construction but as a biological imperative. Second, the concept of the family is never problematized in their thesis and by now there are very few families that will actually reflect the nuclear model inferred by their analysis. The third big lack is the Rapoports' almost total neglect of social class: that is, notwithstanding its recognition of the importance of individuals' immediate social context as a key factor in the way that leisure choices are made, their thesis ignores the central importance of social class as something that structures family life and in the process this allows for patriarchal domination in both the household and in leisure, which in turn justifies and legitimizes the status quo.

The theme of family, gender and leisure is taken up by Green, Hebron and Woodward (1990), who carried out research with 707 women between 18 and 59 years, using a social survey method in combination with unstructured interviews and discussion groups. Green et al. wanted to collect both general information about the types and levels of women's leisure participation and more detailed knowledge about their perceptions and attitudes to leisure. The findings of their research confirmed that women's access to experiences of 'free time' and leisure opportunities was structured by gender, social class, income level, age, ethnicity, work and their domestic situation. They also identified the key constraints on women's leisure, such as time, money, the non-availability of safe transport, childcare, number of children, sexual orientation, and so on. Here they found that the women who were most constrained were those who were not in paid employment, those who had unemployed partners, those who were lone parents and those who were married/living together with children. This study also showed that domestic work firmly remained women's work, even if men helped out with it sometimes. Green et al.'s research suggests that a number of equally pertinent factors – social class, ethnicity, income, time and family – work alongside gender when trying to understand women's leisure opportunities throughout the life course.

Roberts (1999) also attributes much more importance to the life course than most other leisure scholars, who in his view in the main tend to put too much emphasis on the relationship between leisure and work (e.g., Parker, 1971, 1983). For Roberts, leisure is defined as a matter of choice and is characterized by its plurality and diversity. There are undoubtedly some social influences and constraints on leisure, but compared to work it is an area of life in which individuals can enjoy great freedom. Nonetheless, he recognizes that:

- Gender is an important issue and women have less leisure time than men.
- Education is also a strong influence on people's leisure choices.
- Styles of marriage are also important. For example, married couples who have joint conjugal roles tend to engage in more home-centred leisure. For example, he found that unmarried people under 30 spent less time in the home and much more time socializing than their married counterparts.

According to Bramham, with postmodernity life appears to have stopped going round in cycles. As he points out people's lives today are 'about flexibility, irrationality and play, whereas leisure was a modernist, bounded and rational experience. Postmodern culture is characterized by hyperreality and hypermobility, by restlessness and disengagement. Individuals carry polysemic identities: fixed commitments are resisted in postmodern life' (2002: 231). Postmodern life is necessarily episodic. Instead of following the predictable cycle described by the Rapoports, men and women now concentrate themselves on living their lives as a series of episodes, particular moments when life and time are elided.

As Roberts points out, though, if there is no longer a straightforward lifecycle there is still a life course, and the relationship between biographical events and wider sociohistorical processes has not become totally meaningless. As he concludes: 'Social and economic trends have not shattered any of the main leisure patterns: the gender differences, the tendency for the economically privileged to do more of most things, or childhood and youth being the life stages were the foundations are laid for long-term leisure careers. As with financial arrangements, the best time to begin preparing for leisure in later life appears to be as young as possible' (Roberts, 1999: 140).

Tony Blackshaw

Associated Concepts Ageing and Leisure; Class; Feminism; Leisure Society; Marxism; Work-Leisure; Youth.

LEISURE AS A VALUE-SPHERE

Adopted from Max Weber's belief that culture, science, art, religion, law, politics, the economy and the like must be understood as autonomous or distinct realms of human activity which have their own 'inherent dignity' (Brubaker, 1984), the idea of leisure as a value-sphere suggests that not only is leisure governed by a particular set of norms, rules, ethics and obligations that are inherent, but also that those who commit

themselves to leisure often do so as a vocation. In other words, and to paraphrase what Zinzendorf (cited in Weber, 1930: 264, note 24) said about work, in making an existential commitment to leisure they not only do leisure in order to live but live for the sake of their leisure, and if there is no more leisure to do they suffer or go to sleep. The concept of value-spheres is useful because not only does it challenge the functionalist tendency to understand society as a totality, but it also understands that the modern world is not one in which 'everyone is related to a greater or lesser extent to the same ethical powers' (Heller, 1999: 37) and that men and women are capable of succeeding in establishing different ways of life in order to find meaning based on the shared values of their own communities of interest.

One particular, and obvious, criticism is that the guiding philosophy of the contemporary liquid modern individualized and consumer society runs counter to the sort of dedication and moral principles associated with value-spheres. Indeed, the evidence would seem to suggest that the majority of men and women are more likely to be seen engaged in one-off leisure (and consumerist) pastimes rather than vocational leisure which tends to be life-long.

Tony Blackshaw

Associated Concepts Authenticity; Consumer Society; Consumption; Crafts and Craftsmanship; Dionysian Leisure; Extreme Leisure; Functionalism; Individualization; Leisure; Leisure in the Community; Leisure Life-Style; Leisure Life-World; Liquid Modernity; Serious Leisure.

LEISURE BODIES

The world of leisure is filled with bodies: pliable bodies, hard bodies, sexy bodies, hybrid bodies, fast bodies, languorous bodies, pleasuring bodies. Among them sports fans, strippers, dancers, men and women in the gym sculpting and re-sculpting their bodies ... the list is endless. Bodies competing, bodies hurting, bodies dancing, bodies playing, bodies posing, bodies being exploited, all of them, most of all, performing. People put themselves together and announce themselves to the world through what they put on their bodies. What this tells us is that bodies are not just bound by their biology but are also shaped in the social, cultural and economic positions of their owners, as well as being moulded to their relaxations and exertions.

As the above examples suggest, debates about corporeality in leisure studies are also complicated. This has been reflected in epistemological and ontological arguments about the mind–body split that have been subject to an enormous and as yet ongoing debate from at least Descartes onwards. Having said that, most leisure scholars would reject such a dualism, emphasizing the ways in which men and women are embodied.

One of Pierre Bourdieu's major themes was people struggling with their own embodiment, with the fact of having bodies in the modern sense. If how a body looks makes some individuals happy it can also make others unhappy, particularly when they feel that they are failing to match the social norm. This can persuade some individuals to pretend things are not as they are or may encourage them to pursue leisure pursuits which will give them a better 'look'. It can also lead some individuals to follow conventions which, while they compliment some bodies, must be stretched over others; this can also lead to a situation where those (deviants) who contravene the social norm are over-identified with and through their bodily 'look' and deportment. In other words, as Bourdieu would say, violence is exercised upon individuals in symbolic rather than in physical ways.

What this suggests is we live with the knowledge that our bodies are looked at, are everywhere under surveillance, and that leisure scholars should be concerned about imagining how this makes people feel and think about themselves, about their own subjectivity. As Foucault points out, modern social norms and societal conventions are established and lived through bodies. For example, in modern societies, the 'ideal' modern professional sportsman or woman is, to paraphrase Foucault, 'something that can be made; out of a formless clay, an inapt body, the machine required can be constructed; posture is gradually corrected; a calculated constraint runs slowly through each part of the body, mastering it, making it pliable, ready at all times, turning silently into the automatism of habit' (1984: 179). Here Foucault is suggesting that it is not just that we have bodies that is important but also body discipline, or as he would say, having docile bodies.

In his own typically apocalyptic style, Baudrillard takes this position one step further when he describes those who participate in individualized leisure pursuits – such as the skateboarder, the jogger and the bodybuilder – as those who regard the body with the same kind of blank solitude, the same narcissistic obstinacy. For Baudrillard, the cult of the body in modern societies is extraordinary. It is the only object on which everyone today seems to be able to concentrate, not as a source of pleasure, but as an object of frantic concern, in the obsessive fear of failure. In Baudrillard's 'cult of the into' exercise is a kind of self-torture, not only in being painful but also in the way of forcing the body to speak its own truth. Being 'into' leisure is key to all of this. It might be argued that 'my body is different from everyone else's body' is the watchword of our contemporary 'individualized' times and we should recognize that today the value of the body is on its surface. As Debray (2007) points out, in postmodernity (not his chosen term) not only is the body now the subjective centre of gravity but its visibility has also become *the* basis of symbolic authority.

This resonates with the work of Deleuze and Guatarri who understand the body as pure surface, and as such something much more than the physical flesh and bones of a human being. Their idea of a body without organs (BwO) is a radically social constructivist conception of the body which must be distinguished from the body of biology. Developed from the French theatre practitioner Antonin Artuad's idea that 'when you will have made him a body without organs, then you will have delivered him from all his automatic reactions and restored him to his true freedom' (1976: 571), the BwO not only signifies the absence of organs but also suggests that the body cannot be broken down into parts that are distinct from each other.

The BwO is essentially about desire; 'it is that which one desires and by which one desires' (Deleuze and Guattari, 1987: 165). Deleuze and Guattari identify three kinds of BwO: cancerous, empty and full. However, the BwO is about performativity rather than a diagnosis as such, and if it signifies freedom, extreme care is needed for desire to occupy the body freely and prevent it succumbing to the needs of the dominant social order or hegemony. Deleuze and Guattari pay much more attention to the ways in which people's thoughts and longings are shaped and expressed through their bodies and how they can transcend them, demonstrating how body discipline in leisure provides a potential means of expression for social transgression or political resistance. It is in this way that the concept of the BwO is of interest to leisure scholars, because its transformative capacity is suggestive of alternative modes of embodiment that can enable individuals to transcend the vicissitudes of social class, 'race', gender, sexuality and even disability.

Tony Blackshaw

Associated Concepts Bourdieu; Desire; Deviance; Foucault; Identity; 'Into', the; Leisure Life-Style; Performativity; Queer Theory; Social Control; Surveillance.

LEISURE CLASS

An enduring theory within leisure studies, the idea of the leisure class emerged in the work of Veblen (published in 1899), who presented an unambiguous critique of the conspicuous consumption associated with those social elites – aristocracy, *bourgeois*, *nouveau riches* – who perceived that their enjoyment of leisure was what distinguished them from the rest of society. In Veblen's time, conspicuous consumption was, above all else, instrumental (Bauman, in Rojek, 2004): to be in a position not to have to do paid work was to be almost a 'gentleman'. As Bauman points out, it was a way of telling one's 'significant others' (those also selectively admitted to the leisure class) just how high up the social hierarchy one had managed to climb, and that one had the means of settling there for good. Herein it was the display and exhibition of one's ability to consume conspicuously that was important, not the consumption per se. The novelty of consuming was no doubt important to this leisure class but their aspirations for social prestige guaranteed that it was a virtue that they should contain their passions; the consumer goods and experiences accumulated were, as Bauman suggests, valued as possessions first and all the rest after.

In his work on postmodernity and liquid modernity Bauman presents an equally uncompromising assessment of the new leisure class: the celebrities (and those who service and profit from the electronic circus of celebrity culture) whose *raison d'être* is not only to conspicuously consume, but also to be conspicuously consumed in the society of consumers. As Bauman (ibid: 294) makes clear, however, consumption for this new leisure class is not instrumental: 'it is "autotelic", a value in its own right, pursued for its own sake; it is its instrumental functions that have now turned instrumental and are no longer allowed to override or even to push into the second place its erstwhile pleasure-giving task'. This is not to say that the display and exhibition of their ability to consume and be consumed are not important to this new leisure class, but it is not as important as their personal dedication to the task of putting off for as long as possible their own inevitable obsolescence.

Tony Blackshaw

Associated Concepts Bauman; Bourdieu; Celebrity; Consumption; Liquid Modernity; Postmodernity; Veblen.

LEISURE CONSTRAINTS

(ageing and leisure; class; racism and leisure; unemployment, leisure in; women's leisure)

LEISURE EDUCATION

This is a term that has a number of meanings depending on who is using it. Aristotle said that 'we educate ourselves so that we can make a noble use of our leisure'. From the perspective of this author leisure education signifies the circumstances of *skholè*, or what Bourdieu (1999: 1) referred to as 'the free time, free from the urgencies of the world that allows a free and liberated relationship to those urgencies and the world'. More formally, leisure education might be defined as the act or process of acquiring knowledge, skills or experience for their own sake and in ways which will provide the sociability, personal pleasure, challenge and fulfilment usually associated with other leisure activities.

Historically the development of leisure education has had its basis in both community settings (for example, book clubs, local history groups, Working Men's Institutes and so on) and formal educational institutions, especially evening classes in further education where people can engage themselves in all kinds of leisure interests, from learning the guitar to painting to soap making. However, as Harris (2005: 66) points out with regard to the latter, more and more 'it has become almost impossible to discuss the leisure aspects of education in the current political climate ... since a thoroughly instrumental and calculative attitude [to education] prevails'. Indeed, in recent years there has been an obvious waning of the kinds of leisure education aimed at stimulating the imagination (and perhaps even thereby challenging the prevailing social consensus) and a concomitant waxing of institutionalized and professional education targeted at qualifications for the new economy of work focused on entrepreneurship.

Tony Blackshaw

Associated Concepts   Crafts and Craftsmanship; Leisure; Serious Leisure; Work Ethic; Work-Leisure.

LEISURE EXPERIENCE

(happiness; leisure life-world, pleasure)

LEISURE, HISTORY OF

(asceticism; leisure; sport; sportization; work ethic)

LEISURE IN THE COMMUNITY

The idea of leisure in the community has been understood in two ways in leisure studies. The first refers to the large, diverse and conspicuous presence of leisure in everyday life (e.g., every town and city has its formal and informal institutions – restaurants, theatres, shopping centres, pubs and clubs, and so on – which bring people together in order to enjoy their leisure). The second comprises a more critical perspective, found in the work of Bishop and Hoggett (1986), who not only chart the breadth, depth and massive scope of communal, informal or voluntary leisure, but also provide a critique of attempts to subsume these myriad activities under the umbrella of a bureaucratic and centralized programme of 'state'-controlled leisure.

For Bishop and Hoggett, the so-called 'voluntary sector in leisure' is in fact comprised of myriad individuals, groups and organizations. The idea of the existence of a 'voluntary sector of leisure' may be the essential element in the worldview of the leisure profession and the state formations surrounding it, but in their view leisure in the community is very much different from the public sector and the more organized voluntary sector. Making reference to the wider voluntary sector already subsumed under the banner of 'state' provision of services through what they call 'state colonialism', Bishop and Hoggett (page 128) stress that there is 'a key difference between communal leisure organizations and others such as trade unions or tenants' associations. The self-interest of the latter is based upon overt need, whereas in communal leisure we are speaking of that realm of human life beyond such need ... Leisure then begins beyond need. The self-interest underlying forms of communal leisure is ... not based upon neediness, but upon enthusiasm, pleasure and enjoyment. It may perhaps be more useful to talk about an enthusiast's desires than needs'.

Bishop and Hoggett also suggest that we should be very wary of assuming a purely instrumental concept for understanding why people organize around enthusiasms; people organize around leisure for any number reasons to do with communality and mutual interest. Moreover, coming together in leisure may lack the perceived depth associated with long-standing social relations that are in turn associated with neighbourhood or ethnic homogeneity, but under some circumstances leisure can bring people together in circumstances that will yield transitory or ephemeral experiences of belonging that are felt as both deep and meaningful to those involved.

Following this theme Wellman et al. (1988) demonstrated that the question of 'community' is no longer dependent on any notion of place (if it ever was) and that social networks and communities of interest will spread beyond geographical boundaries. Indeed, their research evidence suggests that today the notion of community has been transformed and that we can now see the coexistence of communities which represent, to different degrees, close-knit pre-industrial, or traditional, communities *and* communities which can be described as post-industrial. Community

leisure, in other words, need not be confined to sociological interpretations that emphasize geographical propinquity or all-encompassing forms of communality.

Other recent analyses have also challenged the notion that a sense of belonging, identification with a social group or place making must necessarily involve deep, multiplex and enduring relationships. Dyck (2002), for example, argues that it is in suburban areas in particular where we have witnessed the decline of traditional communal relations, but it is also here where people are more likely to generate a social connectivity out of limited, voluntary and contingent but deeply textured and meaningful leisure activities in what are ostensibly heterogeneous and individualized social settings.

Tony Blackshaw

Associated Concepts   Civil Society; Community; Community Leisure; Leisure Education; Social Capital.

LEISURE LIFE-STYLE

This is a controversial concept which originated in Max Weber's notions of status and status groups, though it came to prominence in leisure studies at the end of the 1980s when some commentators – particularly, though not exclusively, those influenced by postmodernism and cultural studies scholarship – began to argue that social class and work were becoming less significant to understanding leisure behaviour than individual life-style choices centred around patterns of consumerism based on youth, gender and ethnicity. As Veal (2001) points out, at this time there emerged a resistance to the use of the concept, mainly based on the idea that leisure life-styles may change but social classes and their identities essentially remain the same (as coal and diamond are essentially always carbon; e.g., Critcher, 1989). However, such accounts tended to gloss over the changed climatic conditions of advanced capitalism, finding it difficult to re-imagine 'workers' recast as 'consumers' – they merely saw workers consuming – who were increasingly able to occupy the place of consumption in new and imaginative ways through their leisure interests and activities.

During the 1990s the concept continued to grow in significance especially with more and more people rejecting lives made to the measure of social class, and even to some extent age, gender and ethnicity, for those which they perceived did not restrict other potential outlets for credulity. Leisure life-styles today are thus seen as more to do with the individual search for authenticity in a world where authenticity is an impossibility. In this view leisure life-styles have little to do with nation either, except during major international sport tournaments such as the association football or rugby union world cups. Rather, they are seen as identikits constructed and facilitated by global flows of consumer products and culture. The upshot is that, rather than seeing leisure life-styles as being unable to provide the kinds of stable identities associated with a solid modern existence of yesteryear, leisure scholars have now to come to grips with the idea that a liquid modern society has emerged in which there is increasing recognition of the notion of the quick fix self-effacement and reassembly, rather than some gradual shrinking, fading away, ultimately disappearing notion of fixity. The adoption of a new leisure life-style then – we must accept – is often nothing more (and nothing less either) than something more, hopefully much more, potentially exciting and empowering than the last one.

Tony Blackshaw

Associated Concepts Individualization; Leisure Class; Leisure Life-World; Leisure Society; Marxism; Postmodernism; Postmodernity; Rojek; Serious Leisure; Veblen; Virtual Leisure; Work-Leisure.

LEISURE LIFE-WORLD

Derived from the German *lebenswelt*, which is used to describe the realm of lived life and everyday sociability, this term is employed by Blackshaw (2003), following Edward Husserl (1970 [1936]), to deal with the impossibility of examining tacitly understood leisure lives as they are lived just then, at that moment, before the ready-made theories and jargons of academics get in the way, but in such a way as to, nonetheless, try to make those lives live again as well as to excite interest in them. Drawing on the phenomenological approach associated with Husserl, life-world studies assert that it is the embodied character of our being-in-the-world that significantly determines the ways in which we perceive and act. To this extent Blackshaw's analysis charts the ways in which the incumbents of this particular leisure life-world – 'the lads' – live, experience, understand and recognize this world *erlebnis* as both a 'real' and meaningful already existing reality. And in re-presenting 'the lads'' shared leisure experiences as a life-world, his analysis seeks to capture the central importance of the social in the study of this culture.

Blackshaw's thesis is developed through a hermeneutic sociological approach to make knowable the leisure life-world of a group of working-class 'lads' with whom he had grown up. This meant that the study was about their leisure life-world and his leisure life-world, but also his and 'the lads'' shared leisure life-world. Consequently as a researcher he occupied a strange dual position in 'the lads'' universe – Blackshaw as an insider and Blackshaw the ethnographer as an outsider on the inside. He used this special position to not only make sense of how 'the lads' intuitively lived their leisure lives but also allow the reader to know how they and we (he and 'the lads') *felt* that collective experience, individually together.

The crux of his thesis was that 'the lads' may not live in *solid modernity* any more – and likely never have – but their collective consciousness still dwells there and the universe that is their leisure life-world is framed by a *solid modern* discourse, or so it seems. Even though the wider world which they *individually* inhabit has become *liquid modern*, in their leisure lives 'the lads' are still animated by their belief in an imagined community which is perceived as the cornerstone of their shared masculine working-class existence. 'The lads' only feel 'real' in relation to this leisure life-world. There is a warmth, a particular feeling of home about it, which offers 'the lads' a protective cocoon where they are 'naturally' safeguarded from the uncertainties of liquid modern change. They close its shutters to guard against their mutual home-made models of themselves losing credibility and the intricate cogs of their masculine realism from being damaged or lost. The leisure life-world enables them to keep these ready-made narratives alive in their collective memory, their own private gallery, which is the legacy of their youth.

Blackshaw's central argument is that it is this shared passion for a solid modern missing world, sometimes proudly resurrected and celebrated, sometimes merely borne out of the private burden of individuality, which gives this shared leisure life-world its weight and its depth. The book charts 'the lads'' intermittent forays into Leeds city centre on Friday and Saturday nights which constitute a memorable vindication of this missing world. Nights out with 'the lads' tend to spin themselves out into a familiar web which feels like one of those reunions which famous rock bands have when a group gets back together after playing with other people. When 'the lads' are on stage once again it feels great and everything just clicks into place. They drink their beer faster than is good for them and conversation moves from subject to subject. They finish each other's sentences and communicate, more remarkably, without speaking at all. With a real affinity, and in the spirit of the communion that exists between them, they use gestures known only to them.

However, on these nights out 'the lads' do not so much relive their youth as recreate its unheroic aftermath through their leisure. In truth the leisure life-world has, to use the rock band analogy once again, been turned into a sort of heritage museum for ageing lads, which in recent years has become more a duty than a pleasure and whose nagging subliminal power reverberates only on the edges of individual lives lived in the main elsewhere. Indeed, although it is the ultimate experience of a solidly modern leisure life they desire but cannot really capture, it does not deter them from endeavouring to regain the power and certainties of its past and seeking a realm of mutual happiness that was once upon a time theirs.

Outside the leisure life-world, resignation and disillusionment are the nearest things 'the lads' have to freedom, or so it seems. In the fluidity of liquid modernity they have to watch powerless as the Other invades uninvited into their existential and material realms: women controlling their bedrooms and telling them what to do, women and black people taking their jobs, buying their houses, taking over their shops and their schools. But in the leisure life-world 'the lads' are in control. Here they are determined to ensure that their leisure lives are unaffected by difference. In the leisure life-world the features of the Other begin to elongate and liquefy, swell and then resolidify, like Sartre's *le visqueux*, and they are transformed into 'the lads'' own DIY custom-made creations. Take, for example, women, who can never exist as cheerful subjects of their own lives in the leisure life-world but exist merely as scaffolding for 'the lads'' shared dreams – happy and loving shags without another single care except perhaps to go down on working-class white blokes. That these characterizations are not 'real' is neither here nor there, 'the lads' simply have to be convinced that they are. What is important for 'the lads' is the *meaning for them* of these characterizations to their version of truth, which is something that enables them to form what they recognize *is* the world when they are at leisure together. Women have to be wiped out from a *solid modern story* in which they have no place, excluded from the leisure world that has created them. These characterizations of the Other become symbols of subjugation, power and knowledge, the luscious fruit of a *solid* leisure life lived in a *solid* version of truth. This 'universal' truth of the rationality divides 'the lads' and Others into two categories: us and them, same and Other.

In the leisure life-world 'the lads' have the best of both worlds: they have their myth and are able to relativize it as a *contingent* leisure experience which has its own monologic. Indeed, the modus operandi of 'the lads'', leisure together always presumes this form of closure: the conformation of hegemonic masculinity and the restoration of disrupted stability which provide intimations of a past world of communal bliss in a protected time space in which the leisure life-world attempts to impose the fixity of a masculinist, working-class myth on to the ostensible fluidity of contemporary everyday life.

Yet 'the lads'' apparently granite authenticity isn't at all what it seems. In common with other liquid modern men and women they find it difficult to remain authentic for long because they simply have too many other choices in their lives. 'The lads' know that the weekend experience of this life-world is just a leisure break, they understand this and are resigned to their fate. In the event it is only because of its own impossibility that the leisure life-world is possible at all. 'The lads' may be figures carved in the past but their identities are maintained in the present and, in common with other liquid modern men and women, they are *individuals* first and all the rest after. In the words of Bauman, it is this observation that represents the 'irreparable and irredeemable ambivalence' of the leisure life-world of 'the lads'.

Tony Blackshaw

Associated Concepts Authenticity; Bauman; Community; Community Leisure; Individualization; Leisure in the Community; Liquid Modernity.

LEISURE MARKETING

Marketing is principally concerned with exchange or trade and is a generic term that can be used in any sector of commerce, trade and industry. When stripped back to its fundamental principles you might say that it is based on the concept that the customer is the most important person to a company. As Kotler (1997) points out, in order to prosper or survive every company must work hard to retain its existing customers and strive to secure new ones. The leisure sector is no different – services and facilities depend on satisfied customers and without them an organization can quickly go out of business (Torkildsen, 2005).

Historically, marketing has allowed individuals and organizations to specialize in producing particular goods and services and to then exchange them in markets for the goods they needed. Trade flourished during the Industrial Revolution when the opportunities to buy and sell products became increasingly easy. However, as markets expanded businesses began selling to consumers who were no longer within their immediate locality. Businesses in the leisure sector (much like those in other sectors) were also increasingly forced to analyse and interpret the needs and wants of customers and to manufacture products that would fit in with these needs and wants on a much larger scale than ever before. Consequently there was the emergence of mass production, which in turn led to mass consumption.

In the contemporary world in order for a product to be commercially successful it must be produced in sufficient volume. In order for producers to achieve a sufficient level of demand, they must produce products that the market wants to buy. Moreover, to be competitive they not only have to take the needs and wants of the market into consideration but they must also *start* with them.

As markets have grown so has competition. This in turn has led to product differentiation and the realization that selling on its own is not sufficient. This has led to the emergence of a more sophisticated approach to selling goods and services – the so-called 'marketing-led' approach. A marketing-led approach attempts to understand consumers by talking to them and responding positively to changes in their tastes, preferences and opinions. In order to respond to this businesses have had to begin thinking on a much larger and more sophisticated scale. As marketing has emerged it has taken on a whole new set of objectives, including sales, promotion, pricing, packaging, product development, market research, planning and distribution and after-sales service.

Rob Wilson

Associated Concepts Ansoff Matrix; Boston Matrix; Consumption; Marketing Mix for the Leisure Industries; Market Positioning and Market Segmentation.

LEISURE, PHILOSOPHICAL BASES OF

(catharis and cathexsis; extreme leisure; happiness; hedonism; leisure; mimesis; pleasure)

LEISURE POLICY

Although leisure undoubtedly plays an important role in public policy, the term leisure policy is actually a misnomer. It is more useful to refer to the public policy *process* – involving a wide range of politicians, civil services, organizations, professionals and other stakeholders – which uses leisure in both direct and indirect ways to encourage individual health and well-being and promote social inclusion and/or tries to control leisure (e.g., legislation implemented to ban the use of addictive and dangerous drugs). The term public policy is itself generally used interchangeably with the term social policy to refer to the study of, and

participation in, the formation, implementation, monitoring and evaluation of policies in the public domain that are part of the economic, governance, service and social control policies of the state.

Having said that, the idea of public policy is itself a contested term which has different meanings that are largely dependent on the context in which it is used. The term is often understood (though oversimplistically it should be said) as a corporate undertaking in which the state seeks to establish a distinctive set of social policies based on common political and ideological values reflected in the continuum across the social democratic consensus (that is, from 'anti-collectivism' to 'utopian-socialism' – George and Wilding, in Coalter, 1990). However, it should be noted that, while the state has direct control of the legislature of central government, it does not have direct control of either local government or the voluntary and private organizations that are often charged with the responsibility of implementing public policies locally. This is not to say that political and ideological values are not important to understanding public policy for leisure but instead is to recognize that policies are often pragmatically determined, and often in unpredictable ways, both as a response to contradictions between different policy goals and in the light of political and community resistance and/or non-cooperation.

Notwithstanding these observations, critics of contemporary public policy have argued that no matter what shape opposition to policy takes this can, and invariably has been (and without much difficulty), incorporated into the current government's commitment to a 'Third Way' model of market-managerialism which, on the back of the Thatcherite turn to the market, has superseded the social democratic consensus and traditional alternatives in public policy.

The introduction of Compulsory Competitive Tendering (CCT) of services for various public services is a good illustration of the break up of the social democratic consensus. CCT was introduced by the Conservative governments in the UK in the 1980s, beginning in service industries such as cleaning, hospitals, school meals and refuse collecting, before being extended to leisure facilities. The Conservatives rejected the pump-priming Keynesian economic model which had hitherto been used by governments since 1945 and replaced it with the New Right commitment to an economic theory based on monetarism, with the objective of imposing the disciplines of the market on public services. Whilst CCT for leisure aimed to make services more efficient, many argued that it ultimately led to services simply being run more economically (that is, run more cheaply, but with a decline in the quality of output). The election of a new Labour government in 1997 led to a recognition of the limitations of CCT for leisure facilities. The result was a switch of policy in favour of Best Value, which allowed for services to be considered in terms of their effectiveness (that is, the best-quality output, irrespective of the input costs) and based on greater community involvement.

However, critics have argued that the 'Third Way' model for leisure policy based on initiatives such as Best Value has little to do with community other than what's in their labelling, namely because they do not have the essential conditions or purpose that can sustain a community. Marxist critics would also point out that this shift in public policy is merely part of a deeper continuing political struggle, formed and implemented in the interests of neoliberalism in order to maintain the prevailing hegemony.

with little conceptual precision. As an idea it oscillates between the views of those who merely observe that work is losing its former centrality and its most ardent adherents who suggest that it is only with the emergence of leisure society proper (rather than a society of work based on the work ethic) that humankind will be able to realize its fullest and free expression of creativity and sociability. The former view usually pivots on the observation of momentous changes that have occurred since the nineteenth century, suggesting that advances in science and technology have eased the lot of the majority of people, thereby bringing them more time for leisure. From the 1970s, this view has been most notably associated with the sharp decline in the ideology of social class and the emergence of post-industrial society (Bell, 1973), suggesting that fewer hours in paid work means more time for leisure. However, critics have argued that the ostensible benefits of such changes have neither been clear nor equally distributed. The strongest adherents of the leisure society thesis, who also tend to offer the most radical critiques of technological advancement, changes in the class structure and post-industrial debates (e.g., Kane, 2006; Seabrook, 1988), offer some compelling accounts of the alienating effects of the relationship between work and compensatory leisure which, in their view, by the turn of the twenty-first century, for the majority of people adds up to nothing less than an existential crisis of meaning and purpose.

Tony Blackshaw

Tony Blackshaw

Associated Concepts Civil Society; Community; Hegemony; Leisure; Marxism; Third Way; Well-Being.

Associated Concepts Leisure; Play; Play Ethic; Pleasure; Well-Being; Work Ethic.

LEISURE SOCIETY

This term has undergone considerable debate in leisure studies, but it is still often used

Leisure studies, in the broadest sense, is a discursive formation concerned with the systematic interpretation of the whole 'economy' of leisure as a contested realm of society and culture. Its primary task is the elucidation of the meaning of leisure. This discursive formation includes a wide variety of *disciplines* (especially sociology, psychology, philosophy, geography and social history), *perspectives* (Marxism, feminism, figurationalism, postmodernism, and so on) and *institutions* (leisure departments in universities, historical archives, key associations, journals, conferences, and so on) within the category of 'leisure' that it uses to produce its own ideas, concepts and theories, and to then generate its own strategies for dealing with this *knowledge*.

Rojek et al. (2007: 2–3) argue that notwithstanding its interdisciplinary nature leisure studies has by now reached a sufficient level of maturity to be classed as a branch of learning in its own right. They also credibly suggest that the aims and methods of contemporary leisure studies have emerged in considering four primary facts.

- *Globalization*: the growing economic, cultural and political interconnectedness and interdependence of human relations.
- *Power*: the positioning of leisure forms and practice in relations of power.
- *Process*: the recognition that a leisure activity is sensuous, variable, multidimensional and mobile rather than simply the expression of economic, cultural and social reproduction.
- *Context*: the location of leisure forms and practice in the central questions of individualistic citizenship, especially issues of moral tolerance, social inclusion and distributive justice.

Tony Blackshaw

Associated Concepts Decentring Leisure; Deconstruction; Discursive Formations; Free Time; Leisure; Leisure Class; Leisure Life-Style; Leisure Life-World; Leisure Society; Serious Leisure; Virtual Leisure; Work-Leisure.

LIFE COURSE

(leisure and the life course)

LIFE-STYLE

(leisure life-style)

LIMINALITY

Derived from the Latin word *limen* (literally meaning a 'threshold'), this term connotes the idea of the 'betwixt and the between' or a place of movement 'in and out of time'. As expounded in the works of Van Gennep and Victor Turner, liminality describes the indefinable social and spiritual locations involved in religious rites of passage. This is a perennial concept in leisure studies most usually identified with those rituals common to shared leisure experiences that signal a 'spatial separation from the familiar and habitual' and which in the process open up channels of communication to create cultural domains that transcend the limitations of class, gender, race, nationality, politics, religion or even geography. Insights gleaned from the work of Turner suggest that these domains may well have a powerful cosmological significance, conveyed largely through the emotions to affirm an alternative (dis)order of things, which stress 'generic rather than particularistic relationships'.

Turner describes the shared experiences of liminality through the concept of *communitas*, which not only entertains cultural and social difference but also 'strains towards' an openness that provides a 'return' to the social group denied by the manifest inequalities inherent in bourgeois society. *Communitas* is captured within situations of liminal 'margin' and 'remains open and specialized, a spring of pure possibility as well as the immediate realization of release from day-to-day structural necessities and obligatoriness' (Turner, 1973: 217).

There are three types of communitas. *Existential communitas* represents an explicit, total and authentic coming together of a social group, which undermines the capitalistic commodification of relationships encountered in a sociality founded on economic alienation and class, gender and racial inequalities. Participation in existential communitas involves, for the individual, a total dependence on the dialectic of the self in relation to others and when existential communitas occurs it is liable to provide those experiencing it with a return to the unfettered social group of a 'homogeneous, unstructured, and free community'. For these reasons the existential communitas experience is always likely to be transient. However, this is not necessarily so, and Turner defines *ideological communitas* as 'a label one can apply to a variety of utopian models or blueprints of societies believed by their authors to exemplify or supply the optimal conditions of *existential communitas*' (1973: 194).

Normative communitas develops where existential communitas persists and the social group develops a need to organize and make its position more secure. Turner stresses, however, that this more durable form of existential communitas should not be confused with a utilitarian social togetherness, such as a Durkheimian mechanical solidarity, which is likely to have structural antecedents and to have been built on bourgeois-rational, *gesellschaften* foundations. For Turner, communitas-type social groups tend to have non-utilitarian, enchanted and primordial origins and, in this sense, invariably surpass 'the utilitarian and functionalist aspect prevailing in the surrounding economic order' (Maffesoli, 1996: 79).

According to Turner, the concept of social *anti-structure* most fittingly evinces the sense of interpolation experienced in thresholds of liminality. This concept is useful because it connotes the dispensation with definite pattern and structure associated with day-to-day existence during liminal experiences, giving the go-ahead to 'the whim of the moment' (Thompson, 1981), and at the same time signalling an abrogation of the dominant social order of things.

In his discussion of liminality in relation to leisure spaces, leisure practices, configurations of association and identity formation, Rojek suggests that liminal conventions and practices are ultimately so appealing because individuals recognize in them the promise of freedom and the opportunity to 'be oneself'. Liminal zones offer this 'because they appear to be "free spaces" beyond the control of civilized order' (Rojek, 1995: 88). A good example of leisure studies liminality scholarship is Shields' (1991, 1992) work which explores the significance of leisure experiences 'to thresholds of controlled and legitimated breaks from the routines of everyday, proper behaviour' (1991: 7). In the light of Shields' work, it is possible to see that liminality abounds in leisure situations: from the beach to the dance floor, from the massage parlour to the sports arena, leisure offers innumerable betwixt and between spaces where the 'normal' social order can be subverted.

Critics have suggested that the idea of liminality is ultimately an empty concept. Fulgham (1995) argues that paradoxically (and contrary to the assertions of Turner) the most powerful dimension of liminality is its solitariness – the way it emphasizes, not so much a sense of coming together, but the individual's existential separateness from others. Thompson, in his discussion of liminality and holiday experiences, argues that the concepts of communitas and the liminal are in themselves problematic. He makes the key point that they evince little more than the commonsensical point that social collectivity can generate a sense of 'community spirit' and that this is more likely to occur when people are relieved from the structural constraints of day-to-day existence, such as when they are on holiday. Consequently, for Thompson, liminality remains a rather insubstantial concept, because it is essentially without any conceptual 'content', in the sense that it leaves undisturbed the normative order of things. Indeed, what Bernice Martin once said of cultural life more generally is true of liminal leisure more specifically: far from having any powerful cosmological significance, it is often 'pretty carefully programmed as a kind of inversion of workaday role play ... like switching over the TV channel or changing to a new script; everyone knows his (sic) part in both channels and both scripts' (1981: 73).

Tony Blackshaw

Associated Concepts Abnormal Leisure; Bohemians; Carnivalesque; Edgework; Extreme Leisure; Flow; Mimesis; Zones.

LIQUID MODERNITY

This is the term employed by the sociologist Zygmunt Bauman in his attempt to move the debates about modernity and postmodernity on to another level. The critical moment of showing this tactical shift in his work was with the publication of *Liquid Modernity* (2000) in which, to use a film analogy, Bauman offered a *Full-Monty*-ish exposition of industrial decline and personal renewal. In other words, he provided an alternative to the modernity/postmodernity dualism which brought to our attention the redundancy of 'heavy' and 'solid' hardware-focused modernity with its largely 'predictable and therefore manageable' habitat and its replacement with a more 'light' and 'liquid' software-focused modernity. In other words, the world has developed into a particular form of modernity, the most striking feature of which is its lability.

The foremost difference between 'solid' and 'liquid' is that the latter does not tolerate the pressure differences between any two points, and in adopting this law of physics as an analogy what Bauman is suggesting is

that sociology (and leisure studies) must reject the dichotomies and binary oppositions that have nagged it since its inception, and which it has for far too long imagined are the mainstay of the human condition, at the same time as recognizing that it is *individualization* that is liquid modernity's own indelible force. As Bauman suggests, in marked contrast to the producer society of solid modernity, liquid modernity is a *consumer* sociality in which individuals have simultaneously become the promoters of commodities and the commodities they endorse (Bauman, 2007).

Liquid modernity is also a sociality which '"unbinds" time, weakens the constraining impact of the past and effectively prevents colonization of the future' (Bauman, 1992: 190). That is, it is underpatterned rather than patterned, accompanied by many branchings and extensions, trunk lines and switchback tracks, yards and sidings, its trains of experience busy with unremitting new arrivals and speedy departures, as well as unexpected diversions, derailments and cancellations, rather than the secure tracks that once sustained modernity in its formative years. It is a world that slips out of reach just when you think you have a grasp of where it's going. What this suggests is that any understanding of leisure in liquid modernity must also be able to grasp the meaning of uncertainty, risk and fragmentation, which are the hallmarks of liquid modern times.

Tony Blackshaw

Associated Concepts Bauman; Consumption; Consumer Society; Dromology and Speed; Individualization; Leisure Life-World; Modernity; Postmodernism; Postmodernity.

M

MANAGEMENT STYLES

There are a number of management styles which can be utilized by leisure managers in the day-to-day operation of an organization. These have an important role to play in motivating staff and can have a significant role in improving productivity. In leisure industries, management styles can vary enormously but they can be summarized in the following way.

- *Autocratic management* is directive and characterized by order and dictating to staff with little or no consultation in the decision-making process. Generally the manager likes to feel in total control of the situation and decisions will be made quickly (due to the lack of discussion). The major limitation to this style of management is lack of motivation in staff, as they are likely to feel isolated and disenfranchized. This management style is often related to high staff turnover.
- *Democratic management* is characterized by managers involving staff more in both the decision-making process and the execution of work-related tasks. Often staff members will feel a sense of empowerment, consequently becoming more motivated and more efficient in their roles. However, because they are allowed to carry out their jobs with a degree of flexibility there can often be problems with slow decision making (due to drawn-out consultations) and occasionally a reduction in productivity as some individuals take advantage of the democratic situation.
- *The laissez-faire approach* to management requires little involvement from the manager as the employees are basically left to 'get on with the job'. That is not to say the manager sits back and takes no notice, but he or she acts as a guide or coach to staff members, helping them through their designated roles. Again increased empowerment and responsibility can increase motivation, although the associated limitations of taking advantage can often persist. Moreover, the lack of direction can often result in certain individuals 'feeling lost' or not knowing what to do.
- *Motivational management* is accompanied by mutual goal setting between managers and staff. The motivational manager will consult widely with members of staff and will make clear decisions about who is responsible for what. A good example of motivational management is Management by Objectives (MBO), which involves managers defining objectives for individual staff and then directing and comparing their performances against these. Other key MBO principles are cascading management objectives through the organization; participative decision making; time framing; performance evaluation; and feedback.

It should be borne in mind that these different approaches are not mutually exclusive and managers may choose to use more than one of them, or even combinations, as and when the circumstances dictate.

Rob Wilson

Associated Concepts Human Resource Management; Motivation; Training and Development and Appraisals.

MARKETING

(leisure marketing)

MARKETING MIX FOR THE LEISURE INDUSTRIES

This is probably one of the best-known marketing terms of all. Essentially the marketing mix is a process that businesses use to develop products to fit consumer needs and wants. Its major components – price, product, place and promotion – make up some of the most important sections in a marketing plan. However, there are three additional Ps that are equally important to the leisure industries: people, process and physical evidence. By offering the product with the right combination of the seven Ps, marketers can improve business results through better market penetration.

- *Price*: this is one of the most important features of the marketing mix, as it is the only element of the mix that generates a turnover for the organization. Pricing can often be difficult and must reflect the supply and demand relationship. Pricing a product too high or too low could mean a loss of sales for the organization. Consequently pricing must take into account the following factors: fixed and variable costs; the competition; the company objectives; positioning strategies; and target markets (see also Pricing Strategies).

- *Product*: the product is simply the tangible, physical entity that is bought or sold. Examples in the leisure industries include anything from buying a meal in a restaurant to the purchase of a football season ticket to a swim at the local pool. What you buy is the product.

- *Place*: this covers not only the physical location where an organization sells its goods but also the way in which it gets its goods to the customer and the distribution channels it uses to achieve this goal. As such, the term place, in the context of the marketing mix, is also known as the channel, distribution or intermediary. It is the mechanism through which goods and/or services are moved from the manufacturer/service provider to the user or consumer. There are several elements to this process, including: distribution channels; distribution coverage; outlet locations; sales territories; inventory levels and locations; and transportation carriers.
  Kotler (1997) claims that care with this aspect of the marketing mix is essential to achieving good sales. The phrase 'location, location, location' is often be used in conjunction with the term place, due to the fact that consumers will only buy the goods they want if they are available to buy. Consequently the right stock must be in the right place and in the right quantities.

- *Promotion*: this is the specific mix of advertising, personal selling, sales promotion, sponsorship and public relations which a company uses to pursue its advertising and marketing objectives. In short, it is an organization's attempt to stimulate sales by directing persuasive communications to its buyers.
  An organization could have a number of promotional objectives including: company growth through increased sales; the creation of greater brand awareness; the differentiation of a product; and strategies for educating the market. According to Kotler (1997), the objectives that are met by promotion are to move the target market through the following phases: from unawareness to awareness, to beliefs/

knowledge, to attitude, to purchase intention and, finally, to purchase. He points out that marketers need to recognize that all consumers will go through each of these phases.

- *People*: as leisure industries are predominantly service based it is essential to have the appropriate staff who can relate effectively to customers. Recruitment of such staff and training them effectively are essential if an organization is to succeed. If done successfully, the organization will benefit from a competitive advantage.

- *Process*: this refers to the basic systems used by an organization to assist it in its delivery – for example, when you attend your local leisure centre for a swim you will engage in the facilities process to get to the pool. The key stages of the process in this example are: check-in at reception; pay for the session; change; swim; change; and exit. Generally speaking, an efficient process will help an organization to gain customer loyalty and will therefore generate additional future revenues.

- *Physical Evidence*: this term relates to the process whereby a service is delivered. As such it is one element of the marketing mix that allows the consumer to make informed judgements about an organization. It concerns the general environment of a product (e.g., the cleanliness of a facility such as a toilet area).

- *Pricing Strategies*: ensuring that a product is priced effectively is not easy. As a means to help out, a number of different pricing strategies have been established. Although some specific objectives may alter by strategy, there are two common goals that can be identified: maximizing the profit and maintaining the market share. In the leisure industry the common pricing strategies are market skimming and market penetration. However, some more general ones may also be used such as: psychological pricing; premium pricing; competition pricing; product line pricing; and bundle pricing.

Market skimming enables a business to set an initial high price to 'skim' revenue layer by layer from the market. It can be an effective strategy, especially when the quality and image can support a higher price; when there are enough buyers who want the product at that price; when the cost of producing a small volume isn't too high; and when competitors are not able to enter the market easily.

Market penetration is essentially the opposite of market skimming. Businesses will set low initial prices in order to penetrate the market quickly and deeply to win a large market share. This type of strategy can be most effective when: there is a market that is highly price-sensitive; when the production and distribution costs fall as the sales volume increases; and when low prices are required to help keep out any new market competition.

In addition to the predominant pricing strategies in the leisure industry there are a number of other lesser-known ones. Competition pricing relates to setting a price in comparison with competitors. Product line pricing concerns different products within the same product range but at different price points. As its nomenclature suggests, bundle pricing bundles a group of products at a reduced price. Psychological pricing considers the psychology and positioning of price within the marketplace. In very simple terms, a seller might decide to charge 99p instead of £1 for an item. Premium pricing is concerned with prices that can reflect the exclusiveness of the product.

Rob Wilson

Associated Concepts   Ansoff Matrix; Boston Matrix; Branding, Brand Awareness and Brand Image; Leisure Marketing; Market Positioning and Market Segmentation.

MARKET POSITIONING AND MARKET SEGMENTATION

Market positioning is a well-debated term that can mean slightly different things depending on the organization that is under discussion. Kotler (1997) suggests that it is the act of designing the company's 'offering' and 'image' so that they occupy a meaningful and distinct competitive position in target customers' minds. Essentially, for leisure organizations this means where a product or service fits into the marketplace (e.g., how a GP referral scheme fits into a leisure centre's product portfolio and its market). In a nutshell, effective positioning will put you first in the queue in the minds of potential customers.

It is vital that an organization establishes a market position before it begins a marketing exercise because it needs to understand how products are differentiated between competitors so it can decide why a customer would choose one product over another. Ideally, a product will be different from what others can offer and should be difficult for competitors to reproduce.

Marketers also need to understand that customers do not operate in one homogeneous market and that they have different characteristics, tastes and preferences. As such marketers need to break the market up into segments, so that products are targeted specifically at potential customers. In this regard, let us consider how fitness centres operate. There might be a local authority-run centre that is relatively cheap to use, and at the other end of the market a more expensive and exclusive centre run by a private company – the local authority centre will not, and also cannot, charge private centre prices. This process is called market segmentation.

Effective market segmentation will enable organizations to serve their customers more effectively, compete successfully with other companies in the same markets and achieve organizational goals. There are three basic market segmentation strategies that are followed in the leisure industry: undifferentiated marketing, concentrated marketing and multiple segmentation.

Undifferentiated marketing does not recognize the existence of segmentation in the marketplace, whereas concentrated marketing will focus on a single target market with a single marketing mix. Multiple segmentation, instead, puts an emphasis on several distinct target markets and develops a separate marketing mix for each of these.

Rob Wilson

Associated Concepts   Boston Matrix; Leisure Marketing; Marketing Mix for the Leisure Industries.

MARXISM

This term is founded on the ideas of the German philosopher and economic historian Karl Marx. Marxism is a *materialist* philosophy, in that it seeks to explain the existence of social life without assuming the existence of a *natural* social world, but, rather, looks at concrete, scientific, logical explanations of the world. Yet Marxism is more than just a philosophy that only aims to understand the world, it is also a political force or perspective that seeks to change the world.

In particular, Marx was concerned with the exploitation of workers (the proletariat) by the capitalist bourgeoisie. He highlighted the inevitable conflict between the workers and the capitalists as rooted in the production process – in that workers wanted higher wages to improve their standard of living but the capitalists wanted to ensure that wages were as low as possible to maximize their profit. Marx suggested that this conflict would end only when the capitalist system was abolished or overthrown and replaced by the more equitable system of communism.

For Marx all societies are composed of social institutions and the one system or institution that dominates all others is the economy. He drew on the idea of *historical materialism*, which asserts that the way in which humans produce material goods shapes the rest of society. This is often known as Marx's *base/superstructure* model, where the economic basis of society (the base or infrastructure) shapes the nature of that society (its superstructure).

Marx suggested that societies had advanced through a series of historical periods, or 'epochs', beginning with hunter-gatherers which he believed constituted a primitive form of communist society, where the production of food and other material goods was shared more or less equally by members of society. After this basic form of communism, Marx believed that all other epochs had been characterized by class struggle – as he and Friedrich Engles famously wrote in *The Communist Manifesto* in 1848: 'the history of all hitherto existing society is the history of class struggle'.

Marx laid out what he thought the workers should and would do to overcome their oppressors. In particular, he suggested that they must become aware of their shared oppression and see capitalism as the true oppressor. Marx saw this as a shift away from what he referred to as a 'class in itself' (simply a social group) to a 'class for itself' (where members have a class consciousness and solidarity). He suggested that the workers must organize and act to address their problems. This meant that workers should come together to replace their false consciousness with a class-consciousness, which recognized the importance of their unity.

Marx saw inherent weaknesses in the capitalist system and believed that these would lead to its downfall because, as capitalists are motivated by their individual desire for personal gain, they actually fear the competition from other capitalists. He thought that capitalists would therefore be reluctant to band together even though they shared common interests. In addition, the longer they kept workers' wages low the more they would alienate these workers and the more likely a conflict of interests would occur. Marxism is often criticized for being too deterministic and, in particular, for overemphasizing the power of the economy to shape all aspects of society. Notably, for most of the early to mid-twentieth century Marxism remained on the peripheries of social theory, often being seen as too radical and deeply flawed.

However, a new political and social radicalism in the late 1960s and early 1970s brought Marxism to the front of many social theoretical debates. A term often (loosely) applied to this new interest and writing on Marxism from the 1960s onwards is neo-Marxism. This is a post Second World War term, which succeed the earlier twentieth-century term of Western Marxism, which was used to distinguish contemporary thinking from 'classical Marxism'. Key neo-Marxist writers included Herbert Marcuse, who argued that the standardization of work and leisure experience in modern capitalist societies had created the 'one-dimensional man' whose freedom has been reduced to the pursuit of pleasure through the market, consumerism and popular culture. Neo-Marxism also tends to move away from the economic determinism of Marx's original writing and incorporates the consideration of other social forces, such as the culture industry.

Marxist (and neo-Marxist) influences have found their way into many writings on leisure. As early as the 1930s Theodor Adorno (1991) was writing about contemporary sport as 'a shadowy continuation of labour' and the role it played in exploitation. In the 1970s and 1980s the writers of the Birmingham School applied the neo-Marist ideas of Antonio Gramsci to various aspects of contemporary culture and, in particular, Clarke and Critcher's (1985) book *The Devil Makes Work* offers a (now classic) neo-Marxist consideration of leisure – highlighting several key class-based dimensions of leisure, such as how leisure is also shaped by middle-class ideals and capitalist commercial interest and is used as a form of social control of the working classes.

Other significant neo-Marxist accounts of leisure have included Ian Taylor's (1969) consideration of football hooliganism. Here Taylor suggested that for most of its history football has always been a working-class sport, but from the 1960s onwards football had became increasingly taken over by big businesses. The working-class fans therefore became alienated from what was once *their* sport, leading many of them to rebel by engaging in violent ('hooligan') acts. Also, Jean-Marie Brohm's neo-Marxist critique of sport participation argues that sport in capitalist societies ultimately leads athletes to become alienated from their own bodies, as the body is experienced by the athlete as a technical means to an end and the result of this is that the body ceases to be a source of pleasure and fulfilment in itself.

Garry Crawford

Associated Concepts Alienation; Birmingham School; Critical Theory; False Consciousness; Football Hooliganism; Hegemony.

MASCULINITY AND MASCULINITIES

Masculinities refers to 'the set of social practices and cultural representations associated with being a man' (Pilcher and Whelehan, 2004: 82). Hence, what is deemed as masculine varies across time and societies and, some would argue, within cultures also.

There is a long history of writing that links masculinity to our biology and physiology (see, for example, Goldberg, 1979) and suggests that masculine norms and practices are 'natural' and 'innate'. However, sociology would argue that the norms and practices commonly associated with masculinity are learnt values, taught to individuals through a process of socialization. In particular, Hearn (1996: 214) points out that we need to understand men's practices, social relations, assumptions and beliefs which are 'masculinized' rather than speaking of some independent substance of masculinity itself.

For instance, Connell has developed a sociological analysis of masculinity within wider discussions of gender. For Connell (1995) gender is the outcome of ongoing reinterpretations and definitions of the reproductive and sexual capacities of the human body. Masculinity can then be understood as the result of the socially and culturally defined norms and values that we associate with reproductive biology. Connell suggests that within our culture there exists a 'gender hierarchy', in which masculinity is placed above and as superior to femininity.

In particular, Connell asserts that at the top of this hierarchy is 'hegemonic masculinity', which provides a 'traditional' and 'ideal' definition of masculinity based upon the ideas of physical and emotional strength and heterosexuality. According to Connell (1995: 77) hegemonic masculinity can be defined as 'the configuration of gender practice which embodies the currently accepted answer to the problem of the legitimacy of patriarchy, which guarantees (or is taken to guarantee) the dominant position of men and the subordination of women'. However, while few men live up to this, most will gain advantages from being associated with it and hence below this in the hierarchy is 'complicit masculinity'. Below that is 'subordinate masculinities', such as homosexuality, and below these comes femininities. These too can take different forms, such as 'emphasized', 'compliant' or 'resistant' femininities, but, Connell suggests, these are always subordinate to masculinities.

Sport is a good example of how masculinity is valued and reinforced within our culture. For instance, Horrocks (1995: 4) argues that sport reinforces 'masculine images and lifestyles' and, hence, Messner and Sabo (1990) suggest that sport is an ideal site from which to explore how the gender order is produced, maintained and challenged within our society.

However, it has been argued that social changes throughout the twentieth century have challenged this gender hierarchy and sexual and gender identities have become much more questioned in some quarters. For instance, MacInnes (1998) suggests that many authors only seem to think that (biologically defined) men can be masculine, but argues that masculinity is not just the property of men. MacInnes also points out that masculinity should be understood as an ideology about what men should be like and this is developed by both men and women.

In recent years, more poststructuralist and postmodern accounts have developed that see sexuality and gender as much more fluid and Connell's more recent (2000) work suggests that masculine behaviour and traits do not only belong only to men, but can sometimes be demonstrated by women. Hence, masculinities should be understood as sets of practices and not as necessarily belonging to any one (biologically defined) type of person.

However, this questioning of gender roles has also led to a solidification and reinforcement of traditional ideas of masculinity and femininity by others. For instance, the rise of 'lads' mags' such as *Maxim*, *FHM* and *Loaded* in the 1990s with their recipe of sexism and overt masculinity can be understood as a response to the advances made by feminism in the 1970s and 1980s. There is also a long history of popular life-style guidebooks which talk about the need for men to reinforce and rediscover their masculinity. This includes Robert Bly's (1991) book *Iron John*, which suggests that masculinity has been damaged by modern society and that men need to regain this through 'male bonding' and 'men-only' activities that will reinforce their 'natural' masculinity. This is also something that popular fiction has tapped into – for example, in the novel by Chuck Palahniuk (later turned into a film) *Fight Club*, which likewise seems to suggest that masculinity is being eroded by modern consumerism and glorifies a group of men's attempts to regain this through violence.

However, leisure research, such as Blackshaw's (2003) *Leisure Life*, suggests that on the contrary 'solidly' modern men still exist who not only perceive that they grew up as 'real' men, as part of a dominant masculinist hegemony, but also that this is a distinction they will not relinquish willingly. For these 'lads' their fate, their collective weekend leisure experience, is just a break from their 'ordinary' lives. However, more than this, it is created by 'the lads' as (hyper) 'real' life, where in between times they go on rehearsing their parts, biding their time, until 'real' life in the hegemonic masculine social order of

the leisure life-world resumes as normal on a Friday or Saturday night.

Garry Crawford

Associated Concepts Feminism; Hegemony; Identity; Ideology; Power; Women's Leisure.

MASS MEDIA

Technically, when talking about the mass media we should say 'the mass media are … ' rather than 'the mass media is … ', because the word 'media' is the plural of 'medium'. Hence, when we say 'media' we are talking about many things, including television, newspapers, magazines, the internet, and so on.

The word medium means a midway point or a form of carrying communication – such as how a 'spiritualist' (or 'medium') acts as the midway point between the 'physical' and 'spiritual' worlds. Hence, its plural ('media') refers to multiple forms of communication and, when prefixed with the term mass, means forms of media that can communicate to large (mass) audiences.

The advent of the mass media is tied in with the history of printing. Block printing probably dates back to as early as the seventh century AD in China, but did not become commonplace in Europe until the fourteenth century. The advent of the 'mass media' is usually attributed to what are referred to as 'popular prints', which became popular in Europe from the fifteenth century onwards. These were commonly produced by woodcut printing, which were then crudely coloured by hand.

The mechanical printing press, invented by German goldsmith Johannes Gutenberg in 1447, greatly increased printing capabilities and the speed and reduced costs, and would subsequently lead to the production of the first newspaper in Strasburg, Germany, in the early seventeenth century. Throughout the seventeenth century there were many types of publications featuring 'news' stories, but across Europe in this period there started to develop more regular and periodical publications, which we associate with contemporary newspapers.

The development of the mass media was then greatly enhanced by several key inventions in the nineteenth century, such as photography, the telephone, the phonograph, cinematography, the wireless telegram and loudspeakers. Shortly after, the early twentieth century brought radio, talking films and television, and we can see the importance of the mass media in our society began to increase to the level of saturation (seeping into every corner of our lives) that it has reached today.

However, it is also important that we do not see the mass media as simply 'a window on the world', showing us 'truth' and 'reality'. The mass media do not simply 'present' the world but instead offer various 'representations' of it. There can never be an unbiased, objective representation of the world, as all representations come from humans and hence are created from a particular position or viewpoint (O'Shaughnessy, 1999). As Nowell-Smith has argued, the mass media always present a point of view, 'an angle ... coming from somewhere and directed somewhere' (1981: 160).

One distinction that is often made is between 'new' and old' media forms. Generally the term old media is used to refer to older (usually analogue) media forms, such television, radio and print publishing, whereas the term new media (usually digital) refers to media forms such as the internet and digital television. However, answering the question 'What is new about new media?' is very difficult. First, it is evident that media technologies will enter different countries and regions at different times, making it difficult to define one piece of technology as necessarily 'new'. For instance, in many rapidly developing nations (such as some in East Asia) technologies such as the internet are entering many people's homes at the same time as television, thereby making both of these technologies 'new' for many people there. In addition, a lot of new technologies are 'recombinant', simply combining existing media forms into new media, such as the internet, which consists mainly of written text,

pictures and video, all of which predate the World Wide Web (Flew, 2002). Therefore the question of 'What is "new" about new technologies?', Livingstone (1999: 60) suggests, should be rephrased to ask 'What is "new" about these technologies *for society?*' (emphasis in original, cited in Flew, 2002: 10).

There are numerous theories and approaches to the study of the mass media. One of the earliest approaches to the study of the mass media is offered by the Frankfurt School, in their consideration of the 'culture industry' and its role as a means of (class-based) social control. Another tradition with media studies is that of 'media effects', which considers the impact media texts (such as violent films and digital games) have on audiences. Communications studies, and in particular the work of Toronto School writer Marshall McLuan and Harold Innis, are interested in the ways the mass media have transformed our lives, such as by making global mass communication possible. In Britain a cultural studies approach to the mass media was most notably developed by writers at the Birmingham School, who focused their attention on the role of the mass media as a form of state apparatus and a source of social control, but crucially one that could be resisted by its audience.

A more 'positive' reading and analysis of the mass media is offered by a 'uses and gratification' approach, which looks at the uses of the mass media in forming our personal relationships and social identities. For instance, Dennis McQuail (1987) suggests that the mass media is a source of information and education, social integration and interaction, as well as entertainment, and helps to develop our sense of identity and personal values. As Homer Simpson (of *The Simpsons*) once said of his television, the mass media can be 'teacher, mother, secret lover'.

Garry Crawford

Associated Concepts Audiences; Birmingham School; Communication; Critical Theory; Digital Gaming; Fans; Hegemony; Identity; Violence.

MASS-OBSERVATION

This is the nomenclature associated with the work of a research organization established in 1937 by Tom Harrison and Charles Madge, which carried out the world's largest ever participant observation study. Known as the Mass-Observation 'Worktown' project, this involved an investigation into the habits and habitats of the Northern working class in England, a good deal of which took place in leisure settings such as the pub, the cinema and sporting events, and was carried out by a panel of 500 volunteers who recorded their observations in diaries. Some of Mass-Observation's volunteers were also directed to take photographs. Humphrey Spender took hundreds of pictures in Bolton, some of which were displayed at the Ancient and Modern Gallery in London in 2007.

There is no doubt that Mass-Observation is a wonderful archive, but two particular, and oft-voiced, criticisms of it are that the observers tended either to emphasize the out of the ordinary rather than the typical or the reverse – 'the boring flatness of life, the extreme social distance between the ordinary people and the elites, and the popular indifference to political parties and programmes' (McKibbin, 2008: 31). Indeed, the mass observers might have had their eyes on the small moments of the quotidian that defy orchestration, ideology and indoctrination, but as theorists of everyday life have demonstrated that is precisely what it is about human life that is the most difficult to capture. This problem was further exacerbated in the case of Mass-Observation because Harrison and Madge never really considered the social distance between themselves and their research subjects and what this implied for either their chosen social research method or their research findings.

Tony Blackshaw

Associated Concepts Ethnography; Everyday Life; Leisure in the Community.

MCDONALDIZATION

George Ritzer's concept of McDonaldization is largely built upon the ideas of rationalization developed in the nineteenth century by Max Weber, who argued that modernity or modern life has resulted in a decline in traditionalism, where we rely less on religion and tradition and more on reason and rationality. For Weber, modern capitalist society has become increasingly bureaucratic and rule-bound.

Ritzer (1993: 1) defines the concept of McDonaldization as 'the process by which the principles of the fast-food restaurant are coming to dominate more and more sectors of American society as well as the rest of the world'. In particular, Ritzer suggests that this fast-food, restaurant-inspired business model has spread into many other leisure-sector industries – such as indicated in Ritzer and Stillman's (2001b) argument that the building of many new ballparks involves the creation of McDonaldized 'inauthentic' and 'simulated' environments.

Ritzer suggests that McDonaldization is characterized by four components: efficiency, calculability, predictability and control. First, the McDonald's restaurant, and other 'McDonaldized' corporations (i.e., companies that draw on the style and format and way of doing business of the fast-food restaurant sector) emphasize 'efficiency'. In a time-pressured and consumer-based society, service needs to be fast and efficient. Increasingly people do not want to wait for things – they expect a fast and reliable service, and consumer desires are not based upon waiting but, rather, on immediate (but short-lived) gratification. Calculability involves the quantification of services and products: everything centres on size and quantity, rather than quality or style. Burgers, fries and other McDonaldized products are measured by size and product names emphasize this, such as the 'Big Mac'. McDonaldization also breeds 'predictability' – the products, services and even the style and nature of restaurants are standardized so they are the same everywhere, every time. In most places around the world in McDonalds, Pizza Hut, Burger King, KFC and other fast-food chains, each chain outlet will offer similar (if not the same) menus, in very similar restaurants, so customers will know what to expect. The final aspect of McDonaldization is 'control' – wherever possible technology will replace humans, so the processes can become automated and easily controllable. For instance, in fast-food restaurants most of the food is pre-prepared so it is simply (re)heated while automated machines measure out the portions and time how long food needs to be cooked (or reheated) for.

However, Ritzer suggests that these four dimensions lead to a fifth (unforeseen) dimension or consequence: 'the irrationality of rationality'. As Ritzer (1994: 154) writes: 'Most specifically, irrationality means that rational systems are *unreasonable* systems. By that I mean that they deny the basic humanity, the human reason, of the people who work within or are served by them' – that is to say, that this emphasis on so-called 'rational' ways of operating leads to irrational consequences. These irrational consequences can be summarized under the headings of 'illusion', 'dehumanization' and 'externalities' (Aldridge, 2003).

That is to say, McDonaldized corporations only give the illusion of efficiency. The staff members are so fast and efficient because the customers are required to take care of some of their work, such as queue up, pay immediately, carry food to their tables and clean up afterwards. Also, because staff (in their McJobs) are monitored so closely, there is low moral, low productivity and a high labour turnover – so they are rarely friendly or nice to customers.

The whole process of engaging with these corporations is dehumanized as both staff and customers go through preset routines with the latter eating standardized repetitive food in standardized repetitive settings. Also companies such as McDonalds frequently suffer external pressure from outside as films such as *Super Size Me* (Morgan Spurlock, 2004) and books such as *Fast-Food Nation* (Schlosser, 2001) have highlighted the unhealthy and even immoral practices of these kinds of corporations. What McDonaldized corporations rely on most commonly is expensive and powerful legal action to crush those people who dare to criticize them (such as the McLibel case, where McDonalds stopped people handing out leaflets outside one of its restaurants). As Aldridge (2003: 114) puts it: 'corporations with a loveable image are apt to turn nasty if you refuse to love them'.

Garry Crawford

Associated Concepts Bureaucracy; Capitalism; Consumer Society; Consumption; Disneyization; Modernity; Postmodernity; Theming.

METHODOLOGY

This term is often mistakenly used to refer to the research methods employed within a research project. For instance, it is common to find a 'methodology' section within books, projects and dissertations, which discusses what research methods (such as interviews, questionnaires and observations) were employed in the study and how these were utilized and administered. However, the term does have a second wider meaning and, hence, to save confusion, many researchers and authors will refer to the discussion of their research tools simply as 'research methods' or 'research design'.

The second, and more correct, use of the term refers to wider and deeper epistemological and philosophical approaches to research. In other words, this refers to underlying assumptions and beliefs that inform a researcher's particular research approach and strategies. For instance, in the social sciences a key methodological debate exists between those who advocate positivistic/scientific quantitative research and those who adopt a more interpretivist/qualitative research approach and philosophy. Hence, one's epistemological assumptions about social reality, and how we can understand this, will inform the particular research tools and methods that we employ. An example of this kind of methodological discussion can be found in Blackshaw's (2003) *Leisure Life*, where he offers a critique and rejection of the usefulness of traditional ethnographic methods and tools in studying leisure in a 'liquid modern' world.

Garry Crawford

Associated Concepts Content Analysis; Conversational Analysis; Ethnography; Interviews; Observation; Oral/Life History; Qualitative Research; Quantitative Research; Questionnaires; Sampling.

MIMESIS

Derived from the Greek *mimeisthai*, meaning 'to imitiate', this concept, at its most basic, describes the relationship between imitative leisure forms and reality. For example, a piece of artwork can often be described as a copy of something in the 'real' world, just as some sports will be described as facsimiles of battles. What these two examples suggest is that mimesis describes both the products of our leisure and our actions in leisure. However, as Matthew Potolsky points out, mimesis is also much more than these two things; it is a concept that has taken on 'different guises in different historical contexts, masquerading under a variety of related terms and translations: emulation, mimicry, dissimulation, doubling, theatricality, realism, identification, correspondence, depiction, verisimilitude, resemblance' (2006 :1).

In all these senses mimesis is always a double. With this in mind it is possible to argue that some aspects of leisure, such as following the fortunes of your favourite sports team, bear an apt resemblance to a double human existence, as the fortunes of your team move through the seasons but also include the sense of life, birth, death and drama that takes place in modern societies. To this extent, it might be argued that sport gives meaning to the grim and the exciting sense of the mortality of life itself.

Elias and Dunning (1986) used the concept of mimesis in two ways: on the one hand they depicted the ways in which sport elicits different emotions and, on the other, they showed how people can act out strong feelings in sport without running the risk of sanctions. As Dunning suggested, it is in sport that you 'can vicariously experience hatred and the desire to kill, defeating opponents and humiliating enemies' (1999: 27) – in other words, what is normally not condoned in social life is often made acceptable in leisure situations. Taking this understanding of mimesis to another level by highlighting the mimicry implicit in 'sports-entertainment', Atkinson also argues that the cultural appeal of professional wrestling is derived from the ways in which it is able to stage contrived hyper-violent athletic competition to mass audiences in ways that still feel 'sporting' and maintain the excitement of 'real' sport.

What Elias and Dunning's understanding of mimesis perhaps overlooks is the persistence of real violence in sport. For example, some people continue to pursue blood sports because they obviously enjoy hunting animals and killing them. What this suggests is that, for some people, mimesis is simply not enough and the 'hot' blood of the hunt is some kind of compensation for the 'cold' bloodedness of modern life.

Tony Blackshaw

Associated Concepts Blood Sports; Carnivalesque; Elias; Figurations/Figurationalism; Flow; Liminality; Serious Leisure; Sportization.

MODERNISM

Modernism refers to forward-looking and 'modern' forms of thought and practices, particularly in relation to art, architecture and design, which are closely linked to the traditions of the Enlightenment, suggesting that human life, environment and creations can be improved by science, technology and rationality.

The birth of modernism occured in Europe around the turn of the twentieth century and is invariably linked to the dawn of modernity and mass production, as the manufacture of objects (such as furniture) moved away from bespoke, hand-crafted items to mass production (the Arts and Crafts movement of the same period being an attempt to keep alive the 'traditional', individually and hand-made crafts and arts). The height of modernist fashion in Europe came between 1910 and the 1930s (as typified in Art Deco fashions and styles) and spread to America in the 1930s and 1940s, though the influences of modernism continued on into the 1960s with Pop Art (e.g., in the work of Roy Lichtenstein) and beyond.

A key example of modernist thought and its aesthetics can be seen in the architecture of Bauhaus. Bauhaus was a German school of architecture that between 1919 and 1933 advocated functional and rational styles of architecture, with buildings utilizing straight lines and stark, simplified designs. Similarly, the architecture and designs of Le Corbusier present a significant example of modernist thought, such as Le Corbusier's ideas for a modern city ('the radiant city'), which proposed that people should live highly structured lives in functional and rationalized tower blocks, surrounded by parks for recreation and super highways joining together these modern metropolises. In art, Cubism, which utilized simplified shapes such as squares, circles and straight lines and can be most famously seen in Pablo Picasso's Cubist work (such as *Le Guitariste* in 1910), signifies another key example of modernism.

Garry Crawford

Associated Concepts Capitalism; Class; Crafts and Craftsmanship; Fashion; Modernity; Postmodernism; Postmodernity.

MODERNITY

Modernity is a slippery concept that is not easy to define. Generally speaking, it is associated with the dawning of the history of progress, the loosening stranglehold of religion and community, and the emergence of a rational commitment to robust individualism, together with the concomitant rise in humanism and secular, utopian values. Giddens (1990: 1) argues that modernity 'refers to the modes of social life and organization which emerged in Europe from about the seventeenth century onwards and which subsequently became more or less worldwide in their influence'. But if this definition tells us something about the timing of the historical emergence of modernity and its geographical location it also tells us little about its core institutional features underpinning the modern way of understanding the world. The idea of modernity (or modernization) refers to the emergence of a new faith in the processes of scientific knowledge and technological advance, which marks the beginning of modernity's separation from traditional society.

There are a number of important precursors and drivers in the origins of modernity. One of the most important of these was the Enlightenment, which was a philosophical movement that challenged religious and traditional beliefs and advocated a society based upon science and rationality. This was also an important precursor to the Industrial Revolution, which in turn was another driver in modernity. The Industrial Revolution can be traced back to the latter part of the eighteenth century in England and brought about massive changes not only to the production process but also to social life. Coupled with this we also saw great population movement. In particular, industrialization moved people off the land and away from rural communities into cities and factories, but there also occurred great international movement of people, as millions of Europeans emigrated to North America and Australia and millions of African slaves were forcibly brought into North America and Europe.

Capitalism had existed before industrialization and was an important precursor to this, but industrialization allowed the rapid expansion of capitalist modes of business and helped spread this as a/the dominant organizing force within modern society. Modernity also saw the development of new forms of government. This period saw the rise of the nation state, along with new political ideas such as nationalism and citizenship. Coupled with this, there was a rise in Western power and global domination. From the fifteenth century onwards European power had been colonizing and conquering the world, leading to a concentration of power and wealth in Europe and a spread of Western ideals and culture, but the rapid development of Western nations in this period saw their global influence and importance increase vastly.

Modernity brought about massive changes to social life, including leisure. With the division between work and home, leisure time occupied distinct periods, rather than, as in pre-industrial times, it often merging with work time. In particular, leisure and recreation were increasingly advocated by the middle classes and capitalists to improve the lives of unhealthy workers. The advent of the railways also made travel increasingly easy and possible for a greater proportion of the population, and we can also see the birth of the 'package holiday', such as Thomas Cook's first organized group excursion, which left Leicester train station in 1841. In addition, with the Industrial Revolution came a consumer revolution, where cities offered a rapid expansion of sites for shopping and entertainment and ushered in the rise of the department store, music halls, pubs and, later, cinemas. We can also acknowledge the changes in consumer attitudes, such as the rising importance of fashion and trends and also the growing number of industries based around consumption, such as those in design, advertising and marketing.

The question of whether or not we still live in modernity or a modern age is a highly contentious one. Many have argued that the society in which we live today is very different from that seen in the eighteenth and nineteenth centuries, with rapid industrialization and urbanization. In particular, many societies (such as in the UK and the USA) have shifted from a production-based society to a consumer society, which is post-industrial. This has led some to state that we now live in a world that has passed beyond what was described as the modern and, hence, it should be seen as 'postmodern'. However, postmodernity is a term which carries with it many philosophical, political and theoretical connotations and, hence, some authors have chosen to adopt other terms to describe contemporary society, such as 'late modernity', 'advanced capitalism', 'second modernity' or 'liquid modernity.

Garry Crawford and Tony Blackshaw

Associated Concepts   Bauman; Capitalism; Consumer Society; Consumption; Fashion; Globalization; Liquid Modernity; Modernism; Postmodernity; Shopping.

MONOPOLISTIC COMPETITION

Monopolistic competition usually occurs when there is a large number of companies operating within one particular market, offering very similar (but not identical) products. This tends to occur when the companies' products are suitably differentiated or if they are operating in a different geographical location. When such competition exists a firm has the opportunity to increase its price without losing its customers. A good example of this type of competition can be seen in the pub trade. It is usual to have a number of pubs within a certain part of town. When this occurs, the basic commodities that are on offer are essentially the same, but the brands of drinks and some other goods will often differ, as will the consistency and quality of these products. Consumers will display different characteristics and will therefore prefer one establishment over another. Consequently the pub attracting more customers can charge higher prices without this having a detrimental effect on trade.

Rob Wilson

Associated Concepts Demand; Elasticity; Supply.

MORAL PANICS

(folk devils and moral panics)

MOTIVATION

Hannahgan (2002) has argued that motivation consists of all the drives, forces and influences – conscious and unconscious – that will cause an individual to want to achieve certain aims. It is important that managers understand their own motivations and those of their staff. Some individuals will chase money, some will be motivated by challenges and excitement, others by responsibility. We all have different reasons for going to work, but broadly speaking there are two distinct motivators. Intrinsic motivators are those factors external to the individual, such as when a line manager says 'thank you' for a job well done and it leads to personal fulfilment. External motivators are where the rewards are external, such as when an individual gains a pay rise or promotion. The aim of motivational management is to try and understand the needs and objectives of individuals in an organization and to arrive at a position where both their individual needs and those of the organization are met. Schein (1987) calls this the establishment of a psychological contract.

Rob Wilson

Associated Concepts Human Resource Management; Management Styles; Training and Development and Appraisals.

MULTIPLIER ANALYSIS

As developed by UK Sport (2000: 17), this term indicates the conversion of 'the total amount of additional expenditure in the host city to a net amount of income retained within the city'. For example, during a major sport event the total amount of money spent at a hotel will not necessarily be recirculated in a city. Some of the money will be required to pay wages, food suppliers, beverage suppliers, and so on, with such recipients possibly residing outside of the local economy. A multiplier is a device which is used to convert the total additional expenditure figure into the amount of local income retained within the local economy (UK Sport, 2000). There are many different multipliers. However, the one most commonly used for economic impact studies is the proportional income multiplier. The calculation will often be illustrated with the following formula:

$$\frac{\text{Direct + Indirect + Induced Income}}{\text{Initial Visitor Expenditure}}$$

Rob Wilson

Associated Concepts Economic Impact of Sport Events.

NEO-CLASSICAL ANALYSIS

In order to analyse the demand for leisure, economists will utilize the neo-classical approach to consumer behaviour, which regards the consumer as having a given set of tastes and preferences which results in individuals allocating their income so as to maximize utility. This requires us to define what we mean by quantity demanded in a particular leisure context. The first approach involves a hierarchical modelling of demand for leisure, with the *actual demand* for a leisure activity playing the role of the *parent demand function*, while the demands for leisure facilities, equipment, clothing, and so on are treated as *derived demands*.

The quantity demanded is a measure of the leisure participation, while the derived demands give an estimate of a consumer's expenditure on leisure goods and services. This can be illustrated with an example. In the sport of golf, we can identify the parent and derived demand functions easily. The parent demand function is the individual consumer's actual decision on the extent to which he or she will participate in the sport. Following a decision to play golf the derived demands will include clubs, golf balls, clothing and shoes, plus travel to and from the golf course. All of these derived demands are dependent on the individual consumer's decision to participate or not.

These observations notwithstanding, Gratton and Taylor (2000) argue that not all kinds of leisure will fit into this approach, making it unsuitable for understanding leisure activities where it is hard to distinguish between parent demand and derived demand

relationships. For example, a skiing package holiday is a composite holiday, for which a consumer can pay a single price and could well include the costs of travel, equipment, clothing, accommodation and food.

Rob Wilson

Associated Concepts Demand for Health Model; Household Production Function Approach, The; Income–Leisure Time Trade-Off and Time Dating; Neo-classical analysis; Price; Supply.

NEO-MARXISM

(marxism)

NEO-TRIBES

Neo-tribes are social groups distinguished by shared leisure life-styles and leisure tastes. As Rob Shields (1996b) points out, they are not tribes in the anthropological sense because their social bonds are associated with neither fixity nor durability. They are what Michel Maffesoli (1996) describes as the 'little masses' of the uncertain and fragmenting consumer society that is postmodernity.

Bauman's (1992) discussion of neo-tribes is used as further evidence to support his assertion that we are moving towards a more individualistic society. Bauman argues that individuals, increasingly detached from traditional social categories such as social class, gender and ethnicity, engage in new and fluid communities (neo-tribes) out of a desperate search for community. However, this is still a largely individual act as membership of these neo-tribes is largely based upon the ownership and individual use of consumer goods.

Maffesoli's (1991, 1993, 1996) discussion of (postmodern or pseudo) tribes (or *tribus*, as Maffesoli refers to them) places more emphasis on collectivity than Bauman, though significantly Maffesoli's *tribus* are also fluid and often temporary. Rob Shields (1996: xi) in his introduction to Maffesoli's (1996) book *The Time of the Tribes* provides a clear introduction to Maffesoli's use of the term *tribus* and defines these as 'not only fashion victims, or youth subcultures' but also 'hobbyists; sport enthusiasts; and many more – environmental movements, user-groups of state services and consumer lobbies'. Significantly these groups, due to their fluid and often temporary nature, possess little social power apart from the ability of integration and inclusion that is displayed through the habits and rituals of the group, yet can still 'elicit a strict conformity among its members' (Maffesoli, 1996: 15). Hence, Maffesoli emphasizes the continued importance of social belonging and social networks – socializing with friends, conversations and numerous other social interactions, he argues – which bind us together in tribalism.

Garry Crawford

Associated Concepts Audiences; Bauman; Class; Community; Consumer Culture; Consumption; Crafts and Craftsmanship; Fans; Hobbies; New Social Movements; Power; Subcultures.

NETWORK SOCIETY

Manuel Castells, in his three-volume work *The Information Age: Economy, Society and Culture* (1996, 1997, 1998), argued that since the 1980s a new type of economy and society has developed. Though Castells was not the first person to suggest that information communication technologies have changed the nature of global life (for instance, a similar argument was made by Nora and Minc in their book, *Computerization of Society*, in 1980), he remains the theorist most commonly associated with this argument.

Castells has highlighted that, while societies have remained capitalist in nature, what has changed is a shift away from an 'industrial mode of development' towards an 'informational mode of development'. At the centre of this informational mode of development are networks, and Castells terms the development of this new social structure as a 'network society'. Though social networks have existed in 'other times and spaces', Castells (1996: 469) has argued that 'the new information technology paradigm provides the material basis for its pervasive expansion throughout the entire social structure'.

Information becomes the basis of economic activity. It is both the resources and the product of new technologies (Flew, 2002) and information communication technologies are having an increasing influence and impact on our everyday lives. Ideas surrounding a network society have been picked up and developed in many areas of leisure studies, but probably nowhere more so than in studies regarding use of the internet in patterns of everyday life, such as can be found in the work of Wellman and Haythornthwaite (2002).

With the emergence of the network society, Castells suggests this has led to a transformation in the nature of work, where structures, organizations and individuals need to be flexible. In an information-based society changes happen quickly and frequently, therefore for businesses, organizations and individuals to survive they must also be able to adapt and change quickly. Hence, labour has become less standardized and more flexible and the working classes have become 'de-massified'. As labour becomes fragmented, diverse and flexible, social class identities and commonalities become less apparent and social inequalities increase based around inclusion or exclusion from global networks. Castells also suggests that there has been a transformation of social power and communities in the network society. Nation states are becoming less relevant and important as economies, the media and electronic communication become increasingly global. As with Ulrich Beck, Castells emphasizes the importance of new social movements, and communities for Castells become elective communities – communities we join because we want to (such as hobby and interest groups), rather than those attributed to us by society.

Castells (1997: 321) also points out that politics has become a 'race for audience ratings', competing with the entertainment industries to get our attention. For him power increasingly exists within information networks, but this power is organized around certain 'spaces of flows' – that is to say, certain places will become hubs or nodes or links within this global network. Metropolises like London, Paris and New York, Castells suggests, are 'global cities', points or links within a global network, as too are production centres such as Silicon Valley in California where much of the world's computer industry is based (which Castells refers to as 'technopoles'). People will also form cultural links within this network society. Hence power is less located within the hands of political leaders, but more based in the cultural, economic and information flows of a networked society.

The spread and rapid increase of access to information can have positive consequences, but it can have negative ones as well. Castells like many others warns about the rise of a surveillance society, where information is increasingly gathered and stored on ordinary individuals. However, unlike many other writers on a surveillance society, Castells (1997: 299–303) argues that we should be less concerned with 'big brother' and more worried about 'little sister' – that the global networks society may have reduced the power and influence of nation states, but what are rising in importance and power are the privately owned corporations which are increasingly monitoring, observing and recording our behaviour.

However, by way of critiquing the idea of a 'network society' it could be said that there is nothing particularly new about Castells' arguments. For instance, numerous other authors (such as Norbert Elias) have considered the importance of social networks as the basis of social structure. May (2002) has also pointed to the fact that authors such as Castells have greatly exaggerated the impact of new technologies on societies, which still remain capitalist and have changed little in their fundamental nature in recent decades. Castells has also been criticized for being overly deterministic. For instance, Calhoun (2000) has argued that Castells sees network society as inevitable and unavoidable, that there are no alternatives and the power of information and globality will continue and increase. This, however, ignores other possibilities of how society could or should develop. The future is not written for us and societies do not necessarily have to develop as Castells believes they will continue to.

Garry Crawford

Associated Concepts Capitalism; Community; Consumer Society; Elias; Globalization; New Social Movements; Paradigms; Power; Risk Society.

NEW SOCIAL MOVEMENTS

New Social Movements (NSM) is a term given to new forms of social collectives that appeared from the 1960s onwards. However, the systematic study of NSM and the development of NSM theory did not occur until the 1980s. Where 'old' social movements can be understood as being primarily focused around class divisions and, in particular, were primarily working-class based, NSM tend to be more 'issue'-based, (such as environmentalist, animal or human rights groups) or will form around social divisions other than class (such as race, ethnicity or age). Class does remain important in understanding NSM, in that membership of these groups tends to be largely middle class (or at least affluent working class), but class is not central to these movements and membership can cut across class groups.

As such, NSM tend to be less concerned with the acquisition of materialistic rights or goods, but more focused upon identity and meanings. This shifts the arena of political contestation and struggle away from traditional political spheres into the 'everyday' and 'cultural' domain, where 'political' action and resistance take more diverse paths and strategies (some 'old', others 'new'), such as employing websites, e-mail campaigns, leafleting, protest songs and concerts, T-shirts, slogans and media campaigns, 'sit-ins' and numerous other means of protest. NSM also tend to be less hierarchical, less bureaucratic and more participatory than older political movements and, for many members of NSM, this is more a way of life than isolated 'political' acts. NSM therefore blur the boundaries between leisure and political action, as NSM become sites of socializing, leisure and everyday life, such as peace protestor encampments, or fundraising concerts or events.

Key theorists on NSM include Alain Touraine (1981), who has written on political struggle in post-industrial societies and the rise of new political groups such as *Solidarnosc* (Solidarity) in Poland, and Jürgen Habermas (1987), who sees everyday life as the new battleground being colonized by advanced capitalism and simultaneously resisted by grass roots-level collectives. Similarly, Manuel Castells (1996) sees NSM as indicative of the changing nature of advanced capitalist societies and locates a consideration of NSM within his discussion of a 'network society', while

Beck locates these within his discussion of a 'risk society'.

Garry Crawford

Associated Concepts Bureaucracy; Class; Consumer Society; Consumption; Identity; Network Society; Power; Risk Society.

NON-PARTICIPANT OBSERVATION

(observation (participant and non-participant observation))

NON-PLACE

The idea of the non-place is an anthropological notion put forward by Marc Auge who argued that 'if place can be defined as rational, historical and concerned with identity, then a space which cannot be defined as rational, or historical, or concerned with identity will be a non-place' (1995: 77). Such non-places, according to Auge, unlike certain 'places' of modernity where the ancient and the modern coexist, exhibit a state of excesses, solitude and self-containment, all of which are products of what he calls 'supermodernity'.

Auge highlights that, as the world gets smaller through cheaper and more available means of transport, as well as through technological advances in communication equipment such as satellite and the internet, combined with an extension of life expectancy and an ageing global population, there is an excess of space, time and ego and that these three excesses result in supermodernity.

Supermodernity, for Auge, is characterized by the temporary spaces it produces, which are specifically created for travel, communication or consumption. These 'non-places' exist simply to fulfil the requirements of the increasingly self-centred consumer. Examples of such non-places are airports, motorways, petrol or motorway service stations, large supermarkets and theme parks, which are often interchangeable and similar in their appearance and layout.

Auge accepts that 'places' do still exist and that such places have a history and local significance. He believes, however, that where such places are evident, super-modernity manifests them as 'a specific spectacle, as it does with all exoticism and all local particularity' (1995: 110). He also states that it is possible for such places to appear within a non-place. An example of this may be a culturally significant monu-ment being situated within an airport ter-minal. It is also the case that theme parks and shopping malls will attempt to create a pseudo-real spectacle, aimed at satisfying consumers' desire for historical or cultural identity, before ejecting them back on to the motorway, railway terminal or airport departure lounge.

The impact of supermodernity and non-places therefore marks the decline of the public 'man' and the rise of the self-obsessed individuals, who will spend 'more and more effort wondering where they are going [only] because they are less and less sure where they are' (1995: 115).

Jeremy Coulton

Associated Concepts Communication; Consumption; Liminality; McDonaldization; Modernity; Postmodernity.

NOSTALGIA

This word is used of modern ways of think-ing which understand the human relation-ship to the world as one of permanent homesickness or longing. As the great Czech novelist-cum-philosopher Milan Kundera (2002) points out in his novel *Ignorance*, the word is derived immediately from the Greek

Nostos (return) and *Algos* (suffering). In its primary sense, therefore, Kundera suggests that the idea of nostalgia is suggestive of the sort of suffering that is caused by 'an unap-peased yearning to return'. Full of the ache and melancholy of reminiscence, its meaning freighted with implication, nostalgia is the word for what will always be yet has never quite been.

Kundera goes on to suggest that we tend to think of nostalgia as something that con-cerns us the more we get older and that as such it is the preserve of the old: 'the more vast time the amount of time we've left behind us, the more irresistible is the voice calling us to return to it' (ibid.: 77). This is really a facade. The truth is that as we get older each moment of our lives becomes more and more precious and we are there-fore more likely to stop wasting our time over recollections about the past. According to Kundera this is the 'mathematical para-dox' of nostalgia: it is at its most powerful in our youth, when the amount of our lives that has passed is still somewhat small.

What Kundera is suggesting here is that we live in an age when even nostalgia isn't what it used to be. This theme has been taken up by Zygmunt Bauman in his books about *liquid modernity*, where he argues that, just as our contemporary age is one of rapid techno-logical advancements, it is also one where our social relationships have become mere mechanical ways of relating that are built on speeded-up separations. He also suggests that the overriding ethos of the *Zeitgeist* is the preservation of youth combined with an obsession for specificity, for 'really' *feeling* what you do and living life to the full. What all this suggests is that not only are we con-stantly trying to authenticate our realities in going about our everyday lives but also in this beginning and ending formula of experience and expectations we are all inevitably drawn to loss, to nostalgia.

The evidence would seem to suggest that it is in our leisure time that we look to fulfil the perpetual 'homesickness' or 'longing', obsessed as we are with pottering about those virtual spaces which connote past encounters as well as those spurned or not acted upon. High on the familiarity of it all, we log on to eBay to bid for old albums and childhood comics and toys, to download clips of concerts and pop videos from YouTube we never quite got around to seeing, to sign on to Friends Reunited or Classmates and reconnect with people we never much liked in the first place and to join Second Life as 'avatars' (hot chicks, rock chicks, chick magnets, sporty types, and so on), or what we have always wanted to be or couldn't be or were too embarrassed to make the effort to be. Nostalgia seems to have caught up with all of us, then – it's as if it's always biting our heels.

Tony Blackshaw

Associated Concepts Digital Gaming; Dromology and Speed; Flow; Liminality; Liquid Modernity; Mimesis; Postmodernism; Postmodernity; Serious Leisure.

0

OBSERVATION (PARTICIPANT AND NON-PARTICIPANT OBSERVATION)

Methodological observation refers to the process of watching and recording social phenomena. As with most methods of investigation, observation is a research tool which may, on the face of it, seem quite straightforward and unproblematic, but can still be extremely complex and difficult to successfully undertake.

Generally speaking, observations will take the form of two ideal types: participant and non-participant. Generally, non-participant observation is where observers remain detached and separate from the phenomenon they are observing, while with participant observation they become an active (though not necessarily 'full') participant within the social world under scrutiny. Non-participant observation is often found in laboratory-style (often psychological) experiments, where research participants are observed (sometimes covertly) by researchers, who will sometimes use recording equipment and/or one-way mirrors or similar. However, most social research tends to involve some degree of (even if relatively limited) participation by the researcher.

In particular, the separation between non- and participant observation is often far from clear and in many research projects the researcher may find their position within the research shifting continuously between these two. Hence, it is better to understand participant observation and non-participant observation not as polar opposites, but rather as end points on a sliding scale of levels of participation. This is most clearly illustrated by Gold (1969) who offers a scale of the roles of an observer on a continuum ranging from the completely detached (non-participant) *complete observer* to the *observer as participant*, through *participant as observer* to *complete participant* – that is, at this final point on the scale, the observer becomes a complete and full participant in the activities he or she is observing.

Observation can be conducted covertly (where the participants do not know that they are being observed or the researcher's 'true' identity) or overtly (where the participants have full knowledge of their being observed). Obviously both of these raise different methodological and ethical issues and problems. For instance, individuals who know they are being observed are often less likely to behave in a 'natural' manner, bringing into question the whole validity of a researcher's observations. This is known as the 'Hawthorne Effect', a name taken from the Western Electric Company-owned 'Hawthorne' plant in Chicago, where in the 1920–1930s research on its workers showed that workers' productivity increased when they knew they were being observed. In turn, covert research raises massive ethical questions over whether or not researchers have the right to conduct research on individuals without their informed consent. Also, with both overt and covert research, researchers still have to be wary of their own biases. As Ely et al. (1991: 53) suggest 'a great concern of many beginning participant observers as well as more seasoned researchers is that of reaching for objectivity'. However, as Ely et al. continue: 'observations can never be objective ... this is because observation comes out of what the observer selects to see and chooses to not. All we can work for is that our vision is not too skewed by our subjectivities'.

One great advantage of observational research is that it allows a researcher to see the respondents in a (relatively) 'natural' setting and so this method has been employed by numerous studies of leisure, such as Blackshaw's (2003) observations of the leisure life-worlds of the group of 'lads' he studied in Leeds. However, one of the main difficulties encountered, especially with participant observation, is that this often involves the (three-stage) problem of gaining access to a group, maintaining a stable (i.e., engaged, but not too deep) position within this and finally withdrawing from the field – put simply, getting in, staying in and getting out. However, these potential difficulties are reduced if the researcher is already a member of the group under study, such as was the case for Blackshaw, but then again this raises other methodological and ethical questions such as is it possible 'to see the wood for the trees' (e.g., make insightful observations) in a group in which you are already so well established?

Garry Crawford

Associated Concepts Ethnography; Everyday Life; Flâneurs, Flâneurie and Psychogeography; Interviews; Leisure Life-World; Mass-Observation; Methodology; Qualitative Methods; Sampling.

ORAL/LIFE HISTORY

This is a method of research and documentation used primarily within the study of history and anthropology and it is based upon either individual or collective verbal accounts that usually have been collected via interviews. The oral and life history approach involves a researcher asking his or her respondents to recall the past through reference to personal recollections memories and evocations of life stories, where they are encouraged to talk

about their experiences, attitudes and values. The enduring value of these approaches is in their ability to recover the power of life (and its emotions) decayed and lost in time. Memory is both private and public, an individual and social affair, and these approaches use the memories of their respondents not only to explore the ways in which they understand their own personal autobiographies, but also to unpack how individual *and* collective memory can speak about the important issues of continuity and change, power and oppression, love and hate, myth and desire, which are usually omitted or are not taken seriously enough in historical accounts.

Oral and life histories are particularly useful for gathering accounts of people's everyday lived experiences and personal histories and can also provide insight into traditions which may be dieing out or people's experiences of times of crisis or of great social and/or historical importance. These histories can be audio recorded (such as on tape or digitally) or written down and then constructed into individual or interweaving biographies of the participants. This has often been used in leisure studies. Good examples are Clare Langhamer's (2000) history of women's leisure between 1920 and 1960 and the work of John Williams and other researchers at the Sir Norman Chester Centre for Football Research at Leicester University, who conducted an oral history of an Afro-Caribbean football club in Leicester which the centre then published as the book *Highfield Rangers* (1994) that was drawn on by Williams in the chapter 'Rangers is a Black Club'.

Garry Crawford and Tony Blackshaw

Associated Concepts Ethnomethodology; Everyday Life; Interviews; Methodology; Qualitative Methods; Sampling.

OVERWORKED AMERICAN THESIS, THE

(Schor, Juliet B.)

P

PARADIGMS

Much is written today on 'paradigms' – 'alternative paradigms', 'paradigm shifts', 'multi-paradigmatic social science', and so on – in leisure studies. This run-of-the-mill usage of the paradigm conception is an indication of the significance of Kuhn's (1970) seminal work *The Structure of Scientific Revolutions*, first published in 1962, which changed the way we think about the philosophy of science and knowledge. According to Kuhn a paradigm is a framework of theories, ideas and/or methods which essentially shapes and determines our understanding of the world.

For Kuhn, there is no such thing as a 'scientific community' characterized by a 'paradigm' or a collective acceptance of an agreed framework of theories, ideas or methods. What exists are 'scientific communities' that focus on their own particular disciplines and areas of research. For example, the sociology of leisure is a paradigm dedicated to analysing leisure as far as it is a social phenomenon. These communities work on shared paradigms, which they are strongly committed to validating and defending at all costs. But every paradigm has its anomalies and, while scientists will attempt to refine their own frameworks of ideas, theories and methods to counter criticism, these anomalies may still accumulate over time. At some juncture, researchers may come to doubt the validity of the paradigm and the community in question reaches a point of no turning back. This crisis can only be resolved when a new paradigm emerges. Kuhn called these scientific revolutions 'paradigm shifts'.

Tony Blackshaw

Associated Concepts Discursive Formations; Hegemony; Methodology; Network Society; Structure of Feeling.

PARKER, STANLEY

(work-leisure)

PARTICIPANT OBSERVATION

(observation (participant and non-participant observation))

PERFORMATIVITY

The traditional meaning of this term in leisure studies lies with the act, process, or art of performing, particularly with reference to performance arts such as theatrical productions which incorporate acting, song or dance. Erving Goffman (1959) was one of the first major theorists to develop the term in a more critical way. According to him, it is not just actors, musicians, singers and dancers who perform. In the modern world we are all performers (even those of us who are not performers) and everyday life as a whole is guided by performativity. Drawing on a number of theatre analogies, he set out a categorization of dramaturgical contingencies by which he identified the key 'stage props' or strategies that individual actors might draw on in order to negotiate their way through the ups and downs, the challenges and embarrassments, that we are all confronted with in our everyday life.

At the same time that Goffman was developing these ideas about performativity in the 1960s, studies in ethnomethodology, which set out to uncover the 'methods' by which actors construct their everyday lives, were also being developed. These sought to show that, during these performances, individuals are not only able to convince others about their social identities – through the structures of everyday activities which they ordinarily and routinely produce and maintain – but sociologists are also better able to understand human interaction by disrupting tacitly agreed and taken-for-granted assumptions about everyday life through 'breaching experiments' (see Garfinkel, 1967).

As with the ethnomethodologists, Goffman centred his own analysis on individual actors and the ways in which they presented themselves in everyday life, but in addition to them what he was also offering was a form of analysis that took more account of the institutional and structural aspects of the interaction order. In this respect Goffman was wise to the fact that, while individual actors can draw on a range of techniques in order to maintain the presentation of the self, performativity comprises not merely singular acts in order to perform a 'personal front' but also established or institutionalized roles. For Goffman, then, dramaturgical performances tend to be embedded in an existing reality and are selected rather than individually created (Ritzer, 2003). In other words, and notwithstanding our individual ability to act, this suggests that our leisure still tends to reflect everything about what it means to be born in a particular place and time as well as our class, gender and ethnicity.

However, given these latter points, the 'centring' of the self remained at the very heart of Goffman's analysis and from Judith Butler's (1990) poststructuralist perspective this reflects the major weakness of his sociology. Even though Goffman takes into account both institutional and structural aspects of the interaction order, he also understands the individual presentation of the self as a performance rather than the 'front end' of performativity. Goffman's understanding of the self is 'fixed' and 'deep' rather than 'liquid' and 'aesthetic'; he constructs an understanding of the self at the 'centre' of things and this understanding is underpinned by a foundationalism which, in Butler's terminology, 'presumes, fixes and constrains' the individual subject.

What Butler is suggesting is that conventional wisdom tends to not only be preoccupied with the 'individual' or 'individual experience' but also understands the human *habitus* as something that lies deep in the human condition, like some sort of trace that is deep-rooted and a seemingly 'natural' basis for people's interaction with the world. Yet what her critique of Goffman is suggesting is that there is actually nothing below the surface of the self as it is presented in everyday life, that the individual does not exist outside discourse – what you see is what you get – and what the self performs is merely performativity, which, contrary to conventional wisdom, actually turns assumptions about the 'natural' back on themselves. As Butler (1990: 186) argues, 'just as bodily surfaces are enacted as natural, so these surfaces can become a site of dissonant and denaturalized performance that reveals the performative status of the natural itself'. Contrary to Goffman, from Butler's perspective it is a waste of time attempting to find or uncover the 'true' or 'real' self; the self is always defined in the performativity of the business of everyday life and this performativity is always a transaction with others. This is the central difference between Goffman and the poststructuralist interpretations of individual subjectivity.

The most radical use of the term is to be found in the work of the postmodernist thinker Jean-François Lyotard (1984 [1979]), who uses it to suggest that what Bauman (in Rojek, 2004) calls the *market-mediated mode of life* has become *the* central feature of contemporary existence. The key issue this work raises for leisure scholars is to what extent leisure devised, established and maintained by ordinary people themselves has been superseded by commercial leisure and consumerism.

Lyotard's basic premise is that modern knowledge established its monopoly of *Truth* through the use of grand narratives (e.g., Marxism, Hegelianism), which not only promised justice at the end of an inquiry but were also able to legitimate themselves in such compelling ways that they were hardly questioned. In modern society, it emerged that it was science (rather than religion) that would be the chief criterion by which the most convincing of these knowledge claims were made. However, with the emergence of postmodernity we have witnessed the collapse of all grand narratives. Basically, in keeping with the social, cultural, political and economic changes that are consistent with postmodern change, there has been a conspicuous shift in the way in which knowledge claims come to be legitimated.

Lyotard's key argument is that the idea of performativity is coterminous with this new 'generalized spirit' of knowledge. Basically, with the advent of postmodernity, capitalism has become so pervasive that there is no one thing left that is not commodifiable. Inevitably science (like leisure, religion, sex, sport, and so on) became merely another commodity and in turn *truth* is now determined not by its ability to tell the *Truth* but by its exchange value. If modern society stood for the language game of denotation (the difference between true or false), postmodern society stands for an alternative, 'technical' game of efficiency versus inefficiency. As a result performativity will become the new criterion of the legitimacy of knowledge claims.

For Lyotard, then, in postmodernity the status of knowledge is altered and performativity comes to represent a kind of hyper-capitalist efficiency which is able to bring the 'pragmatic functions of knowledge clearly to light and elevate all language games to self-knowledge' (Lyotard, 1984 [1979]: 114). Truth is now performative rather than constative and the most convincing truth claims are those that the market will determine are the most performatively efficient. In a nutshell, everything in postmodernity, including leisure, has to be judged by its market value and if it doesn't sell it is not what is wanted, pure and simple. Truth today is in the manner of its performance. The upshot is that if branding was once upon a time solely the language of the market it has now become the language of leisure and, not only that, but the language of the world as a whole.

Tony Blackshaw

Associated Concepts Authenticity; Ethnomethodology; Goffman; Habitus, Field and Capital; Postmodernism; Postmodernity; Poststructuralism; Symbolic Interactionism.

PILOT STUDY

This is a small-scale empirical 'testing' of the validity of research methods and/or a sample, usually used before engaging in more large-scale research. For instance, if a researcher was planning to conduct a questionnaire-based survey of followers of a particular football team, they might first distribute the questionnaire to a small sample of supporters to see if the questions asked were understandable and if these questions (and the sample selected) were able to provide the kinds of data/information they were hoping to gather.

Piloting can be used with most method types, such as interviews, questionnaires, focus group, content analysis, experiments, and so on. It is an important, but all too often overlooked, stage in the research process. Researchers are usually pressed for time, finances or only have a limited sample to choose from and so will try to avoid undertaking a pilot study, but piloting can prove crucial as it can uncover important flaws in the method, tools or sample, which could in the long run significantly undermine (or even render useless) the research.

Garry Crawford

Associated Concepts Ethnography; Interviews; Methodology; Observations; Oral/Life Histories; Qualitative Methods; Quantitative Methods; Questionnaires; Sampling.

PLAY

According to Plato, the faculty of play is the highest attribute of humanity (Reith, 1999). Likewise, the Dutch historian Huizinga saw it as the basis of human culture. He argued that the origins of rituals and laws of human civilization could all be found in play and crucially this is where civilization continues to reside. As he put it 'civilization ... does not come _from_ play like a babe detaching itself from the womb: it arises _in_ and _as_ play, and never leaves it' (1949 [1938]: 173, emphasis in original). In particular, in his classic (1949 [1938]) book _Homo Ludens_ (which roughly translates as 'human player' or 'human play'), Huizinga discusses the central role of play in the construction of language, civilization, law, war, knowledge, poetry, mythologies, philosophy and art.

Another important contribution to our understanding of play (which builds on the work of Huizinga) was offered by Roger Caillois (1962) who defines play (in a similar fashion to Huizinga) as materially unproductive activities that are free and voluntary, involve uncertainty, are isolated in space and time and have broadly set rules. Caillois also identified four different forms of play: _agon_ (competition), _alea_ (chance), _mimicry_ (simulation) and _ilinx_ (vertigo and disorientation). He argued that play has an important functional role in providing an outlet for emotions that are suppressed elsewhere in social life. This is an idea which was also developed by both Erving Goffman (1967) and Norbert Elias

(1982) who both considered the sociopsychological functions of play. In particular, Goffman argued that play was central to our social lives and provided an opportunity for risk and adventure that was often denied in other aspects of contemporary society. Likewise, Elias pointed out that play represented a human need for stimulation and that our human well-being depends on being able to experience periods of heightened arousal – which, as with Goffman and Caillois, Elias suggests, are frequently denied in other areas of contemporary (or more specifically as Elias would argue a 'civilized') society.

It is also important to note that play has an important role in processes of socialization, helping individuals to learn social roles and an adherence to the rules and social conventions. In particular, Roberts and Sutton-Smith (1971) argued that games have the dual function of diffusing the conflict that inevitably arises between children and their parents as they are disciplined to conform to the adult world and 'enculturation', as game play encourages rule-governed behaviour, and exemplifies values that society holds to be important.

Theoretical considerations of play have been particularly important in understanding many aspects of leisure. In particular, the study of patterns of play (or 'ludology' as it is sometimes referred to) has been influential in research on digital games. The term ludology has previously been used to describe the study of games more generally, but its use has caught on more specifically in the study of digital games. In particular, ludology presents a particular attitude to the study of digital games that suggests they cannot be studied simply as media 'texts', but, rather, a focus is needed on aspects of game-play, such as rituals, rules and interactivity. Another important aspect of play in digital gaming is how play is seen as separate from normal everyday life. For instance, Kerr et al. (2004: 13) in their discussion of gaming pleasures draw on the work of Huizinga to suggest that one of the key pleasures of digital gaming is that it allows the gamer to step out of 'real' life and participate in a 'virtual' gaming world.

However, the idea that gaming is 'separate' from real life has been challenged by many authors, including Crawford (2006), who would argue for a consideration of gaming within its wider social setting.

Garry Crawford

Associated Concepts Digital Gaming; Elias; Goffman; Mimesis; Play Ethic; Virtual Leisure.

PLAY ETHIC

This term has emerged from two ideas: that play is an indelible part of the human experience and that work in modern societies does not offer the fulfilment or creativity that it should. It was coined by Pat Kane (2004), who subverted the early eighteenth-century proverb 'the devil makes work for idle hands to do' to argue that we are moving towards a new sociality in which play will prevail and 'angels will make for idle hands in the players' republic'. Here Kane is dissolving the assumption of the Protestant ethic that leisure is secondary to and earned through work.

In developing the idea of the play ethic Kane drew on the philosophy of James Carse (1986) to challenge the notion that games should be finite and played for the purpose of winning by arguing that we need to recognize that games can also be infinite and played only for the purpose of continuing to play. What Carse's thesis suggests is that infinite playing doesn't come without an obligation to care: that is, our individual desire to continue to play is only possible precisely because others wish to go on with the game. What this means is that any entitlement to play must be counterbalanced with actively taking responsibility for the Other.

What Kane's hopelessly utopian vision fails to address, however, is the implications suggested by this obligation to care. As the sociology of Bauman has consistently shown, the contemporary world is one in which people increasingly do not put down deep roots. One of the upshots of this is that their empathy for the Other is often sincere but also superficial. Another problem is that even when people are interested in binding themselves to other people, a sense of obligation to care can often quickly turn into the feeling that they are a burden; sometimes it can even turn into hatred if the Other's weakness becomes too much of a drain on the carer's strength. The other side of care is that it can also easily lead to domination, especially when the carer begins to define the Other's needs against their will (see Smith, 1999: 164).

Tony Blackshaw

Associated Concepts Leisure; Play; Pleasure; Work Ethic.

PLEASURE

In commonsense usage this is used to indicate either an enjoyable sensation or something that gives a sensational experience. We all know the pleasure of anticipation, just as we have all experienced the kind of pleasure which makes us feel freshly grateful for being alive (for example, for the simple pleasure of reading or for the alchemy of watching a favourite boxer drawing flesh and blood from the mouth of an opponent). What these observations suggest is that pleasure is something that belongs to the person who is experiencing it; as Harris (2005) points out, however, what they also signify is that the presence of a pleasure might be one of the defining characteristics of leisure.

More precise meanings attached to the term will depend upon whether one is considering its psychological, philosophical or sociological meaning – though it must be said that, for the majority of theorizations, none of these tends to be mutually exclusive. The most basic scholarly understandings tend to treat pleasure as the binary opposite of either pain or reality. With regard to the first, pleasure is often referred to as a positive bodily sensation, while pain is seen as negative one. In competitive sport, for example, it is often said that failure brings pain while success brings pleasure. In terms of the relationship between pleasure and reality, it has been forcibly argued that with the emergence of modernity bourgeois values came to rest on the puritan belief that pleasure was one thing and reality another. This dichotomy is enshrined in Freud's concepts of the pleasure principle and the reality principle: the former evincing the tendency inherent in the wishes of human beings to seek self-satisfaction independent of all other considerations (instant gratification), the latter being suggestive of the social conditions imposed on the satisfaction of the pleasure principle (deferred gratification).

Building a sociological interpretation of this Freudian dichotomy, Bauman has argued that the ideal bourgeois citizen of modernity in its 'solid', formative stage was cautious and apprehensive, was given to deferred gratification, considered the rainy days ahead and was prepared to pay the price of present pleasures forgone, while the ideal 'liquid' modern bourgeois citizen of today is not averse to throwing caution to the wind and is, on the contrary, given to instant gratification, to putting off until further notice planning for future hardships and unwilling to forgo present pleasures. 'Liquid' modern men and women find it impossible to censure and repress unconscious forces within them. Indeed, the pleasure of fun is not the type of sin it used to be. The puritanical notion that having fun was wrong has by now almost entirely disappeared and has been replaced by a civic duty to happiness.

Terry Eagleton (1990) argues that, despite his interest in the correct management of pleasure, it was none other than Freud himself who deconstructed the binary opposite between the pragmatic and the pleasurable which was vital to modernity in its formative stage. As Ferguson (1989) points out, at the core of his psychology was the idea of fun rather than pleasure. However, Lacan (1977) asserts that, notwithstanding Freud's understanding that fun has to be all or nothing, the dichotomy between the reality principle and pleasure principle is in the end an obstacle to our understanding of the kinds of higher pleasure that can take us to that extreme where the erotic meets death.

What Lacan's work also alerts us to is the point that pleasure can also be understood as something enjoyable in itself which is closely wrapped up with our desires – and, as we have seen already, even death. In this sense pleasure must be understood not as something to be managed, but as a quality of our individual subjectivity that is intimately tied up with our pursuit of happiness. As Harris (1995) states, Roland Barthes identified the two kinds of pleasure that could motivate us: *plaisir* and *jouissance*. Making reference to our engagement with film and print media, Harris shows that the Barthesian understanding of *plaisir* merely refers to the pleasure we gain from our passive engagement with novels and film, while *jouissance*, which hints at the idea of sexual pleasure, 'refers to something more intellectually ecstatic, the pleasures detectable in being able to recognize the effects of narrative on yourself, and, maybe, to begin to play with the novel or film, to weave your own narratives in and around it' (ibid.: 197). What Barthes is referring to here is something like a confrontation with the sublime, which, as Kant suggested, is the pleasurable fear we have to deal with when we cannot fully grasp or understand something that is overwhelming us, but which all the same prompts us to strive towards such an understanding of it.

In a much more negative vein, Lyotard, in his book *Libidinal Economy* (1993 [1974]), takes Kant's idea of the sublime one step further to argue that, in a postmodern world where hyper-capitalist efficiency seems to have replaced all other values, our desires will create nothing else other than happenings. Anticipating his later work on *The Postmodern*

Condition: A Report on Knowledge(1984 [1979]), Lyotard sees these happenings as both limiting and nihilistic, in the sense that they deny the full possibilities of the expression of pleasure. In other words, our desires have no purpose other than to produce feelings of the highest intensity or what he describes as pointless pleasures. This is because there is no longer any purpose to pleasure other than its own instantaneous sensation. Taking a rather different tack, Slavoj Žižek argues that, because of the postmodern obsession with self-preservation, most of our pleasures today have simply been stripped of the things that make them pleasurable – beer without alcohol, coffee without caffeine, sex without intimacy.

Tony Blackshaw

Associated Concepts   Aesthetics; Asceticism; Desire; Flow; Happiness; Hedonism; Intertextuality; Liminality.

POLICY

(leisure policy)

POPULAR CULTURE

(cultural intermediaries; culture; fans; neo-tribes; postmodernism; structure of feeling; subcultures)

POPULAR CULTURE

Popular culture (such as cinema, pop music, popular novels and digital games) is often compared with 'high' or 'elite' culture (such as 'serious' art, opera and more 'difficult' literature), where popular activities are seen as more widespread than minority tastes in high/elite culture. It is also often contrasted with the concept of 'mass culture', where the term popular culture is often used to avoid the more negative connotations associated with a critique of 'mass culture' as inauthentic by the likes of Oretago Y Gassett (1994 [1932]). In this respect, popular culture is associated more with working-class culture than the idea of an all-consuming mass of 'culture dopes'.

There are numerous academic approaches and attitudes towards popular culture. From a (neoclassical) economic perspective, where what is 'popular' is seen to be defined by the market and its value is determined by competition (Miller, 2007). From a classical Marxist perspective, popular culture is seen as a vehicle of the dominant ideology and/or domination. For instance, for Antonio Gramsci (1971), popular culture plays a significant role in legitimizing domination (hegemony), while for Frankfurt School scholars such as Theodor Adorno (1991) the 'culture industry' can be seen to produce standardized and formulaic products that are imposed upon (rather than created by) the masses.

However, others have been keen to emphasize the more 'positive' aspects of popular culture, including some early writers at the Birmingham School such as Richard Hoggart and Raymond Williams, who highlighted (even celebrated) the importance of working-class culture. This was a tradition continued by later Birmingham School scholars such as Dick Hebdige, who pointed out the resistant nature of working-class youth subcultures, such as Mods, Punks and Teddy Boys. Beyond these Michel de Certeau (1984), and those who have drawn upon his work such as John Fiske (1989), have emphasized how everyday culture can provide opportunities for rebellion. However, beyond these ideas of popular culture as 'good' or 'bad', others have sought to address the way culture (both popular and elite) is used as forms of social distinction and membership, and most notable here would be the work of Pierre Bourdieu.

In recent years there has been an increased emphasis on the globalization of popular culture, both in its production and consumption, as well as an increased awareness that popular and elitist tastes are becoming less class-specific as many consumers become more 'omnivorous' in their tastes.

Garry Crawford

Associated Concepts Authenticity; Bourdieu; Consumption; Critical Theory; Cultural Omnivores; Distinction; Everyday Life; Fanzines; Globalization; Ideology; Subcultures.

PORNOGRAPHY

In both the literature and ordinary language, pornography, or 'porn', is used to describe the use of visual or literary representations of humans, animals and other objects to arouse and satisfy sexual desire and, in the case of 'hard' (as opposed to 'soft') pornography, in ways that are often described as perverted. Pornography is a major global 'leisure' industry worth billions of dollars that has helped drive many mainstream hi-tech advances, such as the internet and video technology.

A distinction is often drawn between 'pornography', which is intended to be sexually stimulating, and 'erotica', which uses sexual images or words in more artistic and/or aesthetic ways. However, making such distinctions is difficult because what constitutes 'sexually explicit material' is often culturally specific. In particular, Foucault (1979) suggests that Western ideas of sexuality developed quite differently from those of Eastern cultures, where sex and sexuality were more openly visible in society (for example, one would think of the Kama Sutra). Even throughout Western history there has been a long history of sexually explicit material dating back to antiquity, as well as examples of Renaissance art and also literature such as the writings of the eighteenth-century French aristocrat the Marquis (Donatien Alphonse-François) de Sade. Even today, the parameters of what constitutes pornography are extremely blurred as there are cases of mainstream films such as *Nine Songs* (dir. Michael Winterbottom, 2005) and *Batalla en el cielo* (trans: 'Battle in Heaven') (dir. Carlos Reygadas, 2005) that have featured highly explicit sexual acts, but were not deemed as 'pornographic' by British film classifiers due to their perceived artistic merits.

One understandable response to the idea that using pornography might be described as a leisure activity is anger and offence. Indeed, as in the case of discussions about other kinds of abnormal leisure, discussions about pornography are often expressed with a sense of moral outrage. Critics argue that pornography involves social harm, more often than not, to women and other vulnerable groups, particularly children, invariably by men. The way in which these vulnerable bodies are objectified in pornography for visual pleasure is often explained through the concept of the male gaze (Mulvey, 1975) which, it is argued, renders men unable to make a proper distinction between real women as living beings and women as objects of sexual desire, which if they cared to look would enable them to sense their feelings as other human beings.

Pornography, and the sexual depiction of women for the delectation of the male gaze, became a major concern for the second wave feminism of the 1970s and 1980s, which saw these as key examples of the objectification and devaluation of women within society. In particular, a key anti-pornography writer was Andrea Dworkin (1988) who saw pornography as employing sex as a tool of male power and aggression. In particular, Dworkin pointed to the propensity of pornography to include images of violence (such as bondage) against women and suggested that pornography was a form of 'sexual terrorism' (page 201).

However, where the value consensus in leisure studies seems to offer a wholly negative critique of pornography, more psychoanalytical and sociologically inclined approaches have tended to offer greater critical deconstruction, suggesting that the use of pornographic material is not only more widespread than we imagine and used by both men and women (straight and gay) (see Smith, 2007), but its use actually also reveals a great deal about men's fears of women, in particular about their sexual fantasies and desires, which are destined to remain unknowable to the male gaze. In particular, authors such as Carole Vance (1992) suggested that the root of the problem was not pornography, but, rather, sexism and patriarchy within the wider society and culture and that therefore it might be possible to imagine erotica that was non-patriarchal. Similarly, Bryson (1999) has called for a more open discussion on pornography, which may recognize the need to develop erotic material made by, and for, women.

Tony Blackshaw and Garry Crawford

Associated Concepts Abnormal Leisure; Addictions; Desire; Deviance; Feminism; Masculinity and Masculinities; Power; Sex; Surveillance.

POSTCOLONIALISM

(acculturation)

POSTMODERNISM

This term has been used to describe the wave of self-conscious novelty and experimentation as well as developments in fashion, social attitudes and culture that began to emerge with the period that the historian Arthur Marwick called the 'long sixties', when radicals in fields as diverse as architecture, historiography and philosophy were creating their own styles of intellectual exposition and, not only that, were using them to dismember some of the putative ideals which had prevailed in their disciplines since the Enlightenment (the age of modern reason bound to the twin ideas of rational inquiry and scientific method which emerged in the seventeenth and eighteenth centuries). What came to be called 'postmodernism' seemed to be transforming these 'modern' disciplines into something radically

different by, on the one hand, moving them away from science and more closely to art and, on the other, by breaking down assumed barriers between 'higher' and 'lower' forms of culture by paying keen attention to the quotidian of new and alternative sociocultural developments, while at the same time celebrating their plurality in the process.

With the dissipation of the distinction between high and low culture, there emerged the assumption among postmodernists that the study of leisure could also be about taking things that previously had not been considered worthy of concern – or even beneath contempt – and putting them centre stage in leisure studies. What postmodernism taught leisure scholars was that humankind had finally crossed the line from innocence to knowledge and from now on it would always be like this. Those prepared to listen (e.g., Rojek, 1995) not only began to argue that we must 'decentre leisure', but also that there was nothing about the world that was quite what it seemed and the way that we understand leisure should run in channels that are shallow as well as deep. This was essentially a critical response to 'modernist' leisure studies that had hitherto evinced a tendency to sacrifice surface to depth in the hope of revealing the innermost truths about our leisure experiences.

The urge to wards playfulness and pastiche is part and parcel of the postmodern outlook. Reality, invention and all kinds of cultural borrowings are playfully intertwined. Art, like leisure, is not about representing things, it is about acting things out. In other words, art is performative, which implies that life itself might be interpreted as a work of art. Yet there is little to be gained from individuals' life and their art because they are constantly staging both; postmodern men and women merely select the details of the world that interest them and make them decorative. According to Umberto Eco, one of the upshots of this aesthetic approach to life is that there are no social judgments that are untouched by irony. In his view the postmodernist attitude is 'that of a man who loves a very cultivated woman and knows he cannot say to her "I love you madly" because he knows that she knows (and that she knows he knows) that these words have already been written by Barbara Cartland. Still, there is a solution. He can say, "As Barbara Cartland would put it, I love you madly" (quoted in French, 2006).

As Lyotard (1984 [1979]) has argued, this postmodern attitude is also marked by an incredulity towards metanarratives. In other words, the collapse, in our time, of the illusions (including love) that gave energy to the modern imagination and modern systems of thought – whether rationalism, functionalism, Marxism, feminism or any other kind of 'ism' – which are futile or comedic, depending on which way you look at them. The arrival of postmodernism signalled an age when any kind of certainty is suspect, when cynicism has become the key signifier of cool. At the heart of postmodernism is the idea that the moral universe is no longer stable, that the areas of agreement about values and ethics have disappeared. There is no such thing as objective truth, which is a bad faith we would be better off without.

According to its critics, postmodernism is nothing less (and nothing more either) than the triumphant celebration of relativism, which assumes that truth (as opposed to Truth) is not absolute but contingent to particular individuals, cognitive systems or cultures. Morally speaking, with relativism there is no right or wrong and anybody is logically allowed to pursue any kind of activity (should they so wish). In other words, nobody has the right to chastise anybody else for enjoying their leisure in one way rather than other or at the expense of anyone else, because there is no leisure that is 'better' than any other kind of leisure.

Critics have also argued that the arrival of postmodernism has led to a world that is a depthless, hyperized asociality, where individual agency is irrelevant and thus this gives priority to the 'code' over subjective ideas and in the process marks the victory of the 'anti-social sign over the social sign' (Harland, 1987). It signals a paranoid, anomic world where renegades from the consumer society can create their own paroxysm while a corrupt, capitalist state seeks to control and exploit both conformists and nonconformists alike – postmodern life is thus a hell of inauthenticity. In other words, the world of postmodernism is simply the outrider of a vast marketing strategy, a place where leisure is 'any consumption of unproductive time' (Baudrillard, 1981: 76). Human lives no longer proceed through a gradual cycle of ripening and rot. The hyper-capitalist economy attempts to abolish adulthood altogether, mobilizing teenagers as consumer guide trainers, Big Macs and electronic toys. Leisure (if we can be bothered with it or can afford it) merely enables us to keep fit in order to postpone the ageing process. In this way, leisure becomes 'irrevocably an *activity*, an *obligatory* social phenomenon. Time is not in this instance "free" ... the individual is not free to escape it. No one needs leisure, but everyone is called upon to provide evidence of his availability for *unproductive* labour' (Baudrillard, quoted in Rojek, 1990: 9). It is not ironic that, in a world so lacking in originality and dramatic finesse, leisure should be so steeped in commercial calculation.

However, other critics have questioned the assumption that we really do live in a world that is so cool, shrugging and impervious, suggesting that the postmodern outlook is a nihilistic fantasy from which we all need to be shaken. As they point out, postmodernism's adherents have a tendency to reduce everything to irony and self-conscious cleverness. It is often complained that postmodernists discuss the world only in aesthetic terms and don't engage with its deeper material content. To this extent postmodernism has also been criticized for being too coldly clever at respinning abstract philosophical ideas rather than embodying its analyses in real human lives – what first of all appeared to be a seamless thread of original ideas now turns out on closer examination to be a patchwork of theoretical borrowings.

Some have begun to argue about when postmodernism began and ended (if it has indeed done so). However, it is perhaps more useful to trace the life course of postmodernism in various stages. It went from being a revolutionary practice to an art form, from an art form to a sensibility, from a sensibility to a domesticated academic perspective and finally became a form of contempt. If postmodernism began as a programme of disruption in leisure studies, today it is a way of thinking that is largely derided.

Tony Blackshaw

Associated Concepts Abnormal Leisure; Authenticity; Baudrillard; Bauman; Cool; Modernism; Modernity; Postmodernity; Performativity; Play.

POSTMODERNITY

Not to be confused with the term postmodernism, at its most basic this concept refers to a historical period subsequent to modernity. With the idea of postmodernity there is the assumption that one phase of modernity has more or less ended and another, however ill understood, has begun, which is accompanied by a distinct self-awareness of its own contingency. In this sense postmodernity needs to be understood as modernity 'coming to terms with its own impossibility; a self-monitoring modernity, one that consciously discards what it was once unconsciously doing' (Bauman, 1991: 272).

Although the idea of postmodernity is expressed in a great variety of ways (e.g., late modernity, liquid modernity, second modernity, reflexive modernization), with some of these difficult to distinguish from modern experiences, it has been largely orientated by leisure scholars into four categories – social, cultural, economic and political – which are nonetheless difficult to conceive in any mutually exclusive manner.

According to Bauman, the modern social and economic conditions that brought with them a society in which the ideal bourgeois citizen was assumed to be cautious and apprehensive, content to defer gratification and to pay the price of present pleasures forgone, has been superseded by a sociality in which individuality dominates more than anything else and where identity is largely achieved through consumption. The postmodern citizen unencumbered by his or her social class is not averse to throwing caution to the wind. On the contrary he or she is given to instant gratification, to putting off planning for future hardships until further notice and unwilling to forgo pleasures. Self-transformation is not merely a possibility, it is a duty to one's individuality, because in postmodernity the lived life is the only life worth living.

Bauman argues that postmodern lives are first and foremost guided by a 'will to happiness' which is progressively more individualized and where social relationships are increasingly lifted out of their more traditional social class contexts to form new *habitats*, which will 'unbind' time and weaken the coercive impact of the past. In a nutshell, with the onset of postmodernity life has increasingly come to be experienced in *pointillist* time (Bauman, 2007), marked by ruptures and discontinuity. Postmodern lives exude an uncalculated lack of concern for sequentiality or consequentiality and postmodern men and women are like the characters in Borges' world of Tlön, who feel that their everyday world, their past and the past of their forebears are always slipping away from them, as if they are drowning in a new and overwhelming world that they cannot make out. It is not so much a deep sinking as a surface trawl – that's the thing about postmodern life: its vicissitudes are underpatterned rather than patterned, ephemeral rather than lasting, ultimately unfulfilling rather than satiating.

The upshot is that men and women are likely to look in two directions for guidance on how to live their lives: on the one hand towards the past, whose shaping of them they have a duty to ludicly explore (even if this is a false nostalgia or a nostalgia for a life that wasn't lived) and, on the other, towards a present they are constantly trying to keep up with. The past, like the present, seems up for grabs, available for playful reinvention. As Terry Eagleton (2005) has suggested, in postmodernity our leisure experiences, once a silent mechanism for resisting the dominance of consumer culture, are now merely another 'species of it'. As he puts it:

> Instead of wandering along Hadrian's Wall, we have the Hadrian's Wall Experience: instead of the Giant's Causeway, the Giant's Causeway Experience. What we consume now is not objects but our sensations of them … In an ultimate postmodern irony, a commodified experience compensates for the commodity's impoverishment of experience. The term 'experience' dwindles to an empty signifier. (p. 3)

In other words, the heritage industry pitches consumers into a fascinating but ultimately domesticated leisure experience which is prepackaged by the market for their individual consumption. What this suggests is that postmodernity is a world marked by the individualization of consumer patterns and consumed by patterns of individualization.

If modernity was a world of men and women beset by fear that they would never arrive but would always be passing through, postmodernity is a world in which passing through is an obligation. Bauman (1992) alerts us to the different paths that a postmodern life can take and what he suggests is that men and women are not so much challenged with finding their essential identity as being open to the challenge of making and remaking it; they act, are compelled to act, in a world which is always on the move and where no one thing stays the same for very long. Postmodernity is episodic and contingent and life's essential incompleteness doesn't merely invite its denizens to fill its gaps, it compels them to do so. Yet it is also a world of cultural confusion.

It is no wonder men and women these days are always on the lookout for those leisure experiences which tell them how to live – how to pose, what music to listen to, where to shop, what to eat and drink and where to go for their holidays.

If modernity was the world of the nation state and big government, with the emergence of postmodernity we have witnessed an uncoupling of life from the hard stuff of politics. Postmodernity is a world in which there is little political life, where capitalism without questions takes hold and inattention is routine, where designer labels and celebrities are the only political emblems and figures to whom men and women are prepared to respond. Others see this shift away from big government in a more positive light, in terms of the identification of emancipatory politics (freedom oppressive, top-down state apparatuses) to a 'life politics' negotiated via 'dialogic democracy' in the space of civil society, signalling the opportunity for politics proper.

This last observation has a great deal in common with Bauman's (1992) idea that postmodernity offers intimations of the re-enchantment of everyday life and the idea that, after all, modernity had not 'progressed' as far as it thought it had. It also signals the idea that humankind is still touched by a kind of magic that can change lives and that love, not rationality, is what will open us to the possibility of as yet unimagined and alternative forms of human happiness. Bauman's message is clear: what all men and women need to do is develop the ability to get away from the dominant reusable language of consumerism to an alternative discourse that speaks itself for the first time. Instead of greedily consuming, they need to get greedy for the small, true details of life. It is only when they are able to grasp this possibility that they will be able to step clear of their cluttered consumer lives into a new relationship with the world, one that is at once simpler and more profound than their present circumstances allow – and the best that leisure can do is help facilitate this kind of magic.

Tony Blackshaw

Associated Concepts Celebrity; Civil Society; Consumer Society; Consumption; Everyday Life; Happiness; Hedonism;

Heritage; Liquid Modernity; Modernity; Nostalgia; Performativity; Postmodernism; Social Control; Surveillance.

POWER

Power is one of the most complex and difficult concepts to define. At its simplest, this can be done in the following way: 'A has power over B to the extent that he [sic] can get B to do something that B would not otherwise do' (Dahl, cited in Lukes, 1974: 11). However, as Lukes (1974: 26) suggests, power is an 'essentially contested concept' that will 'inevitably involve endless disputes over [its] ... proper uses'. Use of this term and, more specifically, the relations and mechanisms of social power is invariably linked to our metatheories of the social world and will therefore vary accordingly. However, the concept of power is one of the central narratives of social, political and philosophical theory and, hence, is also one of the most complex areas to define. Fortunately, though, Clegg (1989) offers both a simplified and extremely useful theorization of social power relations, which suggests there are two main traditions within the discussion of societal power relations – those that follow the tradition of Hobbes (1968 [1651]) and those that adopt a similar perspective to that of Machiavelli (1990 [1532]).

For Clegg, the Hobbesian tradition revolves primarily around discussions of sovereignty and community, where power lies within the hands of individuals or agencies. This is a zero-sum model of power, which suggests there is a finite sum of power, therefore the more power one individual or agency has the less others will possess. The most commonly used version of this framework would be the neo-Marxist theorization of dominant ideology offered by authors such as Althusser (1969), Gramsci (1971) and Habermas (1976). The dominant ideology thesis, though often diverse and complex, suggests that (to cite Marx's famous dictum) the ruling ideas are the ideas of the ruling classes. In other words, the dominant ideas and values within a society are those that legitimate and favour the ruling classes and these are imposed on those lower down the social order.

In contrast, the Machiavellian framework of power, Clegg argues, is concerned with strategy and organization, where power does not belong to any one agency or even agencies but instead resides within social mechanisms. Clegg points to the work of several key authors within this framework; however, it is the work of Michel Foucault (1977) that has been most influential in the area and it is here that Clegg places his greatest emphasis. Foucault presented a 'poststructuralist' account of societal power, which Clegg (1989: 17) argues, seeks not to identify 'real interests' but, rather, to understand the strategies and practices of organizations that will bring about social control and discipline. Here, power relations are not understood as zero-sum models of a top-down or dominant ideological oppression by agents or agencies but, rather, as multilayered and diffuse networks (or, as Clegg asserts, 'circuits') of infinite flows of power. In particular, within a Machiavellian framework, power is often seen to operate through discourses, which are institutionalized ways of thinking.

Power is central to *all* leisure activities and literatures on leisure, though this is not always as explicit in some activities and debates as others. All that we do somehow and at some point will involve social power relations. For instance, simply being 'who we are' and doing 'what we do' involve social norms and values, such as what it means to be a 'man' or a 'woman', and consequently what is expected and demanded of us in society because of this – all of which is defined by social intuitions and/or discourses of power (depending on your perspective on power relations) and enforced through social mechanisms of control and discipline. These power relations are central to many discussions of leisure: for instance, many feminist or Marxist considerations of leisure will explicitly set out how patriarchy and/or capitalism shape leisure. However, even where social power relations are not directly considered, the existence of these must be seen as crucial in understanding all aspects of leisure, as social power relations underpin all aspects of social life (including leisure).

Garry Crawford

Associated Concepts   Discursive Formations; False Consciousness; Feminism; Foucault; Hegemony; Ideology; Marxism.

PROFIT AND UTILITY MAXIMIZATION

Profit maximization is an extension strategy based on the principles of utility maximization. The ability to maximize utility is accepted when individuals are in charge of their own decisions and want to maximize their own advantage in the marketplace. For example, Sloane (1971) argues that utility maximization is the primary objective of most professional sport clubs. He suggests that supporters and directors are willing to outlay money without regard to pecuniary rewards, with playing success being the ultimate objective for clubs. His theory leads to the conclusion that a club will strive to get the most from its utility subject to financial viability.

However, many sport and leisure organizations follow a different philosophy. The idea of profit maximization is characterized by a view that owners of organizations will pursue profits in a normal way – that is to say they will attempt to ensure that the total revenues outweigh the total costs for, in the case of many sport and leisure organizations, owners will make decisions about venues, players, broadcasting and sponsorship contracts and so on in order to maximize the difference between total revenue and total costs.

Generally speaking, most American commentators (for example, Neal, 1964; El Hodiri and Quirk, 1971; Quirk and Fort, 1992) would claim that profit maximization is *the* principle goal of professional sport

organizations, however Fort and Quirk (1992) point out that it is more complex than that. Granted, owners love to field winning teams or run successful organizations if there is money in it, but they will be equally satisfied to keep costs low, field less competitive teams and make as much money as possible in the process.

Rob Wilson

Associated Concepts   Budgeting; Economic Impact of Hosting Major Sport Events; Profitability, Liquidity, Growth and Breaking Even.

PROFITABILITY, LIQUIDITY, GROWTH AND BREAKING EVEN

Profitability is the measure of a company's ability to yield a surplus in relation to other factors (e.g., turnover). In order to create a meaningful assessment of how commercially successful a company is, the amount of profit made should be considered in relation to the size of the business. Moreover, to interpret accounts effectively, there is a need to relate calculations to specific items from the organization in question. To make a profit a company has to ensure that it sells its goods and/or services at a higher price than the cost of producing them. However, in the leisure industry there will be exceptions when determining the internal capability to generate profits due to factors such as the acquisition of grants, television revenue, sponsorship agreements and the like.

Cash is the lifeblood of any business. A business must be capable of paying its debts as they arise or will risk financial failure. Liquidity (and liquidity ratios) are tools for measuring the solvency and financial stability of a business so that an assessment can be made as to how effectively it has managed its working capital. Liquidity is therefore about a business' ability to generate sufficient cash to meet its liabilities as they fall due. It should also be noted that much like the fact that profit is different from cash, profitability should not be confused with liquidity here. A company could be very profitable but not liquid and will therefore not be able to meet its immediate obligations.

The growth of a business is vital if it is to continue, develop, succeed and meet the ever-changing demands of consumers in the marketplace. Indeed, failure to grow might result in a loss of competitiveness, a decline in demand, and, in some cases, eventual closure. Growth also enables past trends to be examined and predictions of performance to be made in the future. In English professional football, for example, growth is essential. A club as a whole must grow in terms of membership and fan base in order to generate increased income through ticket and merchandise sales, in order that it can remain competitive on the field of play. However, if a club does not grow it will not have the resources to match larger (and growing) clubs in terms of player wages and squad sizes. The best way to calculate growth is by examining year-on-year changes, which facilitates the analysis of how the organization has progressed over a period of time. This analysis can then be coupled with other factors that will appear in an organization's annual report, such as commercial activities, sponsorship, television deals and other revenue.

All businesses will try to make a profit. However, this does not always happen and some companies can make substantial losses. The term break-even (B/E) signifies the point at which a firm is no longer in danger of making a loss (i.e., at what point all the costs have been covered by revenue). This is therefore an important point to reach. All managers should know where this is and when they have reached it.

Rob Wilson

Associated Concepts Budgeting; Economic Impact.

PUBLIC AND PRIVATE GOODS

Economists would suggest that the term private goods relates to commodities that are consumed solely by the purchaser unless they have chosen to give them to others. For example, if you purchase a sport drink, only you can drink it. Some goods, however, can be identified as public goods. Such items are characterized by two main issues. Firstly, the consumption of a good by one person does not reduce the amount available for consumption by another. This is called non-rivalry. Secondly, once provided, no single individual can be excluded from benefiting (or suffering) from such items. This is called non-excludability.

Rob Wilson

Associated Concepts Demand; Elasticity; Supply; Three-Sector Provision of Leisure.

Q

QUALITATIVE RESEARCH

Qualitative research involves the gathering and use of non-numerical data, such as words or images. The use of qualitative research is underpinned by the epistemological position that it is more useful to study small-scale samples and gather more detailed information, than gain broader data from larger groups (as would be the case with quantitative research methods). Quantitative research therefore tends to use research methods that gather more in-depth and detailed information about people's leisure lives from relatively small sample sets, such as interviews, focus groups, observations and ethnographies. One example of this would be Hodkinson's (2002) ethnography of goths, in which Hodkinson observed, photographed and interviewed goths at the bi-annual goth weekend in Whitby (North Yorkshire) and beyond.

Drawing on smaller samples, qualitative researchers suggest, allows for greater validity, as these methods allow the research to gain a much greater and more detailed understanding of the reasons and motives of individuals and/or groups. Though researchers employing qualitative research methods have to be wary about drawing sweeping generalizations from relatively small samples, the methods they employ, they would suggest, give a far greater understanding of social life and, therefore, it is still possible to draw generalizations and form theories on the basis of findings from qualitative research.

Qualitative researchers may attempt to remain objective and 'detached' in their research, which can help increase its reliability, though some (such as action researchers, postmodernists or feminist researchers) may forgo any pretensions of objectivity in order to try and gain a more in-depth (and even empathic) understanding of the people they are studying. Though qualitative data cannot be analysed using statistical tests, computer packages (such as *NU*DIST* and *NVivo*) can be employed to help organize and code data, often making it easier to identify commonalties, links and patterns.

Garry Crawford

Associated Concepts Content Analysis; Conversational Analysis; Ethnography; Feminism; Focus Groups; Methodology; Interviews; Observation; Oral/Life History; Quantitative Research; Questionnaires; Sampling; Time Budget Diaries.

QUALITY SYSTEMS

Businesses today can aspire to and obtain a series of quality awards based on systems that indicate that they are achieving excellence in certain areas. The main awards in the leisure industries are the Charter Mark, Quest, Investors in People and the ISO9000 series.

The Charter Mark is a public service-orientated awarded based on the Citizens Charter. It is externally assessed and there are only 100 awards each year. The promoted consultation and publication of standards give this award national standing. Quest is the UK Quality Scheme for Sport and Leisure. It defines industry standards and good practice and encourages their application and development in a customer-focused management framework. The British Quality Foundation recommends Quest for self-assessment in sport and leisure operations. There are two distinct categories for Quest: Quest Facility Management, which is aimed at sports and leisure facilities in the commercial, voluntary and public sectors, and Quest Sports Development, which is aimed at sports development units in local authorities, governing bodies and voluntary organizations.

Investors in People is a standard for the training and development of people in organizations. It was launched in 1991 by the Department for Employment and is accepted as a national quality standard, setting levels of good practice to improve an organization's performance through its people. The main aim of IIP is to promote excellence in the field of human resource management by linking the development of people to the goals and targets of the organization. There are four key elements to the award: a plan and public commitment to develop employees; a regular review of the training and development needs of all employees; action to train and develop individuals; and regular evaluation.

The ISO9000 series is about establishing, documenting and maintaining a quality management system within organizations. It includes work instructions and manuals to ensure that processes are considered in detail and is acclaimed as excellent for its reliability and in supporting staff training. However, its main weakness is that it concentrates on how to reach standards rather than how to maintain them. Moreover, there is no evaluation by auditors and it tends not to be customer-orientated.

Rob Wilson

QUANTITATIVE RESEARCH

Quantitative research involves the gathering and use of numerical data which are often subjected to statistical analysis. The use of quantitative research is underpinned by the epistemological position that it is more useful to study large-scale samples and gather broad information than to gain more individual and in-depth data from smaller groups (as would be the case with qualitative research methods). Quantitative research therefore tends to use research methods that can be applied to large sample sets and will provide numerical data, such as questionnaires or experiments, or else it relies on the analysis of secondary data sources such as official statistics (e.g., census data.

Drawing on large samples, quantitative researchers suggest, allows the generalizations that come from this to be more valid – as they are often sampling a larger proportion of the overall population. Quantitative research usually aims to be objective in its methods, application and analysis, and also more reliable (in that it is easier to repeat these studies and obtain similar results) than using qualitative research methods.

Quantitative research methods also tend to be quicker and cheaper to implement, often lending themselves better to long-term studies, and the data obtained from these can be analysed using statistical tests and computer packages (such as *SPSS*) which can be utilized to find patterns and trends in the data and help reduce any doubts that the results you obtained occurred by chance. One example of the use of quantitative data in leisure- related research would be Crawford's (2001) surveys of ice hockey in Manchester, which were used to find out the demographics (such as age, gender, income category, and so on) and basic attitudinal information of followers of British ice hockey.

Garry Crawford

Associated Concepts Comparative Method; Feminism; Focus Groups; Interviews;

Methodology; Observation; Qualitative Research; Questionnaires; Sampling; Time Budget Diaries.

QUEER THEORY

This is a blanket term used to describe all minority studies and not just those relating to gays and lesbians. It emerged from Foucauldian, feminist, gay and lesbian studies' attention to the social construction of categories of 'normative' and 'deviant' sexual behaviour. In this sense it can be understood as a political response to the civic disenfranchisement of queers of all kinds and their common struggle for recognition on their own terms and equal rights.

While gay and lesbian studies had emerged in the 1970s and 1980s and had focused largely on questions of homosexuality and heterosexuality, queer theory expanded its critical gaze to focus on anything that fell into 'normative' and self-identified 'deviant' categories, particularly, though not necessarily, sexual activities and identities. In the 1990s queer theory began to concern itself with any and all forms of practices, activities, situations, performances, behaviours and 'problems' which were considered to be 'deviant' – that is, 'queer – and with 'normal' behaviours, identities and the like which define what is 'queer' (by being their binary opposites). Consequently queer theory expanded the scope of its analysis to all kinds of behaviours, including those that involved 'gender-bending' (as represented by the American basketball player Dennis Rodman) as well as those involving 'queer' forms of sexuality which were considered to deny the 'norm'.

The major success of queer theory has been in shifting the emphasis from the labellers of 'homosexuals', lesbians', 'drag queens', 'transsexuals', 'deviants' and 'deviance' to the 'homosexuals', lesbians', 'drag queens', 'transsexuals' and 'deviants' themselves and their own *self-identified* understandings of what it was about them

that was 'queer'. Yet if this movement, with its Foucauldian epistemology, recognized and rightly challenged the processes of power–knowledge associated with normalizing dominant categories, what it has also showed us is that *self-identified* 'queer' or 'deviant' behaviour and identities can be not only highly desirable but also that they often involve risky leisure behaviours and identities worth pursuing to make life more exciting, worth living. Indeed, what is most often ignored is queer theory's dread of the absorption of queer into the norm – that is, the idea that it would be intolerable to be tolerated. After all, one of the foremost pleasures of being queer is the specialness that comes from being seen as deviant.

Tony Blackshaw

Associated Concepts   Deconstruction; Deviance; Performativity; Pleasure; Postmodernism; Sex; Social Exclusion.

QUESTIONNAIRES

A questionnaire most commonly consists of a series of questions constructed by one or more individuals with the purpose of it then being distributed to, and completed by, others. Questionnaires are often viewed as one of the simplest, but can be in fact one of the most difficult, research tools to successfully administer.

The key advantages of questionnaires are that they allow the researcher to obtain information on a large sample of subjects, often at little cost in terms of time and finances, when compared with other methods such as interviews, focus groups and observations. What questionnaires are particularly useful for is determining attributes, demographic and behavioural information. For instance, from the mid-1990s through to the early 2000s, the (now defunct) Sir Norman Chester Centre for Football Research (under the directorship of John

Williams) at Leicester University undertook large-scale questionnaire-based surveys of the supporters of (primarily) Premier League football clubs in England (and some in Scotland). These surveys (as with others of this nature) enabled researchers to gather some basic demographic and behavioural information on their samples, such as age, gender, ethnicity, income, attendance patterns at football, and so on What these Premier League surveys also attempted to do was obtain certain (limited) attitudinal information, such as what supporters thought of various aspects of the game, its clubs and its organization. However, the depth of attitudinal information that can be obtained in a questionnaire will always be much more limited than that which can be obtained with other methods, and most notably interviews.

Questionnaires can employ a variety of different types of question. The simplest here are closed questions, which give the respondents a limited number of options to choose from. For instance, 'What is your sex: (a) male or (b) female?' When using closed questions it is important (where relevant) to include non-committal categories, such as 'other' or 'don't know', to ensure that all the options have been covered. For example, 'Do you support (a) Sheffield United (b) Sheffield Wednesday (c) other?' Another typical type of question employed in questionnaires is 'ranking' questions. An example of this would be, 'How do you rate Sheffield Wednesday's performance today: (a) very good (b) good (c) neither good nor bad (d) bad (e) very bad?' This is also referred to as a Likert scale. When using these types of scales or rankings, there should always be a noncommittal/neutral response and the scale must also be balanced (i.e., have an equal number of positive to negative optional responses). Finally, questionnaires can include open questions, which require the respondents to write their own responses to the questions asked. However, open questions are more time-consuming for respondents to complete and (particularly in large-scale surveys) are difficult for the researchers to code, interpret and analyse.

Questionnaires are most typically distributed either by hand or via the post, e-mail or similar methods, and individuals wil be asked to return these at a later time or date to the researchers. This enables a large quantity of questionnaires to be quickly and easily distributed, but response rates from this form of distribution are usually very low (which can bring into question the representativeness of a sample).

Garry Crawford

Associated Concepts Ethnography; Feminism; Focus Groups; Interviews; Methodology; Observation; Oral/Life History; Pilot Study; Quantitative Research; Questionnaires; Sampling.

R

RACISM AND LEISURE

Racism is the belief in the intrinsic superiority of one ethnic or cultural group over another and/or the perverse dislike or hatred of people from that group. In defining racism, a distinction also needs to be drawn between racialization, involving personalized acts of bigotry (which are often dependent on stereotypes about ethnic or cultural characteristics) levelled at other individuals because of their perceived difference, and structural racism involving societal institutions which support racial prejudice and discrimination. It needs to be recognized, therefore, that the opportunities for leisure afforded to ethnic minorities, such as Afro-Caribbean people and the different Asian groups, are not simply a matter of the extent to which they are confronted by racism but are also likely to be influenced by the patterns of prejudice and discrimination they have to face in other social formations, such as the labour market, housing, health, and so on, as well as the attendant forms of psychosocial, cultural, political and economic exclusion which accompany these. What this suggests is that the issue of racism in leisure cannot be divorced from other forms of social stratification such as social class and gender.

In order to make sense of how racism arises in leisure, we must not only recognize that human-being-in-the-world is a corporate undertaking in which people succeed in establishing distinctive ethnic cultures based on common values but also that we must take into account the continuing legacy of colonialism, not just as a form of economic, social, political and judicial imperial rule, but as a cultural and intuitive one too. The sport of cricket is a good example to draw on to illustrate both of these pull and push processes. If during the colonial period cricket was an important part of an English model of sovereignty that had been exported to make India governable and to 'save it' from 'the political and religious despotism of native rule' (Rose, 1999: 108), in a post-colonial world the same sport (along with the allure of Bollywood) has become the focal point for the sense of pride and national identity for what it means to be Indian – for rural farmers subsisting below the poverty line as well as for the new urban middle-class professionals thriving in the wake of the country's recent economic upturn. In this way, cricket has become the glue that holds together the imagined community (Anderson, 1991) of the Indian nation state.

This example notwithstanding, as John Spink (1994:17) points out these two elements of internal ethnicity (pull) and external racism (push) are often difficult to separate, but what is clear is that time and again they can be seen operating together to maintain segregation between different ethnic groups in leisure. Indeed, if we look at popular leisure pursuits in Western countries, they are often marked with a 'very visible black cultural presence' (Harris, 2005: 226), but there is little evidence to suggest that these are representative of leisure more generally. Take, for example, Stephenson and Hughes'

(2005) research on race and tourism trends, which critically explored how black people's perceptions and experiences of tourism were influenced and structured by the social conditions of racialism and institutional racism. In particular, they examined how a penetrating and discriminating 'white gaze' (a racist governing form of surveillance) with racialist representations and stereotypes of black societies and cultures not only contributes to black people's disengagement from tourism, but also even calls into question their explicit right to adopt a tourist identity.

It has also been demonstrated that even when a particular leisure activity or interest exhibits a highly visible ethnic minority presence, it can still be a site for perpetuating racist ideologies. For example, when exploring sports where there is a large Afro-Caribbean cultural presence, Hoberman (1997: 208) found that this is often used to reinforce stereotypes about black criminality by 'merging the black athlete and the black criminal into a single threatening figure ... first, by dramatizing two physically dynamic black male types which are often presumed to be both culturally and biologically deviant; and, second, by putting the violent or otherwise deviant behaviour of black athletes on constant public display so as to reinforce the idea of the black male's characterological instability'.

Drawing on a similar research approach, Blackshaw and Crabbe (2005) considered the ways in which this kind of racism is both consumed and performed in sport, specifically in their research into the context of the mediagenic format of the courtroom trials involving the 'off-field' experiences of white and black players from professional football and rugby league. Building on Back, Crabbe and Solomos' important (2001) research on football, which led them to assert that racialization is often contingent and ambivalent as well as being articulated with other lines of social division, Blackshaw and Crabbe critically explored the ways in which the public performance, media representation and regulation of 'crime' are combined with racial and working-class stereotypes in order to reveal ostensible guilt.

Also by focusing his attention on the role of contingency and ambivalence in the way the media perpetuate racism, Blackshaw (2008) argues forcefully that, while anti-racism campaigns have done a great deal over the last 20 years or so to challenge racial discrimination in football, they have hitherto been poor at including football supporters as active participants through community action. Drawing on research findings gathered through participant observation at a Leeds United versus Blackburn Rovers match during the National Anti-Racism Week of Action in professional English football, he highlighted that campaigning tends to rely on managerial strategies which, on the one hand, draw on the vocabulary of community through the writing of a variety of media discourses and, on the other, undertake stage-managed anti-racist spectacles in the hope that supporters will respond by repudiating racial discrimination and prejudice. He argues that such strategies appear to be based on the idea that it is in the very heart of football's community – the stadiums – and in the hope that the rhetorical effectiveness of media *persuasion* can be effectively combined with the spectacle of *manipulation* that this will challenge the irrationalities of racism in the game.

However, Blackshaw's research showed that not only do these strategies have no large meaning for the majority of football supporters but also that in their culturally blinkered struggle for political correctness they may paradoxically perpetuate some of the very kinds of racism they are attempting to alleviate. Focusing, amongst other things, on the way in which The Mighty Zulu Nation, a young singing and dance group from South Africa, performed during the half-time interval to ostensibly introduce Zulu culture to the crowd, Blackshaw argues that the spectacle of manipulation ultimately led to the day becoming nothing less than a staged portrayal of racialist stereotyping, albeit concocted and performed by 'authentic' Zulus.

What this kind of research suggests, to paraphrase Back et al. (2001: 282), is that the legacy of racism in leisure is unfinished business, not least because of society's ability to combine old racism with new variants.

Tony Blackshaw

Associated Concepts   Culture; Governmentality; Hegemony; Ideology; Leisure Bodies; Liquid Modernity; Postmodernism; Power; Social Exclusion; Surveillance.

RATIONAL RECREATION

(recreation)

RECREATION

The word 'recreation' can be similarly defined as 'leisure' in the sense that it refers to an activity engaged in for relaxation and pleasure. However, beyond this, 'recreation' is more commonly (than the term leisure) associated with the refreshment of the mind and body and therefore is typically applied to 'physical' and 'outdoors'-type activities. In particular, this specific use of the term can be clearly seen in the kinds of activities and subjects available and covered on a 'recreation management' course or at 'outdoor recreation' centres.

This contemporary use of the term 'recreation' also bears a direct relationship to the Victorian ideals of 'rational recreation'. From the early nineteenth century British public schools became key to the development of modern forms of sport, adapting and formalizing earlier 'folk' sports and laying down organizing rules and regulations. The focus and purpose of these activities were not of mere leisure and enjoyment, but following the Enlightenment philosophies of the likes of Rousseau's emphasis on the relationship between the mind and body, about the transfer and instilment of values and morals. This can clearly be seen in the attitude of Eustace Miles (1904) regarding the value of cricket: 'co-operation, division of labour, specialisation, obedience to a single organiser ... national character, geography, and its influences, art and artistic anatomy, physiology and hygiene [and] ethics ... can be learnt [through cricket] (cited in Horne et al., 1999: 11).

Concurrent with the development of organized sport (as well as other forms of 'moral' recreation) in Britain's public schools was a marked decline in the leisure time and health of the Victorian working classes, who had been forced into cities and factories by urbanization and industrialization. Coupled with this were middle-class (and capitalist) concerns about the moral bankruptcy of the working classes, with their interest in drinking, gambling and (vulgar) blood sports such as cockfighting, and also the potentially rebellious and troublesome nature of the undisciplined masses. Hence, the (perceived) educating and disciplining benefits of sport and recreation began to trickle down through government, religious, philanthropic and industrial organizations (sometimes through enforcement) to the working classes.

During the late nineteenth century there was a rapid expansion of facilities and organized activities for the working classes, such as the opening of museums, public parks and the establishment of numerous sporting clubs. In particular, many contemporary sport clubs have their origins in these philanthropic and/or industrial organizations, such as football (soccer) clubs including Aston Villa, Bolton, and Wolverhampton Wanderers, which all began as church-instigated teams, and Preston and Sheffield, which were founded by employers.

Rational recreation was, then, primarily about 'order and control' (Cunningham, 1980: 90, cited in Horne et al., 1999: 17); however, it was not only a class-based control, as recreation was also employed by the Victorians as a means of teaching women their place and role within society and the proper morals and behaviour expected of a lady. However, by the end of the nineteenth century a massive increase in the popularity of watching sport saw the start of a shift in emphasis away from sport (and other forms of recreation) as a moral educator towards its potential for economic gain. Yet the old ideals of sport as a moral educator and controlling influence can still be seen in the policies of governments and non-governmental organizations right through the twentieth century and continuing today.

Garry Crawford

Associated Concepts Blood Sports; Class; Leisure; Modernity; Sport; Sportization.

RELIGION

The manner in which religion is understood is open to debate, which suggests that the focus of any definition obviously affects the way in which the concept is used. For example, from a Christian perspective, religion is typically understood as being concerned with a belief in, or the worship of, a supernatural power such as a god, while, from a Buddhist perspective, wherein gods are less important, the accent is instead put on deliverance or liberation. In the academic world, in classical sociology, for example, the concept is understood very much in social terms: as a ritual through which a community periodically reaffirms its collective identity and values, as in the work of Emile Durkheim; as something that gives meaning to social life *vis-à-vis* Max Weber; or, in the words of Marx (1970 [1844]), as 'the sigh of the oppressed creature, the heart of a heartless world ... the opium of the people'.

If the major debate in contemporary sociology has been about the extent to which modern societies could ever be secular, in leisure studies it has been about whether the concept of religion should include within its compass the study of secular world-views that are, to all intents and purposes, sacred in orientation. To say, for example, that sport is a religion and that the stadiums in which sports fans worship their clubs are cathedrals, is much more than to draw on a religious analogy, for it can signify an adherence to a secular experience that is nonetheless guided by a strength of belief that animates people's lives to the extent that it enables them to reach out to a mutual spiritual reality.

Indeed, as Baker (2007: 2) argues, for all their ostensible differences, 'religion and sport seem to have been made in the image of each other. Both are bathed in myth and sustained by ritual; both reward faith and patience; both thrive on passion tempered with discipline'.

Tony Blackshaw

Associated Concepts Asceticism; authenticity; Leisure; Liminality; Sport; Work Ethic.

RETIREMENT, LEISURE IN

(ageing and leisure)

RISK MANAGEMENT

The concept of risk is today an important feature of debates in both academia and the workplace. Its increase in usage can be attributed to various factors, including academic responses to the emergence of postmodernity and workplace reactions to legal compulsions, attempts at rational decision making and debates about economic and financial speculation. In leisure management, the management of risk has become essential, with some arguing that it has now become an additional primary function, mainly because of the increase in legal regulation and media interest, particularly when accidents occur and the people involved are vulnerable in some way.

Despite the ubiquity of the concept, this does not necessarily mean there is consistency in the understandings and applications of risk. However, examining the origins and development of the concept can help explain why there are many different ways in which risk can be understood and used. Risk is thought to have two possible roots: it is either attributed to the Arabic word *risq*, which signifies anything given by God that creates or brings fortune, or the Latin word *riscum*, which refers to the challenge a barrier reef presents to a sailor for good or bad (Merna and Faisal, 2005: 9). Whatever its initial origins, it seems to have entered the English language in the mid-seventeenth century, having derived from the French word *risqué*, which was used to refer to the chance of a negative or positive outcome and was strongly associated with the burgeoning maritime and insurance industries of the time.

What is of particular interest here is how risk has evolved and changed as a paradigm for understanding the world, which is often presented in three key ages. In the first age, risk was viewed as an objective danger or a neutral idea or an act of God, which excluded the idea of human fault or responsibility, with management actions primarily of a defensive type. In the second age, it was recognized that it was not just nature that generated risks, but also human beings through negligence or some other kind of inattention. During this second age, a belief developed that, as the science of statistics and probabilities grew, human beings would develop a better understanding of risk predicted through calculations. Risk therefore became contrasted with uncertainty, an event which could not be assigned a probability, together with the outcomes of risk, primarily focusing on the notion of loss (asymmetric risks). The third age of risk, or the modernistic age, is viewed in a more neutral manner, which can create both opportunities/upsides and threats/downsides (symmetrical risks). This third-age understanding of risk is increasingly evident in literature relating to both general business management and leisure management, whereby risk is embraced because, it is argued, without risk there can be no business opportunities and a central part of the adventure associated with leisure experiences will be lost.

This historical evolution in the application and understanding of risk illustrates two points. The first is that it reveals the subjective nature or the social construction of risk, in that its usage reflects the concerns of people at a particular time. The second is that it helps show two key ways that risk can be understood: on the one hand as a 'culture' and, on the other, as a practical 'management process'. Risk culture refers to how risk and change are viewed and understood, which, as has been illustrated, has gone through a number of paradigmal shifts. The risk process deals with the practical methods and stages through which data are collected, analysed, assessed and controlled, and can take place at both operational and strategic levels. As part of this practical process, it can be common to identify three core conceptual strands: risk probability, risk severity and the notion of hazard. Risk probability relates to the notion of the likelihood that a risk will occur. Risk severity relates to the magnitude of the risk event's impact, for good or bad, which can be measured in financial, physical, reputational and ethical terms. Finally, whilst the term hazard is often used as a synonym for risk, it is more helpful to maintain its conceptual distinction, with some arguing that it relates to the cause of the risk but is perhaps better understood as the source of the risk.

By now there are many influential texts relating to our understanding of risk. In a more practical management sense the publication produced by the Royal Society in 1992 stands out. The initial intention of reports such as this was to try and establish some form of conceptual clarity between various subject fields and disciplines. Such works have been important in framing how risk management is approached and the conceptual understanding of risk, particularly in terms of its relationship to a hazard, probability, severity and uncertainty. Furthermore, they have also been useful in making a distinction between the notion of *perceived risk*, described as the layperson's interpretation, and *objective risks*, described from an expert point of view.

Mark Piekarz

Associated Concepts Paradigms; Postmodernity; Risk Society.

RISK SOCIETY

Since its publication in 1986 in German, and its English version in 1992, *Risk Society* by Ulrich Beck has become one of the best-known and most influential pieces of sociological work in recent decades. For Beck, the 'second modernity' in which we currently live is characterized by increased globalization and the decline of traditions and customs in everyday life – where the old industrial society is being replaced by a new 'risk society', which is characterized by uncertainty and increased globalization.

In this new form of modern society, risk becomes a central concern and Beck suggests that this has occurred for a number of reasons. However, he primarily suggests that advances in science and technology have led to the creation of new risks. Though science and technology have undoubtedly benefited our lives in many ways, Beck argues that they have also created new fears and risks, such as the fear of a nuclear holocaust. Furthermore, Giddens (1990) has stated that the risks that concern people today are primarily 'manufactured' risks, as a result of human actions. For instance, even many so-called 'natural' disasters such as famines are the result of environmental changes brought about by global, industrial practices and mass tourism.

Everyday life has also become filled with risk and uncertainty. For instance, Beck suggests that where marriage was once a quite straightforward and solid process, today fewer people marry, they leave it much later in life and more and more relationships are ending in separation and divorce. Hence, Beck believes that relationships are now much more risky, as each individual has to make a careful judgement about the likelihood of it securing his or her future happiness. Similarly, our leisure lives become about calculated risks, examples of which are included in Mitchell, Bunton, and Green's (2004) edited collection on *Young People, Risk and Leisure*, which case studies (amongst other things) road racing in Sydney, gender and risky leisure pursuits, teenage lifestyles and the fear of crime and the pleasures and risks of young motherhood.

Beck is not necessarily arguing that the world we live in today is any more risky or dangerous than previously, but, rather, that the nature of the risks we face is changing. However, there is an increased awareness of risks that not only affect our lives but also have global consequences, and this global awareness is driven by the mass media which provide information and access to issues of global risk and disaster. Hence, the mass media help to raise awareness of modern (real) risks, which in turn helps generate a sense of anxiety in people and a fear that we live in a dangerous world over which we have little control.

Beck argues that many of the risks we face today cannot be understood in economic or class terms – for instance, the nuclear threat. However, by way of a critique, Marxist writers such as Rustin (1994) would also argue that these threats are often not driven by technology but by capitalism. For example, nuclear power is used as it is cheaper (and hence more profitable) than other forms of power, and nuclear weapons are built as they help create jobs (thereby helping to support the economy) and give people a sense of security (secure people shop more and are happier, as well as more supportive of the state). Another example here is genetic engineering. Again, it could be argued that what drives a genetics engineer is not merely scientific discovery and advancement but capitalist profit. For example, crops are genetically engineered to last longer, look better or taste better, and all to increase profit margins. Rustin also questions if new forms of political movements (such as New Social Movements, or what Beck calls 'subpolitics') have any real power and argues that these tend to have very little influence on global capitalism.

Garry Crawford

Associated Concepts Class; Consumer Society; Consumption; Deviance; Elias;

Extreme Leisure; Globalization; Leisure and the Environment; Mass Media; Modernity; Network Society; New Social Movements; Postmodernity; Postmodernism; Power; Risk Management; Tourism.

ROBERTS, KEN

(decentring leisure; leisure and the life course; well-being; youth)

ROJEK, CHRIS (1954–)

Chris Rojek began his academic career at the University of Leicester, under the tutelage of Ilya Neustadt and Eric Dunning, where he encountered the sociology of Norbert Elias and the figurational approach to leisure studies. After completing his MPhil at Leicester on 'Convergence and the Problem of Divergence', he became Lecturer in Sociology at the College of St Mark and St John in Plymouth, where he taught for two years before taking up another sociology lectureship at The Queen's College, Glasgow. In 1986 he put his teaching career on hold for eight years when he became Senior Editor for Sociology with the publishers Routledge in London. During this time he also completed a PhD in sociology at Glasgow University (1993) on 'Ways of Escape: Transformations in Modern Leisure and Tourism'. In 1994 he became Publisher in Social Science at Sage in London and Professor of Sociology at Staffordshire University. He subsequently moved to Nottingham Trent University in 1996 where he was Professor of Sociology and Culture for ten years. He is currently Professor of Sociology and Culture at Brunel University, West London.

Leisure studies is unimaginable without Rojek, but Rojek is not unimaginable without leisure studies. As the proof of his biographical details and publications record suggests, Rojek may be a leisure scholar but he is also

more than that. He is a practitioner of the sociological imagination with a great enthusiasm for culture. He is also a seriously good social theorist and an observant critic of the contemporary cultural scene, as well as being a passionate publisher whose own writings cover a wide range of subjects, from leisure to social work to sociology to celebrity, from Norbert Elias to Jean Baudrillard to Stuart Hall to Frank Sinatra.

While Rojek's work is still very much in progress, he has already made two major contributions to leisure studies. The first can be attributed to this gift of polishing the sociological imagination like Aladdin's lamp to produce ideas of penetrating insight. He might not be an original thinker in the mode of say an Elias or a Bauman and his books might be baked using the ingredients found in the work of other thinkers, but he is the kind of sociologist who likes to rub stock assumptions in his hands, feel them and turn them into something new. As Bramham (2002) points out, in his first major book contribution to leisure studies Rojek demonstrated why the subject field could no longer be business-as-usual by offering a penetrating critique of the dominant tradition of social formalism that had hitherto dominated the discipline, while at the same time outlining four new rules of method for leisure studies.

1. Leisure activity is an adult phenomenon which is defined in opposition to the play world of children.
2. Leisure practice is an accomplishment of skilled and knowledgeable actors.
3. The structure and development of leisure relations is an effect of the legitimating rules of pleasure and unpleasure.
4. Leisure relations must be sociologically examined as dynamic, relatively open-ended processes. (Rojek, 1985: 180–181)

This important work on understanding, modern leisure notwithstanding it was Rojek's interest in the puzzle of postmodernism which came to the forefront in leisure studies in the late 1980s that provided his most telling contribution to the discipline.

Here was a dramatic irony – by the mid-1990s postmodernism had lost its magnesium flare fame, but at the very moment when some were gleefully driving a stake through its heart Rojek was using it to give leisure studies a second blood transfusion in his book *Decentring Leisure* (1995). As Bramham (2002: 231) points out, it was this seminal publication that led Rojek to conclude that:

> postmodern analysis corrected the modernist notion that leisure was segmented from the rest of life, as a charmed realm of self-fulfillment. It also reverses the tendency to oppose authentic experience with inauthenticity. It challenges any notion of an integrated self. Postmodern analysis acknowledges identity politics, the difference and divisions of ethnicity, gender, and class. It highlights failures of government, of public policies; consequently, it destabilizes elitist authority structures and those cultural missionaries keen to bind citizens into the 'imaginary community' of the nation state.

Given these two important contributions, what difference has it made to leisure studies to have had Rojek in its precincts for the last 20 years or so? In one sense, hardly any. As Bramham intimates, a good many leisure 'experts' go on theorizing in bad ways, writing bad work – all tugging their forelock to a man utterly unlike themselves whose language they find interesting, but not interesting enough to make sense of, or to value, his important contributions to leisure studies.

In evincing this critique, Bramham argues that one of the problems with Rojek's work is that is often uneven and difficult to pin down and in due course criticizes it for having no overarching consensus. But he surprisingly misses the point about Rojek: his work couldn't have any overarching consensus because he couldn't be a Marxist, a figurationalist, a postmodernist or any other 'ist'. This is because Rojek has always refused to take positions that are closed. His understanding of leisure doesn't even have a cumulative look about it; this should come as no surprise, however, for he seldom reiterates his earlier work. His is an inversion of the kind of leisure studies that preceded it: instead of telling us what we already knew about leisure and inviting us to admire its by now ordinary concepts, theories and methodologies like comfy cultural artefacts that it had preserved intact in its museum gallery, he is always inviting us to rethink leisure studies anew, in extraordinarily different ways.

Rojek sees that it is his role to expand the sociological imagination in leisure studies, leaving endings open for reinterpretation and further scrutiny. The major difference between his version of leisure studies and the version of leisure studies practised by the majority of other leisure scholars is reminiscent of the distinction between the sociology of sport and sport sociology. Whereas practitioners of the latter are content to be absorbed with sport's meaning, accepting the fate of its own 'insidedness', those of the former are concerned with the inherent plurality of the world as a whole and what this adds to widening the horizons of our understanding of sport. Widening the horizons of leisure studies is the reflexive task that Rojek has set himself.

We can conclude that, rather than adhering to disciplinary strictures, Rojek's version of doing leisure studies is about understanding the modern condition, its atmosphere, its unsolvable riddles and the never fully explainable. In this way, his work is true to culture – to the atmosphere of the street, to the way that people live their leisure lives, gloss their memories and jumble life together. It is in this inimitable way that Rojek offers his 'readers *routes* through the changing landscapes of leisure studies rather than providing deep *roots* of one single solid theoretical perspective' (Bramham, 2002: 222).

Tony Blackshaw

Associated Concepts Abnormal Leisure; Decentring Leisure; Leisure; Modernity; Postmodernism; Postmodernity; Serious Leisure.

S

SAMPLING

A 'sample' is anything that is taken to be representative of who, what and/or where a researcher chooses to study. The sample used in any piece of research is one of, if not *the* most important aspects of any piece of research, as this will determine what data can be gathered and what conclusions (and possibly generalizations) can be drawn from this. The first stage of sampling is to select a 'population' – in other words, who (or what) is to be studied. For instance, researchers may decide to study football supporters. From this, they will then need to consider how they are going to select (sample) individuals and also how many.

Generally speaking, sampling can be split into two types: *probability* and *non-probability* sampling. Probability sampling (also known as *random sampling*) is where every individual in the population has a chance of appearing within the sample selected. Probability sampling is most useful if the researcher is undertaking 'analytical' or 'scientific' types of research, such as using a hypothesis (and a null hypothesis), as random sampling is usually helpful in ensuring that a representative sample is drawn from a population (though of course this cannot be guaranteed) and it allows for more stringent statistical testing of the data.

The easiest way to obtain a probability sample is to employ a list containing every member of the population concerned (this is called a *sampling frame*) and to use a computer to randomly select a certain number of individuals from this. For instance, it is may be possible to obtain a list of all of Manchester United's season ticket holders and, from this, to randomly select certain individuals to research. This is known as a simple random sample. However, it would not be possible to obtain a random/probability sample of *all* Manchester United supporters, as there is no list which includes *all* of the supporters of this team. In this instance, the researcher would probably have to rely on non-probability sampling techniques (which we will come to in a moment).

There are various forms of probability sampling, such as *systematic*, *stratified* and *cluster* sampling. Systematic sampling is where the researcher selects every nth person, such as every fifth or tenth, and so on, person. Stratified sampling is where the sampling frame is subdivided on the basis of a particular variable (such as age or gender) and then a sample is randomly (though not necessarily equally) selected from these (such as selecting 10 men and 20 women from the population). Cluster sampling (or multistage cluster sampling, as it is sometimes referred to) uses pre-existing 'clusters', such as electoral wards or districts. In this, researchers would randomly select certain 'clusters' and then for each of these would randomly select certain individuals to study.

Non-probability sampling is usually employed if a sampling frame does not exist from which a random sample can be drawn. Again, there are different types of non-probability sampling, such as *quota*, *snowballing* and *convenience* sampling. Quota sampling seeks to gather a sample based upon certain quotas. For example, the researcher may want to interview twice as many men as women, so they will purposefully select twice as many men in their sample. The main reason why this is usually done is to obtain some degree of representativeness in the sample. For instance, if a researcher wanted to interview 'typical' fans attending football matches in the UK, it would be logical to interview more men than women (as on average more men usually attend football games in the UK than women). Snowballing (or network sampling) is where one individual used in the research is asked to put the researcher in touch with others who could also be researched. For instance, one Manchester United fan might put the researcher in touch with his or her friends who are also Manchester United fans, who in turn can put the researcher in touch with friends or people they know who likewise follow Manchester United. Finally, convenience sampling is the simplest form of sampling of all and involves the researcher selecting those individuals they have access to. This is usually not representative of the wider population, but it is often the case (due to financial, time and other constraints) that we will research those we can easily get access to.

Garry Crawford

Associated Concepts Comparative Method; Ethnography; Feminism; Focus Groups; Interviews; Methodology; Observation; Oral/Life History; Pilot Study; Quantitative Research; Questionnaires; Sampling.

SCHOR, JULIET B. (1955–)

Schor is an economist-cum-sociologist whose work is primarily concerned with consumerism and leisure. She studied for her BA at Wesleyan University and completed her PhD in economics at the University of Massachusetts. Thereafter she taught for 17 years in the Department of Economics and the Committee on Degrees in Women's Studies at Harvard and was Visiting Professor of the Economics of Leisure Studies at the University of Tilburg in the Netherlands between 1995 and 2001. She has been Professor of Sociology at Boston College since 2001.

Before publishing a number of important studies on consumerism, Schor wrote the American bestseller *The Overworked American: The Unexpected Decline of Leisure* in 1992. In this book she argued that, after almost 100 years of steady decline, the number of hours that Americans work in a week had begun to accelerate in the 1940s, signalling the beginning of a new era in 'worktime'. Schor higlighted that not only was this change barely noticed but it also marked a notable departure from the hours worked in Europe, which continued to decline. Schor went on to argue that since 1948 the economic productivity of each American worker had doubled, but crucially there had been no concomitant reduction in the hours they worked. At the same time the standard of living of most Americans had increased to the extent that by 1991 most of them owned twice as much as they did in 1948. One of the upshots of this increase in relative prosperity was that during the same period consumption had also doubled.

The main casualty of these two trends has been leisure. Schor explained that the major cause of this lies in the difference between the markets for consumer products and free time: there is a massive market of consumerism and only a tiny market for free time, and what this means is that Americans crowd increasingly expensive forms of consumptive leisure spending into smaller periods of time. Schor argues that the most conspicuous casualty of this work–consumption trend is leisure. She also points out that the 'worktime' era has contributed significantly to the growth of societal problems such as stress-related illness, poor sleep patterns, divorce and family breakdown.

Tony Blackshaw

Associated Concepts Consumption; Work-Leisure; Work Ethic.

SELF, THE

(identity)

SEMIOTICS/SEMIOLOGY

The study (or science) of 'signs' is known in Europe as 'semiology' (a term coined by Ferdinand de Saussure, a Swiss linguist) and in North America as 'semiotics' (a name devised by C.S. Peirce for his independently developed philosophical system that shared many common premises with de Saussure's).

The simplest way to define what a sign is, is to consider the components or parts that make it up. At its most basic a sign consists of two components. First, there is a spoken, written or visual symbol (such as a word or a road sign or an advertisement) – this is known as the signifier. Second, associated with this symbol there will be a certain concept or idea – this is the signified. For example, the word 'cat' (the signifier) along with our understanding of what a cat is (a small furry domestic animal – this is the signified) together provide us with an understanding of or meaning for 'cat'. This then is the sign – the sum of both the word and the meaning we attach to it.

One of the key suggestions from de Saussure is that the relationship between a sign and its meaning is arbitrary. That is to say, the meaning is not straightforward. For example there is no reason why the three letters that make up the word 'cat' should mean a small furry domestic animal. These three letters could just as easily have been used to refer to what we call a 'dog' or a 'fish' or a 'banana'.

Saussure's most influential ideas were set out in lectures given between 1907 and 1911 and published posthumously in 1916 as *Cours de Linguistique Général*, edited from Saussure's papers and his students' notes. Saussure emphasized that what a sign stands for is simply a matter of cultural convention, of how things are done in a given culture. This can clearly be seen in the way different people attach different meanings to a word or the way

people use different words to refer to the same object/thing. For instance, the word 'pig' could refer to a farmyard animal. However, in a different context, or to a different person, a 'pig' could refer to a greedy person or even a police officer. Likewise to a French-speaking person the farmyard animal in question is not called a 'pig' at all, but rather a 'cochon' or 'porc'. This is also the case for all signs and symbols. For instance, many Western cultures see black as a colour for mourning and funerals; however, in many Asian nations it is white (and not black) that is associated with death (Newsom, 2007). If the sign is arbitrary, then its meaning can only be established by considering its relation to other signs. It is thus necessary to look for the relationship between signs. These can be classified in two broad ways.

- *Syntagmatically* – the linear or sequential relations between signs (thus a traditional English meal consists of a starter, followed by a main course, then a dessert).
- *Paradigmatically* – the 'vertical' relations, the particular combination of signs (thus soup or melon but not apple pie for a starter).

Semiologists will also speak of different levels of signification. The skilled semiologist can proceed from the level of denotation, the obvious meaning of the sign (e.g., a picture of a cowboy smoking a cigarette in a Marlboro advertisement), to the connotation of the sign, which is what is implied by this (e.g., that smoking Marlboros is something that tough 'real' men do). In this way the ideological nature of signs can be exposed and considered.

A further influential distinction suggested by Saussure is between language as a patterned system (langue) and language as embodied in actual speech (parole) – and, in particular, Saussure himself concentrated most of his studies on language systems (langue) which are relatively stable, unlike spoken language (parole) that are much more fluid and dynamic.

This is because Saussure located the study of language as part of a larger science devoted to 'the study of the life of signs within society'. In particular, semiologists maintain that it is possible to discern certain logics or structures or codes which underpin the multiplicity of cultural life as we experience it. Saussure's ideas have been developed effectively in the broader sphere of culture by Roland Barthes. His writings explicate the latent meanings (the myths and codes) that inform such diverse cultural phenomena as guidebooks, steak and chips, electoral photography, all-in wrestling, margarine and the Eiffel Tower.

Greg Smith and Garry Crawford

Associated Concepts Binary Oppositions; Communication; Content Analysis; Deconstruction; Ideology; Intertextuality; Mass Media; Paradigms.

SERIOUS LEISURE

This term is used interchangeably with casual leisure in an attempt to get to grips with a fast-changing world in which work appears to be becoming less meaningful for a significant number of people. For Robert Stebbins, casual leisure is in the main consumptive and involves largely non-productive leisure activities, such as 'hanging around', drinking and smoking. Serious leisure, as the term suggests, is essentially a form of leisure participation that is 'craftsman-like' and allows the individual to develop a sense of career from free-time activities.

Stebbins (1999) discusses three types of serious leisure: amateurism, hobbyist pursuits and volunteerism. Each of these has a special capacity to support enduring careers of leisure which are marked by historical turning points and stages of achievement. Serious leisure also tends to be built on the kind of perseverance which, although at times might be experienced as particularly challenging for those involved, enables its participants to build special skills and knowledge; this in turn tends to engender self-confidence

through achievement when they are successful. There are also other long-lasting benefits to be had through engaging with serious leisure that will go beyond individual and personal self-enhancement, such as material products and long-lasting personal relationships.

As Rojek (2000: 18) observes, serious leisure is built on a strong sense of the moral foundations of social behaviour and tends to give primacy to the integrative dimensions of companionship and community. In this sense, serious leisure plays a largely integrative function and as such should be understood as 'a vehicle for the cultural and moral reaffirmation of communities as places in which the individual recognizes relations of belonging'. In this regard, Stebbins takes the debate about leisure in a new direction from other more conventional approaches which largely tend to focus their critical gaze on the dichotomy between work and leisure. However, there are some problems with his analysis.

As Rojek (2000: 19) goes on to point out, Stebbins' fondness for serious leisure tends to 'emphasize the integrative effect of leisure in reinforcing the social order', at the expense of recognizing the efficacy of casual leisure for individuals and social groups. As he concludes, Stebbins ends up reducing serious leisure to a 'rational-purposive activity'. To this extent his use of the concept has a conservative bias and is underpinned by the tacit functionalist assumption that its contribution to the larger whole of social life makes serious leisure a 'good' thing.

On a more broadly philosophical basis, Stebbins' claims for the originality of the 'serious leisure' perspective have to be called into question. The concept can be traced back to the Greek term *skholē* (see Leisure) and Plato's *Republic*, where Plato's 'serious play' or 'playful seriousness' provides the source for much discussion on the threats that mimesis (e.g., leisure activities such as painting, play, poetry, and so on) poses to knowledge and truth. Plato 'seriously' deplored imitators because imitations are realities that interfere with the generation of character in the guardians of society who have 'true' knowledge. Another direct link from Stebbins' work is to the *Timaeus*, an imaginative interpretation of the world's creation by a 'craftsman' who modelled his work on the Forms (e.g., ideas surrounding good, justice, and so on). In both regards Stebbins fails to consider the extent to which his celebration of serious leisure is itself ironic, since it might be argued that what amateur, hobbyist and volunteerist pursuits are themselves is simply approximations which merely imitate (rather than initiate) values such as authenticity, pleasure, good, truth and justice, and so on.

Tony Blackshaw

Associated Concepts Authenticity; Crafts and Craftsmanship; Free Time; Leisure; Leisure Education; Mimesis; Play; Play Ethic; Social Capital.

SEX

Sex is an ambiguous but powerful word. Its reference to, on the one hand, gender differences between men and women and, on the other, sexual intercourse, overlaps with ideas such as sexual identity and the ways in which individuals have the freedom (or not) to express themselves through their sexual activities and relations.

Freud argued that every minute of our lives we are sexual beings, but because we are taught to keep our thoughts about sex deep inside ourselves, the very air of sex in society ends up clouded with repression. What this suggests is that historically sex must be understood as both a driving force and a burden. This relationship is perfectly summed up by the philosopher Michel Foucault in his *History of Sexuality* (1979) where he suggests that in early modern society sex was hidden by keeping it everywhere on view.

Notwithstanding the debate about whether or not abnormal leisure activities, such as the consumption of pornography, should be considered leisure at all, it is clear that sex permeates many leisure activities and in ways which still resonate with Freud's and Foucault's theses. Indeed, that sex is important to understanding leisure can be demonstrated quite easily. In common with leisure, sex often involves play. We can think of it as a game, an act, even a performance. It induces in us passion and ecstasy, orgasmic and even comedic feelings. Like leisure, sex is often thought of as something rather beautiful, an expression of love; while for some people it is a form of filth, the dirtier the better. Both leisure and sex often involve different kinds of war: chases, hunts, battles, sometimes resulting in violence. Like many leisure activities, sex is also inclusive and exclusive: homogeneous and homophobic; masculine and feminine; queer and straight. Sex like leisure can also induce medical problems. Sex like leisure is often used as a commodity to be bought and sold.

What is perhaps more interesting about the relationship between leisure and sex, however, is that, notwithstanding the greater tolerance of sexual diversity in contemporary society, same-sex relations that are suggestive of homo-erotic connotations are still by and large a burden that many individuals find too much to handle. Yet these same-sex relations are in the main not hidden and occur in many of our leisure activities, clearly on view. For example, sport puts men in situations where they are nude together, celebrates male camaraderie and venerates the muscular male form: These situations and attributes are not necessarily homosexual, but they contain homo-erotic elements that some men consciously and unconsciously take to. In this way, it might be said that such leisure activities allow men (and women) to live out homo-erotic fantasies that are more difficult to fulfil in other contexts.

Tony Blackshaw

Associated Concepts Abnormal Leisure; Desire; Deviance; Fantasy Leisure; Pornography; Sexual Exploitation.

SEXUAL EXPLOITATION

Sexual exploitation refers to the traumas caused by sex-related physical abuse and emotional abuse and neglect. Though writers are unanimous in their assertion that it is a serious problem in leisure, the actual ways in which they try to account for it differ in a number of key aspects. One understandable response to the problem of sexual exploitation is extreme anger and offence. Such a standpoint is often reflected in media reports that scream out at us in the news seemingly every day, encompassing a blame culture that points to the incompetence of the government and the prison service for not dealing effectively enough with perverts and paedophiles. From this standpoint sexual exploitation is often described as symptomatic of a more general moral malaise in society, though not always. Invariably the upshot of this is that perpetrators are held to be firmly responsible for their actions and there is an emphasis on retribution against those who are (usually adults) in powerful positions, who are perceived to have failed (usually young) people. Solutions to the problem of sexual exploitation are more often than not seen in terms of harsher punishments and greater legal powers and controls over the perpetrators. The major problem with this approach is that in exciting such levels of moral repugnance it leads to unreflexive condemnation.

The 'experts' who study sexual exploitation tend to adopt a rather different approach, seeing it as a technico-administrative problem to be solved rather than a *moral* issue, in the sense that their approach involves trying to separating the 'facts' from values. In other words, this is an approach to sexual exploitation that aims to eliminate subjective judgements in order to concentrate on the known 'facts' about the problem. This approach often involves studying the statistical distribution of abuse in particular leisure settings or comparing a group of known abusers with a group of non-abusers in order to identify and isolate the factors that make it more likely that some adults will abuse young people under their care. For example, Celia Brackenridge (2001) has called sport 'the last bastion of child abuse', estimating that as many as one in five young athletes may have experienced sexual victimization by the adults overseeing their careers.

Brackenridge says that there is still little research on sexual abuse in sport. For this reason it is unclear which sports are most at risk, although she argues abuse cases in the media tend to involve sports that require a high degree of intimacy between coach and athlete, including visits to the coach's home and shared accommodation. The stage just before peak performance, known as the 'stage of imminent achievement', is a particularly critical period; sports where this stage coincides with puberty are thought to pose the greatest risk of exploitation. Most cases, Brackenridge suggests, will involve the power to reward and coerce and will centre on an older male authority figure, who will also have the expert and charismatic power to exploit dependent young female athletes.

In attempting to establish a 'realistic' policy agenda, Brackenridge (2001) acknowledges the dilemmas presented by contemporary theoretical deconstructions of gender for institutions that have been built on sex segregation. However, it is significant that discussions of 'the dominant ideologies of "heterosexual masculinity" and "family" combine inside sporting subworlds to preserve male power and to stifle female autonomy' (ibid.: 99), providing the *starting point* for the consideration of theory. Ultimately, whilst a contingency model of sexual exploitation is offered it is centred on the (positivist) assertion that 'sexual contact with an athlete is always wrong and always the responsibility of the coach or authority figure' (ibid.: 240) whose judgements are a factor of the 'gender order of sport' (ibid.: 238).

As Blackshaw and Crabbe (2004) point out, in many respects this understanding of sexual exploitation in sport can be related to wider populist concerns with rising levels of 'crime' and its material consequences, which has evolved into what Downes and Rock (1998) refer to as a 'practical administrative criminology of the Left', which has abandoned the search for 'causes' by preferring to fall back upon the functionalist pursuit of social cohesion.

Echoing Foucault's exploration of the implications for judging 'dangerous individuals' through expert knowledge, other recent analyses (e.g., Lianos with Douglas, 2000) have been equally concerned with the ways in which public perceptions have become more sensitized to danger and how the right to censure as a result of dangerization has come to feature more extensively in relation to crime control. They suggest that this 'new attitude to deviance is a side-effect of new forms of social regulation' based on dangerization, which has seen society develop the tendency to perceive and analyse the world through categories of menace which invoke the tacit assumption that the world 'out there' is unsafe and that as a consequence it becomes essential to continuously scan and assess public and private spaces for potential threats (i.e., perverts and paedophiles).

As a result of these factors threats of danger are exaggerated – as are the identities of individuals perceived as threatening – to the extent that the probability of becoming a victim of a dangerous crime seems to be omnipresent. Nowhere is the ubiquitous probability of victimization felt more than in relation to the threat of sexual abuse by 'paedophiles' in sport. According to Brackenridge, sport faces two particular problems in relation to this threat. First, committed paedophiles will use it as a way to gain access to young people and, second, a culture has developed in sporting circles under which sexual liaison and banter are widely and sometimes inappropriately tolerated.

As Blackshaw and Crabbe point out, as much as is possible, Brackenridge's technico-administrative approach to abuse in sport aims to eliminate the subjective and value judgements associated with paedophilia in order to concentrate on the known 'facts' about the problem in sport. However, the key problem with this approach is that it evidences an *essentialist* and *absolutist* view of sexual exploitation in which the problem of paedophilia is thus seen to be shaped by intrinsic, instinctual and overpowering forces in the individual that not only shape the personal but the social as well. From this perspective, then, it is biological and instinctual forces (which are basically male) that will form the perversion for paedophilia. Consequently, the question of whether sexual exploitation is really an autonomous realm or a 'natural' force which the 'social' controls is never really considered.

This approach to managing the risk of paedophilia in sport reflects what Feeley and Simon (1992) have described as the new penology, which is basically concerned with the efficient administration of danger in contemporary societies. The problem here is that this approach not only increases public perceptions about the probability of paedophiles operating in sport but it also provides the general public with tangible targets of dangerousness that can be dealt with. Ultimately this technico-administrative approach ends up paying exclusive attention to coaches and the 'abused' at the expense of including the study of the 'experts' and others who are charged with the identification and protection of young people at 'risk' of 'danger' in sport. This does not mean that we should not consider as important the influences which relate to abusers and abused, but it does suggest that the issue of how and why some individuals and not others come to be labelled as abused is also a problem in its own right.

Tony Blackshaw

Associated Concepts Abnormal Leisure; Deviance; Folk Devils and Moral Panics; Social Control; Surveillance.

SEXUALITY

(compulsory heterosexuality; masculinity and masculinities; queer theory)

SHOPPING

Because of a general growth in affluence in the UK, North America and beyond (particularly in the post-war period), the rise of a consumer society, a dominating retail industry and the need to acknowledge the role of women within leisure, there has been a growing recognition of the social importance of shopping. It is evident that the nature, and importance, of shopping have changed significantly over recent decades. In particular, the mass media and new information technologies (such as the internet) have made the promotion, desire and purchase of goods and services a much more central theme of everyday social life. Moreover, shopping's role in leisure is no longer restricted to merely the purchase of goods and services for leisure activities, with shopping itself having become a major leisure activity. In particular, Oh and Arditi (2000) have suggested that shopping is key in helping us to understand contemporary postmodern (consumer) society. However, they also suggest this is not as easy as it may first appear as 'shopping' is not a single coherent activity but, rather, a 'fuzzy' practice that involves a variety of different, often complex and multi-dimensional meanings and practices.

One important aspect of shopping is its gendered nature. Mica Nava (1997) argues that shopping has until very recently been considered as primarily a female practice, due to the traditionally (patriarchal) defined roles of men as workers and women as managers of the household, which inevitably involves feeding and clothing the family and, hence, shopping. Nava suggests, therefore, that (historically) men have become increasingly disconnected from shopping because it has been seen as first and foremost a 'woman's' activity. Shopping also helps to reinforce gender roles and inequalities through the promotion and requirement that women purchase an ever-growing range of beauty and fashion items to conform to feminine ideals. As Sylvia Walby (1990) has argued, the shift from private to public patriarchy has simply allowed women to be exploited in the public sphere (such as in their paid employment and their shopping) as well as in their own homes. It is also important to recognize that not all shopping is a pleasurable leisure activity.

For instance, in Miller's *A Theory of Shopping* (1998) he carried out an ethnographic study of 76 households in North London, looking primarily at the role of women in shopping, and argued that this activity was an illustration of the personal relations within households. That is to say, women's shopping patterns would primarily reflect their devotion and duties to their families and that they would often sacrifice their own needs for those of other family members. Hence, in many cases shopping (for both men and women) could be understood as a chore and work-like. As Edwards (2000: 120) writes 'although shopping is a seductive, pleasure-seeking experience for some people some of the time, for many people a lot of the time it is simply a mundane if not tiresome chore that has all the excitement of wiping the floor'.

However, shifts towards a consumer society have seen shopping and consumption become much more central in most people's everyday lives and not just women as consumer goods are becoming ever more targeted towards male shoppers. Significantly, our cities and lives have been increasingly focused on shopping and consumption. City centres continue to become centres for shopping (rather than sites of political office or education, as public facilities such as libraries become marginal within city centres) and ever greater numbers of out-of-town retail parks and malls spring up around the outskirts of our cities. Even our leisure becomes largely reduced to shopping, as not only does shopping become a major leisure activity, but, similarly, most other leisure activities now involve some degree of shopping and consumption.

As well as the gendered nature of shopping and the feminist critique of this, it is also possible to analyse shopping from a neo-Marxist perspective and to see shopping as a form of class-based exploitation (see Clarke and Critcher, 1985). However, rather than shopping being seen in wholly negative terms, it is important to recognize the potential freedoms and pleasures that shopping can offer to many of us. For instance, and with respect to gender, it has been suggested that shopping provides many women with a legitimate reason to move outside of the home and to occupy public spaces where they can encounter and socialize with other women. It has also been suggested that shopping can involve certain levels of skill and knowledge, so should not be undervalued, and that shopping is a very important (if not central) activity in our contemporary economy, as well as in the formation of our identities (Nava, 1997).

Fiske (1989) also considers how shopping can be a form of social resistance, as individuals use items capitalism sells them to be disruptive, such as punks ripping their clothes, or youths being disruptive in shopping malls. Morris (1993) also suggests that shops and malls can become the locations for local and personal narratives, such as specific places where people meet: a good illustration of this is Richard Hawley's 2005 album, which takes its name from 'Cole's Corner' in Sheffield (named after the shop, Cole Brothers, that had been located on this corner) where family and lovers had arranged to meet for generation.

Garry Crawford

Associated Concepts   Consumption; Consumer Society; Mass Media; Theming; Subcultures; Youth; Women's Leisure.

SOCIAL CAPITAL

This term has recently come much into vogue to describe those social networks and relationships associated with civic virtue and social responsibility which involve communities and other social groups establishing common values, trust and cooperative ways of being and working together for mutual benefit.

In their critical discussion of the ways in which social capitalism has been incorporated into leisure policy discourse, Blackshaw and Long (2005) extend this basic definition to show that, in the work of Robert Putnam

(2000), social capital tends to be accompanied by two kinds of reciprocity.

- Bonding ties, which signify the interaction between 'like people' whose social networks are inward-looking and exclusive.
- Bridging ties or inter-group links, which are more outward-looking and inclusive.

As the same authors point out, in Putnam's work social capital has some further important characteristics.

- It is both a public and a private 'good' in that, just as individuals benefit from their contribution to social capital, so do others.
- It is evidenced in many different kinds of social networks – family, neighbours, church groups, personal social circles, civic organizations, e-groups. Some of these networks are repeated and intensive; some involve strong ties, while others involve weak ties; some are episodic and casual; some are formal, some informal.
- Its networks and reciprocity are largely positive for those inside particular communities and social groups, but its external effects are by no means always positive.

Putnam observes that we have witnessed a decline in social capital and points out that the bowling leagues of his youth with their legions of teams are no longer a dominant form of leisure participation and people now tend to 'bowl alone'. Obviously they don't actually bowl alone but in small, closed groups, such that the activity does not involve any interaction with new people. Insisting that this concern with the decline of social capital is not just a hankering for the nostalgia of the community of his youth, Putnam presents a wealth of research data contending that there is a positive relationship between social capital and education, economic prosperity, health and well-being and the democratic process overall. Through social capital the problems of civil society are resolved more easily, business and social transactions are less costly, personal coping is facilitated, information flows are better and increased awareness promotes tolerance as well as challenging ignorance and distrust.

Blackshaw and Long (2005) argue that what Putnam overlooks is Bourdieu's important point that what he calls 'the profits of membership' of civic associations and social networks are not available to everybody. As they indicate, drawing on the work of Ball (2003), the point of all 'capitals' – not just social capital – is that they are resources to be exploited and it is their exclusivity that gives them their value. In a nutshell, people are able to realize social capital through their social networks precisely because they are able to exclude others. This ostensible failing of Putnam's thesis is normally presented as a bonus in that some aspects of social capital are seen not as positional goods in a zero-sum game – those contributing to trust, support and security might be seen to be strengthened if shared. Moreover, in using it, social capital can be seen to grow.

Blackshaw and Long (2005) conclude that social capital has two decisive (and divisive) features: on the one hand it is a tangible resource created by the advantage of social networks and, on the other, as with all forms of capital, it has a symbolic dimension, which contrives to hide networks of power woven into the fibres of familiarity. In the event they suggest, following Bourdieu, that in understanding social capital we must take into account the extent, quality and quantity of social actors' networks *and* their ability to mobilize these, which is always governed by the mutual understanding that any given field is an arena of struggle. In other words, it is the battle for distinction that gives social capital its ostensible qualities.

Tony Blackshaw

Associated Concepts   Bourdieu; Community; Cultural Capital; Cultural Intermediaries; Serious Leisure; Social Network Analysis; Third Way.

SOCIAL CLASS

(class)

SOCIAL CONTROL

This is an enduring if often poorly defined concept in leisure studies. The view that social control denotes the patterned and systematic ways in which society on the one hand enforces or encourages conformity and on the other deals with any form of deviance that violates its accepted norms and values was once taken as read. Foremost among the reasons responsible for this oversimplistic reading is the explanation that under the auspices of orthodox sociology the concept emerged merely miming the reifying habits of the functionalist approach through which it was developed. Social control was, in Foucault's terminology, 'normalized' and, in its obsession with the circumstances of human conformity and obedience, orthodox sociology allowed the concept to emerge as unexceptional. Consequently the major assumption made about social control at this time was the idea that human behaviour is just that: tacitly and routinely socially controlled. If not exactly saying so, sociology thus conceptualized a category which yoked socialization and social control together as one and the same: connecting the idea that the social order is maintained not only, or even namely, by the state – judiciary, legal systems, police forces and prisons – but also by public opinion, culture, leisure patterns, religion, popular beliefs, family, education, and so on and so forth. To this extent it was assumed that social control converged around all efforts that induce the populace to behave willingly and voluntarily in ways that the 'value consensus' considers proper and appropriate.

Talcott Parsons (1951) made this functionalist perspective more analytically complex when he suggested that social control mechanisms are both necessary and inevitable 'secondary defences' to combat the deviance that is inevitable in all societies. Foremost amongst these is the utilization of sanctions that are filtered through individuals and institutions. Positive sanctions (e.g., leisure) are used to reward desirable social behaviour, while negative sanctions in the form of punishments are aimed at deterring unwelcome social behaviour. Formal sanctions tend to be institutionally rooted, while informal sanctions are in most cases exercised through the immediate 'off the record' responses of significant others. But according to functionalism the backbone of any system of sanctions is 'the basic and irreducible' functions of social institutions, such as the occupational structure and leisure, driven as they are by the pervasive authority of the work ethic.

If not entirely shaking off the pervasive influence of functionalism, Lemert's (1967) work on 'primary' and 'secondary' deviance and Becker's (1963) influential study of the sociohistorical context of marihuana usage both neatly encapsulated the growing influence of labelling theory, which offered the view that if society creates deviance, in the sense that the application of deviant labels may produce more deviance than it prevents, it follows that we cannot understand deviance without understanding social control in the form of the response of society to rule-breaking behaviour. Labelling theorists suggested that it should be the role of micro social analysis to examine the social audience and its reaction to deviance, since labels are not automatically imposed on all rule-breakers and some people escape labelling altogether. From this perspective, then, social control was seen to be coercive and repressive, its main aim being to bring under control those perceived to be troublesome.

The upshot was that this 'new' sociology of deviance came more and more to focus its critical gaze on the actions of powerful groups. What unified what was essentially a fast-emerging subdiscipline of theoretically divergent perspectives was their collective willingness to 'side with the underdog'. Indeed, there was no logical reason why structural Marxists should necessarily concern themselves with developments in the anti-structuralist interests of symbolic interactionism, yet such interchanges became characteristic of a number of important studies of social control. In Britain Paul Willis' classic (1977) study of cultural reproduction and subcultural resistance in education was a case in point. Drawing on a theoretical blend which encompassed different aspects of structural and cultural Marxism and symbolic interactionism, Willis offered an understanding of the ambivalence of an education system which ostensibly prepared working-class boys for their subordinate and inferior adult roles in society, but in its crystallization did not appear to be particularly effective as an agency of social control.

Also writing from a neo-Marxist perspective, Clarke and Critcher (1985) argued that capitalism and the state played a key role in shaping work and leisure though the regulation of individuals and groups and certain activities and public spaces. In Policing the Crisis, Hall et al. (1978) added the issues of 'race' and ethnicity to this class-based approach to deal with the racial motivations behind what they called the moral panic generated around the category of 'mugging' in Britain in the early 1970s. Drawing on a Marxist theoretical amalgam inspired by Althusser and Gramsci and augmented through an adaptation of Cohen's (1972) theorization of Folk Devils and Moral Panics, Hall et al. turned their attention to the role of establishment authority figures and institutional arrangements in the assignment of social control to young, unemployed, black populations. In a nutshell they argued that, if the involvement in street crime by young black men could to some extent be attributed to their social, economic and political marginalization, their criminality was more a result of institutional social control intensified through a mass media-inspired moral panic about 'mugging'. Regardless of its originality Policing the Crisis was subject to widespread criticism, not only because of its dubious empirical consistency but also for being silent on the matter of the social control of women.

It was left to feminist critics to put the issue of gender and social control on the political agenda and they demonstrated how women's leisure is constrained not only directly due to the narrow range of activity options open to them but also because of the temporal, spatial, economic, ideological and sociopsychological factors involved, as well as the influences on this process of the categories of social class, 'race', ethnicity and familial and other gender roles (see Deem, 1986).

Another important factor in considering social control in relation to these categories was that it brought to our attention the pervasive significance of power. In the 1980s increasing numbers of materialist and structuralist thinkers were diverting their theoretical interests across to poststructuralism and in particular the work of Foucault. If classical Marxism had emphasized a reductive economy of power related to the means of production it was Foucault who exposed in a dialectical fashion the imbrication of social control in a 'microphysics of power' with the normalizing judgements that persisted through this collusion. Foucault offered an alternative view which understood power as having no substantive content and in an innovative twist he suggested it would be more profitable to analyse it as a technology of knowledge, rather than being something possessed or centralized in the state or some other institution.

More recent analyses of social control have been concerned with the ways in which public perceptions of certain kinds of leisure activities have become sensitized to danger and how the right to censure as a result of 'dangerization' has come to feature more extensively in social control (Lianos with Douglas, 2000). It has also been argued quite forcefully by Bauman that the configuration of economic arrangements associated with consumer capitalism may be of far greater importance for explaining patterns social control today. To put it another way, social control, like much else in liberal democracies (including leisure), has by and large been commodified and privatized. The comfortable majority no longer live in the shadow of tyranny by state; instead they create their own paroxysm, driven by market forces that they have no authority over, but at the same time have no final authority over them. In what Bauman (2000) calls 'liquid modernity', private consumption replaces work as the backbone of the reward system in a society which is underpatterned rather than patterned, disorganized rather than ordered. It is only the poor – the 'flawed consumers' – who are still controlled through the work ethic.

Tony Blackshaw

Associated Concepts Abnormal Leisure; Birmingham School; Consumer Society; Consumption; Deviance; Folk Devils and Moral Panics; Football Hooliganism; Foucault; Functionalism; Power; Racism and Leisure; Surveillance; Work Ethic.

SOCIAL NETWORK ANALYSIS

Social networks are used by researchers to depict the ways in which social relations between individual agents are intertwined in manifold sets of interdependent relations or webs of attachment. The aim of social network analysis is to explain the ties or patterns manifest in those configurations. As social network theorists might argue, most people belong to some sort of network and can be involved in any number of relationships which may be reciprocated by others to a greater or lesser extent – who interacts with whom is dependent on a number of factors, including class, ethnicity, gender and age. As Stokowski (1994) demonstrates in her discussion of organizational networks in leisure, some networks will be equally reciprocated but not all ties are necessarily symmetrical and people are most likely to experience non-reciprocal relations with those of a higher social status.

Blackshaw and Long (1998) identified four distinctive, though not mutually exclusive, approaches to social network analysis: graph theory, which uses statistical analysis, sociograms and network density to plot social relationships diagrammatically; the structural sociology of Barry Wellman (1979, 1988) and his colleagues at the University of Toronto, which to a large extent has been concerned with the question of social networks as personal communities; the network structural approach to leisure research (Stokowski, 1994), which has attempted to merge structural analysis with more action-based perspectives *vis-à-vis* Giddens' structuration theory; and the work of Phillip Abrams (1986), which used the idea figuratively rather than structurally.

Tony Blackshaw

Associated Concepts   Community; Giddens; Network Society; Social Capital.

SPECTACLE

This is a concept which does not permit a precise definition. Like the Latin terms *specere* 'to look at', *spectare* 'to watch' and *spectaculum* 'show', the idea of the spectacle represents a number of different things. As a consequence it has been used repeatedly in the literature to formulate different ideas surrounding extraordinary public performances of mass leisure, from rock concerts to sporting cup finals to state-sponsored ceremonies. Having said that what unites most, if not all, of these interpretations is the idea that, in marked contrast to the carnival, where leisure is part and parcel of a disorganization of spontaneous and anarchic proceedings, the spectacle implies a structured organization of proscribed events that tend to render participation dutiful and often socially controlled, leaving only the illusion of ecstatic release.

Key amongst these interpretations is Guy Debord's seminal publication *The Society of the Spectacle* (1995 [1967]), which suggested the encounters that shape sport spectacles are banal in the way that they have reduced the carnivalesque to spectator status, or what

Bauman (2007) calls the 'momentary resuscitation(s) of the togetherness that [have] sunk into a coma', making manifest 'unreal unities' that mask 'the class divisions on which the real unity of the capitalist mode of production is based' (Debord: thesis 72). In Debord's sense, the notion of the spectacle is a sham, suggesting that sporting spectacles are merely material constructions of consumerist illusions. What is more, their inexorable significance in modern societies means that our encounters with sport are disposed to become mere images, because of their complicity in the capitalistic relations of production and consumption.

In Debord's scheme of things, however, there remains hope of escape from the spectacle, for 'it is not a collection of images; rather, it is a social relationship between people that is mediated by images' (thesis 4). There is an explicit link here between Debord and the Frankfurt School, in the sense that he infers our relationships to the spectacle present new possibilities for exploitation. However, for Debord there is also an attempt to distinguish between the commodified (that is, distorted and fetishized) situations of the spectacle and 'authentic' or essential situations, which are undistorted by capitalistic relations. What Debord's work suggests is that, by moving away from the spectacle, which imposes on us an existence that is not really ours, to a more 'authentic' practice, we can gain a sense of the real meaning of our leisure lives.

Tony Blackshaw

Associated Concepts   Audiences; Authenticity; Carnivalesque; Celebrity; Commodity Fetishism; Consumption; Critical Theory; Dionysian Leisure; Social Control.

SPORT

This modern term is a shortened version of the word *disport*, which literally means 'to indulge (oneself) in pleasure'. Disport is in turn a facsimile of the French word *desporter*, which is derived from the Latin etymological root *disportare*, meaning 'to carry away'. In getting carried away with their own eagerness to define the term some leisure scholars have been much more specific in attempting to identify what they see as the range of qualities which together establish an activity as a sport proper. While some have merely reduced the idea to modern recreational pursuits in which the outcome is affected by physical skills and prowess (Loy et al., 1978), others have identified what they see as being sport's essential features (Haywood et al., 1995). In contrast social theorists have found it impossible to set limits on what constitutes a sport, because culturally sport is experienced in myriad ways. Accordingly they have explicitly rejected the kind of nuts-and-bolts definitions that emphasize the essentialist structural properties of sport forms, or which focus their attention on elite performance, as these sidestep the really interesting and difficult questions suggested by the role of sport in both historical and contemporary sociocultural formations.

In relation to questions about the historical development of sport, the figurationalist sociologist Norbert Elias convincingly argued that most modern forms of organized sport had their antecedents in eighteenth-century Britain, where they developed through the 'sportization' of pastimes in two main phases, which saw the emergence of sports such as cricket, boxing, fox hunting and horse racing, followed by association football, rugby, tennis and track and field games in the mid-nineteenth century. Elias developed the concept of sportization to argue that what came to be known as 'sport' emerged as part of a wider civilizing tendency where the rules governing 'sporting' contests became not only more exacting, but also established a balance between the ability to gain a high degree of 'combat-tension' with what was perceived to be an acceptable use of protection against injury (Elias and Dunning, 1986). What Elias was in effect offering was a domesticated modern understanding of the Aristotelian concept of *mimesis* or, in other words, a processual theory of the 'imitation of men in action' which despite the protestations of his followers was latently functionalist.

Functionalist sociologists have themselves considered the ways in which sport meets the 'needs' of the social system by concentrating their attentions on the way it not only contributes to individual personal development, but more importantly maintains value consensus and social order. Yet functionalism has been heavily criticized not least because it underplays the extent to which sport may actually discourage people from participation because the way in which it is structured in capitalist societies allows for few 'winners'. If this counterargument acknowledges that some individuals might rationally conclude that their own efforts might not be enough and instead might resort to dishonest ways of improving their chances of winning, it also suggests that sport, whatever its public and moral hegemony, offers multiple opportunities for the pursuit of deviance, from the ritualized rule-breaking activities, such as football violence, to the more abhorrent crimes against the vulnerable, such as sexual exploitation.

As well as criticizing functionalism for overlooking the multifaceted ways in which sports manifest themselves in various social formations, social theorists writing for Marxist, feminist and 'race' and ethnicity perspectives have in their own ways viewed the social relationship with sport as one of domination and social inequality which maintains unequal power relations in support of social class and patriarchal and racist conditions. Neo-Marxist accounts have also suggested that sport in capitalist societies merely serves as a spectacle (Debord, 1995 [1967]) or opiate (Brohm, 1978) which diverts people's attention away from more pressing issues and that sport participation ultimately leads to alienation, because the body is reduced to an instrumental means to an end – a virtual machine set with the task of maximizing capitalist production.

As Debray (2007) points out, not only has the body become the subjective centre of gravity in the contemporary age, visibility has also become the basis of symbolic authority. What this means is that the body is now central to current theorizing about sport, but in relation to consumption rather than production. This interest in consumer culture has often been combined with a growing interest in the reciprocal relationship between sport and the media. An increasing recognition has also developed that if people's experiences of sport are better understood through their contingency rather than their fixity, sport also presents numerous possibilities for identity – both individualized and communal – and this has initiated a range of innovative studies which have drawn their inspiration from poststructuralism, postmodernism and queer theory. In this sense the study of sport, as with leisure more generally, has increasingly become subsumed under the rubric of cultural studies.

Tony Blackshaw

Associated Concepts Consumer Society; Consumption; Elias; Extreme Leisure; Leisure Bodies; Pleasure; Postmodernism; Play Ethic; Pleasure; Sexual Exploitation; Spectacle; Sportization.

SPORTIZATION

This term was coined by Norbert Elias and ties into his wider civilization process thesis; it is also linked to debates on globalization. Elias (1986) suggests that during a period from the seventeenth through to the nineteenth centuries the 'parliamentalization of political conflict' occurred across Europe, which saw a shift towards centralized state control and parliamentary democracy. Along with this civilizing trend of politics and social life, came an emphasis on changes in individual conduct, including new forms of morality and controlled, ordered and organized forms of sporting competition, which Elias refers to as the 'sportization of pastimes'. For Elias, this then constitutes the formation of our contemporary understanding of what 'sport' is, as a form of organized ritualized and relatively non-violent (compared with what had gone before) play.

Elias argues that this process of sportization occurred first in eighteenth- and nineteenth-century England (and to a lesser extent Scotland) and then over time spread through Europe, the British Empire and beyond. However, it is important that the process of sportization is not seen as a simple matter of colonialisms as the figurational sociology of Elias emphasizes the two-way process of cultural interaction between established groups (such as between the West and non-Western nations) (Maguire, 2000).

The concept of sportization is then developed further by Maguire (1999), who, by drawing on the work of Roland Robertson (1995), updates this theorization for a global world. In particular, Maguire uses the term sportization to describe the 'transformation of English pastimes into sports and the export of some of them on a global scale (Maguire, 1999: 79), and suggests that there have been five phases of global sportization.

- *Phase 1: The Germinal Phase (1400–1750)* – characterized by the growth of new nation communities; a rise in Catholicism; new conceptions of the individual; the birth of geography and the calendar.
- *Phase 2: The Incipient Phase (1750–1802)* – the emergence of nation states in the 'West'; international trade; the domination of the 'West'.
- *Phase 3: The Take-Off Phase (1870s–1920s)* – a strong notion of the modern ideal to which all societies should adhere; the organization of international events; the onset of global warfare.
- *Phase 4: The Struggle-for-Hegemony Phase (1920–1960s)* – continuing conflict between world states (Second World War, Cold War); the nuclear age; Third World poverty.
- *Phase 5: The Uncertainty Phase (1960s–1990s)* – new awareness of global concerns, challenge to materialist values; end of the Cold War; global cultural patterns; postsocialism; renewed belief in religious traditions such as Islam.

Garry Crawford

Associated Concepts Elias; Globalization; Play; Sport; Violence.

STATUS

The word 'status' derives from Latin to mean a person's condition as defined by law, but, in its usage within leisure studies, and the social sciences and more generally, it has come to mean a person's social standing.

For Marx, a person's position within the social hierarchy was simply determined by their relationship to the means of production – such as, if they were factory owners or workers. This simple economic determinist model was challenged by the writings of Max Weber who suggested that a person's social standing, as well as being determined by their economic position ('class'), was also shaped by other social factors, such as their political affiliations and memberships ('party') and their social 'status'. For Weber (1922), status refers to a social system of stratification based upon customs, traditions and legalities. However, this is still closely intertwined with social class, where status groups are able to use their position to acquire greater wealth and power.

After Weber, the concept of status was most notably developed by Ralph Linton in the 1930s. Linton (1936: 113) defined status as 'a position within a particular system'. Linton is particularly useful as he developed an understanding of how status operated at an individual level. Linton suggested that an individual's particular social status was determined by the sum of all the various statuses they occupied (such as their ethnicity, gender, and so on), and that this status would then provide them with certain privileges as well as responsibilities.

Status is a useful concept within leisure studies, as it recognizes that individual and collective social positions within society, and the privileges and rights that these afford (and restrict), are not solely determined by economic position and social class but by other factors also, such as gender, age, ethnicity and the like, which will all go towards determining status and position within a social hierarchy. In particular, Veal (1989) suggests that Weber's consideration of status offers a much more profitable way of understanding contemporary leisure and life-style patterns than a traditional Marxist (class- based) analysis, as status allows for an understanding of how social factors beyond class (such as ethnicity and gender) help to shape leisure patterns, participation and opportunities.

Garry Crawford

Associated Concepts Bourdieu; Class; Habitus, Field and Capital; Leisure Life-Style; Marxism.

STEBBINS, ROBERT A.

(serious leisure)

STRUCTURE AND AGENCY

This is a juxtaposition, a conceptual couplet or dichotomy that highlights the debate about the extent to which human action is either determined or undetermined by social structures. The 'structure and agency' debate deals with how we can best understand what people do and think. Structural explanations are those that explain activities with reference to people's social circumstances. A fan of a particular football team, for instance, might be a supporter because he or she grew up in an area where everyone else was a supporter, with a family of supporters and where supporting rival neighbouring teams would be seen as a disloyal action to be negatively sanctioned. A fan's support can be explained without thinking that he or she made any 'choice' in the matter at all – the social structures surrounding him or her 'make' that person the supporter of a particular team, and the thought of supporting another team simply would not occur to him or her. Perhaps the most extreme variant of structuralism was Louis Althusser, who argued that there is no such thing as an 'individual' at all – that all our ideas, motivations and beliefs are merely the products of social–structural and ideological forces – and that all human activities are ultimately driven by social forces acting 'behind our backs' (Althusser, 1969).

'Agency' explanations, however, account for people's activities by looking at how people understand their circumstances, then decide what to do on the basis of those understandings. In such an approach, people are treated as fundamentally rational – as reasonable decision makers – and what they do is the result of their making what seem to them to be the most sensible choices open to them given a particular situation. In this sense, then, someone might support a particular team because it is very successful (thus accruing such a status on its supporters) or because going to see the team play is affordable (thus allowing a supporter to see more games and become more involved). A choice *between* teams is made by weighing up these different possibilities, and that choice is made by the individual in question. Most economic explanations are based on these notions of rational actors seeking to maximize the benefit they can accrue from making particular decisions.

Most contemporary sociologists would argue that neither approach allows us to explain people's activities very well. Most notably, Anthony Giddens, Pierre Bourdieu and Jürgen Habermas have attempted to theoretically 'reconcile' structure and agency into grand theories that can encompass both forms of explanation simultaneously. Bourdieu's (1984) book *Distinction*, for example, tries to show how people *tend towards* particular tastes and leisure pursuits on the basis of their social positions and change these tastes as they move (or seek to move) socially. Other theorists, however, have argued that very few thinkers have ever seriously advanced 'structuralist' or 'agency' explanations in the ways that these are conventionally portrayed. Anthony King (2004), for instance, argues that all the attempts to 'reconcile' structure and agency are theoretically flawed and that no respectable social theorist has ever 'chosen' between them in the first place.

Alex Dennis

Associated Concepts Binary Oppositions; Bourdieu; Functionalism; Giddens; Marxism; Power; Symbolic Interactionism.

STRUCTURE OF FEELING

This term emerged out of the work of Raymond Williams. He used the idea as a key organizing concept with which to make sense of, and find expression for, the day-to-day experience of culture as it is lived by generation or during a particular historical period. In Williams' early (1961) work the structure of feeling of any generation tends to be embodied in the 'dominant' social group in the more general culture, while in his later writings (1977) it is more closely aligned with 'emergent' (as opposed to 'dominant' or 'residual') cultural formations 'in solution', in the process attaching to the idea counter-hegemonic possibilities. We can grasp this idea best if we try to understand how an explicit emotion arises out of the structuration between the official consensus of any historical period, as codified in its societal and legislating institutions, and the everyday lived experiences which together define the meanings, justifications and values articulated. However, because the structure of feeling also emerges out of the interaction between unconscious and conscious awareness, as well as the feelings of the culture rather than its thoughts, the full extent of these meanings, justifications and values can never be fully articulated. It is this attention to tacit knowing that led Blackshaw in his (2003) ethnography of the leisure life-world of 'the lads' to argue that, if there will always be more about culture than we are able to say, it is nonetheless intuition, with all its 'large, daring short cuts and approximations', to paraphrase Bruno Schulz (1998), rather than analysis in the scientific meaning, which is better suited to revealing the truth about culture.

Tony Blackshaw

Associated Concepts Culture; Community; Ethnography; Giddens; Habitus, Field and Captial; Hegemony; Leisure Life-World; Marxism; Postmodernism.

SUBCULTURES

The origins of subcultural theory can be found in the Chicago School (a group of scholars at the University of Chicago), who studied deviant groups that were said to have different norms and values from those of wider society – such as Howard Becker's (1963) study of marihuana users or Albert Cohen's (1955) book *Delinquent Boys*. In this, Cohen suggests working-class boys, deprived of social status and opportunities, would commit 'deviant' acts which contrasted with the dominant middle-class values. This then results in 'pressure' and the formation of a subculture with its own value system in which members can find status and rewards.

However, the theory of subcultures was most notably developed by a group of scholars working at the Birmingham School. In particular, the Birmingham School was responsible for associating the idea of subculture with particular style groups, such as, Mods, Punks, Skinheads and Teddy boys. In particular, Hebdige (1979) suggested that subcultures engaged in a process of 'bricolage', whereby they will draw on existing consumer goods, but will redefine and combine these to develop a distinct style to mark themselves out from the general public and as a form of social subversion and resistance.

Subcultural theories have been extensively criticized for neglecting to consider the internal diversity, overlaps and movement between subcultures, the instability of these groups and their often permeable and ill-defined boundaries. Also, adopting a traditional subcultural approach suggests that these groups form as a response to structural social processes (like the alienation of these youths). This overlooks levels of choice (and the agency) of individuals. It also overlooks the power and influence of the mass media and consumption in helping to form and define these groups. In these accounts the mass media tend to be viewed as part of 'the Establishment' and, hence, detached and even opposed to these subcultures rather than playing an important role within them (Hodkinson, 2002). There is also often a general belief, even by subcultural writers (such as Hebdige, 1988), that subcultures are tied to a particular era and are less applicable to understanding contemporary forms of youth culture or social groupings. For it is questionable today, if youth cultures (such as 'Skaters', 'Goths', 'Emos', and so on), which are often more numerous, diverse in their membership and have more permeable boundaries, would constitute subcultures in the same way as groups such as the Mods, Punks, Skins and Rockers once did.

Since the demise of the Birmingham School, several authors have offered updated (post)modern alternatives to the idea of subculture, such as the 'neo-tribe' (Bauman, 1992; Maffesoli, 1996) or 'life-style' (Jenkins, 1983; Chaney, 1996), amongst numerous others, to counter the weakness inherent in a subcultural framework and to account for the changing (and more fluid) nature of contemporary social groupings. However, certain authors such as Muggleton (2000) and Hodkinson (2002) would argue for the continued use, though an updated version, of the concept.

Garry Crawford

Associated Concepts Alienation; Birmingham School; Consumption; Deviance; Fashion; Folk Devils and Moral Panics; Leisure Life-World; Mass Media; Neo-Tribes; Power; Structure and Agency; Youth.

SUPERMODERNITY

(non-place)

SUPPLY

Supply is basically the quantity of goods that suppliers are willing to sell at a given price and at a certain point in time. Changes in supply (in response to demand) can have an effect on price. Generally speaking the supply of products and services to the leisure industry is split into three sectors: the voluntary sector, the public sector and the commercial sector.

The voluntary sector is dominant at the club level, often operating in conjunction with the public sector, to provide leisure opportunities within a relatively small radius of the club-house or sports facility. Local government coordinates both the voluntary-sector and the public-sector facilities at the broader community level. Thus it has strategic responsibility over its administrative area for the provision of leisure opportunities. It will do this independently by direct supply. However, it will increasingly do it in partnership with voluntary-sector clubs and charitable trusts across all the different kinds of leisure activities in that area. It will also have an interface with the commercial sector in the area, at the very least through the application of planning regulations.

If the government and the voluntary sector operate primarily at the local level, there is an important and strategic national presence for these two sectors. We can see this relationship in sport. The first national impact is through the governing bodies of sport, which have the responsibility for the organization and administration of national and international competitions. The second impact is through national government sports agencies, which have responsibility for the 'production' of international sporting success.

The commercial sector is the most diverse and fragmented of the three sectors involved in the provision of leisure opportunities. It has an increasingly strong presence at the local level, in direct competition with both local government and the voluntary sector in the provision of opportunities for leisure, particularly through the provision of sport, health and fitness facilities. However, it will only compete in certain sectors of the leisure market: fitness centres, country clubs, golf clubs and the like. In these areas, the commercial sector will aim to give similar products but also provide a higher-quality product at a higher price. This allows the sector to have a national presence in the sense of a national network of leisure facilities with an established brand and quality.

With reference to the national presence of the commercial sector in sport specifically, this has increasingly become dominated by the professional sports sector, which grew enormously in importance in the 1990s through an escalation in the price of broadcasting rights for major national and international sport competitions. The alliance between professional sport and the changing structure of broadcasting (involving terrestrial, cable, satellite and digital) is the largest single factor that influenced the economics of sport in the 1990s.

Other items of sport-related consumer expenditure are also part of the 'non-sport' commercial sector; this means that they are sport-related expenditure by consumers but the firms that supply these demands would not classify themselves as being in the sport industry. These include the providers of things like travel, gambling, magazines and newspapers. Additionally, there is sport employment, which provides jobs for a sizeable number of people. For example, sport retailers and manufacturers in the UK alone employ 18 per cent of the total estimated for sport in the UK.

Gratton and Taylor (1991) explained how the commercial sector has dominated expenditure on sporting excellence through spending on sport sponsorship and professional team sports. On the other hand, the market for mass participation sport has given a large role to the voluntary and government sectors. Since 1991, government resources devoted to excellence have increased and more commercial market activity has been seen in the mass participation sector. Additionally, the voluntary sector has seen more of its economic activity taking place in the formal market economy, as paid labour time has replaced volunteer labour and as some voluntary-sector clubs have become commercial operations.

Rob Wilson

Associated Concepts Demand; Three-Sector Provision of Leisure.

SURVEILLANCE

This concept is important in the thought of Michel Foucault. It originated in his work on madness and became part of his general philosophy, being fully discussed in *Discipline and Punish* (1977), where he used a startling juxtaposition to chart the unfolding of the machinery of a new modern disciplinary society. Here Foucault suggested that in modern societies there had been an historical movement from brutal, overt repression and social control to rational, scientific and bureaucratic control of 'deviant' populations through surveillance. In this most illuminating work Foucault evoked the image of Jeremy Bentham's *Panopticon* in order to argue that an all-seeing gaze (*le regard*) comes to serve as a metaphor for surveillance connected with governmentality in the modern state.

A significant feature of Panopticonism is that, like Orwell's 'Big Brother' surveillance, it is indiscernible: those under surveillance are always unsure of whether or not they are being watched, and as a consequence the 'watched' simply act in accordance with the Panopticon, because they never know 'when' or 'who' may be watching. From this analysis it follows that what is surveillance is self-surveillance. It is not clear whether Foucault consulted the work of Gaston Bachelard in developing his theory, but it is Bachelard who perfectly sums up how self-surveillance is fully assured under the Panopticon: 'it must somehow be itself held under surveillance. Thus, there come into existence forms of surveillance of surveillance to which, for sake of brevity, we shall give the exponential notation (surveillance). We shall, moreover, set out the elements of a surveillance of surveillance, in other words, of (surveillance)' (Bachelard, quoted in Raban, 2006: i).

Foucault argued that this surveillance of surveillance – the Panopticonisms of everyday life found in leisure activities such as dance, swimming and aerobics but also sport stadiums, which have 'changed from being open, public spaces to privatized spaces of segmented confinement' (Bale, 1994: 84) – micro-manages individuals more efficiently than carceral systems because it thwarts deviant behaviour through self-actuating prohibitions, reinforced by the subject's own certainty in the omnipresence of the all-seeing power of the normalizing gaze.

It has been argued by some (e.g., Garland, 1990) that Foucault's historical claims are overgeneralized and that he provides little by way of empirical evidence for his assertions, but there is no doubt that new surveillance technologies have today become widespread, thus placing more limits on our privacy and freedom. As O'Hagan (2003: 5) points out, for example, Britain has the highest density of surveillance equipment in the world and since 1994 'British Governments have spent more than £205 million on CCTV installation in towns and cities, supporting 1400 projects, far more than any other country in Europe'.

These observations notwithstanding, Bauman has argued that today it is only the poor who experience the hard edge of exclusionary and repressive surveillance. In his (1992) critical theory, experts and expert systems play an important role – they become crucial to the enforcement and preservation of the weapons of *seduction* and *repression*. Contra Foucault, Bauman (1998) suggests that the *repressive* apparatus of the Panopticon has largely been supplemented by the *seductive* allure of Synopticon watching. So in our present-day society social control is by and large not about *the few who watch the many* (Panopticon), but, rather, *the many who watch the few* (Synopticon). For the comfortable majority, *normalization* is thus replaced by *precarization* and, when the 'normal' lost its authority, people became committed, as Bauman might say, to revealing themselves. Those most adept at revealing themselves are the celebrities, who the rest of us perceive have the ability to fulfil our collective fantasies about stardom, and it is they who are the principal target of the Synopticon gaze. In this sense surveillance for the most part today has become rather more like the world of Endemol's *Big Brother* than Orwell's dystopia.

Tony Blackshaw

Associated Concepts Abnormal Leisure; Celebrity; Consumer Society; Consumption; Deviance; Folk Devils and Moral Panics; Football Hooliganism; Foucault; Social Control.

SYMBOLIC INTERACTIONISM

Herbert Blumer (1900–1987) originated this term (also called SI) in the mid-1930s as a means of identifying elements in the Chicago sociological tradition in which he had been trained, convergent with the ideas of US pragmatist philosophers. In particular, SI was designed to codify the sociological implications of the work of George Herbert Mead (1863–1931), a philosopher who had emphasized the role of shared symbols such as language and non-verbal codes in addressing questions about the nature of human action and the self. However, SI was not widely identified as a major sociological perspective until the late 1960s. By this time Blumer's (1969) theoretical and methodological presuppositions had been put into practice through a series of influential studies by sociologists linked to the 'second Chicago School' (Fine, 1995), including Becker (1963), Goffman (1959, 1961a, 1963), Hughes (1958) and Strauss (1959; Strauss et al., 1964). These studies are now regarded as exemplars of the SI approach to social life.

The process of interpretation lies at the heart of the SI approach. Blumer (1969) suggests that humans act towards things on the basis of their meanings, which arise in social interaction and contribute to the definition of the situation. People must interpret objects and events and act upon the definitions they arrive at or devise. Language and other shared symbols are the medium of these everywhere present and utterly unavoidable processes of interpretation. SI works with a distinctive view of society, seeing it as a vast array of interactions that are best conceived as fluid social processes, not as a set of rigid social structures. SI suggests that positivistic methods of variable analysis have not proved successful in the social sciences and do not adequately capture the interpretive character of social life. As Robert E. Park, one of the leading figures of the first Chicago School, put it, 'What sociologists most need to know is what goes on behind the faces of men [sic], what it is that makes life for each of us either dull or thrilling' (Park, 1950: v–vi). Accordingly, SI favours observation, open-ended interviewing, documentary analysis and other methods best able to access the point of view of the person and the meanings that guide interaction.

SI has long been interested in the informal processes of social life that occur in leisure settings. Its major philosophical forerunner, George Herbert Mead (1934), paid especial attention to play and games, identifying these as important stages in the development of the self. In the play stage the child is able to act out roles familiar to it, such as parent or teacher. By 'taking the role of the other' through play activity, the child as it were tries on an identity for size, experiencing the rights and expectations that go with that role in a not-real, playful context. The further development of the child's self occurs through games, which are organized according to universalistic rules that apply to particular roles in the game (e.g., the kinds of moves that a goalkeeper is entitled to undertake in the game of soccer). Once a child can play a game, it begins to develop a self that can recognize the authority of what Mead called the 'generalized other' – the impersonal moral codes of society. Play and games are thus central to the emergence of adult identities.

SI concerns were introduced into leisure studies via John R. Kelly's *Leisure Identities and Interactions* (1983; see also Kelly, 1994). This book distinguished an interpretive approach that was at odds with the structural–functional and conflict theorizing that had dominated the field of leisure studies. It emphasized the need for leisure researchers to identify the situated meanings and social contexts of leisure, to attend to the identity implications of participation, to distinguish the constructed and skilled character of leisure activity and to recognize how leisure was embedded in emergent processes of symbolically mediated interaction. These emphases have been evident in SI studies of a diverse range of leisure activities, from going shopping, examining museum exhibits and interacting with fellow sport fans in a crowd, to attending Bluegrass music festivals, collecting mushrooms and playing little league baseball. 'Leisure' is likely to continue to prove an enduringly problematic designation of a class of human activities. SI has helped to produce a more complex and nuanced understanding of the social organization of leisure activities, casting unexpected light on the pleasures, rewards and identities they sustain.

Greg Smith

Associated Concepts Goffman; Folk Devils and Moral Panics; Pleasure; Shopping; Structure and Agency.

T

TASTE

(distinction)

THEMING

This concept refers to the creation of an 'artificial' environment within a particular setting. The archetypal example of a themed environment is of course the 'theme park', where a certain location containing (most typically) fairground rides, amusement arcades, cafés and shops is united under a common theme, such as characters and concepts from Disney films and cartoons, Warner Brothers films, medieval Europe, 'Wild West' America or any other number of potential 'themes'. However, theming extends beyond the theme park and can be witnessed in numerous other environments, such as casinos, shopping malls, restaurants, bars and even museums and sport venues.

One of the most important discussions of the theming is offered by Mark Gottdiener in his book *The Theming of America* (1997). Gottdiener argues that symbolism was at the centre of pre-industrial societies, with religion and spirituality signifying the centre of peoples' lives and also the physical focus of many communities, as towns and villages were often unified around religious buildings or places of worship. Modernity brought a much greater rationality to our everyday lives and the urban planning of our towns and cities, as symbolism and spirituality were replaced by an emphasis on the economic and the material. However, the desire for symbolism in our lives did not disappear and, in particular, has re-emerged, though this time to a much greater extent, within post-industrial societies.

At one level, theming can be understood simply as a need for businesses, within a highly competitive environment, to distinguish themselves from their competition. Businesses can no longer rely on merely offering a product, but must also offer an 'experience'. However, Gottdiener suggests that theming is also indicative of other deeper changes within society. In particular, Gottdiener aligns the growth of theming with the decline of traditional urban spaces and, further, public 'downtown' spaces within American cities. As the town/city centre has declined as the focus of community life and identity, this void has been filled by new 'artificially' created 'centres', such as shopping malls. These themed locations, Gottdiener suggests, offer people a sense of place, belonging and ultimately identity – as people buy into and identify with the themes they are presented with. Gottdiener fears that our ideas of history and culture will not be taught to us through books or education, but increasingly through themed locations, such as Caesar's Palace in Las Vegas, which provides a 'themed' (and Americanized) version of ancient Rome and Egypt.

However, themes do not necessarily always have to be *borrowed* from other sources and can be created around existing products or themes, and this is particularly noticeable in sport, where many major sport teams have turned the club, its venues and its symbols into merchandising themes. For instance, as Crawford (2004: 80) writes, 'the key to initiating a theme for a leisure site is to create a brand and an experience for the consumer, and many sports have proved very successful at creating a brand image'. A good example of this would be Manchester United, the football club which has been very successful in turning its name and image into a global theme used, not only in merchandising, but also in Red Cafés in places such as Dublin and Singapore, and superstores as far away as Kuala Lumpur.

Garry Crawford

Associated Concepts Consumption; Consumer Society; Modernity; Identity; Shopping.

THIRD WAY

The 'Third Way' is, according to the sociologist Anthony Giddens, a re-evaluation of leftist politics in the light of the 'social revolutions of our time' or the altered societal conditions associated with the second stage of modernity. Giddens argues that, as a result of a combination of social, cultural, economic and political changes, such as de-industrialization, individualization, consumerism, information technology-driven globalization and the emergence of 'life politics' at the expense of 'class politics' – all of which have undermined the viability of post-war social democratic politics and policies – modernity has been altered inexorably. Thus it no longer makes sense to understand politics from either the perspective of the 'Right' or the 'Left'. Writing in the 1990s, Giddens argued that this dichotomy needed to be replaced by a radical Centre–Left politics embodied a 'utopian realist' outlook. If communism and capitalism had been central to the world

order in modernity, in late modernity it was now the time of the 'Third Way', a political ethic (ostensibly not an ideology) in its own right, defensible in its own terms and self-supporting, which would provide the necessary impetus for renewing social democracy, especially by encouraging an active civil society. There are various criticisms that have been made of the 'Third Way', not least with regard to its inherent vagueness, philosophical incoherence and dubious ideological origins.

Tony Blackshaw

Associated Concepts Civil Society; Giddens; Globalization; Individualization; Liquid Modernity; Modernity; Postmodernism; Postmodernity.

THREE-SECTOR PROVISION OF LEISURE

The supply of leisure has traditionally been placed within a three-sector model: the public, private and voluntary sectors. The private sector is market-orientated and exists to generate profit. The public sector, however, takes place in the state but outside the private sector, because the market finds it unprofitable. According to the Marxist sociologist Castells (1976: 148), leisure, sport, the arts and other cultural services constitute a major part of this consumption of goods and services, whose site of reproduction is the city, which is 'a unit of collective consumption corresponding more or less to the daily organization of a section of labour power'.

Taking a more conservative approach, economists argue that it is the responsibility of the public sector to deal with 'merit' goods and services which can provide social benefits to the individual and to society as a whole. Education and health services are the classic examples of merit goods, which often include leisure services. One of the reasons for seeing leisure as a merit good is because of the externalities it produces. The externalities of leisure primarily relate to health benefits, which have proved politically attractive to both politicians and economists who often see the encouragement to take up active leisure as a means of tackling issues such as the growing problem of obesity and the increasing financial pressures this problem places on the health service. What is rarely discussed is that externalities can also provide costs, such as sport injuries, which also represent a burden to the health service. While the health benefits of leisure have become a key social objective for politicians and economists, clearly there are others which give an insight into why the state intervenes in leisure, such as on the grounds of equality or using it as a tool of social control in order to reduce crime and antisocial behaviour.

These observations notwithstanding, there is no doubt that the idea of collective consumption raises some issues that are crucial to people's rights to leisure. However, it is essential to distinguish between collective consumption as *provision* and collective consumption as *use*. Though it is not obvious that collective provision will actually lead to collective use – after all most people consume leisure individually – distinguishing between the two can help providers to identify the kinds of problems which will exclude or put people off state-provided leisure services, as well helping them to develop participative and consultative practices which can better include them.

The voluntary sector constitutes those organizations and individuals who provide leisure services for no commercial gain and have a strong social objective orientation. The primary reason for the existence of the voluntary sector is that, just as there are market failures, there are also failures of the state, whereby it is either impractical or unfeasible for government to meet an identified need. Castells argues it is because the state is persistently unable to meet the costs of collective consumption that this often leads it to make cuts in provision, which have sometimes been translated into political struggle in the form of urban social movements.

What is of particular interest with the emergence of postmodernity is the implosion or collapse of the traditional three-sector model, which has led to shifting relationships between the traditional private (profit), public (need) and voluntary (aid organization and self-organized enthusiasms) sectors and tacit assumptions about their roles, especially public-sector leisure organizations which are increasingly run on market lines. Both the public and voluntary sectors have been required to adopt many business practices in the drive to be more efficient and effective, particularly since funding has been reduced and the need to justify any funding has increased. The public and private sectors have also increasingly been required to consider methods of generating greater amounts of revenue, which has seen a growth in partnerships, particularly in urban regeneration projects. An additional factor for the voluntary sector has been the professionalization of volunteers, notably as a response to the emergence of the risk society and increasing litigation. The upshot of all this is that it has become a requirement for volunteers involved in leisure services to be properly qualified and police checked as a precaution against the potential abuse of minors. The private sector has also been affected by changes in social attitudes, which means that it is more and more having to consider the ethical implications of its actions (such as in relation to the environment or negative impacts on health).

Mark Piekarz and Tony Blackshaw

Associated Concepts   New Social Movements; Risk; Sexual Exploitation.

TIME BUDGET DIARIES

Time budget diaries require respondents to itemize the nature of the leisure activities that they undertake during a set period. They are a useful research tool, which involves subjects keeping a written, audio or video record of their activities and/or thoughts. The key writer and advocate of time budget diaries in leisure research is Jonathan Gershuny, who has used these in several key studies of leisure and household patterns, such as in understanding the continuing work/leisure divide and relationship (see, for example, Gershuny, 2000).

Diaries can be quite structured, asking individuals only to record certain activities or information, either quantitatively (such as ticking boxes each time they undertake a certain task) or in a more open-ended manner (such as asking individuals to record their thoughts and emotions each day). As with all research it is important that the researcher knows from the outset what they are looking for and what they hope to get out of the method they are employing. When using diaries for research it is vital to specify what individuals are expected to record, as being too vague may result in them either recording lots of irrelevant information or overlooking what the researcher wants them to record. The easiest way to do this is to list a set of examples or questions that the researcher wants the individual (diarists) to consider or address in their diaries.

It is also important to set a specific time period for keeping the diary, which should not be too long (as diarists are likely to get bored or more forgetful the longer they are asked to keep this for) but still long enough to record the information required. For instance, a researcher may ask an individual to keep a written diary of each time they play a digital game and also to include such information as who they played with, what they played and how long they played for. With a diary of this type, it would probably be suitable to ask an individual to keep this for one to three weeks, as this would probably be long enough to gain enough information on their typical gaming patterns. The finished diaries are then analysed by the researcher with the principle aim of looking at categories and the diversity of leisure activities and patterns, as well as the location of these, and to then draw comparisons with other diarists.

Garry Crawford

Associated Concepts Methodology; Oral/Life History; Qualitative Research.

TOTAL QUALITY MANAGEMENT

Markets, including those the business of which is leisure, have become increasingly competitive with quality, pricing and delivery now key performance issues for customer satisfaction and increasing market share. Total quality management (or TQM) can be defined as an approach to quality within an organization which is committed to total customer satisfaction through a continuous process of improvement and the contribution and involvement of people (Mullins, 2005). This is a preferred method in the leisure industry. Embedding such a strategy in an organization means that quality and management are seen as a holistic product that has the aim of guaranteeing the efficiency and effectiveness of the organization and its employees. There are six key factors to take into account when considering such a distinctive management philosophy: customer orientation; clear and appropriate organizational objectives; commitment to the involvement of all staff in the running of the organization; using systems and procedures to ensure quality; monitoring and evaluating operations; and education and training for all staff. To this extent TQM goes further than IIP in achieving organizational aspirations, but it is no quick fix for organizational problems.

Rob Wilson

Associated Concepts Event Management; Financial and Management Accounting; Risk Management.

TOURISM

Tourism is an economic and social phenomenon that is an increasingly prominent feature of contemporary life. There have been many attempts to define this complex term. The official definition from the World Tourism Organization (WTO) claims that tourism comprises 'the activities of persons travelling to and staying in places outside their usual environment for not more than one consecutive year for leisure, business, or other purposes' (World Tourism Organization, 1991). A much-used and broader definition has been provided by Mathieson and Wall, who suggested that tourism is 'the temporary movement of people to destinations outside their normal places of work and residence, the activities undertaken during their stay in those destinations, and the facilities created to cater to their needs' (1982: 1). Key to these definitions is an attempt to encapsulate three crucial features of tourism: displacement (being outside the usual environment); the purpose of that travel; and the duration (the time spent there). In an attempt to more fully capture both the social and economic dimensions of tourism, Macintosh and Goeldner (1986) highlight the importance of the relationship and interaction between those who supply tourism, such as business, those who consume it, such as tourists, and those who host it, such as governments and destination communities. Tourism has experienced continued growth and deepening diversification in recent times. This global expansion and diversification has led to a growing number of tourist destinations and the segmentation of the tourist industry, leading in turn to the development of niche areas of tourism such as disaster tourism or culinary tourism.

An influential contributor to debates around tourism is John Urry. In *The Tourist Gaze* (2002) he identified a number of key features of contemporary tourism and suggested that travel and tourism were central aspects of contemporary or modern social life. One of his most important ideas is that of the 'tourist gaze', which he argues is central to the tourist experience. Urry maintains that practices of looking, such as the taking of photographs and the purchasing of postcards, are at the core of the tourist activity. He emphasizes the role of the visual in tourism, and links the centrality of this to modernity and the abundance of visual technologies in contemporary society. A parallel is suggested between the tourist gaze and the medical gaze articulated by Michel Foucault, in that it is 'socially organized and systematized' (2002: 1). Urry generated ideal types of different forms of the tourist gaze which obtain in different contexts. He argued that, in particular, there are two different forms of the tourist gaze: the 'romantic' and the 'collective'. The romantic tourist gaze is where the emphasis is 'upon solitude, privacy and a personal, semi-spiritual relationship with the object of the gaze' (ibid.:43). The collective gaze 'necessitates the presence of large numbers of other people' (ibid.: 43), as it is the interaction between such large numbers that creates the atmosphere of the tourist place. In an attempt to capture the diversity of tourism and tourists' experiences Urry has developed further categories of gaze, including the 'mediatized gaze', which is an attempt to capture the way that places made famous in the media-worlds of popular culture become tourist destinations, as people travel to these actual places to experience virtual places.

Urry has been criticized for placing too much emphasis on the visual, as tourism is an embodied experience. Taste, smell, touch and sound are all key to tourism: indeed it has been suggested that Urry is in danger of writing the body and pleasure out of tourism (Franklin and Crang, 2001; Bagnall, 2003). Urry has responded by claiming that in emphasizing the gaze he did not want to denigrate or play down other aspects of the tourists' experiences (smell, taste, and so on). Nevertheless, he has argued that it is the visual that is dominant or organizes this range of experience (Franklin, 2001). As his analysis clearly shows, the visual environment in which ostensibly mundane activities, such as shopping and walking along the street, are carried out can transform them into a tourist activity.

Gaynor Bagnall

Associated Concepts Aesthetics; Bohemians; Commodity Fetishism; Cruising; Disneyization; Flâneurs, Flâneurie and Psychogeography; Heritage; Leisure; McDonaldization; Non-Place; Nostalgia; Theming.

TOURIST GAZE

(tourism)

TRAINING AND DEVELOPMENT AND APPRAISALS

It is now very common to see the ideas of training and development used in the same context. However, it is worth considering each concept separately to begin with. This is because leisure industry training is often a legal requirement, whereas development is down to the individual employee and his or her employer.

Training endeavours to impart the knowledge, skills and attitudes necessary to perform the functions of a job. Consider the training that pool lifeguards need to undertake. They must be trained to rescue swimmers from the water and to perform a variety of first aid tasks. Additionally they should be able to communicate effectively and manage situations under pressure. In this regard, training enables a person to offer the 'bottom line' service that is required for work in the leisure industries.

In contrast, development is more concerned with refining skills and ensuring that a person becomes more competent at their job. As such it is not a legal requirement. Consider the lifeguard example once more. Once trained a person is deemed able to work. However, they may wish to develop the skills they have learnt to make them more effective in their job. Together, training and development combine to form an integral part of an organization's human resource management strategy, which can contribute to an organization's efficiency and effectiveness.

Appraisals are the systems that provide an analysis of a person's overall capabilities and the potential related to their job and, to this extent, are a key aspect of training and development. This allows managers to make informed decisions regarding particular purposes and aspirations for the organization. An important part of the process is assessment, whereby data on an individual's past and current work practices and performance are collected and reviewed. The outcome of the appraisal process may well have an impact on any training and development opportunities that staff may have during the next year.

Rob Wilson

Associated Concepts Human Resource Management; Quality Systems.

U

UNEMPLOYMENT, LEISURE IN

Unemployment, otherwise known as the involuntary or voluntary lack of paid work, has considerable implications for people's leisure opportunities. Unemployment is a complex process but it can nonetheless be divided into a number of subcategories: *frictional* unemployment, which arises as a result of movement in the job market as people move from one job to another; *seasonal* unemployment, such as occurs in the leisure and tourism industries as a result of changes in supply and demand; *cyclical* unemployment, caused by the swinging pendulums that are the business and trade cycles; and *structural* unemployment, where significant changes in the global economy lead to large numbers of people losing their jobs.

On the face of it the major trend in Western economies since the mid-1960s has seen employment in services grow and employment in manufacturing decline. However, this trend masks the fact that the decline in manufacturing has also been accompanied by technological changes as well as changes in production, such as the substitution of (flexible) post-Fordist work practices for (inflexible) Fordist work practices (see Harvey, 1989) and the global restructuring of industrial labour along neoliberal lines – two processes which have increased productivity while dispensing with the need for unskilled and semi-skilled workers, and sometimes even highly skilled workers. The upshot of

these changes is that, compared with the period of relative full employment (which occurred in the late-1950s and 1960s) unemployment rates in Western countries have increased dramatically and long-term unemployment is by now a persistent problem. It should also be noted that unemployment is, on the whole, a *selective* process: different *social groups* will experience different levels of unemployment. For example, it tends to be higher for women, ethnic minority groups and young people and, as job losses tend to be regional, as a result these are experienced as *geographically* uneven.

In her pioneering book *Leisure and Unemployment*, She Glyptis (1989: 159) observed that 'work and leisure are not just a conceptual couplet, twinned for the convenience of testing theories. They are experienced as a couplet, the one deriving meaning from the other'. Indeed, the loss of work through unemployment has some profound implications for patterns of participation in leisure activities as well as for individuals and society more generally. When individuals become unemployed they lose the income, social networks, identity, status and self-esteem which are obtained through work. If their unemployment is long term, the incessant search for work and the stigma associated with welfare dependence are likely to lead to the development of shame and the sense of personal failing. One of the foremost consequences of long-term unemployment is social isolation, with the loss of friendships garnered through work; this situation is exacerbated because individuals have little disposable income to spend on by now taken-for-granted leisure activities, such as going to the cinema, eating out and having a drink at the local pub. In a nutshell, unemployment means more 'free time' for individuals with little money, confidence or inclination to enjoy it.

What should not be overlooked, however, is that unemployment can provide an unprecedented opportunity to get involved in new leisure activities and leisure education, which can in turn lead to hitherto unimagined experiences and may even offer new openings in the job market. Nevertheless this view is highly contested, not least because work remains the major source of value in society.

The consequences of unemployment for society are less obvious but equally significant for leisure participation. Evidence shows that, in societies where high levels of unemployment persist, the likelihood is that more discipline will emerge in the workplace, leading to increased working hours and more uncertainty amongst the employed. As Pat Kane (2006) argues, in such a scenario work tends to make individuals less happy, unhealthy and confused, at the same time as dissolving the dignity and respect it affords them in conditions of full employment. It is

the unemployed themselves who bear the brunt of high unemployment, however, with society seeing rising levels of poverty, homelessness and family breakdown, as well as concomitant problems such as mental illness, increased levels of crime, violence, alcoholism, drug misuse and suicide. Evidence also shows that another significant societal trend that emerges in such circumstances is more racism, as those most affected by unemployment come to lay the blame for their circumstances on ethnic minority and immigrant groups.

What the foregoing discussion suggests is that not only are the symptoms and pain of unemployment both *private* and concealed within people's homes and *public* and revealed in the way that a society constitutes and imagines itself but that they also have massive implications for how people experience leisure both individually and collectively.

Tony Blackshaw

Associated Concepts Free Time; Leisure; Leisure Class; Leisure Education; Leisure Society; Racism and Leisure; Work Ethic; Work-Leisure.

V

VEAL, TONY

(leisure life-style; leisure studies)

VEBLEN, THORSTEIN BUNDE (1857–1929)

The economist-cum-sociologist who developed the theory of the leisure class, Veblen was born into a family of Norwegian immigrant farmers who had settled into the Scandinavian farming community in Wato, Wisconsin, in the USA. After receiving his doctorate in economics from Yale University, he spent some time working on farms before taking up a teaching position at Cornell University. The crux of Veblen's theory of the leisure class is this: the pointlessness of the competition for social status embedded within the conspicuous consumption activities associated with those social elites who perceive that their enjoyment of leisure is what distinguishes them from the rest of society. Notwithstanding his coining of the idea of conspicuous consumption, Veblen's work was also instrumental in developing a processual understanding of the economy which took into account extant societal power structures as well as the way in which these evolve over time. Perhaps his main legacy to a contemporary world facing imminent environmental crisis, however, is that there is a powerful critique of the wastefulness embedded in his theory of the leisure class.

Tony Blackshaw

Associated Concepts Celebrity; Consumer Society; Consumption; Leisure Class.

VIDEO GAMES

(digital gaming)

VIOLENCE

Violence usually refers to the use of physical power to harm others (either human or animal) or objects, but the term can also be applied to images, words or ideas. It is evident that historically violence has been an integral part of many leisure activities, as it continues to be today. In particular, there is evidence of killing for both survival and pleasure throughout human history, and this remains evident in leisure activities (such as blood sports) right up to the current day.

The control of violence is central to Norbert Elias' theorization of 'the civilizing process'. Elias suggests that violence is an inherently pleasurable experience, but, through the formation of the modern nation state, an individual's ability to conduct violence on a day-to-day basis has been removed, as the state monopolizes the legitimate use of violence. This creates a 'paradox of pacification' (Goudsblom, 2001) where control of violence within nation states allows for a greater opportunity for violence to be directed against other nation states or peoples, most notably in wars and conflicts. Therefore, the civilizing of violence reduces the likelihood of individual 'expressive' (e.g., emotional) violence, but continues to allow certain forms of (most commonly state-directed) 'instrumental' violence – a key illustration of which would be the Holocaust (see Bauman, 1989a).

Certain arenas within a civilized society do continue to allow 'controlled' bouts of violence, such as participation in sport, and, likewise, the civilizing process has been extensively applied to our understanding of football hooliganism. However, Elias argues that, largely, the control and repression of individual violence within a 'civilized society' leads to the transfer of violent pleasures away from participation towards watching violence. This would include watching both 'aggressive' and 'contact' sports and would also help account for its popularity in violent films, digital games and other mass media forms. Violence in mass media images and texts has often raised concerns about the 'effect' on audiences, such as in the work of Dolf Zillmann (2000) who suggests that violence within the mass media can 'amplify' the behaviour of audiences and may lead them to become violent. The debate over 'media effects' dates back to at least the birth of film and, most probably, long before this and has taken many forms and focused on several different media types, including most recently digital games.

However, the relationship between violence and violent media images is far from conclusive, the main problem being that it is impossible to attribute changes in behaviour to one stimulus when on a day-to-day basis individuals are surrounded by millions of images and influences, with each person interpreting these differently based upon their own understanding of these and their personal histories. As David Trend (2007) argues, we are looking in the wrong place for the origins of violent behaviour. It is not the mass media that create violence in society, but, rather, the violent society in which we live that creates the media we consume. As he concludes: 'more restrictions on what is available on TV or the internet won't help the situation very much. But more discussions and more consumer choices will. By discussing the various ways we understand, dislike, enjoy, and use media violence, we move the conversation forward' (Trend, 2007: 123).

Garry Crawford

Associated Concepts Abnormal Leisure; Bauman; Blood Sports; Deviance; Digital Gaming; Elias; Football Hooliganism; Mass Media; Power.

VIRTUAL LEISURE

This concept refers to the idea of undertaking leisure activities in a 'virtual' (i.e., computer-generated) environment and is closely tied to the idea of 'virtual reality'. Virtual reality is the idea of occupying spaces or personas outside of the 'real world'. The idea of a virtual reality has existed since the 1960s; however, it was the rise of the internet and digital gaming, particularly in the 1990s, that led many to begin to explore these ideas further (Flew, 2002). For instance, Turkle (1995) argues that the internet has allowed people to play with their identities and personas, providing a new opportunity to project their fantasies and ideas on to this virtual reality. Similarities can be drawn here with the concepts of cyborgism (such as in the work of Donna Haraway, 1991). The 'cyborg' constitutes the intersection between machines and humans, such as the implanting of mechanical technologies into the human body, but more importantly raises the idea of blurring identities, where the boundaries between humans and machines become less fixed and more malleable. These are ideas that have also been explored in both science fiction films such as *The Matrix* trilogy and David Cronenberg's *eXistenZ* (1999), as well as in cyberpunk writings (such as the work of William Gibson), which are set in (dystopian) futures, telling of a blurring between the 'real' and the 'unreal' as cyborgs (human-machine hybrids) stretch the boundaries of our known world and the possibilities within this.

Though contemporary leisure technologies have not reached the levels of human–machine integration that are outlined in many fictional literatures (such as the cyber-punk geure) and cinematic accounts, contemporary digital gaming does provide gamers with the opportunity to play out 'alternative' lives and realities. For instance, one of the biggest phenomena in digital gaming in recent years has been the rapid growth and popularity of massively multiplayer online role playing games (MMORPGs), such as *World of Warcraft*, *EverQuest* and *Lineage*, as well as virtual online 'worlds' such as *Second Life*. These games allow a player to create characters (avatars) that they can control and to play out adventures in an online world inhabited by other players from all over the ('real') world. These games will also often allow characters to develop careers, not just as warriors or wizards but also in professions such as dancing, mining or medicine; some games will allow players to own vehicles, pets and property (such as houses and shops) and even to get married and have virtual (cyber) sex. However, even more common than these games are the hugely popular online social networking sites (such as Facebook, MySpace and Bebo), which require users to create a profile page on which they upload information, music, pictures and programmes and, through these, interact, socialize and network with other users.

Turkle and Haraway, in their consideration of online identities, adopted a similar perspective to that of Jean Baudrillard and his ideas on hyperreality to suggest that new media and information communication technologies offer a blurring between the 'real' and 'unreal'. However, distinctions between what is 'virtual' and what is 'real' are problematic. For instance, Murray and Jenkins (n.d.: 2) suggested that many digital games contain a level of 'immersion', which involves 'being transported to another place, of losing our sense of reality and extending ourselves into a seemingly limitless, enclosing, other realm'. However, digital gamers, as with the users of any other information technologies, are not 'transported to another world' but, rather, are physically and socially located. All technologies (both 'new' and 'old') are used and located in certain physical locations, which can have important social consequences. For instance, it has been noted that the propensity for digital games machines to be located within certain 'male' household spaces, such as male siblings' bedrooms, means these are restricted for many women (Green, 2001). As Shields (1996: 3) argues, 'it is essential to treat telecommunications and computer-mediated communications networks as *local* phenomena, as well as global networks ... [and] embedded within locally specific routines of daily schedules and the "place-ballets" of individuals' (emphasis in original).

Garry Crawford

Associated Concepts   Baudrillard; Cyberculture; Digital Gaming; Mass Media; Network Society; Play; Postmodernism.

VOLUNTEERS AND VOLUNTEERING

Volunteering is a feature of leisure that has only recently begun to be seriously considered within leisure studies, as it is typically an area that has been considered as more relevant to discussions of work. However, for many people, participating in any number of voluntary organizations or providing other forms of unpaid work can constitute an important and rewarding form of leisure. Considering voluntary work is also important as it highlights the ambiguities between drawing clear distinctions between what is 'work' and what is 'leisure'.

Stebbins (2004: 5) defines voluntary work as 'uncoerced help offered either formally or informally with no, or at most, token pay done for the benefit of both other people and the volunteer'. Stebbins locates his discussion of volunteering within his framework of serious and casual types of leisure and, similarly, suggests that there can be 'serious', 'casual' and 'project-based' forms of volunteering.

Stebbins (1992) defines serious leisure as a non-work activity that provides a career where the participant can acquire a combination of special skills, knowledge and experience. Corresponding to this, serious volunteering includes activities such as care work, working for political organizations and coaching an amateur sport team, which, similarly, can provide the possibility of (non-work) career progression and knowledge and skill acquisition. Casual leisure refers to pleasurable activities that are immediately and intrinsically rewarding, relatively short term and require no specialist skills. Hence casual volunteering, Stebbins suggests, would include activities such as cooking hot dogs at a church or school fête. Finally, project-based leisure is a 'short-term, reasonably complicated, one-off or occasional, though infrequent, creative undertaking carried out in free time' (Stebbins, 2004: 7), an example of which would include fundraising for charitable causes or appeals.

The idea of volunteering has become particularly important in British politics since the late 1970s, with the increasing 'rolling back' of state provision and a growing emphasis on local community participation in providing welfare assistance. Volunteering has been seen by successive governments as a way of involving local communities in overcoming local problems and as a means of providing the experience and training that many unemployed people will need to return to work (Levitas, 1998). However, there are major weaknesses and limitations with this strategy. These include that, first, voluntary organizations are having to compete (rather than cooperate) with each other for funding. Second, the work and training offered by voluntary organizations are often generic and many involve little skills attainment, as well as tending to not be targeted towards gaining specific paid work. Third, the services offered by voluntary organizations can be seen as little more than a way of governments ensuring that crucial services are provided free of change to them (see Gosling, 2008).

Garry Crawford

Associated Concepts Community; Community Leisure; Hobbies; Leisure as a Value-Sphere; Leisure in the Community; Serious/Casual Leisure.

W

WEBER, MAX

(asceticism; bureaucracy; capitalism; leisure as a value-sphere; mcdonaldization; status; work ethic)

WEISBROD'S HYPOTHESES

Weisbrod (1978) established a set of hypotheses that help to explain the reasons why leisure output is split between the voluntary, private and public sectors. He divided all outputs into three types – publicly provided goods; private good substitutes for collective goods; and pure private goods.

Weisbrod's first hypothesis was that consumers will first look to the public sector for the provision of collective goods. However, they are likely to be dissatisfied with the level of public provision for any particular collective good and as a result will look for additional output from the voluntary and commercial sectors. His second hypothesis relates to the nature of demand, in particular its heterogeneity. The lesser the heterogeneity, then the more likely it is that government will provide the major share of output. The greater the heterogeneity of demand, the larger the share of total output jointly provided by the voluntary and commercial sectors. The reason for this is that government output is determined on the basis of a simple majority vote. If consumers for a particular collective good are not numerous enough to be an important influence on the

voting process, they are unlikely to see a public provision of the good. The third argument is what Weisbrod calls the 'income hypothesis'. He argues that, from a consumer's point of view, there is likely to be an important disadvantage with the collective good compared with a private good substitute for it: the consumer will have a lower degree of individual control over its form, type of availability and the times of availability.

Weisbrod argued that private market substitutes will cater more to specific consumer demands in niche markets. Since the degree of individual control desired by consumers is likely to be positively related to their income, the commercial supplier is likely to 'skim' the market and cater to the demands of the higher-income consumers. The consumers who turn to the private market option will expect to pay a higher charge in return for a product that is closer to individual demands. Consumers are also likely to choose a form of the good that maximizes their personal benefits and minimizes external benefits. In relation to the leisure market there is a dominance of provision by the public and voluntary sectors. The nature of the product provided is also more likely to be of an individual-type 'good' rather than a collective-type 'good'.

Weisbrod's second hypothesis indicates that the greater the heterogeneity of demand, then the greater the share of total output provided by the voluntary and commercial sectors. Demand for leisure is clearly heterogeneous with many leisure activities involving a small minority of the population. Most of the demand for minority sports, for example, is provided by the voluntary and commercial sectors. Sporting activities with a demand across a wider range of the population, such as indoor swimming, exhibit greater involvement by the public sector.

Rob Wilson

Associated Concepts Demand; Elasticity; Supply; Three-Sector Provision of Leisure.

WELL-BEING

Well-being is an extremely ambiguous, multifaceted and subjective concept. At its most basic level it refers to a state of happiness, health and satisfaction, and relates to a person's welfare. Hence, it is physically, mentally and culturally defined and subjective – what one person describes as 'well', another (certainly in another culture or time) may not. Therefore, defining what well-being is and measuring it in an objective way can prove extremely difficult. However, the idea of well-being continues to be pertinent to discussions of leisure, particularly in relation to the perceived benefits that certain leisure actives may offer.

In particular, Roberts (1999) suggests that leisure contributes more to our levels of satisfaction than both income and health. He suggests that this is particularly apparent with older people, where leisure can provide individuals with both a distraction and social networks. However, Roberts is right to be wary of overstating this relationship, as social factors such as income and health, as well as numerous other relations like age, class, gender and ethnicity, can all shape and limit our leisure opportunities and choices. Roberts also warns that the perceived benefits of certain physical leisure activities (like sport) are often overstated – as a healthy diet, not smoking and not drinking heavily can often contribute more significantly to our health than engaging in activities such as sport.

However, Stebbins (1997b) suggests that certain leisure activities, and in particular 'serious' leisure activities, can positively contribute to an individual's well-being and points out that hobbyists, amateurs and volunteers all regularly derive satisfaction from their leisure. However, as with Roberts, Stebbins is keen not to overstate this point and argues that the relationship between serious leisure and well-being is a correlation rather than a causality, as leisure can at times cause unrest and conflict (such as between married couples with differing interests).

All of these factors can be seen in Ingham's (1991: 247) definition of well-being, which describes this as the right balance between integration in a social world and the extent of agency afforded within that social world. This can be clearly seen in Hendry et al.'s (1991) study of youth leisure patterns, which suggests that the satisfaction and benefits of sport (in terms of an individual's well-being) are not derived from the health benefits of sport, but, rather, its social networks and the entry into a social world that this offers.

Garry Crawford

Associated Concepts Amateur and Amateurism; Happiness; Hobbies; Pleasure; Serious/Casual Leisure; Sport; Volunteers and Volunteering.

WOMEN'S LEISURE

In the late 1970s and 1980s there developed a new and significant focus within leisure studies on women's leisure patterns. In particular, Talbot's (1979) research report *Women and Leisure: A State of the Art Review* is generally viewed as the first contemporary consideration of women's leisure, but this was followed by a number of key workshops, seminars and publications on the subject in the early 1980s (Aitchison, 2004).

It is evident that a large proportion of the literature on women's leisure patterns (see, for example, Deem, 1982, 1986; Wimbush and Talbot, 1988) has focused upon the constraints placed upon their leisure opportunities. These accounts indicate how women's leisure is constrained due to numerous social factors, such as restrictions placed upon their presence in many 'public' places; economic constraints; domestic and caring responsibilities; the limited and fragmented leisure time of many women; and social expectations of women's location and roles within society.

Key studies on women's leisure as constrained include Dixey and Talbot's (1982) study of women and bingo, which served to highlight issues around gendered leisure spaces and, in particular, the male domination of many public spaces and the safety and freedom afforded to women by the bingo hall. Deem (1982, 1986) conducted research on the leisure patterns of women in Milton Keynes in the early 1980s and identified the constraints placed upon their leisure participation, such as male attitudes towards women going out alone or with friends, childcare and domestic labour responsibilities, a lack of money and friends and poor access to transport. Significantly, Deem's research also highlighted the differences (as well as the similarities) between different women's leisure opportunities and patterns, for instance by suggesting that working-class women have fewer leisure opportunities than those available to middle-class women. Likewise, Wimbush's (1986) study of mothers of young children in Edinburgh identified similar constraints placed upon women's leisure participation and suggested steps, such as increased crèche facilities and women-only evening and weekend sessions, which could help increase women's sport and leisure participation.

The largest, and probably one of the most cited studies of women's leisure, is Green et al's study of over 700 women between the ages of 18 and 59, conducted in Sheffield between 1984 and 1987, the findings of which formed the basis of the book *Women's Leisure, What Leisure?* (1990). This supported earlier research by Talbot, Deem and others, in suggesting that women's leisure was constrained both within and outside of their homes.

Aitchison (2004) suggests that research on women's leisure declined in the 1990s, primarily due to shifts towards a more practical and management-based approach to leisure studies that saw the decline of links between leisure studies and its parent disciplines of sociology and geography, which had given the discipline its critical and reflexive edge. However, the 1990s did provide a new focus on women's sport participation, including most notably Hargreaves' (1995) book *Sporting Females* and Brackenridge's (1994) study of sexual abuse in sport.

However, as well as focusing on leisure as constrained (and/or also constraining, such as by reinforcing traditional gender roles; see Alcoff, 1988), other writers have identified the potential opportunities, and even resistance, that leisure can offer some women. Key here is the work of Freysinger and Flannery (1992), which argued that women's leisure is potentially empowering as it allows them to take on social roles that are different from (and challenge) their traditional gender-specific labels of 'wives' and 'mothers'. Similarly, Wilson (1991) suggested the contemporary city can offer women freedom, such that leisure activities like shopping can offer the opportunity for women to enter the public domain and to also mix and meet with other women.

A significant shift within research on women's leisure occurred in the late 1990s and into the new century, when several writers on women's leisure began to try and catch up some of the lost ground in sociology by starting to engage with poststructuralist debates. This can be seen as a response to the critique of 'traditional' (structuralist) feminist perspectives on leisure which had been extensively criticized by authors such as Rojek (1995) amongst others for seeing all women as sharing a 'common world'. In seeking to meet the challenges of these critics, writers on women's leisure increasingly sought to engage with a poststructuralist perspective, most frequently seen in the work of Foucault, to the point that Green (1998: 174) suggested that postmodernity and poststructuralism are becoming the 'new orthodoxies' in feminist writings on leisure.

In particular, 'poststructuralist' writers on women's leisure (see, for example, Wearing, 1998; Shaw, 2001; Aitchison, 2004) focus much more attention on individual rather than collective leisure patterns and experiences, shifting their analyses towards more 'cultural' concerns and debates, such as postmodernity. However, not all have so warmly embraced a poststructuralist approach on women's leisure. In particular, Scraton (1994) and Watson and Scraton (1998) warn that this new interest in cultural patterns offers a predominantly male perspective on culture and marginalizes concerns for continuing (structural) constraints and inequalities. Furthermore, poststructuralism can be accused of being 'anti-humanist in orientation, dealing with signs, language and writing' (Blackshaw, 2003: 32). Post-structuralist research tends to focus on discourses and how these operate in specific situations, and (as with structuralism) decentres the individual. This potentially conflicts with many feminist approaches, which often seek to prioritize and give voice to the experiences of women (Aitchison, 2004).

Garry Crawford

Associated Concepts Class; Discursive Formations; Feminism; Foucault; Power; Shopping.

WORK ETHIC

Most leisure scholars will adopt the designations 'Protestant' or 'puritan' at the beginning of their definitions. This is a reflection of the power of Max Weber's classic study of the *Protestant Ethic and the Spirit of Capitalism* (1930), which made the controversial argument that Protestantism or, more specifically, the Calvinist belief in predestination and the spirituality of wealth) and the rationalization of the economy were the twin driving forces in developing Western capitalism. In other words, productive labour as something valued in and for itself had a God-like significance and sense of moral obligation, which originated in the asceticism of Protestantism in the Reformation in Western Christianity and, when combined with fiscal prudence, was to become a unique feature of Western European culture. Weber also argued, equally controversially, that the religious facet of this affirmation of the virtues of hard daily work was soon extinguished by the very ethic it had produced. In other words, God's calling to humankind's work role in society was no longer necessary to industrial capitalism once it had become established because labour could be 'performed as if it was an absolute end in itself'.

The 'Weber thesis' has been widely criticized on the basis of its lack of empirical evidence, especially its author's lack of attention to the influences and changes contiguous with Catholicism, the fact that the ability of industrial capitalism to sustain itself was dependent on the consumption of commodities, as well as a willingness to forgo immediate pleasures and plan for future hardship and his propensity to overlook the fact that, if Protestantism was a religion of great variety, it was nonetheless in many ways at odds with a nascent industrial capitalism.

Notwithstanding these criticisms, there is no doubting the import of understanding the work ethic as the attitudinal base on which industrial capitalism developed and the implications of this for understanding modern leisure. Indeed, the definition of leisure as a compensatory activity is to be found in the idea of the work ethic: the prescribed time free from hard industrial toil that was available to recuperate workers in order to extract the maximum output from them when they returned to the workplace. This model is the basis of Marxist interpretations of leisure, which view leisure as constrained by work.

Numerous other leisure scholars have also explored this connection and among some of the issues that have attracted their attention has been the relationship between the work ethic and social control and the social and psychological implications of the stigma of unemployment for leisure. What this kind of research demonstrates is that the work ethic continues to shape leisure but also shapes society and culture in ways that reflect the new inequalities associated with the social structure.

Zygmunt Bauman has consistently argued that today it is only the poor – the weakest members of our society – who are controlled by the work ethic. Leisure scholars have also begun to explore the implications of the consequences of the work ethic as it has ostensibly become a central plank of government thinking, proclaimed by the then Chancellor and later Prime Minister Gordon Brown as what should be the attitudinal base of 'every community of Britain' (Kane, 2004: 64).To this extent the work ethic remains a powerful feature of debates about how society should go. In fact, in historicist terms, it might be argued that, since the work ethic was very much a phenomenon of the genesis of industrial capitalism, whose star began to wane with the debates about the coming of the leisure society in the 1970s, we have recently witnessed its return with a vengeance.

Tony Blackshaw

Associated Concepts Asceticism; Capitalism; Leisure; Leisure Society; Play Ethic; Social Capital; Third Way; Unemployment, Leisure in; Work-Leisure.

WORK-LEISURE

This conceptual couplet has undergone considerable debate in leisure studies. There was once a tendency to treat the relationship between work and leisure in overly simplistic terms, with the latter understood as a residual category of, or an oppositional response to, the former (i.e., leisure is something that people do on an evening or at the weekend when they are not at work or it symbolizes an act of resistance to people's dissatisfaction with work). In

this view, leisure is seen as something that is 'ostensibly private, individual and free as opposed to work which is public, social and regulated' (Slater, 1998: 396).

Writing in the 1970s and early 1980s, Stanley Parker suggested that, although work takes up only a portion of people's lives, their leisure activities are undoubtedly conditioned by the various factors associated with the ways they work. People who work together are not only assembled in the same time and space but are also required to focus their collective attention on a common objective or activity, which means that they also share a common experience of work, whether it is positive, negative or neutral. Consequently, Parker concluded that, for most people, their leisure is shaped by how they react to work and its authority predominates over other influences, such as class and gender (Clarke and Critcher, 1985). What this suggests is that leisure cannot simply be understood as reflecting a particular form of work; it is necessary to understand the specific nature and conditions of that work experience, which are pervasive.

Parker's research led him to conclude that the relationship between work and leisure tends to fall into three categories: the opposition pattern (e.g., those in physically hard and dangerous occupations will often try to escape from the hardships of work through drinking and gambling with workmates), the neutrality pattern (repetitive or routine work has a tendency to lead to apathy and indifference in the workplace and this is reflected in people's leisure activities, which tend to be monotonous and passive) and the extension pattern (those who have high levels of personal commitment to their work and get a good deal of job satisfaction are more likely to extend work-related social networks and activities into their leisure time).

While such research was important to an understanding of how inextricably intertwined the relationship between leisure and work has been in modern societies and how any adequate theory of leisure must take work into account, it has been criticized on a number of counts. First, there are simply too many exceptions to the work-leisure couplet, the most conspicuous being the non-employed, such as the elderly, and those people not in paid work, such as the unemployed and carers (especially many women), whose experiences of leisure are often fragmented and unpredictable. This leads to a second problem with the work-leisure couplet – it marginalizes the extent to which the home is for many women a place of work (e.g., domestic labour, home-working), albeit one that is not recognized by society as such. Third, the work-leisure couplet focuses its attention much less on what people do in their leisure time and more on leisure as a residual category of work and, to this extent, it offers an overly functionalist understanding of leisure. Indeed, contrary to Parker, many people today would argue that it is their leisure that is utterly bound up with who they are and their identities, not their work.

This last point notwithstanding, it has been compellingly argued by a number of scholars that, in a work-based society dominated by capitalist accumulation, leisure itself has become functionalist in the sense that it deeply commodified and used to accomplish the need to sell more consumer goods. As Slater (1998: 401) points out, in this way leisure ends up being 'ideologically sold to us as a sphere of freedom from work, from public responsibilities and obligations ... it is part of a deal that in exchange for all this "freedom" and "pleasure" – it secures docile workers and citizens'.

More recent evidence suggests that there has been a relaxing of the societal hold that the work ethic once had and this has been supplanted by an aesthetic of consumerism (for an alternative perspective see the entry for Work Ethic). As Rutherford (2007: 46) points out, the puritan's anxiety about 'How can I be good?' has by now turned into the secular 'How can I be happy?' Moreover, there is increasing evidence to suggest that, with the consolidation of post-Fordist working practices, work and leisure have once again become dedifferentiated. Poder's (2007) research suggests that it is increasingly the case that people do not so much value their leisure time over work, but think of work in similar ways to what they think and feel about consuming. That is, the point of being in work is not just to have a job: it should be exciting, stimulating and challenging and make us happy. One of the upshots of this is that work (like leisure) has developed an aesthetic significance, which not only means that it increasingly individualizes our experiences of employment so that they are not easily shared with others but also therefore makes shared responses to discontent in the workplace more unlikely.

Any consideration of the relationship between work and leisure must also take into account Veblen's assertion that it is not leisure but work that gives humankind the possibility to embrace the opportunity for an authentic existence that is both magical and moral (Slater, 1998). This theme has recently been taken up by Sennett (2005), who argues that what people often lack in the contemporary world is the cultural anchor of a more coherent and secure work existence, suggesting three critical values that might just fill this void: narrative, usefulness and craftsmanship.

Tony Blackshaw

Associated Concepts Authenticity; Binary Oppositions; Class; Crafts and Craftsmanship; Happiness; Leisure; Leisure Life-Style; Veblen; Unemployment, Leisure in; Work Ethic.

X, Y

YOUTH

The idea of youth is both a socially constructed label and a biological condition associated with the formative stages of the life course. Young people and youth cultures have long been a subject of study in leisure studies (such as Ken Robert's (1983) study, *Youth and Leisure*) and more generally within the social sciences. It was G. Stanley Hall in *Adolescence*, published in 1904, who invented the modern concept of problematic youth. However, our contemporary understanding of 'youth cultures' is seen to have developed since the 1950s, due to changing patterns of employment and associated cultural changes leading to a more affluent society, coupled with the rise in the cultural importance of the mass media (and most notably film and popular music), which are seen to have given birth to the contemporary idea of 'the teenager'.

Youth is often seen as a period of transition between childhood and adulthood. It is a period when lives and leisure choices are still being shaped by families and formal education, but where young people seek to define their own identities and sense of who they are. It is also a period, for most, of greater free time and few responsibilities and a period of change, both physically and emotionally, but also in terms of fashions and trends as young people experiment and play with identities. Balzac listed three paths in life available to the young: obedience, struggle and revolt. He stressed that the first is dull,

the latter is impossible and the middle one is too much of an effort. Of those outcomes it is clear that young people themselves have traditionally feared dullness the most. Hence, it is probably during youth that leisure is at its most significant, as it is here (as with after retirement) that leisure fills the greatest proportion of an individual's time, but also contributes significantly to youth's development of an individual identity.

Our contemporary understanding of youth cultures is greatly informed by the work of some of the Birmingham School's authors, such as Hebdige (1979) and Willis (1977), who saw the formation of youth subcultures as primarily the outcome of young people's (class-based) alienation and subsequent attempts to resist and rebel against dominant cultures. Youth has often been seen by wider society as 'problematic' and Bernard Davies (1986) suggests that the state often employs strategies to combat youth-related issues, particularly in periods of high unemployment, such as in the UK in the 1980s.

However, in recent years there has been an increased fragmentation and individualization of youth cultures. In an increasingly consumer-based society the myriad of popular culture and consumer choices becomes even greater and young people are presented with an ever-wider (almost infinite) combination of cultural artefacts to choose from in defining their own identities – therefore this has led many to question if 'coherent' youth subcultures still exist.

Youth is also becoming increasingly elongated. A larger proportion of individuals are now remaining in full-time education for much longer and many are living with their parent(s) for longer and postponing starting families of their own. There is also less distinction between the leisure and popular culture choices of teenagers and those in their twenties, thirties and even beyond – particularly in relation to music tastes and choices (Longhurst, 1995). At the other end of the age scale, in recent years there has been a growth in the phenomenon of what is sometimes referred to as 'tweenagers'. 'Tweenagers' refers to pre-teens around the ages of 10 to 13 who are increasingly being targeted by the fashion and popular culture industries, marketing older 'teenage' culture to pre-teens, and in 2000 the BBC suggested that this new 'market sector' constituted 'the group with the fastest-rising spending power on the High Street' (BBC Online, 2000). This has led to some concerns about the 'sexualization' of pre-teens, such as the debate over dolls (and their associated merchandising and products) named 'Bratz', which their official website describes as 'girls with a passion for fashion', but which the *Daily Mail Online* (2006) accused of being 'tarty' and 'bring[ing] "hooker chic" into the bedroom of pre-teens'.

Garry Crawford and Tony Blackshaw

Associated Concepts   Alienation; Birmingham School; Class; Consumption; Consumer Society; Fashion; Folk Devils and Moral Panics; Leisure Life-Course; Mass Media, Identity; Subcultures.

Z

ZOMBIE CATEGORIES

In both ordinary language and in sociology the term zombie refers to the idea of the 'living dead'. The concept zombie category was developed by Ulrich Beck (2002) as a response to the major epochal changes that have transformed the relationship between sociology, individuals and existing social formations and institutions. For Beck, zombie categories are essentially stock sociological concepts which, if they seem self-apparent, have in fact lost their conceptual and explanatory power.

Drawing on Beck's thesis it is possible to argue that the stock concepts that once upon a time sustained leisure studies have become fictitious or at least shadowlike going's on that stalk the living. There are those zombie categories that are too faded to have any toehold on the world (e.g., social class) and those so driven by the events that smashed them that they cannot lie down (e.g., community). Even leisure itself has come to feel like a ghost from a different time.

Beck is on to something significant here. He has taken the halfway house between the living and the dead (the dead and the living) to offer an alternative way of thinking which spooks those who would not otherwise throw off their conceptual blinkers and forces them to try something they might have not done otherwise. This raises a number of questions for leisure scholars. Is leisure at best merely a ghost of its former self or a concept with an identity crisis? Are extant understandings of leisure too dated to be convincing? That is, is the kind of leisure that the discursive formation known as leisure studies theorizes and looks for in its empirical research simply that which fills the heads of leisure scholars, while by and large the sociality of ordinary men and women has no idea what this leisure is any more? Does the past in leisure studies refuse a decent burial, instead preying on the living in zombie form? Is the leisure of leisure studies like one of those old pop acts from the 1970s – the performances are still adequate, but its theories in their application are by now largely hollow affairs, the same old ideas being sung as the band played on? Would it be better to reconceive leisure studies as cultural studies? Here one can only speculate, but the value of such a speculation is that it shows the idea of leisure beyond a death-in-life zombie existence is conceivable, and by no means nonsense.

Tony Blackshaw

Associated Concepts Decentring Leisure; Deconstruction; Individualization; Leisure.

ZONES

This is a term that has its roots in urban studies where it was used to describe an area of a city known as the zone of transition, on the periphery of the central business district, the sociocultural makeup of which is diverse and forever in flux and is generally inhabited by the temporarily and not so temporarily poor, such as less fortunate working-class groups, bohemians, immigrants and students. In the 1970s and 1980s the term was replaced by the more ideologically loaded concept of the inner city, which was used to indicate the pathological features of the persistent social problems associated with such areas, such as rundown housing, poor leisure amenities and high rates of poverty, disease and crime.

More recent analyses have begun to explore how patterns of social differentiation in the contemporary city and other urban spaces are reflected in processes that entail the waning of social structures and their concomitant substitution by a configuration of global flows – flows of money, information, images, books and any number of cultural products (Lash, 2002). Drawing on the work of Tim Luke, Lash argues that, where global flows are particularly 'heavy', cities witness the emergence of 'live zones', literally the social, cultural and economic 'happening' places. Conversely, where flows are 'light', they see the emergence of 'dead zones', which are socially, culturally and economically lacking. For this reason Lash suggests that social inequality today has become less a matter of location in place and more a matter of location in space and, for this reason, social differentiation must be understood in relation to the spatialization of zones.

In his discussion of the deterritorialization and reterritorialization of these urban spaces Lash also analyses the displacement of fixed identities. In so doing, he identifies two other types of zone: wild and tame. He suggests that, generally speaking, 'tame zones' are often found in 'live zones' and 'wild zones' in

'dead zones', but not necessarily always. 'Live and tame zones' are inhabited by the 'utilitarian wing' of the new bourgeoisie, while the 'live and wild zones', or newly gentrified cultural spaces with their myriad choice of entertainment including cinemas, clubs and restaurants, are inhabited by the 'new-media cultural intellectuals'. 'Live and tame zones' encourage the kind of leisure life-styles that encourage the consolidation of ethnic cafés and restaurants, concert halls and galleries selling exotic art, all of which the French sociologist Jacques Diderot argues are the 'symbols of prestige that developers have learned to encourage in order to bestow upon certain areas the global brand that will attract those aspiring to membership of this global community' (cited in Ruffin, 2007).

Dead zones on the other hand tend to be either moribund or 'dead and wild zones'. In the latter, 'identities are fluid, disintegrated, social disorganization is the rule. These zones, in comparison with those of the expressive middle classes ... are *seriously* wild' (Lash, 2002: 29). Presdee (2000) suggests that the kinds of leisure associated with 'wild' zones, such as street racing with cars, incorporate some of the important features of Bakhtin's classic carnival, including pleasure seeking related to edgework and its oppositional status, as well as the pursuit of leisure identities that subvert the dominant hegemony.

Tony Blackshaw

Associated Concepts Abnormal Leisure; Bohemians; Carnivalesque; Cruising; Deviance; Edgework; Hegemony; Identity; Pleasure.

Bibliography

Aaker, D. A. (1991) *Managing Brand Equity: Capitalising on the Value of a Brand Name*. New York: Free.

Abercrombie, N., Hill, S. and Turner, B. (1980) *The Dominant Ideology Thesis*. London: Allen & Unwin.

Abercrombie, N. and Longhurst, B. (1998) *Audiences*. London: Sage.

Abrams, P. (1986) *Neighbours: The Work of Philip Abrams* (edited by M. Bulmer). Cambridge: Cambridge University Press.

Adorno, T. (1991) *The Culture Industry*. London: Routledge.

Adorno, T. (1996) *Negative Dialectics*. London: Routledge.

Arnold, A. (1986) 'The impact of the Grand Prix on the transport sector', in J. P. A. Burns, J. H. Hatch and T. J. Mules (eds), *The Adelaide Grand Prix: The Impact of a Special Event*. Adelaide: The Centre for South Australian Economic Studies. pp. 58–81.

Aitchison, C. C. (2004) *Gender and Leisure: Social and Cultural Perspectives*. Abingdon: Routledge.

Alcoff, L. (1988) 'Cultural Feminism versus Post-Structuralism: The Identity Crisis in Feminist Theory', *Signs*, 13: 405–435.

Aldridge, A. (2003) *Consumption*. Cambridge: Polity.

Althusser, L. (1969) *For Marx*. Harmondsworth: Penguin.

Althusser, L. (1977) *Lenin and Philosophy and Other Essays*. London: New Left.

Anderson, B. (1991) *Imagined Communities: Reflections on the Origin and Spread of Nationalism* (2nd edition). London: Verso.

Anderton, A. (1991) *Economics*. Ormskirk: Causeway.

Ang, I. (1985) *Watching 'Dallas': Soap Opera and the Melodramatic Imagination*. Routledge, London.

Annandale, D. (2006) 'The Subversive Carnival of Grand Theft Auto: San Andreas', in N. Garrelts (ed.), *The Meaning and Culture of Grand Theft Auto: Critical Essays*. London: McFarland.

Ansoff, I. (1957) 'Strategies for Diversification', *Harvard Business Review*, 35 (5): 113–124.

Appadurai, A. (1989) 'Global Ethnoscapes: Notes & Queries for a Transnational Anthropology', in R. G. Fox (ed.), *Interventions: Anthropology of the Present*. Santa Fe, NM: School of American Research Press.

Appadurai, A. (1990) 'Disjuncture and Difference in the Global Economy', *Theory, Culture & Society*, 7: 295–310.

Appadurai, A. (1993) 'Disjuncture and Difference in Global Cultural Economy', in B. Robins (ed.), *The Phantom Public Sphere*. Minneapolis, MN: University of Minesota Press.

Armitage, J. (ed.) (2000) *Paul Virilio: From Modernism to Hypermodernism and Beyond*. London: Sage.

Armstrong, G. (1998) *Football Hooligans: Knowing the Score*. Oxford: Berg.

Armstrong, M. (2003) *A Handbook of Personnel Management Practice* (9th edition). London: Kogan Page.

Artaud, A. (1976) *Selected Writings*. Edited and Introduction written by Susan Sontag. Berkeley, CA: University of California Press.

Asam, B., Beck, U. and Loon, J. (eds) (2000) *The Risk Society and Beyond: Critical Issues for Social Theory*. London: Sage.

Atkinson, M. (2002) 'Fifty Million Viewers Can't Be Wrong: Professional Wrestling,

Sports Entertainment, and Mimesis', *Sociology of Sport Journal*, 19 (1): 47–66.

Atkinson, M. and Young, K. (2005) 'Reservoir Dogs: Greyhound Racing, Mimesis and Sport-Related Violence', *International Review for the Sociology of Sport*, 40 (3): 335–356.

Auge, M. (1995) *Non-Places: Introduction to an Anthropology of Supermodernity* (trans. John Howe). London: Verso.

Back, L., Crabbe, T. and Solomos, J. (2001) *The Changing Face of Football: Racism, Identity and Multiculture in the English Game*. Oxford: Berg.

Badiou, A. (2005) 'The Adventure of French Philosophy', *New Left Review*, 35, September/October: 67–77.

Bagnall, G. (1996) 'Consuming the Past', in S. Edgell, K. Hetherington and A. Warde (eds), *Consumption Matters*. Oxford: Blackwell/The Sociological Review.

Bagnall, G. (2003) 'Performance and Performativity at Heritage Sites', *Museum & Society*, 1 (2): 87–103 (http://www.le.ac.uk/ms/m&s/ msbagnall.pdf).

Bailey, P. C. (1989) 'Leisure, Culture and the Historian', *Leisure Studies*, 8: 109–122.

Baker, W. J. (2007) *Playing with God: Religion and Modern Sport*. Cambridge, MA: Harvard University Press.

Bakhtin, M. M. (1984a [1968]) *Rabelais and His World*. Bloomington, IN: Indiana University Press.

Bakhtin, M. M. (1984b) *Problems of Dostoevsky's Poetics*. Manchester: Manchester University Press.

Bale, J. (1994) *Landscapes of Modern Sport*. Leicester: Leicester University Press.

Ball, S. J. (2003) 'It's Not What You Know: Education and Social Capital' in *Sociology Review*, November.

Barker, C. (2004) *The Sage Dictionary of Cultural Studies*. London: Sage.

Barthes, R. (1957) 'Histoire et Sociologie de Vêtement: Quelques Observations Méthodologiques', *Annales*, 3: 430–441.

Barton, C. (1994) 'Savage Miracles: Redemption of Lost Honor in Roman Society and the Sacrament of the Gladiator and the Martyr', *Representations*, 45: 41–71.

Baudrillard, J. (1981) *For A Critique of the Political Economy of the Sign*. St Louis, MO: Telos.

Baudrillard, J. (1989) *America*. London: Verso.

Baudrillard, J. (1990 [1983]) *Fatal Stratgies*. London: Pluto.

Baudrillard, J. (1998 [1970]) *The Consumer Society: Myths and Structures*. London: Sage.

Baudrillard, J. (2001) *Impossible Exchange*. London: Verso.

Baudrillard, J. (2005) *The Intelligence of Evil or the Lucidity Pact*. Oxford: Berg.

Bauman, Z. (1976) *Socialism: The Active Utopia*. London: Allen & Unwin.

Bauman, Z. (1987) *Legislators and Interpreters: On Modernity, Post-Modernity and Intellectuals*. Cambridge: Polity.

Bauman, Z. (1989a) *Modernity and the Holocaust*. Oxford: Blackwell.

Bauman, Z. (1989b) 'Hermeneutics and Modern Social Theory', in D. Held and J. B. Thompson (eds), *Social Theory and Modern Societies: Anthony Giddens and His Critics*. Cambridge: Cambridge University Press.

Bauman, Z. (1991) *Modernity and Ambivalence*. Cambridge: Polity.

Bauman, Z. (1992) *Intimations of Postmodernity*. London: Routledge.

Bauman, Z. (1993) *Postmodern Ethics*. Oxford: Blackwell.

Bauman, Z. (1994) 'Desert Spectacular', in K. Tester (ed.), *The Flâneur*. London: Routledge.

Bauman, Z. (1997) *Postmodernity and its Discontents*. Cambridge: Polity.

Bauman, Z. (1998) *Work, Consumerism and the New Poor*. Buckingham: Open University Press.

Bauman, Z. (2000) *Liquid Modernity*. Cambridge: Polity.

Bauman, Z. (2001) *Community: Seeking Safety in an Insecure World*. Cambridge: Polity.

Bauman, Z. (2002) 'Foreword: Individually, Together', in U. Beck and E. Beck-Gernsheim (eds), *Individualization*. London: Sage.

Bauman, Z. (2004) *Identity: Conversations with Bendetto Vecchi*. Cambridge: Polity.

Bauman, Z. (2007) *Consuming Life*. Cambridge: Polity.

BBC Online (2000) 'Tweenagers Rule the High Street'. http://news.bbc.co.uk/1/hi/business/88260.stm.

Beck, U. (1992) *Risk Society: Towards a New Modernity*. London: Sage.

Beck, U. (2002) 'Zombie Categories: Interview with Ulrich Beck', in U. Beck and E. Beck-Gernsheim (eds), *Individualization: Institutionalized Individualism and its Social and Political Consequences*. London: Sage.

Becker, G. S. (1965) 'A Theory of the Allocation of Time', *Economic Journal*, 75: 3.

Becker, H. S. (1953) 'Becoming a Marihuana User', *The American Journal of Sociology*, 59: 235–242.

Becker, H. S. (1963) *Outsiders: Studies in the Sociology of Deviance*. New York: Free.

Beech, J. and Chadwick, S. (eds) (2004) *The Business of Sport Management*. Harlow: Prentice Hall.

Beilharz, P. (2000) *Zygmunt Bauman: Dialectic of Modernity*. London: Sage.

Bell, C. R. and Newby, H. (1971) *Community Studies*. London: Allen & Unwin.

Bell, D. (1973) *The Coming of Post-Industrial Society*. New York: Basic.

Bell, J. (1993) *Doing your Research Project*. Buckingham: Open University Press.

Bellah, R., Madsen, R., Sullivan, W., Swidler, A. and Tipton, S. (1987) *Habits of the Heart*. Berkeley, CA: University of California Press.

Berelson, B. (1952) *Content Analysis in Communication Research*. Glencoe, IL: Free.

Bhabha, H. (1994) *The Location of Culture*. London: Routledge.

Bilton, T., Bonnett, K., Jones, P., Skinner, D., Stanworth, M. and Webster, A. (1987) *Introductory Soiology* (2nd edition). Basingstoke: Macmillan.

Birrell, S. and Donnelly, P. (2004) 'Reclaiming Goffman: Erving Goffman's Influence on the Sociology of Sport', in R. Giulianotti (ed.), *Sport and Modern Social Theorists*. Basingstoke: Palgrave Macmillan.

Bishop, J. and Hoggett, P. (1986) *Organizing Around Enthusiasms: Mutual Aid in Leisure*. London: Comedia.

Blackshaw, T. (2003) *Leisure Life: Myth Masculinity and Modernity*. London: Routledge.

Blackshaw, T. (2005) *Zygmunt Bauman*. Abingdon: Routledge.

Blackshaw, T. (2008) 'Contemporary Community Theory and Football', in A. Brown, T. Crabbe and G. Mellor (eds), *Football and Community in the Global Context: Studies in Theory and Practice*. Abingdon: Routledge.

Blackshaw, T. (2008) 'Zygmunt Bauman', in Rob Stones (ed.), *Key Sociological Thinkers* (2nd edition). Basingstoke: Palgrave Macmillan.

Blackshaw, T. and Crabbe, T. (2004) *New Perspectives on Sport and 'Deviance': Consumption, Performativity and Social Control*. Abingdon: Routledge.

Blackshaw, T. and Crabbe, T. (2005) 'Leeds on Trial: Soap Opera, Performativity and the Racialization of Sports-Related Violence', *Patterns of Prejudice*, 39 (3): 327–342.

Blackshaw, T. and Long, J. (1998) 'A Critical Examination of the Advantages of Investigating Community and Leisure from a Social Network Perspective', *Leisure Studies*, 17 (4): 233–248.

Blackshaw, T. and Long, J. (2005) 'What's the Big Idea? A Critical Exploration of the Concept of Social Capital and its Incorporation into Leisure Policy Discourse', *Leisure Studies*, 24 (3): 239–258.

Blumer, H. (1969) *Symbolic Interactionism: Perspective and Method*. Englewood Cliffs, NJ: Prentice Hall.

Bly, R. (1991) *Iron John: A Book about Men*. Dorset: Element.

Born, G. and Hesmondhalgh, D. (eds) (2000) *Western Music and Its Others: Difference, Representation, and Appropriation in Music*. Berkeley, CA: University of California Press.

Bourdieu, P. (1977) *Outline of a Theory of Practice*. Cambridge: Cambridge University Press.

Bourdieu, P. (1984) *Distinction: A Social Critique of the Judgment of Taste*. London: Routledge.

Bourdieu, P. (1999) *Pascalian Meditations*. Cambridge: Polity.

Bourdieu, P. and Wacquant, L. (1992) *An Invitation to Reflexive Sociology*. Cambridge: Polity.

BPP Professional Education (2003) *Financial Accounting Fundamentals*. London: BPP.

Brackenridge, C. H. (1994) 'Fair Play or Fair Game?: Child Sexual Abuse in Sport Organisations', *International Review for the Sociology of Sport*, 29 (3): 287–299.

Brackenridge, C. H. (2001) *Spoilsports: Understanding and Preventing Sexual Exploitation in Sports*. London: Routledge.

Brackenridge, C. H. and Fasting, K. (eds) (2002) *Sexual Harassment and Abuse in Sport: International Research and Policy Perspectives*. London: Whiting & Birch.

Bramham, P. (1994) 'Community Arts', in L. Haywood (ed.), *Community Leisure and Recreation: Theory and Practice*. Oxford: Butterworth-Heinemann.

Bramham, P. (2002) 'Rojek, the Sociological Imagination and Leisure', *Leisure Studies*, 21 (3/4): 221–234.

Bramham, P. and Henry, I. P. (1985) 'Political Ideology and Leisure Policy in the United Kingdom', *Leisure Studies*, (4): 1.

Brassington, F. and Pettitt, S. (2000) *Principles of Marketing*. Harlow: Prentice Hall.

Bratton, J. and Gold, J. (1994) *Human Resource Management: Theory and Practice*. London: Macmillan.

Bratz (no date) www.bratz.com.

Breivik, G. (ed.) (1999) *Empirical Studies of Risk Sports*. Oslo: Norges idrettshøgskole, Institutt for sammfunnsfag.

Brewster, C., Dowling, P., Grobler, P., Holland, P. and Warnich, S. (2000) *Contemporary Issues in Human Resource Management: Gaining a Competitive Advantage*. Oxford: Oxford University Press.

Brohm, J.-M. (1978) *Sport: A Prison of Measured Time*. London: Ink Links.

Brown, A., Crabbe, T. and Mellor, G. (2008) 'FC United of Manchester: Supporter Communities and Contesting Corporate Football', in A. Brown, T. Crabbe and G. Mellor (eds), *Football and Community in the Global Context: Studies in Theory and Practice*. Abingdon: Routledge.

Bratton, J. and Gold, J. (1994) *Human Resource Management: Theory and Practice*. London: Macmillan.

Brubaker, R. (1984) *The Limits of Rationality: An Essay on the Social and Moral Thought of Max Weber*. London: Allen & Unwin.

Bryant, C. (1995) *Practical Sociology: Post-Empiricism and Reconstruction of Theory and Application*. Cambridge: Polity.

Bryce, J. and Rutter, J. (2001) 'In the Game – In the Flow: Presence in Public Computer Gaming'. Poster presented at Computer Games and Digital Textualities, IT University of Copenhagen, March (www.digiplay.org.uk/Game.php).

Bryman, A. E. (1999) *The Disneyization of Society*. London: Sage.

Bryson, V. (1999) *Feminist Debates: Issues of Theory and Political Practice*. London: Macmillan.

Burchell, G., Gordon, C. and Miller, P. (eds) (1991) *The Foucault Effect: Studies in Governmentality*. Chicago, IL: University of Chicago Press.

Burns, J. A., Hatch, J. H. and Mules, T. J. (eds) (1986) *The Adelaide Grand Prix*. Adelaide: The Centre for South Australian Economic Studies.

Butcher, H., Glen, A., Henderson, P. and Smith, J. (eds) (1993) *Community and Public Policy*. London: Pluto.

Butler, J. (1990) *Gender Trouble: Feminism and the Subversion of Identity*. London: Routledge.

Caillois, R. (1962) *Man, Play and Games* (trans. M. Barash). London: Thames & Hudson.

Calder, A. and Sheridan, D. (eds) (1985) *Speak for Yourself: A Mass-Observation Anthology, 1937–49*. Oxford: Oxford University Press.

Caletato, P. (2004) *The Clothed Body*. Oxford: Berg.

Calhoun, C. (2000) 'Resisting Globalisation or Shaping It?', *Prometheus*, 3: 28–47.

Carse, J. (1986) *Finite and Infinite Games: A Vision of Life as Play and Possibility*. New York: Ballantine.

Castells, M. (1976) 'Theoretical Propositions for an Experimental Study of Urban Social Movements', in C. G. Pickvance (ed.), *Urban Sociology: Critical Essays*. London: Methuen.

Castells, M. (1996) *The Rise of Network Society*, Vol. 1. *The Information Age: Economy, Society and Culture*. Oxford: Blackwell.

Castells, M. (1997) *The Power of Identity*, Vol. 2. *The Information Age: Economy, Society and Culture*. Oxford: Blackwell.

Castells, M. (1998) *End of the Millennium*, Vol. 3. *The Information Age: Economy, Society and Culture*. Oxford: Blackwell.

Certeau, M. de (1984) *The Practice of Everyday Life*. Berkeley, CA: University of California Press.

Chaney, D. (1996) *Lifestyles*. London: Routledge.

Chartered Institute of Management Accountants (CIMA) (2003) *Financial Accounting Fundamentals*. London: BPP Professional Education.

Clarke, A. (1992) 'Figuring a Brighter Future', in E. Dunning and C. Rojek (eds), *Sport and Leisure in the Civilizing Process*. London: Macmillan.

Clarke, J. and Critcher, C. (1985) *The Devil Makes Work*. London: Macmillan.

Clavel-Lévéque, M. (1984) *L'Empire en Jeux*. Paris: éditions du CNRS.

Clegg, S. R. (1989) *Frameworks of Power*. London: Sage.

Coakley, J. (1998) *Sport in Society: Issues & Controversies* (6th edition). Boston, MA: McGraw-Hill.

Coakley, J. and Dunning, E. (eds) (2000) *Handbook of Sports Studies*. London: Sage.

Coalter, F. (1990) 'Analysing Leisure Policy', in Ian P. Henry (ed.), *Management and Planning in the Leisure Industries*. London: Macmillan.

Cohen, A. (1955) *Delinquent Boys: The Culture of the Gang*. London: Macmillan.

Cohen, A. (1985) *The Symbolic Construction of Community*. London: Tavistock.

Cohen, S. (1972) *Folk Devils and Moral Panics*. London: MacGibbon & Kee.

Connell, R. W. (1995) *Masculinities*. Cambridge: Polity.

Connell, R. W. (2000) *The Men and the Boys*. Cambridge: Polity.

Coverley, M. (2006) *Psychogeography*. Harpenden: Pocket Essentials.

Crawford, G. (2001) 'Characteristics of a British Ice Hockey Audience: Major Findings of the 1998 and 1999 Manchester Storm Ice Hockey Club Supporter Surveys', *International Review for the Sociology of Sport*, 36 (1): 71–81.

Crawford, G. (2002) 'Cultural Tourists and Cultural Trends: Commercialization and the Coming of The Storm', *Culture, Sport, Society*, 5 (1): 21–38.

Crawford, G. (2004) *Consuming Sport: Sport, Fans and Culture*. London: Routledge.

Crawford, G. (2006) 'The Cult of Champ Man: The Culture and Pleasures of Championship Manager/Football Manager Gamers', *Information, Communication and Society*, 9 (4): 496–514.

Crawford, G. and Gosling, V. K. (2005) 'Toys of Boy? The Continued Marginalization and Participation of Women as Digital Gamers', *Sociological Research Online*, 10 (1) (www.socresonline.org.uk/10/1/ crawford.html).

Crawford, G. and Rutter, J. (2007) 'Playing the Game: Performance in Digital Game Audiences', in J. Gray, C. Sandvoss and C. L. Harrington (eds), *Fandom: Identities and Communities in a Mediated World*. New York: New York University Press.

Critcher, C. (1989) 'A Communication in Response to Leisure, Lifestyle and Status: A Pluralist Framework for Analysis', *Leisure Studies*, 8 (2): 159–162.

Crompton, J. L. (1995) 'Economic Impact Analysis of Sport Facilities and Events: 11 Sources of Misapplication', *Journal of Sport Management*, 9: 14–35.

Crompton, J. L. (2001) 'Public Subsidies to Professional Team Sport Facilities in the USA', in C. Gratton and I. Henry (eds), *Sport in the City: The Role of Sport in Economic and Social Regeneration*. London: Routledge.

Csikszentmihalyi, M. (1974) *Flow: Studies of Enjoyment*. Chicago, IL: University of Chicago Press.

Csikszentmihalyi, M. (1990) *Flow: The Psychology of Optimal Experience*. New York: HarperPerennial.

Csikszentmihalyi, M. (1997) *Living Well: The Psychology of Everyday Life*. London: Weidenfeld & Nicholson.

Cunningham, H. (1980) *Leisure in the Industrial Revolution c.1780–1880*. London: Croom Helm.

Dahl, R. A. (1957) 'The Concept of Power', *Behavioural Science*, 2: 201–215.

Daily Mail Online (2006) 'Over-Sexed and Over Here: The "Tarty" Bratz Doll' www. daily-mail.co.uk/pages/live/femail/artile.html? in_article_id = 411266& in_page_id =1879.

Davies, B. (1986) *Threatening Youth*. Buckingham: Open University Press.

Dean, M. (1994) *Critical and Effective Histories: Foucault's Methods and Historical Sociology*. London: Routledge.

Dean, M. (1999) *Governmentality: Power and Rule in Modern Society*. London: Sage.

Debord, G. (1995 [1967]) *The Society of the Spectacle*. New York: Zone.

Debray, R. (2007) 'Socialism: A Life-Cycle', *New Left Review*, 46: 5–28.

Deem, R. (1982) 'Women, Leisure and Inequality', *Leisure Studies*, 1 (1): 29–46.

Deem, R. (1986) *All Work and No Play?* Buckingham: Open University Press.

Delanty, G. (2003) *Community*. Abingdon: Routledge.

Deleuze, G. and Guattari, F. (1983) *Anti-Oedipus: Capitalism and Schizophrenia*. Minneapolis, MN: University of Minnesota Press.

Deleuze, G. and Guattari, F. (1987) *A Thousand Plateaus: Capitalism and Schizophrenia II*. Minneapolis, MN: University of Minnesota Press.

Dennis, N., Henriques, F. and Slaughter, C. (1969) *Coal is Our Life: An Analysis of a Yorkshire Mining Community*. London: Tavistock.

Derrida, J. (1976) *Of Grammatology*. Baltimore: Johns Hopkins University Press.

Dittmar, H. (1992) *The Social Psychology of Material Possessions: To Have is to Be*. Hemel Hempstead: Harvester Wheatsheaf.

Dixey, R. and Talbot, M. (1982) *Women, Leisure and Bingo* (Women and Leisure Research). Leeds: Trinity & All Saints College.

Dobson, N., Gratton, C., and Holliday, S. (1997) *Football Came Home: The Economic Impact of Euro '96*. Sheffield: Hallam University, Sheffield, Leisure Industries Research Centre.

Dominelli, L. (1990) *Women and Community Action*. Birmingham: Venture.

Donnelly, P. (1996) 'The Local & the Global: Globalization in the Sociology of Sport', *Journal of Sport & Social Issues*, 23: 235–257.

Donnison, D. (1989) 'Social Policy: The Community-Based Approach', in M. Bulmer, J. Lewis and D. Piachaud (eds), *The Goals of Social Policy*. London: Unwin Hyman.

Downes, D. and Rock, P. (1998) *Understanding Deviance: A Guide to the Sociology of Crime and Rule Breaking*. Oxford: Oxford University Press.

Duncombe, S. (1997) *Notes from Underground: Zines and the Politics of Alternative Culture*. London: Verso.

Dunning, E. (1999) *Sport Matters: Sociological Studies of Sport, Violence and Civilization*. London: Routledge.

Dunning, E., Williams, J. and Murphy, P. (1987) *The Social Roots of Football Hooliganism*. London: Routledge.

Durkheim, E. (1933 [1893]) *The Division of Labour in Society* (trans. G. Simpson). Glencoe, IL: Free.

Dworkin, A. (1988) *Letters from a War Zone: Writings 1976–1987*. London: Secker & Warburg.

Dyck, N. (2002) '"Have you Been to Hayward Field?": Children's Sport and the Construction of Community in Suburban Canada', in V. Amit (ed.), *Realizing Community*. Abingdon: Routledge.

Eagleton, T. (1990) *The Ideology of the Aesthetic*. Oxford: Blackwell.

Eagleton, T. (2005) 'Lend Me a Fiver', *London Review of Books*, 27 (12).

Eagleton, T. (2007) *The Meaning of Life*. Oxford: Oxford University Press.

Eco, U. (1985) quoted in P. French (2006) 'Watch This Movie or Die', *The Observer Review*, 1 October.

Edgell, S. (1993) *Class*. London: Routledge.

Edwards, T. (2000) *Contradictions of Consumption: Concepts, Practices and the Politics of Consumer Society*. Buckingham: Open University Press.

El Hodiri, M. and Quirk, J. (1971) 'An Economic Model of a Professional Sports League', *Journal of Political Economy*, 79 (6): 1302–1319.

Elias, N. (1970) 'Dynamics of Sport Groups with Special Reference to Football', in E. Dunning (ed.), *The Sociology of Sport*. London: Frank Cass.

Elias, N. (1971) 'The Genesis of Sport as a Sociological Problem', in E. Dunning (ed.), *The Sociology of Sport*. London: Frank Cass.

Elias, N. (1978a) *What is Sociology?* New York: Columbia University Press.

Elias, N. (1978b) *The Civilizing Process* (Vol.I): *The History of Manners*. Oxford: Blackwell.

Elias, N. (1982) *The Civilizing Process* (Vol.2): *State Formation and Civilisation*. Oxford: Blackwell.

Elias, N. (1983) *The Court Society*. Oxford: Blackwell

Elias, N. (1986) 'Introduction', in N. Elias and E. Dunning (eds), *Quest for Excitement: Sport and Leisure in the Civilizing Process*. Oxford: Blackwell.

Elias, N. (1987) *Involvement and Detachment*. Oxford: Blackwell.

Elias, N. (1991 [1939]) *The Society of Individuals*. Oxford: Blackwell.

Elias, N. (1994) *The Civilizing Process: The History of Manners and State-Formation and Civilization* (integrated edition). Oxford: Blackwell.

Elias, N. and Dunning, E. (eds) (1986) *Quest for Excitement: Sport and Leisure in the Civilizing Process*. Oxford: Blackwell.

Ely, M., Anzul, M., Friedman, T., Garner, D. and Steinmetz, A. M. (1991) *Doing Qualitative Research: Circles within Circles*. London: Falmer.

Emes, C. E. (1997) 'Is Pac Man Eating our Children? A Review of the Effects of Video Games on Children', *The Canadian Journal of Psychiatry*, 42: 409–414.

Entertainment Software Association (ESA) (2006) *Essential Facts about the Computer and Video Game Industry* www.theesa.com/archives/files/Essential%20Facts%202006.pdf)

Erickson, B. (1996) 'Culture, Class and Connections', *American Journal of Sociology*, 102: 217–251.

Ewert, A. (1994) 'Playing the Edge: Motivation and Risk Taking in a High-Altitude Wildernesslike Environment', *Environment and Behavior*, 26 (1): 3–24.

Featherstone, M. (1991) *Consumer Culture and Postmodernism*. London: Sage.

Featherstone, M. (1995) *Undoing Culture: Globalisation, Postmodernism and Identity*. London: Sage.

Feeley, M. and Simon, J. (1992) 'The New Penology: Notes on the Emerging Strategy of Corrections and its Implications', *Criminology*, 30 (4): 449–474.

Ferguson, A. (1767) *An Essay on the History of Civil Society*. Edinburgh.

Ferguson, H. (1989) 'Sigmund Freud and the Pursuit of Pleasure', in C. Rojek (ed.), *Leisure for Leisure: Critical Essays*. London: Macmillan.

Fielding, N. (2001) 'Ethnography', in N. Gilbert (ed.), *Researching Social Life* (2nd edition). London: Sage.

Fine, G. A. (ed.) (1995) *A Second Chicago School?* Chicago, IL: University of Chicago Press.

Fiske, J. (1989) *Understanding Popular Culture*. London: Unwin Hyman.

Flew, T. (2002) *New Media*. Melbourne: Oxford University Press.

Forster, J. (1997) *Potential of a Lifetime*. Dunfermline: The Carnegie United Kingdom Trust.

Fort, R. and Quirk, J. (1995) 'Cross Subsidisation, Incentives and Outcomes in Professional Team Sports Leagues', *Journal of Economic Literature*, 33 (3): 1265–1299.

Foucault, M. (1971) *Madness and Civilization: A History of Insanity in the Age of Reason* (trans. R. Howard (1964) of *Histoire de la folie à l' âge classique*). Paris: Gallimard.

Foucault, M. (1972) *The Archaeology of Knowledge*. London: Tavistock.

Foucault, M. (1977) *Discipline and Punish: The Birth of the Prison*. Harmondsworth: Penguin.

Foucault, M. (1979) *The History of Sexuality* (Vol. 1): *An Introduction*. Harmondsworth: Penguin.

Foucault, M. (C. Gordon ed.) (1980) 'Power and Strategies', in M. Foucault, *Power/Knowledge: Selected Interviews and Other Writings 1972–1977*. London: Harvester Wheatsheaf.

Foucault, M. (1984a) 'Docile Bodies', in P. Rabinow (ed.), *The Foucault Reader: An Introduction to Foucault's Thought*. Harmondsworth: Penguin.

Foucault, M. (1984b): 'On Genealogy of Ethics: An Overview of Work in Progress', in P. Rabinow (ed.), *The Foucault Reader: An Introduction to Foucault's Thought*. Harmondsworth: Penguin.

Foucault, M. (1986) *The Order of Things: An Archaeology of the Human Sciences*. London: Routledge.

Foucault, M. (1991) 'Governmentality', in G. Burchell, C. Gordon and P. Miller (eds), *The Foucault Effect: Studies in Governmentality*. Chicago, IL: University of Chicago Press.

Foucault, M. (1997) 'Security, Territory, and Population', in P. Rabinow (ed.), *Michel Foucault: Ethics, Subjectivity and Truth*. New York: The New Press.

Franklin, A. (2001) 'The Tourist Gaze and Beyond: An Interview with John Urry', *Tourist Studies*, 11 (1): 115–132.

Franklin, A. and Crang, M. (2001) 'The Trouble with Tourism and Travel Theory', *Tourist Studies*, 1 (1): 5–22.

Frasca, G. (2003) 'Simulation versus Narrative: Introduction to Ludology', in M. J. P Wolf and B. Perron (eds), *The Video Game Theory Reader*. Abingdon: Routledge.

French, P. (2006) 'Watch This Movie or Die', *The Observer Review*, 1 October.

Freud, S. (1928) 'Dostoevsky and Parricide', in J. E. Strachey (ed.), *Complete Psychological Works of Freud*, 21. London: Hogarth.

Freud, S. (1930) 'Civilisation and Its Discontents', published in P. Gay (ed.) (1995), *The Freud Reader*. London: Vintage.

Freysinger, V. and Flannery, D. (1992) 'Women's Leisure: Affiliation, Self-Determination, Empowerment and Resistance?, *Loisir et Société*, 15 (1): 303–321.

Freire, P. (1970) *Pedagogy of the Oppressed*. New York: Seabury.

Fromme, J. (2003) 'Computer Games as a Part of Children's Culture', *Game Studies*, 3 (1). (www.gamestudies.org/0301/fromme/).

Fulgham, R. (1995) *From Beginning to End*. New York: Ballantine.

Fullagar, S. (2002) 'Governing the Healthy Body: Discourses of Leisure and Lifestyle in Australian Health Policy', *Health: An Interdisciplinary Journal for the Social Study of Health, Illness and Medicine*, 6 (1): 69–84.

Furedi, F. (1994) 'A Plague of Moral Panics', *Living Marxism*, 73.

Gane, M. (2000) *Jean Baudrillard*. London: Pluto.

Gardiner, M. E. (2000) *Critiques of Everyday Life*. London: Routledge.

Garfield, S. (ed.) (2005) *Our Hidden Lives: The Everyday Diaries of Yesterday's Britain*. London: Ebury.

Garfinkel, H. (1967) *Studies in Ethnomethodology*. Englewood Cliffs, NJ: Prentice Hall.

Garland, D. (1990) *Punishment in Modern Society: A Study in Social Theory*. Oxford: Oxford University Press.

Geertz, C. (1973) 'Thick Description: Towards an Interpretive Theory of Culture', in C. Geertz, *The Interpretation of Cultures*. London: Hutchinson.

Gelber, S. M. (1992) 'Free Market Metaphor: The Historical Dynamics of Stamp Collecting', *Comparative Studies in Society and History*, 34 (4): 742–769.

George, V. and Wilding, P. (1976) *Ideology and Social Welfare*. London: Routledge.

Gershuny, J. (2000) *Changing Times: Work and Leisure in Post-industrial Societies*, Oxford: Oxford University Press.

Getz, D. (1997) *Event Management and Event Tourism*. New York: Cognizant Communication.

Giddens, A. (1976) *New Rules of Sociological Method*. London: Hutchinson.

Giddens, A. (1977) *Studies in Social and Political Theory*. London: Hutchinson.

Giddens, A. (1979) *Central Problems in Social Theory*. London: Macmillan.

Giddens, A. (1981) *A Contemporary Critique of Historical Materialism*. London: Macmillan.

Giddens, A. (1984) *The Constitution of Society*. Cambridge: Polity.

Giddens, A. (1990) *The Consequences of Modernity*. Cambridge: Polity.

Giddens, A. (1991) *Modernity and Self-Identity: Self and Society in the Late Modern Age*. Cambridge: Polity.

Giddens, A. (1992) *The Transformation of Intimacy: Sexuality, Love and Eroticism in Modern Societies*. Cambridge: Polity.

Giddens, A. (1998) in A. Giddens and C. Pierson (eds), *Conversations with Anthony Giddens: Making Sense of Modernity*. Cambridge: Polity.

Gilbert, D. (1999) *Retail Marketing Management*. London: Financial Times Management.

Gilroy, P. (1982) *The Empire Strikes Back: Race and Racism in 70s Britain*. London: Routledge, in association with the Centre for Contemporary Cultural Studies, University of Birmingham.

Gilroy, P. (1987) *There Ain't no Black in the Union Jack*. London: Hutchinson.

Giulianotti, R. (1991) 'Scotland's Tartan Army in Italy: The Case for the Carnivalesque', *Sociology Review*, 39 (3): 503–530.

Giulianotti, R. (1999) *Football: A Sociology of the Global Game*. Cambridge: Polity.

Giulianotti, R. (2002) 'Supporters, Followers, Fans, and Flâneurs: A Taxonomy of Spectator Identities in Football', *Journal of Sport and Social Issues*, 26 (1): 25–46.

Glaser, B. and Strauss, A. (1968) *The Discovery of Grounded Theory*. London: Weidenfield & Nicholson.

Glen, A. (1993) 'Methods and Themes in Community practice', in H. Butcher, A. Glen, P. Henderson and J. Smith (eds) *Community and Public Policy*. London: Pluto Press.

Glyptis, S. (1989) *Leisure and Unemployment*. Buckingham: Open University Press.

Goffman, E. (1959) *The Presentation of Self in Everyday Life*. New York: Anchor.

Goffman, E. (1961a) *Asylums: Notes on the Social Situation of Mental Patients and Other Inmates*. New York: Anchor.

Goffman, E. (1961b) 'Fun in Games', in *Encounters: Two Studies in the Sociology of Interaction*. Indianapolis, IN: Bobbs-Merrill. pp. 17–81.

Goffman, E. (1963) *Stigma: Notes on the Management of Spoiled Identity*. Englewood Cliffs, NJ: Prentice Hall.

Goffman, E. (1967) 'Where the action is', in *Interaction Ritual: Essays on Face-to-Face Behavior*. New York: Anchor.

Gold, R. L. (1969) 'Roles in Sociological Field Observations', in G. McCall and J. Simmons (eds), *Issues in Participant Observation*. Boston, MA: Addison Wesley.

Goldberg, S. (1979) *Male Dominance: The Inevitability of Patriarchy*. London: Abacus Sphere.

Goldthorpe, J., Lockwood, D., Platt, J. and Bechhofer, F. (1969) *The Affluent Worker in the Class Structure*. Cambridge: Cambridge University Press.

Gosling, V. K. (2008) 'Regenerating Communities: Women's Experiences of Urban Regeneration', *Urban Studies*, 45(3): 607–26.

Gottdiener, M. (1997) *The Theming of America: Dreams, Visions and Commercial Spaces*. New York: Westview.

Gouldner, A. W. (1973) 'Anti-Minotaur: the Myth of a Value-Free Sociology', in A. W. Gouldner (ed.), *For Sociology*. Harmondsworth: Penguin.

Goudsblom, J. (2001) *Stof waar honger uit ontstond*. Amsterdam: Meulenhoff.

Gramsci, A. (1971) *Selections from the Prison Notebooks*. London: New Left.

Gratton, C., Dobson, N. and Shibli, S. (2000) 'The Economic Importance of Major Sport Events: A Case Study of Six Events', *Managing Leisure*, 5: 17–28.

Gratton, C. and Taylor, P. (1991) *Government and the Economics of Sport*. Harlow: Longman.

Gratton, C. and Taylor, P. (2000) *The Economics of Sport and Recreation*. London: Routledge.

Grazia, D. de (2002) *Animal Rights: A Very Short Introduction*. Oxford: Oxford University Press.

Green, E. (1998) 'Women Doing Friendship: An Analysis of Women's Leisure as a Site of Identity, Empowerment and Resistance', *Leisure Studies*, 17: 171–185.

Green, E. (2001) 'Technology, Leisure and Everyday Practices', in E. Green and A. Adams (eds), *Virtual Gender: Technology, Consumption and Identity*. London: Routledge.

Green, E., Hebron, S. and Woodward, D. (1990) *Women's Leisure, What Leisure?* London: Macmillan.

Greig, D. (2007) 'Lord of the Dance', in *The Guardian Review*, 8 September.

Grossberg, L. (1992) 'Is there a Fan in the House?: The Affective Sensibility of Fandom', in L. A. Lewis (ed.), *The Adoring Audience: Fan Culture and Popular Media*. London: Routledge.

Grossman, M. (1972) 'On the Concept of Health Capital and the Demand for Health', *Journal of Political Economy*, 80 (2): 223–255.

Gruneau, R. (1983) *Class, Sports and Social Development*. Amherst, MA: University of Massachusetts Press.

Gunter, B. G. and Gunter, N. C. (1980) 'Leisure Styles: A Conceptual Framework for Modern Leisure', *The Sociological Quarterly*, 21: 361–374.

Gutting, G. (ed.) (1994) *The Cambridge Companion to Foucault*. Cambridge: Cambridge University Press.

Habermas, J. (1976) *Legitimation Crisis*. London: Heinemann Educational.

Habermas, J. (1987) *The Theory of Communicative Action*. Boston, MA: Beacon.

Hall, G. S. (1904) *Adolescence: Its Psychology and Its Relations to Physiology, Anthropology, Sociology, Sex, Crime, Religion, and Education*. New York: Appleton.

Hall, S. (1978) 'The Treatment of "Football Hooligans" in the Press', in R. Ingham (ed.), *Football Hooliganism: The Wider Context*. London: Inter-Action Inprint.

Hall, S. (1980) 'Encoding and Decoding', in S. Hall, D. Hobson, A. Lowe and P. Willis (eds), *Culture, Media, Language: Working Papers in Cultural Studies, 1972–79*. London: Hutchinson.

Hall, S., Critcher, C., Jefferson, T., Clarke, J. and Roberts, B. (1978) *Policing the Crisis: Mugging, the State and Law and Order*. London: Macmillan.

Hall, S. and Jefferson, T. (eds) (1976) *Resistance through Rituals*. London: Hutchison.

Hannahgan, T. (ed.) (2002) *Management: Concepts and Practices*. Harlow: Prentice Hall.

Haraway, D. (1991) *Simians, Cyborgs and Women: The Reinvention of Nature*. London: Free Association.

Hardie-Bick, J. (forthcoming) 'It's Extreme But it's not Extremely Dangerous: Skydiver's Perceptions of Risk', in M. Kosut and E. Bachner (eds), *Extreme Culture/ Extreme Bodies*.

Hargreaves, J. (1986) *Sport, Power and Culture*. Cambridge: Polity.

Hargreaves, J. (1995) *Sporting Females: Critical Issues in the History and Sociology of Women's Sport*. London: Routledge.

Harland, R. (1987) *Superstructuralism: The Philosophy of Structuralism and Post-Structuralism*. London: Routledge.

Harris, D. (1992) *From Class Struggle to the Politics of Pleasure: The Effects of Gramscianism on Cultural Studies*. London: Routledge.

Harris, D. (2005) *Key Concepts in Leisure Studies*. London: Sage.

Harris, J. C. (1982) 'Sport and Ritual: A Macroscopic Comparison of Forms', in Jon W. Loy (ed.) *The Paradoxes of Play*. West Point, New York, pp. 205–214.

Harvey, D. (1989) *The Condition of Postmodernity*. Oxford: Blackwell.

Harvey, J., Rail, G. and Thibault, L. (1996) 'Globalization and Sport: Sketching a Theoretical Model for Analysis', *Journal of Sport and Social Issues*, 20 (3): 258–277.

Haynes, R. (1995) *The Football Imagination: The Rise of Football Fanzine Culture*. London: Ashgate.

Haywood, L. (ed.) (1994) *Community Leisure and Recreation: Theory and Practice*. Oxford: Butterworth-Heinemann.

Haywood, L. and Kew, F. (1989) 'Community Recreation: New Wine in Old Bottles' in P. Bramham, I. Henry, H. Mommaas and H. van der Poel (eds), *Leisure and the Critical Studies of Leisure Policy in Western European Cities Urban Processes*. London: Routledge.

Haywood, L., Kew, F., Bramham, P., Spink, J., Capenerhurst and Henry, I. (1995) *Understanding Leisure* (2nd edition). Cheltenham: Stanley Thornes.

Hearn, J. (1996) 'Is Masculinity Dead? A Critique of the Concept of Masculinity/-Masculinities', in M. Mac An Ghaill (ed.), *Understanding Masculinities*. Buckingham: Open University Press.

Heathfield, D. and Russell, M. (1992) *Modern Economics*. London: Harvester Wheatsheaf.

Hebdige, D. (1979) *Subculture: The Meaning of Style*. London: Methuen.

Hebdige, D. (1988) *Hiding in the Light: On Images and Things*. London: Routledge.

Heidegger, M. (1962) *Being and Time*. Oxford: Blackwell.

Hekman, S. (ed.) (1996) *Feminist Interpretations of Michel Foucault*. University Park, PA: Pennsylvania State University Press.

Heller, A. (1999) *A Theory of Modernity*. Oxford: Blackwell.

Hendry, L. B., Shucksmith, J. and Cross J. (1991) 'Healthy Minds and Healthy Bodies: A View of the Relationship between Leisure Activity and Patterns and Feelings of Wellbeing among Adolescents', in J. Long (ed.), *Leisure, Health and Wellbeing*. Brighton: Leisure Studies Association. pp. 129–144.

Henry, I. P. (2001) *The Politics of Leisure Policy* (2nd edition). Basingstoke: Palgrave Macmillan.

Hewison, R. (1987) *The Heritage Industry*. London: Methuen.

Hills, M. (2002) *Fan Cultures*. London: Routledge.

Hobbes, T. (1968 [1651]) *Leviathan*. Harmondsworth: Penguin.

Hoberman, J. (1997) *Darwin's Athletes: How Sport Damaged Black America and Preserved the Myth of Race*. Boston, MA: Houghton Mifflin.

Hobsbawm, E. (1995) *Age of Extremes: The Short Twentieth Century 1914–1991*. London: Abacus.

Hodkinson, P. (2002) *Goth: Identity, Style and Subculture*. Oxford: Berg.

Hoggart, R. (1957) *The Uses of Literacy*. London: Chatto & Windus.

Hoggart, R. (1988) *A Local Habitation Life and Times: 1918–1940*. London: Chatto & Windus.

Hopkins, K. (1983) *Death and Renewal: Sociological Studies in Roman History 2*. Cambridge: Cambridge University Press.

Horne, J., Tomlinson, A. and Whannel, G. (1999) *Understanding Sport: An Introduction to the Sociological and Cultural Analysis of Sport*. London: Spon.

Horrocks, C. (1999) *Baudrillard and the Millennium*. New York: Icon.

Horrocks, R. (1995) *Male Myths and Icons: Masculinity in Popular Culture*. Basingstoke: Palgrave Macmillan.

Hughes, E. C. (1958) *Men and Their Work*. Glencoe, IL: Free.

Howard, D. and Crompton, J. (1995) *Financing Sport*. Morgantown, WV: Fitness Information Technology.

Hughes, E. C. (1958) *Men and Their Work*. Glenncoe, IL: Free.

Huizinga, J. (1949 [1938]) *Homo Ludens: A Study of the Play Element in Culture*. London: Routledge.

Husserl, E. (1970 [1936]) *The Crisis of European Sciences and Transcendental Phenomenology*. Evanston, IL: Northwestern University Press.

Hussey, D. E. (1996) *Business Driven Human Resource Management*. London: John Wiley.

Ingham, R. (1991) 'Leisure and Wellbeing: A Perspective from New Social Psychology', in J. Long (ed.), *Leisure, Health and Wellbeing*. Brighton: Leisure Studies Association. pp. 233–252.

Inglis, D. (2004) 'Theodor Adorno on Sport: The Jeu D'Esprit of Despair', in R. Giulianotti (ed.), *Sport and Modern Social Theorists*. Basingstoke: Palgrave Macmillan.

Jarvie, G. (2006) *Sport, Culture and Society: An Introduction*. Abingdon: Routledge.

Jenkins, H. (1992) *Textual Poachers*. London: Routledge.

Jenkins, R. (1983) *Lads, Citizens and Ordinary Kids: Working-Class Youth Life-Styles in Belfast*. London: Routledge.

Jenkins, R. (1992) *Pierre Bourdieu*. London: Routledge.

Jenkins, R. (2002) *Pierre Bourdieu* (2nd edition). London: Routledge.

Kalfus, K. (2006) *A Disorder Peculiar to the Country*. London: Simon & Schuster.

Kane, P. (2004) *Play Ethic: A Manifesto for a Different Way of Living*. Basingstoke: Palgrave Macmillan.

Kane, P. (2006) 'The Power of Play', *Soundings* (summer).

Katz, J. (1988) *Seductions of Crime*. New York: Basic.

Katz, E., Blumer, J. G. and Gurevitch, M. (1974) 'Utilization of Mass Communication by the Individual', in J. G. Blumer and E. Katz (eds), *The Uses of Mass Communication*. London: Sage.

Kawamura, Y. (2005) *Fashion-ology: An Introduction to Fashion*. Oxford: Berg.

Keane, J. (1988) *Democracy and Civil Society*. London: Verso.

Kelly, J. R. (1983) *Leisure Identities and Interactions*. London: Allen & Unwin.

Kelly, J. R. (1994) 'The Symbolic Interaction Metaphor and Leisure: Critical Challenges', *Leisure Studies*, 13: 81–96.

Kern, S. (1983) *The Culture of Time & Space, 1880–1918*. Cambridge, MA: Harvard University Press.

Kerr, A., Brereton, P., Kücklich, J. and Flynn, R. (2004) *New Media: New Media Pleasures?*, STeM Working Paper: Final Research Report of a Pilot Research Project.

Kerr, A., Brereton, P. and Kücklich, J. (2005) 'New Media – New Pleasures?', *International Journal of Cultural Studies*, 8 (3): 375–394.

King, A. (1998) *The End of the Terraces*. Leicester: Leicester University.

King, A. (2000) 'Football Fandom and Post-national Identity in the New Europe', *British Journal of Sociology*, 51 (3): 419–442.

King, A. (2004) *The Structure of Social Theory*. Abingdon: Routledge.

Kirby, S., Greaves, L. and Hankivsky, O. (2000) *The Dome of Silence: Sexual Harassment and Abuse in Sport*. Halifax, NS: Fernwood.

Knott, G. (2004) *Financial Management* (4th edition). Basingstoke: Palgrave Macmillan.

Kotler, P. (1997) *Marketing Management*. Harlow: Prentice Hall.

Kress, G. (1988) *Communication and Culture: An Introduction*. Sydney: University of South Wales Press.

Kristeva, J. (1969) *Semiotikè*. Paris: Points.

Kuhn, T. S. (1970) *The Structure of Scientific Revolutions* (2nd edition). Chicago, IL: University of Chicago Press.

Kundera, M. (2002) *Ignorance* (translated by Linda Asher). London: Faber and Faber.

Lacan, J. (1977) *Ecrits: A Selection*. London: Tavistock.

Lancaster, G. and Massingham, L. (1988) *Essentials of Marketing*. Maidenhead: McGraw-Hill.

Lane, J. F. (2000) *Pierre Bourdieu: A Critical Introduction*. London: Pluto Press.

Langhamer, C. (2000) *Women's Leisure in England 1920–1960*. Manchester: Manchester University Press.

Lash, S. (2002) *Critique of Information*. London: Sage.

Lash, S. (2002) 'Foreword: Individualization in No-Linear Mode', in U. Beck and E. Beck-Gernsheim (eds), *Individualization*. London: Sage.

Lash, S. and Urry, J. (1987) *The End of Organized Capitalism*. Cambridge: Polity.

Laviolette, P. (2006) 'Green and Extreme: Free-flowing Through Seascape and Sewer', *WorldViews: Environment, Culture, Religion*, 10 (2): 178–204.

Layard, R. (2005) *Happiness: Lessons from a New Science*. Harmondsworth: Penguin.

Le Breton, D. (2000) 'Playing Symbolically with Death in Extreme Sports', *Body & Society*, 6 (1): 1–11.

Lefebvre, H. (1991 [1947]) *Critique of Everyday Life: (Volume 1) Introduction*. London: Verso.

Leggett, W. (2005) *After New Labour: Social Theory and Centre-Left Politics*. Basingstoke: Palgrave Macmillan.

Lehnert , G. (1999) *Fashion: A Concise History*. London: Laurence King.

Leisure Industries Research Centre (1998) *An Evaluation of the European Short Course Swimming Championships*. Sheffield: Hallam University, Sheffield, Leisure Industries Research Centre.

Leisure Industries Research Centre (2000) *Flora London Marathon 2000 – The Economics*. Sheffield: Hallam University, Sheffield, Leisure Industries Research Centre.

Lemert, E. (1967) *Human Deviance, Social problems and Social Control*. Englewood Cliffs, NJ: Prentice Hall.

Lengermann, P. and Niebrugge, G. (2007) 'Feminism', in G. Ritzer (ed.), *Blackwell Dictionary of Sociology*. Boston, MA: Blackwell.

Lévi-Strauss, C. (1966) *The Savage Mind*. London: Weidenfield & Nicholson.

Levitas, R. (1998) *The Inclusive Society: Social Exclusion and New Labour*. Basingstoke: Palgrave Macmillan.

Lianos, M. with Douglas, M. (2000) 'Dangerization and the End of Deviance: the Institutional Environment', in D. Garland and R. Sparks (eds), *Criminology and Social Theory*. Oxford: Oxford University Press.

Linton, R. (1936) *The Study of Man*. New York: Appleton-Century.

Livingstone, S. (1999) 'New Media, New Audiences', *New Media and Society*, 1 (1): 59–68.

Long, J. A (2007) *Researching Leisure, Sport and Tourism: The Essential Guide*. London, Sage.

Long, J. and Blackshaw, T. (2000) 'Back to Literacy', *Leisure Studies*, 19 (4): 227–245.

Longhurst, B. (1995) *Popular Music and Society*. Cambridge: Polity.

Longhurst, B., Smith, G., Bagnall, G., Crawford, G., and Ogborn, M. (2008) *Introducing Cultural Studies* (2nd edition). Harlow: Pearson.

Loy, J. W., McPherson, B. D. and Kenyon, G. (1978) *Sport and the Social System*. Reading, MA: Addison-Wesley.

Luke, T. (1995) 'New World Order or Neo-World Orders?: Power, Politics and Ideology in the Informationalizing Global Order', in M. Featherstone, S. Lash and R. Robertson (eds), *Global Modernities*: London: Sage

Lukes, S. (1974) *Power: A Radical View*. Basingstoke: Palgrave Macmillan.

Lury, C. (1996) *Consumer Culture*. Cambridge: Polity.

Lüschen, G. (1967) 'The Interdependence of Sport and Culture', *International Review for the Sociology of Sport*, 2: 127–142.

Lyng, S. (1990) 'Edgework: A Social Psychological Analysis of Voluntary Risk Taking', *American Journal of Sociology*, 95 (4): 851–886.

Lyng, S. (ed.) (2005) *Edgework: The Sociology of Risk-Taking*. Abingdon: Routledge.

Lyotard, J.-F. (1984 [1979]) *The Postmodern Condition: A Report on Knowledge*. Minneapolis, MN: University of Minnesota Press.

Lyotard, J.-F. (1993 [1974]) *Libidinal Economy*. London: Athlone.

MacInnes, J. (1998) *The End of Masculinity*. Buckingham: Open University Press.

Macintosh, R. W. and Goeldner, R. (1986) *Tourism: Principles, Practices, Philosophies*. New York: John Wiley.

Machiavelli, N. (1990 [1532]) *The Prince*. Oxford: Oxford University Press.

Maffesoli , M. (1991) 'The Ethics of Aesthetics', *Theory, Culture & Society*, 8, pp. 7–20.

Maffesoli, M. (1993) *The Shadow of Dionysus: A Contribution to the Sociology of Orgy*. Albany, SUNY.

Maffesoli, M. (1996) The *Time of the Tribes: The Decline of Individualism in a Mass Society*. London: Sage.

Maguire, J. (1999) *Global Sport*. Cambridge: Polity.

Maguire, J. (2000) 'Sport and Globalization', in J. Coakley and E. Dunning (eds), *Handbook of Sports Studies*. London: Sage.

Mannheim, K. (1936) *Ideology and Utopia: An Introduction to the Sociology of Knowledge*. New York: Harvest.

Marsh, P. (1978) 'Life and Careers on the Football Terraces', in R. Ingham (ed.), *Football Hooliganism: The Wider Context*. London: Inter-Action Inprint.

Marshall, P. D. (2002) 'The New Intertextual Commodity', in D. Harries (ed.), *The New Media Book*. London: BFI.

Martin, B. (1981) *A Sociology of Contemporary Cultural Change*. Oxford: Blackwell.

Marx, K. (1963) *Selected Writings in Sociology and Social Philosophy* (edited by T. Bottomore and M. Rubel). Harmondsworth: Penguin.

Marx, K. (1970[1844]) *A Contribution to the Critique of Hegel's Philosophy of Right*. Cambridge: Cambridge University Press. Introduction

Marx, K. and Engels, F. (1965 [1845]) *The German Ideology*. London: Lawrence & Wishart.

Mathieson, A. and Wall, G. (1982) *Tourism: Economic, Physical and Social Impacts*. Harlow: Longman.

May, C. (2002) *The Information Society: A Sceptical View*. Cambridge: Polity.

May, T. (2001) *Social Research: Issues, Methods and Process* (3rd edition). Buckingham: Open University Press.

McCrone, D., Morris, A. and Kiely, R. (1995) *Scotland – The Brand*. Edinburgh: Edinburgh University Press.

McKibbin, R. (2008) 'Not Pleasing the Tidy-Minded', *London Review of Books*, 30 (8).

McMillen, J. (1999) 'Introduction', in J. McMillen (ed.), *Gambling Cultures: Studies in History and Interpretation*. London: Routledge.

McNay, L. (1994) *Foucault: A Critical Introduction*. Cambridge: Polity.

McQuail, D. (1987) *Mass Communication Theory: An Introduction* (2nd edition). London: Sage.

McRobbie, A. (1989) 'Introduction', in A. McRobbie (ed.), *Zoot Suits and Second-Hand Dresses: An Anthology of Fashion & Music*. Basingstoke: Palgrave Macmillan.

McRobbie, A. (1994) 'The Moral Panic in the Age of Postmodern Mass Media', in *Postmodernism and Popular Culture*. London: Routledge.

McRobbie, A. and Garber, J. (2000) 'Girls and Subcultures', in A. McRobbie (ed.), *Feminism and Youth Culture* (2nd edition). London: Routledge.

Mennell, S. (1989) *Norbert Elias: Civilisation and the Human Self-Image*. Oxford: Blackwell.

Mennell, S. (1990) 'The Globalization of Human Society as a Very Long-Term Social Process', in M. Featherstone (ed.), *Global Culture: Nationalism, Globalization and Modernity*. London: Sage.

Merna, T. and Faisal, F. (2005) *Corporate Risk Management: An Organisational Perspective*. Chichester: Wiley.

Merton, R. K. (1938) 'Social Structure and Anomie', *American Sociological Review*, 3: 672–682.

Messner, M. and Sabo, D. (eds) (1990) *Sport, Men and the Gender Order*. Champaign, IL: Human Kinetics.

Michel, F. (2006) '"Here I am, Just off the Plane": Mass-Marketing Sex', *Le Monde Diplomatique*, August (translated by David Hounam).

Miles, E. (1904) *Let's Play the Game, or the Anglo-Saxon Sportsmanlike Spirit*. London.

Miles, S. (1998) *Consumerism – As a Way of Life*. London: Sage.

Miller, D. (1998) *A Theory of Shopping*. Cambridge: Polity.

Miller, J. (1993) *The Passion of Michel Foucault*. London: Harper Collins.

Miller, T. (2007) 'Popular Culture', in G. Ritzer (ed.), *Blackwell Dictionary of Sociology*. Boston, MA: Blackwell.

Mills, C. W. (1959) *The Sociological Imagination*. New York: Harper & Row.

Minseok, A. and Sage, G. H. (1992) 'The Golf Boom in South Korea: Serving Hegemonic Interests', *Sociology of Sport Journal*, 9: 372–384.

Mitchell, W., Bunton, R. and Green, E. (eds) (2004) *Young People, Risk and Leisure: Constructing Identities in Everyday Life*. Basingstroke: Palgrave Macmillan.

Mitra, A. (2000) 'Virtual Commonality: Looking for India on the Internet', in B. Bell and B. M. Kennedy (eds), *The Cybercultures Reader*. London: Routledge.

Moore, S. (1993) *Interpreting Audiences*. London: Sage.

Morris, M. (1993) 'Things to Do with Shopping Centres', in S. During (ed.), *The Cultural Studies Reader*. London: Routledge.

Muggleton, D. (2000) *Inside Subcultures: The Postmodern Meaning of Style*. Oxford: Berg.

Mules, T., and Faulkner, B. (1996) 'An Economic Perspective on Special Events', *Tourism Economics*, 12 (2): 107–117.

Mullins, L. J. (1996) *Management and Organisational Behaviour* (4th edition). London: Pitman.

Mullins, L. J. (2005) *Hospitality Management and Organisational Behaviour* (4th edition). Harlow: Longman.

Mulvey, L. (1975) 'Visual Pleasure and Narrative Cinema', *Screen*, 16 (3).

Murray, J. H. (1997) *Hamlet on the Holodeck: The Future of Narrative in Cyberspace*: New York: Free Press.

Murray, J. and Jenkins, H. (no date) *Before the Holodeck: Translating Star Trek into Digital Media* (http://web.mit.edu/21fms/wwww/faculty/henry3/holodeck.html).

Myerson, R. B. (1991) *Game Theory: Analysis Conflict*. Cambridge, MA: Harvard University Press.

Nash, J. (1950) 'The Bargaining Problem', *Econometrica*, 18: 155–162.

Nava, M. (1997) 'Modernity's Disavowal: Women, the City and the Department Store in Modern Times', in M. Nava and A. O'Shea (eds), *Reflections on a Century of English Modernity*. London: Routledge.

Neal, W. C. (1964) 'The Peculiar Economics of Professional Sport', *Quarterly Journal of Economics*, 78 (1): 1–14.

Newsom, D. (2007) *Bridging the Gaps in Global Communication*. Oxford: Blackwell.

Nora, S. and Minc, A. (1980) *The Computerization of Society*. Cambridge, MA: The MIT Press.

Nowell-Smith, G. (1981) 'Television – Football – The World', in T. Bennett (ed.), *Popular Television and Film*. London: BFI/OU.

Nuryanti, W. (1996) 'Heritage and Postmodern Tourism', *Annals of Tourism Research*, 23 (2): 249–260.

Oh, M. and Arditi, J. (2000) 'Shopping and Postmodernism: Consumption, Production,

Identity, and the Internet', in M. Gottdeiner (ed.), *New Forms of Consumption*. Oxford: Rowman & Littlefield.

O'Hagan, A. (2003) 'Watching Me Watching Them Watching You', *London Review of Books*, 25 (19): 3–9.

Olivier, S. (2006) 'Moral Dilemmas of Participation in Dangerous Leisure Activities', *Leisure Studies*, 25 (1): 95–109.

Oretago Y Gasset, O. (1994 [1932]) *The Revolt of the Mass*. New York: Norton.

O'Shaughnessy, M. (1999) *Media and Society: An Introduction*. Oxford: Oxford University Press.

Owen, G. (1994) *Accounting for Hospitality, Tourism and Leisure*. London: Pitman.

Park, Robert, E. (1950) *Race and Culture*. Glencoe IL: Free.

Parker, S. (1971) *The Future of Work and Leisure*. London: MacGibbon Kee.

Parker, S. (1983) *Leisure and Work*. London: Allen & Unwin.

Peterson, R. and Kern, R. (1996) 'Changing Highbrow Taste: From Snob to Omnivore', *American Sociological Review*, 61: 900–907.

Pilcher, J. and Whelehan, I. (2004) 50 *Key Concepts in Gender Studies*. London: Sage.

Poder, P. (2007) 'Relatively Liquid Interpersonal Relationships in Flexible Work Life', in A. Elliott (ed.), *The Contemporary Bauman*. Abingdon: Routledge.

Poole, S. (2000) *Trigger Happy: The Inner Life of Videogames*, London: Fourth Estate.

Postolsky, M. (2006) *Mimesis*. Abingdon: Routledge.

Pountain, D. and Robins, D. (2000) *Cool Rules: Anatomy of an Attitude*. London: Reaktion.

Presdee, M. (2000) *Cultural Criminology and the Carnival of Crime*. London: Routledge.

Pronger, B. (1999) 'Outta My Endzone: Sport and the Territorial Anus', *Journal of Sport and Social Issues*, 23 (4): 373–389.

Pronger, B. (2002) *Body Fascism: Salvation in the Technology of Physical Fitness*. Toronto: University of Toronto Press.

Putnam, R. D. (2000) *Bowling Alone: The Collapse and Revival of American Community*. New York: Simon & Schuster (Touchstone).

Quirk, J. and Fort, R. D. (1992) *Pay Dirt: The Business of Professional Team Sports*. Princeton, NJ: Princeton University Press.

Raban, J. (2006) *Surveillance: A Novel*. London: Picador.

Rapoport, R. and Rapoport, R. N. (1975) *Leisure and the Family Life-Cycle*. London: Routledge.

Reason, P. (2003) 'Pragmatist Philosophy and Action Research', *Action Research*, 1 (1): 103–123.

Reason, P. and Bradbury, H. (2001) *Handbook of Action Research: Participative Inquiry and Practice*. London: Sage.

Redhead, S. (1997) *Post-Fandom and The Millennial Blues: The Transformation of Soccer Culture*: London: Routledge.

Redhead, S. (2004) *Paul Virilio: Theorist of Accelerated Culture*. Edinburgh: Edinburgh University Press.

Reith, G. (1999) *The Age of Chance: Gambling in Western Culture*. London: Routledge.

Rheingold, H. (1994) *The Virtual Community: Finding Connection in a Computerized World*. London: Secker & Warburg.

Rich, A. C. (1981) *Compulsory Heterosexuality and Lesbian Existence*. London: Only Women.

Ricoeur, P. (1988) *Time and Narrative* (Vol. 3) (trans. Kathleen Blamey and David Pellauer). Chicago, IL: University of Chicago Press.

Ridge, D. T. (2004) '"It was an Incredible Thrill": The Social Meanings and Dynamics of Younger Gay Men's Experiences of Barebacking in Melbourne', *Sexualities*, 7 (3): 259–279.

Rinehart, R. (1998) 'Born-Again Sport: Ethics in Biographical Research', in G. Rail (ed.), *Sport and Postmodern Times*. Albany, NY: SUNY.

Ritchie, J. R. B. and Smith, B. H. (1991) 'The Impact of a Mega Event on Host Region Awareness: A Longitudinal Study', *Journal of Travel Research*, 30 (1): 3–10.

Ritzer, G. (1993) *The McDonaldization of Society*. Newbury Park, CA: Pine Forge.

Ritzer, G. (1994) *Sociological Beginnings: On The Origins of Key Ideas In Sociology*. New York: McGraw-Hill.

Ritzer, G. (2003) *Contemporary Social Theory and its Classical Roots: The Basics*. New York: McGraw Hill.

Ritzer, G. and Stillman, T. (2001a) 'The Modern Las Vegas Casino-Hotel: The

Paradigmatic New Means of Consumption', *M@n@gement*, 4 (3): 83–99.

Ritzer, G. and Stillman, T. (2001b) 'The Postmodern Ballpark as a Leisure Setting: Enchantment and De-McDonaldization', *Leisure Sciences*, 23: 99–113.

Roberts, J. and Sutton-Smith, B. (1971) 'Child Training and Game Involvement', in J. Loy and G. S. Kenyon (eds), *Sport, Culture and Society*. London: Macmillan.

Roberts, K. (1970) *Leisure*. London: Longman.

Roberts, K. (1978) *Contemporary Society and the Growth of Leisure*. London: Longman.

Roberts, K. (1983) *Youth and Leisure*. London: Allen & Unwin.

Roberts, K. (1999) *Leisure in Contemporary Society*. Wallingford: CABI.

Robertson, R. (1995) 'Glocalization: Time-Space and Homogeneity-Heterogeneity' in M. Featherstone, S. Lash and R. Robertson (eds), *Global Modernities*. Sage: London.

Robinson, D. W. (1992) 'A Descriptive Model of Enduring Risk Recreation Involvement', *Journal of Leisure Research*, 24 (1): 52–63.

Robson, G. (1999) *No One Likes Us, We Don't Care: The Myth and Reality of Millwall Fandom*. Oxford: Berg.

Rojek, C. (1984) 'Did Marx Have a Theory of Leisure?, *Leisure Studies*, 3: 163–174.

Rojek, C. (1985) *Capitalism and Leisure Theory*. London: Tavistock.

Rojek, C. (1986) 'The Problems of Involvement and Detachment in the Writings of Norbert Elias', *The British Journal of Sociology*, 37 (4): 584–596.

Rojek, C. (1990) 'Baudrillard and Leisure', *Leisure Studies*, 9 (1): 7–20.

Rojek, C. (1995) *Decentring Leisure: Rethinking Leisure Theory*. London: Sage.

Rojek, C. (2000) *Leisure and Culture*. Basingstoke: Palgrave Macmillan.

Rojek, C. (2004) 'The Consumerist Syndrome in Contemporary Society: An Interview with Zygmunt Bauman', *Journal of Consumer Culture*, 4 (3): 291–312.

Rojek, C. (2005) *Leisure Theory: Principles and Practice*. Basingstoke: Palgrave Macmillan.

Rojek, C., Shaw, S. M. and Veal, A. J. (2007) 'Introduction: Process and Context', in C. Rojek, S. M. Shaw and A. J. Veal (eds), *A*

Handbook of Leisure Studies. Basingstoke: Palgrave Macmillan.

Rorty, R. (1991) *Objectivity, Relativism and Truth: Philosophical Papers 1*. Cambridge: Cambridge University Press.

Rose, N. (1990) *Governing the Soul: the Shaping of the Private Self*. London: Routledge.

Rose, N. (1999) *Powers of Freedom: Reframing Political Thought*. Cambridge: Cambridge University Press.

Ruffin, F. (2007) 'Marseille: Upgrades and Degradation (The Politics of Urban Planning)', *Le Monde Diplomatique* (translated by Donald Hounam), February.

Russell, D., Patel, A., and Wilkinson-Riddle, G. (2002). *Cost Accounting: An Essential Guide*. Harlow: Prentice Hall.

Rustin, M. (1994) 'Incomplete Modernity: Ulrich Beck's Risk Society', *Radical Philosophy*, 67.

Rutherford, J. (2007) *After Identity*. London: Lawrence & Wishart.

Rutter, J. and Bryce, J. (eds) (2006) *Understanding Digital Games*. London: Sage.

Sabo, D. (1993) 'Sociology of Sport and the New World Disorder', *Sport Science Review*, 2 (1): 1–9.

Said, E. (1993) *Culture and Imperalistism*. London: Chatto & Windus.

Sandel, M. (1996) *Democracy's Discontent*. Cambridge: Cambridge University Press.

Sandvoss, C. (2003) *A Game of Two Halves: Football, Television and Globalization*. Abingdon: Routledge.

Sandvoss, C. (2005) *Fans: The Mirror of Consumption*. Cambridge: Polity.

Sandy, R., Sloane, P. J. and Rosentraub, M. S. (2004) *The Economics of Sport: An International Perspective*. Basingstoke: Palgave Macmillan.

Sansone, D. (1988) *Greek Athletics and the Genesis of Sport*. Berkeley, CA: University of California Press.

Saunders, P. (1979) *The New Urban Politics*. London: Hutchinson.

Schein, E. (1987) *The Art of Managing Human Resources*. Oxford: Oxford University Press.

Schlosser, E. (2001) *Fast-Food Nation*. Boston, MA: Houghton Miffin.

Schor, J. B. (1992) *The Overworked American: The Unexpected Decline of Leisure*. New York: Basic.

Schor, J. B. (1998) *The Overspent American: Upscaling, Downshifting and the New Consumer*. New York: Basic.

Schor, J. B. and Taylor, B. (eds) (2002) *Sustainable Planet: Solutions for the 21st Century*. Boston, MA: Beacon.

Schulz, B. (1998) The Collected Works of Bruno Schulz. Edited by Jerzy Ficowski. London: Picador.

Schwery, R. and. Eggenberger-Argote, N. (2003) 'Sport as a Cure to Mitigate Negative Syndromes of Anomie and to Prevent Violent Conflicts'. Paper presented at the ICHREP-SD 2nd Middle East Region Congress, Sport, Development and Peace, Tehran, 1–3 December (www.sport2005bildung.ch/deutsch/files/MA_Ds_SportAsACure.pdf).

Scraton, S. (1994) 'The Changing World of Women and Leisure: "Post-Feminism" and "Leisure"', *Leisure Studies*, 13 (4): 249–261.

Scruton, R. (2008) 'Review of The Craftsman by Richard Sennett', *The Sunday Times*, 10 February.

Seabrook, J. (1988) *The Leisure Society*. London: Blackwell.

Sennett, R. (1977) *The Fall of Public Man: On the Social Psychology of Capitalism*. New York: Knopf.

Sennett, R. (2003) *Respect: The Formation of Character in an Age of Inequality*. London: Allen Lane.

Sennett, R. (2005) *The Culture of the New Capitalism: Castle Lectures in Ethics, Politics, and Economics*. New York: Yale.

Sennett, R. (2008) 'Labours of Love', *The Guardian*, 2 February.

Shaw, S. M. (2001) 'Conceptualizing Resistance: Women's' Leisure as Political Practice', *Journal of Leisure Research*, 33 (2): 186–201.

Shibli, S. (1994) *Leisure Manager's Guide to Budgeting and Budgetary Control*. London: Longman.

Shibli, S. and Wilkinson-Riddle, G. J. (1998) 'The Financial Health of English Cricket – An Analysis Based on the 1995 Annual Reports and Financial Statements of the 18 First-Class Counties', *The Journal of Applied Accounting Research*, 4 (1): 4–36.

Shields, R. (1991) *Places On the Margin*. London: Routledge.

Shields, R. (ed.) (1992) *Lifestyle Shopping*. London: Routledge.

Shields, R. (1996a) 'Virtual Spaces, Real Histories and Living Bodies', in R. Shields (ed.), *Cultures of the Internet*. London: Sage.

Shields, R. (1996b) 'Introduction' in Maffesoli, M. *The Time of the Tribes: The Decline of Individualism in Mass Society*. London: Sage.

Simmel, G. (1997 [1904]) 'Fashion', in G. Simmel, D. Frisby and M. Featherstone (eds), *Simmel on Culture: Selected Writings*. London: Sage.

Simmel, G., Frisby, D. and Featherstone, M. (1997) *Simmel on Culture: Selected Writings*. London: Sage.

Sinclair, I. (1997) *Lights Out for the Territory*. London: Granta.

Sir Norman Chester Centre for Football Research (1994) *Highfield Rangers: An Oral History*. Leicester: Living History Unit.

Slater, D. (1998) 'Work/Leisure', in C. Jenks (ed.), *Core Sociological Dichotomies*. London: Sage.

Sloane, P. J. (1971) 'The Economics of Professional Football: The Football Club as a Utility Maximiser', *Scottish Journal of Political Economy*, 18 (2): 121–146.

Smith, C. (2007) *One For the Girls! The Pleasures and Practices of Reading Women's Porn*. London: Intellect.

Smith, D. (1999) *Zygmunt Bauman: Prophet of Postmodernity*. Cambridge: Polity.

Smith, G. (1996) *Community – Arianism* (www.communities. org.uk/greg/ gsum.html).

Smith, G. (2006) *Erving Goffman*. Abingdon: Routledge.

Smith, P. (2001) *Cultural Theory: An Introduction*. Oxford: Blackwell.

Sparrow, P., Brewster, C. and Harris, H. (2004). *Globalising Human Resource Management*. Abingdon: Routledge.

Spencer, H. (1966 [1896]) *The Principles of Sociology* (Vol. 2). London: D. Appleton.

Spink, J. (1994) *Leisure and the Environment*. Oxford: Butterworth-Heinemann.

Stallybrass, P. and White, A. (1986) *The Politics and Poetics of Transgression*. London: Methuen.

Stebbins, R. A. (1992) *Amateurs, Professionals and Serious Leisure*. London: McGill-Queen's University Press.

Stebbins, R. A. (1997a) 'Casual Leisure: A Conceptual Statement', *Leisure Studies*, 16 (1): 17–25.

Stebbins, R. A. (1997b) 'Serious Leisure and Wellbeing', in J. T. Haworth (ed.), *Work, Leisure and Wellbeing*. London: Routledge. pp. 117–130.

Stebbins, R. A. (1999) 'Serious Leisure', in T. L. Burton and E. L. Jackson (eds), *Leisure Studies: Prospects for the Twenty-First Century*. State College, PN: Venture.

Stebbins, R. A. (2004) 'Introduction' in R. A. Stebbins and M. Graham (eds), *Volunteering as Leisure/Leisure as Volunteering: An International Assessment*. Wallingford: CABI.

Stebbins, R. A. (2006) *Serious Leisure: A Perspective for Our Time*. New Brunswick, NJ: Aldine/Transaction.

Stephenson, M. L. and Hughes, H. L. (2005) 'Racialised Boundaries in Tourism and Travel: A Case Study of the UK Black Caribbean Community', *Leisure Studies*, 24 (2): 137–160.

Stokowski, P. A. (1994) *Leisure in Society: A Network Structural Perspective*. London: Mansell.

Stotlar, D. (2001) *Developing Successful Sport Sponsorship Plans*. Morgantown, WV: Fitness Information Technology.

Strathern, M. (1994) 'Forward: The Mirror of Technology', in R. Silverstone and E. Hirsch (eds), *Consuming Technologies: Media Information in Domestic Spaces*. London: Routledge.

Strauss, A. L. (1959) *Mirrors and Masks: The Search for Identity*. Glencoe, IL: Free.

Strauss, A. L., Schatzman, L., Bucher, R., Erlich, D. and Sabshin, M. (1964) *Psychiatric Ideologies and Institutions*. Glencoe, IL: Free.

Sugden, J. and Tomlinson, A. (1999) 'Digging the Dirt as Staying Clean: Retrieving the Investigative Tradition for a Critical Sociology of Sport', *International Review for the Sociology of Sport*, 34 (4): 385–397.

Sumner, C. (1994) *The Sociology of Deviance: An Obituary*. Buckingham: Open University Press.

Talbot, M. (1979) *Women and Leisure: A State of the Art Review*. London: UK Sports Council/Social Science Research Council.

Taylor, D. J. (2007) 'Working-Class Hero', *The Guardian*, 24 February.

Taylor, I. (1969) 'Hooligans: Soccer's Resistance Movement', *New Society*, 7 August, 204–206.

Taylor, I. (1971) "Football Mad: A Speculative Sociology of Football Hooliganism', in E. Dunning (ed.), *The Sociology of Sport*. London: Frank Cass.

Taylor, I. (1982) 'Soccer Hooliganism Revisited', in J. Hargreaves (ed.), *Sport, Culture and Ideology*. London: Routledge.

Taylor, I. (1987) 'Putting the Boot into Working-Class Sport: British Soccer after Bradford and Brussels', *Sociology of Sport Journal*, 4: 171–191.

Taylor, I. (1989) 'Hillsborough 15 April 1989: Some Personal Contemplations', *New Left Review*, 177: 89–110.

Taylor, I. (1995) 'It's a Whole New Ball Game', *Salford Papers in Sociology*. Salford: University of Salford.

Taylor, R. (1992) *Football and its Fans*. Leicester: Leicester University Press.

Tester, K. (2004) *The Social Thought of Zygmunt Bauman*. Basingstoke: Palgrave Macmillan.

The Audit Commission and Better Government for Older People (2004) *Older People: Independence and Well Being*. London: Audit Commission.

The Royal Society (1992) *Risk: Analysis, Perception and Management: Report of a Royal Society Study Group*. London: The Royal Society.

The Trap, part 1: Fuck You Buddy. (2007) Written and Directed by Adam Curtis. BBC 2. [60 mins].

Thompson, G. (1981) 'Holidays', in *Popular Culture and Everyday Life*. Buckingham: Open University Press.

Torkildsen, G. (2005). *Leisure and Recreation Management* (5th edition). Abingdon: Routledge.

Touraine, A. (1981) *The Voice and the Eye*. Cambridge: Cambridge University Press.

Trenberth, L. (ed.) (2003) *Managing the Business of Sport*. Palmerston North, New Zealand: Dunmore.

Trend, D. (2007) *The Myth of Media Violence: A Critical Introduction*. Oxford: Blackwell.

Tseëlon, E. (1995) *The Masque of Femininity*. London: Sage.

Tunstall, J. (1977) *The Media are American*. London: Constable.

Turco, D. M. and Kelsey, C. W. (1992) *Conducting Economic Impact Studies of Recreation, Parks and Special Events*. Washington, DC: National Recreation and Parks Association.

Turkle, S. (1995) *Life on the Screen: Identity in the Age of the Internet*. New York: Simon & Schuster.

Turner, V. W. (1973) 'The Center Out There: Pilgrim's Goal', *History of Religions*, 12 (3): 191–230.

UK Sport (1999) *Major Events Blueprint: The Economics – A Guide*. Prepared by the Leisure Industries Research Centre. London: UK Sport.

UK Sport (2000) *The Economics: Measuring Success – A Blueprint for Success*. London: UK Sport.

Urry, J. (2002) *The Tourist Gaze* (2nd edition). London: Sage.

Valenti, J. (2007) 'How the Web Became a Sexists' Paradise', *The Guardian, G2*, 6 April, 16–17.

Vance, C. (1992) *Pleasure and Danger: Exploring Female Sexuality*. London: Pandora.

de Vaus, D. A. (1991) *Surveys in Social Research* (3rd edition). London: UCL.

Veal, A. J. (1989) 'Leisure, Lifestyle and Status: A Pluralist Framework for Analysis', *Leisure Studies*, 8 (2): 141–153.

Veal, T. (2001) 'Leisure, Culture and Lifestyle', *Loisir et Société/Society and Leisure*, 24 (2): 359–376.

Veblen, T. (1934 [1899]) *Theory of the Leisure Class: An Economic Study in the Evolution of Institutions*. New York: Modern Library.

Wacquant, L. (1998) 'Pierre Bourdeu', in R. Stones (ed.), *Key Sociological Thinkers*. Basingstoke: Palgrave Macmillan.

Walby, S. (1990) *Theorizing Patriarchy*. Oxford: Blackwell.

Wann, D. L., Melnick, M. J., Russell, G. W. and Pease, D. G. (2001) *Sport Fans: The Psychology and Social Impact of Spectators*. New York: Routledge.

Warde, A. (1990) 'Introduction to the Sociology of Consumption', *Sociology*, 24: 1–4.

Warde, A. (1992) 'Notes on the Relationship Between Production and Consumption', in R. Burrows and C. Marsh (eds), *Consumption and Class: Divisions and Change*. London: Macmillan.

Warde, A. (1994) 'Consumption, Identity-Formation and Uncertainty', *Sociology*, 28 (4): 877–898.

Warde, A. (1996) 'The Future of the Sociology of Consumption', in S. Edgell, K. Hetherington and A. Warde (eds), *Consumption Matters*. Oxford: Blackwell.

Warde, A., Martens, L. and Olsen, W. (1999) 'Consumption and the Problem of Variety: Cultural Omnivorousness, Social Distinction and Dining Out', *Sociology*, 33 (1): 105–127.

Watson, B. and Scraton, S. (1998) 'Gendered Cities: Women and Public Leisure Spaces in the Postmodern City', *Leisure Studies*, 17 (2): 123–137.

Wearing, B. (1998) *Leisure and Feminist Theory*. London: Sage.

Weber, M. (1922) 'The Distribution of Power within the Political Community: Class, Status, and Party' in *Economy and Society*. Berkeley, CA: University of California Press.

Weber, M. (1930) *The Protestant Ethic and the Spirit of Capitalism*. London: Unwin Hyman.

Weber, M. (1978) *Economy and Society: An Outline of Interpretive Sociology*. Berkeley, CA: University of California Press.

Weisbrod, B. A. (1978) *The Voluntary Non-Profit Sector*. Lexington, MA: Lexington.

Wellman, B. (1979) The Community Question: The Intimate Networks of East Yorkers', *American Journal of Sociology*, 84 (5): 1201–1231.

Wellman, B. and Berkowitz, S. (eds) (1988) *Social Structures: A Network Approach*. Cambridge: Cambridge University Press.

Wellman, B., Carrington, P. and Hall, A. (1988) 'Networks as Personal Communities', in B. Wellman and S. Berkowitz (eds), *Social Structures: A Network Approach*. Cambridge: Cambridge University Press.

Wellman, B. and Haythornthwaite, C. (2002) *The Internet in Everyday Life*. Oxford: Blackwell.

Whannel, G. (1979) 'Football, Crowd Behaviour and the Press', *Media, Culture and Society*, 1: 327–342.

Wheaton, B. (ed.) (2004) *Understanding Lifestyle Sports: Consumption, Identity and Difference*. Abingdon: Routledge.

Whyte, W. F. (1993 [1943]) *Street Corner Society: The Social Structure of an Italian Slum* (4th edition). Chicago, IL: University of Chicago Press.

Wilkinson, A. (ed.) (2006) *Contemporary Human Resource Management: Text and Cases*. Harlow: Financial Times/Prentice Hall.

Williams, B. (1993) *Shame and Necessity*. Berkeley, CA: University of California Press.

Williams, J. (1994) 'Rangers is a Black Club: Race, Identity and Local Football in England', in J. Williams and R. Giulianotti (eds), *Games Without Frontiers: Football, Modernity and Identity*. Aldershot: Ashgate.

Williams, J. (2000) 'The Changing Face of Football: A Case of National Regulation?', in S. Hamil, J. Michie, C. Oughton and S. Warby (eds), *Football in the Digital Age: Whose Game is it Anyway?* London: Mainstream.

Williams, R. (1961) *The Long Revolution*. London: Chatto Windus.

Williams, R. (1976) *Keywords: A Vocabulary of Culture and Society*. London: Fontana.

Williams, R. (1977) *Marxism and Literature*. Farnborough: Oxford University Press.

Willis, P. (1977) *Learning to Labour: How Working Class Kids get Working Class Jobs*. Farnborough: Saxon House.

Wills, N. (2000) 'Football Myths No.18: Replica Shirts are a Rip-Off', *When Saturday Comes*, March, 169: 46.

Wilson, E. (1991) *The Sphinx and the City*. Berkeley, CA: University of California Press.

Wilson, E. (1994) *Adorned in Dreams: Fashion and Modernity*. Berkley, CA: University of California Press.

Wilson, E. (2000) *Bohemians: The Glamorous Outcasts*. London: I.B. Tauris and Rutgers University Press.

Wilson, R. and Joyce, J. (2007) *Finance for Sport and Leisure Managers: An Introduction*. Abingdon: Routledge.

Wimbush, E. (1986) *Women, Leisure and Wellbeing*, Edinburgh: Centre for Leisure Research, Moray House College of Education.

Wimbush, E. and Talbot, M. (eds) (1988) *Relative Freedoms: Women and Leisure*. Buckingham: Open University Press.

Winlow, S. and Hall, S. (2006) *Violent Night: Urban Leisure and Contemporary Culture*. Oxford: Berg.

Wolf, N. (1991) *The Beauty Myth: How Images of Beauty Are Used Against Women*. London: Vintage.

Wollen, P. (2007) 'On Gaze Theory', *New Left Review*, 44, March/April: 91–106.

Women's Studies Group (1978) *Women Take Issue: Aspects of Women's Subordination*. London: Hutchinson, in association with the CCCS.

World Tourism Organization (1991) Methodological Notes and Definitions (www.unwto.org/facts/eng/methodological. htm#2).

Wright, E. O. (1976) 'Class Boundaries in Advanced Capitalist Societies', *New Left Review*, 98: 3–41.

Wright, J. and Clarke, G. (1991) 'Sport, the Media and the Construction of Compulsory Heterosexuality', *International Review for the Sociology of Sport*, 34 (3): 227–243.

Wright, P. (1985) *On Living in an Old Country*. London: Verso.

Wright, P. (1989) 'Sneering at Theme Parks: An Encounter with the Heritage Industry: An Interview with Tim Putnam', *Block*, 15: 48–55.

Zillmann, D. (2000) *Media Entertainment: The Psychology of Its Appeal*. New York: Lawrence Erlbaum.

Žižek, S. (2006) *The Pervert's Guide to Cinema 1, 2, 3*. A documentary scripted and presented by Slavoj Žižek and directed by Sophie Fiennes. The documentary is self-distributed by P Guide Ltd.

Index